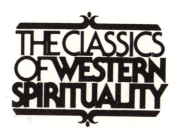

THE CLASSICS OF WESTERN SPIRITUALITY
A Library of the Great Spiritual Masters

President and Publisher
Kevin A. Lynch, C.S.P.

EDITORIAL BOARD

Editor-in-Chief
Bernard McGinn—Professor of Historical Theology and the History of Christianity, Divinity School, University of Chicago, Chicago, Ill.

Editorial Consultant
Ewert H. Cousins—Professor of Theology, Fordham University, Bronx, N.Y.

John E. Booty—Professor of Anglican Studies, School of Theology, University of the South, Sewanee, Tenn.

Joseph Dan—Professor of Kabbalah, Department of Jewish Thought, Hebrew University, Jerusalem, Israel.

Albert Deblaere—Professor of the History of Spirituality, Gregorian University, Rome, Italy.

Louis Dupré—T. L. Riggs Professor of Philosophy of Religion, Yale University, New Haven, Conn.

Rozanne Elder—Executive Vice-President, Cistercian Publications, Kalamazoo, Mich.

Anne Freemantle—Teacher, Editor and Writer, New York, N.Y.

Karlfried Froehlich—Professor of the History of the Early and Medieval Church, Princeton Theological Seminary, Princeton, N.J.

Arthur Green—President, Reconstructionist Rabbinical College, Wyncote, Pa.

Stanley S. Harakas—Archbishop Iakovos Professor of Orthodox Theology, Holy Cross Greek Orthodox Seminary, Brookline, Mass.

Moshe Idel—Professor of Jewish Thought, Department of Jewish Thought, Hebrew University, Jerusalem, Israel.

Bishop Kallistos of Diokleia—Fellow of Pembroke College, Oxford, Spalding Lecturer in Eastern Orthodox Studies, Oxford University, England.

Jean Leclercq—Professor of Spirituality, Institute of Spirituality and of Religious Psychology, Gregorian University, Rome, Italy.

George A. Maloney—Spiritual Writer and Lecturer, Seal Beach, Calif.

Seyyed Hossein Nasr—Professor of Islamic Studies, George Washington University, Washington, D.C.

Heiko A. Oberman—Professor for Medieval, Renaissance and Reformation History, University of Arizona, Tucson, Ariz.

Raimundo Panikkar—Professor, Department of Religious Studies, University of California at Santa Barbara, Calif.

Jaroslav Pelikan—Sterling Professor of History and Religious Studies, Yale University, New Haven, Conn.

Annemarie B. Schimmel—Professor of Indo-Muslim Culture, Harvard University, Cambridge, Mass.

Sandra M. Schneiders—Associate Professor of New Testament Studies and Spirituality, Jesuit School of Theology, Berkeley, Calif.

Huston Smith—Thomas J. Watson Professor of Religion Emeritus, Syracuse University, Syracuse, N.Y.

John R. Sommerfeldt—Professor of History, University of Dallas, Irving, Tex.

David Steindl-Rast—Spiritual Author, Benedictine Grange, West Redding, Conn.

David Tracy—Greeley Professor of Roman Catholic Studies, Divinity School, University of Chicago, Chicago, Ill.

The Rev. Rowan D. Williams—Bishop of Monmouth, Wales.

John Henry Newman
SELECTED SERMONS

EDITED, WITH AN INTRODUCTION BY
IAN KER

PREFACE BY
HENRY CHADWICK

PAULIST PRESS
NEW YORK • MAHWAH

Cover art: NOREEN MALLORY and her husband, the writer Hugh Hood, live in Montréal, Canada. A professional painter since she graduated from the Ontario College of Art, Noreen has exhibited her paintings and drawings in both Toronto and Montréal. Of this cover painting, she says, "I was particularly interested in preparing the Cardinal Newman cover from the point of view of a convert, having myself made the transition from Methodist to Anglican to Roman Catholic almost through what might be called beguilement rather than agonizing interior struggle. There is much for me to learn from Newman's conversion, which was made under intense public scrutiny of the highest, most critical order and which required the surest, clearest, most utterly truthful defense in the name of Christ. I have a small but gratifying family link with this extraordinary man in that my mother-in-law, Margaret Blagdon (Hood), was a founding member of the Newman Club at the University of Toronto in 1916."

Copyright © 1994 by Ian Ker

All rights reserved. No part of this book may be reproduced or transmitted in any form or by any means, electronic or mechanical, including photocopying, recording, or by any information storage and retrieval system without permission in writing from the publisher.

Library of Congress Cataloging-in-Publication Data

Newman, John Henry, 1801–1890.
   [Parochial and plain sermons. Selections]
   Selected sermons / John Henry Newman; edited, with an
introduction by Ian Ker.
      p. cm. — (Classics of Western spirituality)
   All but 4 of the 38 sermons selected are from Parochial and plain
sermons, originally preached in the 1830's and 40's in the Church of
St. Mary the Virgin at Oxford, first published in successive
volumes, then collected in six volumes, then definitively in eight
in 1868.
   Includes bibliographical references and index.
   ISBN 0-8091-0465-2 — ISBN 0-8091-3451-9 (pbk.)
   1. Church of England—Sermons.   2. Anglican Communion—England—
Sermons.   3. Sermons, English.   4. Catholic Church—Sermons.
I. Ker, I. T. (Ian Turnbull)   II. Title.   III. Series.
BX5133.N4P32   1994
252'.03—dc20   93-42475
                                                                                                            CIP

Published by Paulist Press
997 Macarthur Boulevard
Mahwah, New Jersey 07430

Printed and bound in the United States of America

Contents

Foreword 1

Preface 3

Introduction 9
The Scriptural Background 9
The Reaction Against Evangelicalism 13
The Influence of the Greek Fathers 28
Characteristics of Newman's Spirituality 41
Notes 52

PAROCHIAL AND PLAIN SERMONS

Volume I

Sermon II. The Immortality of the Soul 61
Sermon III. Knowledge of God's Will without Obedience 69
Sermon IV. Secret Faults 77
Sermon V. Self-Denial the Test of Religious Earnestness 86
Sermon VII. Sins of Ignorance and Weakness 95
Sermon XIII. Promising without Doing 103
Sermon XXIV. The Religion of the Day 110

Volume II

Sermon XV. Self-Contemplation 120
Sermon XIX. The Indwelling Spirit 127
Sermon XXIII. Tolerance of Religious Error 136
Sermon XXIX. The Powers of Nature 146
Sermon XXX. The Danger of Accomplishments 152

CONTENTS

Volume III

Sermon VIII. Contracted Views in Religion 159
Sermon XI. Bodily Suffering 166
Sermon XXIV. Intercession 176

Volume IV

Sermon I. The Strictness of the Law of Christ 186
Sermon II. Obedience without Love, as instanced in the
    Character of Balaam 197
Sermon IX. The State of Grace 209
Sermon X. The Visible Church for the Sake of the Elect 219
Sermon XIV. The Greatness and Littleness of Human Life 230
Sermon XV. Moral Effects of Communion with God 237
Sermon XVI. Christ Hidden from the World 245
Sermon XVII. Christ Manifested in Remembrance 254
Sermon XXI. Faith and Love 263
Sermon XXII. Watching 270

Volume V

Sermon I. Worship, a Preparation for Christ's Coming 279
Sermon X. Righteousness Not of Us, but in Us 287
Sermon XV. Sins of Infirmity 296
Sermon XVI. Sincerity and Hypocrisy 304
Sermon XXII. The Thought of God, the Stay of the Soul 313

Volume VI

Sermon IV. Christ's Privations a Meditation for Christians 322

Volume VII

Sermon I. The Lapse of Time 330
Sermon VII. The Duty of Self-Denial 337

Volume VIII

Sermon XIII. Truth Hidden When Not Sought After 346

CONTENTS

SERMONS BEARING ON SUBJECTS OF THE DAY

Sermon VII. Faith and the World 357
Sermon XIX. The Apostolical Christian 367

DISCOURSES ADDRESSED TO MIXED CONGREGATIONS

Discourse XVI. Mental Sufferings of Our Lord in His Passion 381

SERMONS PREACHED ON VARIOUS OCCASIONS

Sermon II. The Religion of the Pharisee, the Religion of
    Mankind 395

Select Bibliography 405
1. Primary Sources 405
2. Secondary Sources 406

Indexes 408

Author of the Foreword and Introduction
and Editor of this Volume

IAN KER was formerly a lecturer in English and Related Literature at the University of York, England (1969–1974), holder of the Endowed Chair in Theology and Philosophy at the University of St. Thomas, St. Paul, Minnesota (1987–1989), and a member of the Theology faculty, Oxford University (1989–1990). He is currently Dean of Graduate Research at the Maryvale Institute, Birmingham, England. He has an Oxford B.A. and a Cambridge Ph.D. He is the author of *John Henry Newman: A Biography* (1988), *The Achievement of John Henry Newman* (1990), *Newman on Being a Christian* (1990), *Newman and the Fullness of Christianity* (1993), and *Healing the Wound of Humanity: The Spirituality of John Henry Newman* (1993). He is the editor of the Oxford critical editions of Newman's *The Idea of a University* (1976) and *An Essay in Aid of a Grammar of Assent* (1985), and co-editor of *The Letters and Diaries of John Henry Newman*, vols. 1–4 (1978–1980). He has also edited *The Genius of John Henry Newman: Selections from his Writings* (1989) and *Newman the Theologian: A Reader* (1990), and co-edited *Newman After a Hundred Years* (1990).

Author of the Preface

HENRY CHADWICK has held professorships at both Oxford and Cambridge as well as having served as head of Colleges (Christ Church and Peterhouse) at both universities. Besides studies of Newman, his writings include *Early Christian Thought and the Classical Tradition; Boethius; Augustine;* a translation for the World's Classics of Augustine's *Confessions;* and *The Early Church.* He is a Fellow of the British Academy and a corresponding member of numerous European and American academies.

Foreword

John Henry Newman (1801–1890) was not a writer whose works lend themselves to tidy classification. This is partly because he was not a systematic thinker, partly because he so often wrote to meet a specific problem for a particular occasion, and partly because the deeply personalist cast of his thought encouraged a free-ranging style of writing. His spirituality, then, is not only to be looked for in his sermons and the posthumously published *Meditations and Devotions*. It is to be found as much in his novel *Callista* as in his poem *The Dream of Gerontius*, in his philosophy as well as his theology.

However, it has not seemed right in this selection to stray outside the sermons, as nowhere else is the spirituality of Newman displayed so abundantly and concentratedly. Most of the sermons included here are taken from the eight volumes of his Anglican *Parochial and Plain Sermons*, which is one of the great classics of Christian spirituality. Out of his profound and prolonged study of the sources of Christianity, the Bible and the Fathers, there emerges a spiritual theology that is based on a remarkably balanced and comprehensive grasp of the fullness of the Christian revelation in its primitive purity.

Shortly after Newman became a Roman Catholic, he ceased reading his sermons from a text (as was the Anglican custom) in order to conform to the practice of his adopted Church. As a result, he only thereafter published sermons that were preached for special public occasions and when a script was required. Of the two volumes of those sermons that he published, the first, *Discourses Addressed to Mixed Congregations*, which appeared not long after his conversion, is marked by a certain florid and Italianate element, but it also contains one of his most powerful pieces of spiritual writing (which is included here). However, even out of the much smaller corpus of Catholic preaching, relatively few of the sermons can rival the best of his Anglican preaching, to which most of this volume is devoted.

Preface

John Henry Newman must be reckoned among the greatest writers on Christian faith of the nineteenth century, with an influence extending far beyond that of Oxford common room or Birmingham Oratory. Brought up an Anglican, he experienced an evangelical conversion in adolescence under the influence of a schoolmaster, but then had his mind enlarged and transformed at Oriel College, Oxford, through the conversation of highly intelligent colleagues—E. B. Pusey, John Keble, Richard Whately, above all Hurrell Froude. The secularising of English society and political life was putting question marks against old assumptions about the relation of church and state. Froude convinced Newman that the authority of the Church must be independent of government; that it was no criterion of truth in a doctrine to claim that it happens to be congenial to the English; that the pincer forces of pietism and rationalism in the age of the Enlightenment had combined to make many forget the Catholic heritage of the Anglican communion and to obscure the fact that the reformed Thirty-Nine Articles of 1571 (more negative to Baptists than to Roman Catholics) were sufficiently ambiguous to allow of a Catholic interpretation. Long after he had become a Roman Catholic, Newman kept the anniversary of his evangelical conversion and specially remembered Froude in his prayers.

From 1833 until 1841 Newman and a group of like-minded friends issued the series *Tracts for the Times,* reaffirming themes of classical Anglican theology of the seventeenth century—apostolic succession, the need for frequent communion, the recovery of mystery in worship, above all the assertion that the Church is guardian and witness of revealed religion and has no right or freedom to rewrite its title-deeds to suit the rationalist prejudices of the age. During the 1830s Newman wrote striking, clear-headed books on the doctrine of the Church (*The Prophetical Office of the Church,* 1837) and on the sixteenth-century dispute about Justification by Faith (*Lectures on Justification,* 1838), both being essays in stating a via media, or middle path, between Rome and Protestantism, but implicitly less sympathetic to contemporary Calvin-

PREFACE

ism than to classical Catholicism. The crisis came when, in 1841, he published Tract 90, intended to restrain overenthusiastic disciples who were claiming that Newman's reassertion of the Catholic inheritance of Anglicanism should lead to restoration of communion with the see of Rome. The tract interpreted the Thirty-Nine Articles with hairsplitting exactitude in their literal and grammatical sense, which turned out to be far more Catholic than contemporary Protestants supposed,[1] though not conceding universal Roman jurisdiction or the necessity of expressing Real Presence in the eucharist with the ambivalent term *transubstantiation*. An ex-curate of Newman, whom he had dismissed in 1836 as unsatisfactory, had his revenge by stirring up conservative minds ("two-bottle orthodox," was Newman's phrase for them) to create a storm of anger. In the general panic, a number of bishops attacked what they understood Newman to be saying—though he was for much less liberty of interpretation than was freely practised by liberal theologians with the Articles or by evangelicals with the Book of Common Prayer. His own bishop of Oxford initially supported him, but became intimidated into uttering regret that Newman had caused such bitter controversy. Newman understandably came to feel that he was being pushed out of the Church of his baptism: "If all the world agrees in telling a man he has no place in our Church, he will at length begin to think he has none." Could the Church of England, with its self-image of tolerance, allow all or any beliefs other than those of Catholic tradition? Had liberalism taken such a grip upon this Church that it was turning its back on such great masters as John Bramhall or Herbert Thorndike or even Jeremy Taylor? If so, its torpor explained why it lacked the intellectual resources to combat the prevailing scepticism about revealed religion. Newman became a Roman Catholic in October 1845, impelled by a number of motives, but by none so strong as the conviction that only Catholicism could provide an adequate ark in which to survive the flood of scepticism, and that sooner or later Anglicanism, with its too diffused notion of ecclesial authority, would surrender to the spirit of the age.

Nevertheless, during the thirties and early forties Newman's sermons in the great church of St. Mary the Virgin at Oxford were the dynamo of the Tractarian movement, soon to be called the Oxford Movement. The preacher, at 4:00 or 5:00 on Sunday afternoons, drew large congregations of thoughtful students and professors—and to Newman's surprise even several women. The sermons were not delivered with rhetorical flourish or panache. Newman did what every seminarist today is taught not to do; he buried his head in his carefully com-

PREFACE

posed script. Yet his hearers felt a new pulse, a disturbing voice that did nothing to flatter complacency. The preacher did not strive for effect. But the content is one of high demand under the Gospel, a call for austerity and discipline, an insistence on the scriptural proposition that faith goes hand in hand with a moral conversion of heart. Moreover, Newman hammered home to his hearers that the Church and the Sacraments, the means of grace given by Christ, are not optional adornments that Christians are free to use or not to use according as their fancy takes them. "Forms are the food of faith."

Newman's parochial sermons formulated a programme for the Church where people were taking Justification by Faith to mean justification by feeling. The preacher stressed the continuity of the Christian community in the Gospel, protected by the ministerial succession, endowed with the Sacraments of Baptism and Eucharist, and, in solidarity with the Saints and martyrs, grateful for the benefits not only of the Redeemer but also of His Holy Mother of transcendent purity and "sanctified human nature."

Newman's sermons were in demand, and were soon printed in successive volumes—six at first, then reissued in eight volumes in 1868. John Keble told Newman that reading them was "the next thing to talking with you." The success of the reissue led Newman to republish in succession other books he had written as an Anglican. In his *Apologia* he had enchanted his readers by the affectionate portraits of old Oxford friends who had not followed him to Rome; for, with the exception of H. E. Manning, Newman was the only contributor to the *Tracts for the Times* who became a Roman Catholic.

After October 1845 Newman was never in doubt that his decision for conversion was correct. Yet he quickly discovered that the path of a convert can be uncomfortable, even miserable. Encouraged to found an Oratory, he experienced profound personal tensions between his house in Birmingham and the Oratory in London. Trust between himself and F. W. Faber was minimal. Relations with Archbishop's House at Westminster were prickly. With Cardinal Wiseman he was frankly disappointed, and with his successor Manning abrasions were constant. Manning, a zealous convert, interpreted his own conversion to mean renunciation of everything characteristically Anglican, including a love for the Fathers of the Church. Newman held a more minimizing view of papal infallibility apart from the conciliar consensus of Catholic bishops. He respected the ancient Church's view that the see of Rome held primacy as first among equals. If before 1845 Newman disturbed some An-

PREFACE

glicans by sounding too Roman Catholic, after 1845 he alarmed people by sounding too Anglican, and the distrust came to a nasty head when in 1859 he published his essay "On Consulting the Faithful in Matters of Faith." That essay implied that true authority is in some real degree dependent on consent.

In 1869 the leak of a private letter to his bishop (Ullathorne of Birmingham) disclosed to the world that Newman did not favour the proposed definition of papal infallibility by the Vatican Council. Yet the actual text of 1870 caused him no problems; its language was "vague and comprehensive"[2] of diversity of interpretation. Newman's own exegesis finally appeared in 1875 in the form of his *Letter to the Duke of Norfolk*. It was a "legitimate minimizing" of the Vatican Council's language, which did not affirm popes to be inspired oracles, but only to be negatively protected at critical times from leading the Church astray. In a word, Newman applied to the Vatican Council's text the exact method he once applied to the Thirty-nine Articles in Tract 90. He provided an exegesis wholly compatible with the principles of Tractarian ecclesiology, and his *Letter* contained some of his most positive post-1845 statements about the truth and value of that understanding of the Church.

Not everything in Newman's writings can be taken as a model for ecumenists today, but his influence for mutual rapprochement between separated Christians remains powerful. In January 1991 he was formally accorded the epithet "Venerable" by solemn decision on the part of Pope John Paul II, a few months after the centennial of his death commemorated in August 1990. That act was a step toward the inclusion of his name in the calendar of Saints, a roll of honor surprisingly more generous to men than to women and in recent times much enlarged. To Newman himself the Roman decision would have seemed astounding. Confidence had come late in his career with the award of the cardinal's hat in recognition of his acknowledged place among the masters of the English language and his achievement in undermining the notion that Catholicism is not really for the English. In character he was a humble and unpretentious person. He disowned the title "theologian," saying his métier was that of a controversialist. Certainly he was a master of annihilating satire, never writing more brilliantly than when stating an opponent's position with the subtlest undercurrent of irony. Shy and thin-skinned by nature, he was quick to take offence and could sometimes write the kind of irate letter that he would have suppressed if he had slept on it.

PREFACE

It has to be conceded that there is an important limitation to Newman's horizon. He was well read in the Greek Fathers, and his annotated translation of St. Athanasius remains today a classic of the subject. His notes show him torn between his admiration for the masterly dissertation of Bishop George Bull of Chester (1634–1710) in defence of the Nicene Creed and his apprehensive fears that the subordination of the Church of England to a secular government was anticipated by the Arians of the fourth century. He had acquired the best editions of the Church Fathers before he began to collect editions of the medieval schoolmen and Catholic theologians of the Counter-Reformation period. Nevertheless, the Greek Orthodox tradition of theology and mystical aspiration is at a distance in his mind. This is surprising when one recalls the powerful influence on him in the 1830s of the old patristic scholar, M. J. Routh. He could write unsympathetically about the Greek Orthodox churches that they "have given up dogma, and allow all sorts of opinion."[3] Nationalism prevented them from being Catholic.[4] During the debate about infallibility on the eve of the first Vatican Council he claimed that the Greek Church put itself out of court by not claiming infallibility for itself, as if our Lord intended councils to cease with the Seventh.[5] Yet it was the idea of a universal Church, not Roman authority that moved him to become a Roman Catholic, and he disliked Roman centralization.[6] He never thought it necessary to Catholicism to be authoritarian, legalistic, and intolerant.

Newman's prayers are strikingly simple. Converse with the unseen world is no place for sophistication or satire. His ideal was "the simple and concise expression of our humiliation, fear, hope, and desire, for ourselves and others."[7] The conversion of 1845 would create a larger place for simple devotions in honor of the Blessed Virgin Mary, but with the conscious provisos that such devotions are not necessary for salvation, and that what is beautiful in the language of devotion can sound harsh when expressed as dogma.[8] A book that he particularly liked, and retained his regard for, was Bunyan's *Pilgrim's Progress*.[9] And in 1851 he is found recommending to a friend the use of John Cosin's *Private Devotions*. Prayer for Newman needed to be rooted and grounded in Scripture and the tradition of the ancient Catholic Church. That, as much as anything else, imparted to his writings a power to speak to Christians of persuasions other than his own.

Dr. Ian Ker is an acknowledged master of Newman studies, and his anthology of Newman's sermons is admirably selected.

PREFACE

NOTES

1. It surprised people when Newman pointed out the total silence of the Articles on such matters as the intercession of the saints, prayers for the faithful departed, or monastic vows.
2. *Letters & Diaries* XXIV 377.
3. Ibid. XIV 36 (1850).
4. Ibid. XIV 354 and 373.
5. Ibid. XXIV 390.
6. Ibid. XXII 95; XX 426.
7. *Hymni Ecclesiae* (1838) preface. Lengthy prayers he thought the pride of Pharisees.
8. *Letters & Diaries* XIX 364; XXI 34.
9. Ibid. XXIII 38. Thomas à Kempis's *Imitation of Christ* he found congenial, but he kept clear of Alfonso Liguori. St. John of the Cross was unknown territory to him.

Introduction

THE SCRIPTURAL BACKGROUND

John Henry Newman was not, as is sometimes alleged, brought up as an Evangelical Christian. In fact, he grew up as an ordinary member of the established Church of England. His parents belonged to what their son would later call "the national religion of England" or "Bible Religion," consisting "not in rites or creeds, but mainly in having the Bible read in Church, in the family, and in private."[1] He himself, he recorded, was "brought up from a child to take great delight in reading the Bible."[2] Whatever the disadvantages, from the point of view of doctrine and sacraments, this kind of solid, undogmatic biblical Protestantism, which has so declined in recent decades in traditionally Protestant countries, has the inestimable advantage of instilling its adherents with a deep familiarity with the Scriptures. Newman was to feel its loss when he became a Roman Catholic. Indeed, he attributed the decline of religious practice in European Catholic countries to the lack of a Scripture-based faith. The Bible, he wrote,

> is the best book of meditations which can be, because it is divine. This is why we see such multitudes in France and Italy giving up religion altogether. They have not impressed upon their hearts the life of our Lord and Saviour as given us in the Evangelists. They believe merely with the intellect, not with the heart. Argument may overset a mere assent of the reason, but not a faith founded in a personal love for the Object of Faith. They quarrel with their priests, and then they give up the Church. We can quarrel with men, we cannot quarrel with a book.[3]

As he put it succinctly in a note for one of his Catholic sermons, "to know Christ is to know Scripture."[4]

INTRODUCTION

Newman's own spirituality was deeply scriptural, as the eight volumes of his Anglican *Parochial and Plain Sermons* bring out so vividly. In that great classic of Christian spirituality, his professed aim was "to make the text a living word to the benefit of our souls."[5] Familiar stories and words become fresh again as Newman breathes new life into them. Sometimes it is by giving a completely different twist to a well-known story, as when he suggests that the son in the parable who promises his father to work in his vineyard but fails to keep his promise does so not because he is insincere as we would suppose—given our postromantic preoccupation with the importance of sincerity—but rather the opposite:

> He said, "I go, Sir," sincerely, from the feeling of the moment; but when the words were out of his mouth, then they were forgotten. It was like the wind blowing against a stream, which seems for a moment to change its course in consequence, but in fact flows down as before.[6]

In other words, those two very modern virtues of authenticity and spontaneity are shown not to be lacking but to be insufficient. Again, in his explanation of the parable of the Prodigal Son, Newman draws almost the opposite conclusion to what we would expect, namely, "that it is *not* the same thing in the end to obey or disobey . . . the Christian penitent is not placed on a footing with those who have consistently served God from the first." The father's welcome, on this interpretation, of his younger son is not at all warmer than that of his elder son: "I do not make any outward display of kindness towards *thee*, for it is a thing to be taken for granted. We give praise and make profession to strangers, not to friends."[7]

We may think such an interpretation paradoxical, but Newman loves the unexpected twist, as is shown particularly by his frequent allusions to the paradox of the Old Testament prophet Balaam—"a man divinely favoured, visited, influenced, guided, protected, eminently honoured, illuminated,—a man possessed of an enlightened sense of duty, and of moral and religious acquirements, educated, high-minded, conscientious, honourable, firm; and yet on the side of God's enemies, personally under God's displeasure, and in the end . . . the direct instrument of Satan."[8] Newman also uses Balaam as "a most conspicuous instance of a double mind, or of hypocrisy." Full of specious excuses, Balaam was not really set on obeying God but on serving his own worldly ends.

INTRODUCTION

> Such is the way in which the double-minded approach the Most High,—they have a something private, a hidden self at bottom. They look on themselves, as it were, as independent parties, treating with Almighty God as one of their fellows. Hence, so far from seeking God, they hardly like to be sought by Him. They would rather keep their position and stand where they are,—on earth, and so make terms with God in heaven.

Given that there are "in the estimation of the double-minded man two parties, God and self, it follows . . . that reasoning and argument is the mode in which he approaches his Saviour and Judge; and that for two reasons,—first, because he will not *give* himself up to God, but stands upon his rights and appeals to his notions of fitness: and next, because he has some secret misgiving after all that he is dishonest, or some consciousness that he may appear so to others; and therefore, he goes about to fortify his position, to explain his conduct, or to excuse himself." This interesting and original analysis of hypocrisy or insincerity is then applied to the unprofitable servant in the parable who justified himself, to the argumentative Pharisees, to Adam and Eve so "ready with excuses," and to others.[9] It is similar to the treatment of the rich young man in the Gospel who "flattered himself that he was perfect in heart when he had a reserve in his obedience," for, although in his superficial enthusiasm he had not really counted the cost, "his fault was not merely self-deception, but, in a measure, a reserved devotion."[10]

Newman loves to quote Scripture in his sermons—lavishly, almost extravagantly. As an Anglican, of course, he quoted from the Authorized Version, that great monument to the golden prose of the English Renaissance. He used biblical quotations less profusely in his (fewer) published Catholic sermons, and the effect is correspondingly less compelling as the translation is inferior from the literary point of view. But it is surely also less effective from a spiritual point of view too, as the emotional impact of the language of the Authorized Version is so overwhelming that the preacher frequently and for long periods simply freewheels, as it were, on the strength of what becomes in fact an extended reading from Scripture. Often Newman draws together passages from both Old and New Testaments into a veritable flood of biblical texts to drive home his point.

Thus in the sermon "The Work of the Christian," he wants to make his hearers realize as vividly as possible that the Christian faith

INTRODUCTION

demands a total, life-long commitment to "Labour until the evening! *Until* the evening, not *in* the evening only of life, but serving God from our youth, and not waiting till our years fail us. Until the *evening*, not in the day-time only, lest we begin to run well, but fall away before our course is ended." The great test is whether one can persevere right to the end through the twilight of life, when the natural incentives to devotion are less compelling and strong. A beautiful lyrical passage follows the direct, conversational admonition, "The end is the proof of the matter." It is not simply an aesthetic, literary matter, for the haunting cadences of the Authorized Version actually realize the loss of spiritual energy and enthusiasm that old age brings. Having warned against leaving religion to the end of one's life, it is characteristic of Newman promptly to emphasise the opposite spiritual danger:

> That evening will be the trial: when the heat, and fever, and noise of the noontide are over, and the light fades, and the prospect saddens, and the shades lengthen, and the busy world is still, and "the door shall be shut in the streets, and the daughters of music shall be brought low, and fears shall be in the way, and the almond-tree shall flourish, and the grasshopper shall be a burden, and desire shall fail," and "the pitcher shall be broken at the fountain, and the wheat broken at the cistern"; then, when it is "vanity of vanities, all is vanity"; and the Lord shall come, "who both will bring to light the hidden things of darkness, and will make manifest the counsels of the hearts,"—then shall we "discern between the righteous and the wicked, between him that serveth God and him that serveth Him not."[11]

The most moving example of this kind of densely scriptural preaching is surely the famous "The Parting of Friends," Newman's last sermon as an Anglican, in which his poignant farewell to the Church of England is made virtually entirely through citing the famous farewells of the Old and New Testaments.[12]

There is at least one occasion, on the other hand, a very famous one because it was recalled years later by one of his hearers, on which a single, short quotation is used to devastating effect. The historian James Anthony Froude recounted how in a sermon Newman "described closely some of the incidents of our Lord's passion," and then "paused."

INTRODUCTION

> For a few minutes there was a breathless silence. Then, in a low, clear voice, of which the faintest vibration was audible in the farthest corner of St. Mary's [the university church in Oxford where Newman was vicar], he said, "Now, I bid you recollect that He to whom these things were done was Almighty God." It was as if an electric stroke had gone through the church, as if every person present understood for the first time the meaning of what he had all his life been saying. I suppose it was an epoch in the mental history of more than one of my Oxford contemporaries.[13]

In fact, Froude was not quoting exactly from the sermon in question, "The Incarnate Son, a Sufferer and Sacrifice," where Newman offers a challenge to his congregation:

> Think of this, all ye light-hearted, and consider whether with this thought you can read the last chapters of the four Gospels without fear and trembling.

> For instance; "When He had thus spoken, one of the officers which stood by struck Jesus with the palm of his hand, saying, "Answerest Thou the high priest so?" The words must be said, though I hardly dare say them,—that officer lifted up his hand against God the Son. This is not a figurative way of speaking, or a rhetorical form of words, or a harsh, extreme, and unadvisable statement; it is a literal and simple truth, it is a great Catholic doctrine.[14]

THE REACTION AGAINST EVANGELICALISM

In the summer of 1816, when he was fifteen, Newman underwent an Evangelical-style conversion under the influence of one of his schoolmasters, who had himself only shortly before—although he had already taken holy orders in the Church of England—become what we would now call a born-again Christian. The Wesleyan revival was still in full flood, and only a few years later the novelist George Eliot was herself to undergo a similar conversion at exactly the same age and also under the influence of an Evangelical schoolteacher. Like so many other Victo-

INTRODUCTION

rians, both Newman and George Eliot came to reject the tenets of the Evangelicalism that had so powerfully affected them in adolescence, but in both cases certain formative influences were lasting. It is true that Newman soon became aware that he had not apparently experienced the full emotional experience of what he was to call "the Evangelical process of conversion" with "its stages of conviction of sin, terror, despair, news of the free and full salvation, joy and peace, and so on to final perseverance," for his feelings had not been "*violent*" in the required manner, "but a returning to, a renewing of, principles, under the power of the Holy Spirit, which I had *already* felt, and in a measure acted on, when young." But even if he had not had "those special Evangelical experiences, which, like the grip of the hand or other prescribed signs of a secret society, are the true token of a member," still it was close enough to such a conversion to deceive all but the most doctrinaire, and there was certainly no doubting the Calvinist doctrines which he now accepted as part and parcel of the Christian faith.[15] To understand Newman's preaching (as an Anglican), and therefore his spirituality, it is necessary to set it against the background of his Evangelical period, which lasted for some eight years until about 1824.[16] This is true both in terms of positive influence and in terms of negative reaction.

(i) *Real Christianity*

It was standard Evangelical practice to distinguish "nominal" from "real" Christians, or merely conventional church-going Christians from Christians saved through their personal faith in Christ's Atonement. But a very important factor in Newman's deconversion from Evangelicalism was his practical experience of parish work, when he came to the conclusion that this kind of religion "would not work in a parish; that it was unreal ... that Calvinism was not a key to the phenomena of human nature, as they occur in the world."[17] In other words, one could not sharply separate those who had been saved through faith (in the Evangelical sense) and those who had not. But in spite of this rejection of a fundamental Evangelical tenet, Newman as a preacher is constantly stressing the difference between "real" and "unreal" Christians.

However, for Newman a real Christian is not so much someone who has made a conscious act of faith in Jesus Christ as personal saviour as someone who realizes the reality of the Christian faith. A regular refrain in the Anglican sermons is that "the greater number of those who

INTRODUCTION

are called Christians in no true sense realize it in their own minds at all." For most Christians do not "realize" what it is they profess to believe, but content themselves with an "unreal faith," substituting "a mere outward and nominal profession" for real belief. An "indolent use of words without apprehending them" is the natural concomitant of a merely "passive faith." Instead, religion must be "*real.*" To profess a religious belief as true, and yet not be able to "feel, think, speak, act as if it were true," is to believe "in an unreal way." The reason why people do not "act upon the truths they utter" is "because they do not *realize* what they are so ready to proclaim"; it is only when people "realize a truth" that "it becomes an influential principle within them."[18]

The famous distinction between "notional" and "real" knowledge, to which Newman was to give classic philosophical expression in *An Essay in Aid of a Grammar of Assent* (1870), is anticipated in the preaching in a spiritual way: "Indeed, it is a very difficult thing to bring home to us, and to feel, that we have souls; and there cannot be a more fatal mistake than to suppose we see what the doctrine means, as soon as we can use the words which signify it." It was possible to "talk of the doctrine" and yet be as if one "never had heard of it."[19] The use of words is no guarantee that the person using them really means or understands them: "We all use words... higher and fuller than we really understand."[20] Thus the Pharisees "went on merely talking of religion... till their discourses became but words of course in their mouths, with no true meaning attached to them."[21] When Newman wants to *realize* the fearful nature of the crucifixion, he takes literally the image of the lamb of God and compares Christ to a "poor dumb" animal, "fastened against a wall, pierced, gashed, and so left to linger out its life." Or asks what we would think "if wicked men took and crucified a young Child? What if they deliberately seized its poor little frame, and stretched out its arms, nailed them to a cross bar of wood, drove a stake through its two feet, and fastened them to a beam, and so left it to die?" Or again, if some elderly, kind person was "rudely seized by fierce men, stripped naked in public, insulted, driven about here and there, made a laughingstock, struck, spit on, dressed up in other clothes in ridicule, then severely scourged on the back, then laden with some heavy load till he could carry it no longer, pulled and dragged about, and at last exposed with all his wounds to the gaze of a rude multitude who came and jeered him, what would be our feeling?"[22] But such dreadful comparisons, Newman suggests, pale before the enormity of the passion of the sinless

INTRODUCTION

Son of God. If so many Christians fail to realize the truths of their faith, the opposite is true of holy Christians: "Though religious men have gifts, and though they know it, yet they do not *realize* them."[23]

In a sermon that attempts to describe "The Apostolical Christian," Newman tells his congregation that he will say nothing "but what you know well already," indeed he will do no more than quote texts from Scripture: "And yet you have heard these texts so often, that perhaps they fall dead upon your ear, and they leave you as they found you, impressing no definite image of their meaning upon your minds."[24] So much of Newman's preaching is devoted precisely to this object of making the familiar biblical texts come alive again with fresh meaning. As he wrote in a letter, he intended his sermons above all else to be real and to have "reality in them," by bringing out the Gospels in all their concrete actuality.[25] Evangelical preachers discoursed on the doctrines of the Atonement and of Justification by Faith. But Newman's aim as a preacher was to depict the Person of Christ not in an "unreal way—as a mere idea or vision," but as "Scripture has set Him before us in His actual sojourn on earth, in His gestures, words, and deeds." Instead of using "vague statements about His love, His willingness to receive the sinner, His imparting repentance and spiritual aid, and the like," the sermons try to present "Christ as manifested in the Gospels, the Christ who exists therein, external to our own imaginings ... really a living being."[26] Instead of preaching so-called Christian motives like Evangelicals, Newman wanted "Christ set forth *from the first* as the object of our worship."[27]

(ii) *Faith and Works*

When Newman published his first volume of *Parochial Sermons* in 1835, they were criticized by Evangelicals for being, in effect, unspiritual because of their lack of emphasis on the Holy Spirit in the Christian life. Newman's reply was that he preached as he did because he believed the Spirit normally worked through ordinary human channels, such as the conscience, reason, and feelings, and "does not come immediately to change us." It was in this sense that Newman could go so far as to say that "salvation depends on ourselves." And so in his preaching he has been "led" to "enlarge on our part of the work not on the Spirit's," on the ground that what needed emphasis was "the Law not the Gospel in this age—we want rousing—we want the claims of duty and the details of obedience set before us strongly." It was quite true that Christian

INTRODUCTION

works had to be done "through the Spirit," but that did not alter the fact that they had to be done by ordinary human means. This was something "this age forgets," which was why it was "necessary to bring out the fact in all its details before the world." Evangelicism had led people to assume "that a saving state is one, where the mind merely looks to Christ" as the Saviour who rewards faith with justification.[28] The result was that actual moral behaviour could seem to be virtually irrelevant. It is often alleged that the severity of Newman's preaching was due to a latent Calvinism that survived his deconversion from Evangelicism. In fact, it was a conscious and deliberate reaction (partly) against what Newman saw as a very real tendency on the part of Evangelicals towards antinomianism.

Nor was it just that the doctrine of Justification by Faith seemed to imply that no further moral and spiritual development was needed. But the overwhelming emphasis on the experience of conversion and faith had another effect: It encouraged the Christian believer to concentrate on feelings and words rather than acts and works. If everything depended on having an authentic faith, then inevitably this tended to concentrate the mind on the actual experience of faith, and therefore on words about it. Of course, the temptation to talk rather than to do is a natural infirmity of human nature: "It is easy to make progressions, easy to say fine things in speech or in writing ... [but] Let not your words run on; force every one of them into action."[29] But the insistence with which Newman warns against mere words shows that he is not simply concerned with ordinary laziness and weakness but with a spirituality inclined to verbalize for its own sake. It is not enough to acknowledge one's sins and to rely on Christ's redemption: "Repent," he urges, "in *deeds* ... hasten to commit yourselves to certain definite *acts*." The Evangelical idea of repentance, however, he argues, fosters a certain indulgence in feelings of unworthiness: People "think that to be thus agitated is to be religious; they indulge themselves in these warm feelings for their own sake, resting in them as if they were then engaged in a religious exercise, and boasting of them as if they were an evidence of their own exalted spiritual state." And instead of trying to practise the relevant virtues—"they despise this plain obedience to God as a mere unenlightened morality"—"they seek for potent stimulants to sustain their minds in that state of excitement which they have been taught to consider the essence of a religious life."[30] Newman insists that the real Christian is not someone who can speak "like an angel" or have "good thoughts and emotions" about the necessity "to look for salvation solely to Christ's blessed sacrifice on the cross"; for "there is an immeasurable

INTRODUCTION

distance between feeling right and doing right," and without the appropriate actions there is no evidence, not even to the person concerned, that they have a "true living faith." So-called justifying faith, then, "has no existence independent of its particular definite acts." We shall be looking later at the relentlessly concrete and specific character of Newman's spirituality, but, however typical it is of his whole intellectual approach, it is not unconnected with his rejection of Evangelical spirituality—although again it has to be said that talking without doing is not confined to Evangelicals:

> He who does one little deed of obedience . . . evinces more true faith than could be shown by the most fluent religious conversation, the most intimate knowledge of Scripture doctrine, or the most remarkable agitation and change of religious sentiments. Yet how many are there who sit still with folded hands, dreaming, doing nothing at all, thinking they have done every thing, or need do nothing, when they merely have had those good *thoughts*, which will save no one![31]

Newman sets very high ideals for the Christian, but he is under no illusions about how extremely difficult the Christian life is for fallen human beings, especially as it involves not so much feelings and words as actions and works:

> One secret act of self-denial, one sacrifice of inclination to duty, is worth all the mere good thoughts, warm feelings, passionate prayers, in which idle people indulge themselves. It will give us more comfort on our death-bed to reflect on one deed of self-denying mercy, purity, or humility, than to recollect the shedding of many tears, and the recurrence of frequent transports, and much spiritual exultation.[32]

It is not that Newman, whose own sermons vibrate with more or less repressed emotion, is against feelings in religion—but

> God has made us feel in order that we may *go on to act* in consequence of feeling; if then we allow our feelings to be excited without acting upon them, we do mischief to the moral system within us, just as we might spoil a watch, or other piece of mechanism, by playing with the wheels of it. We weaken its

springs, and they cease to act truly ... and, since it is very difficult to begin any duty *without* some emotion or other ... a grave question arises, how, after destroying the connexion between feeling and acting, how shall we get ourselves to act when circumstances make it our duty to do so?

And so he scornfully dismissed "that entire religious system (miscalled religious) which makes Christian faith consist, not in the honest and plain practice of what is right, but in the luxury of excited religious feeling, in a mere meditating on our Blessed Lord, and dwelling as in a reverie on what He has done for us;—for such indolent contemplation will no more sanctify a man *in fact,* than reading a poem or listening to a chant or psalm-tune." And far from "spiritual conversation" being "the test of a spiritual mind," as Newman accuses Evangelicals of thinking, he dismisses "all formal and intentional expression of religious emotions" as a "religious disorder," as nothing but "*dissipation*" and "a parallel case to that of the sensualist."[33]

It is not so much feelings in themselves that Newman is suspicious of, but rather sudden emotional excitement: "Violent impulse is not the same as a firm *determination* ... men may have their religious feelings roused, without being on that account at all the more likely to obey God in practice, rather the less likely."[34] To reinforce his point, Newman points to the *calmness* of Christ himself in the gospels, "without aught of mental excitement or agitation":

> And can we find any where such calmness and simplicity as marked His devotion and His obedience? When does He ever speak with fervour or vehemence? ... Consider the prayer He gave us.... How plain and unadorned is it! How few are the words of it! How grave and solemn the petitions! What an entire absence of tumult and feverish emotion![35]

And so, although vehement feelings may well be appropriate at a time of conversion and repentance, "all such emotion evidently is not the highest state of a Christian's mind; it is but the first stirring of grace in him," for "the more religious men become, the calmer they become."[36]

Since it is calmness rather than excitement that is the hallmark of the mature Christian, it is not surprising that Newman is anxious to warn against the spiritual dangers of "novel situations or circum-

INTRODUCTION

stances"—"See that you are not *unsettled* by them; this is the danger; fear becoming *unsettled*. Consider that stability of mind is the chief of virtues, for it is Faith."[37] Such strictures against nineteenth-century Evangelical Christianity have not lost their relevance in the twentieth century. In particular, while Newman would be very sympathetic to the emphasis placed by charismatic or pentecostal Christianity on the Holy Spirit, he would be very suspicious of any tendency to downplay the human responsibility to cooperate with God's grace and of any apparent indulgence in emotion as an end in itself.

(iii) *Introspection*

The Evangelical preoccupation with the act of faith not only led to a disproportionate preoccupation with the feelings involved in the faith-experience itself, and with the verbal expression of it, but this emphasis encouraged a distinct tendency to introspection. If, without the right feelings (which one should be able to describe), there was always the possibility that one had not really made the necessary act of faith, without which one could not be saved, then this was bound to arouse an anxiously introspective self-examination. In his sermon "Self-Contemplation," Newman complains:

> Instead of looking off to Jesus, and thinking little of ourselves, it is at present thought necessary, among the mixed multitude of religionists, to examine the heart with a view of ascertaining whether it is in a spiritual state or not. A spiritual frame of mind is considered to be one in which the heinousness of sin is perceived, our utter worthlessness, the impossibility of our saving ourselves, the necessity of some Saviour, the ... Atonement.

Although, he argues, Evangelicals regard the doctrine of Justification by Faith as "the one cardinal point of the Gospel," they are not interested (in practice) in it as a dogma, "but as ascertaining and securing ... a certain state of heart." For they think that it is not enough to believe in it merely as a doctrine, but this faith must be "living" and held with "real feelings," so that the "evidence of spiritual-mindedness" must be "sought for in the frame of mind itself," on the assumption that "faith and spiritual-mindedness ... consist in certain emotions and desires." Spiritually, the "inherent mischief" of Evangelicalism lies in

INTRODUCTION

its necessarily involving a continual self-contemplation and reference to self, in all departments of conduct. He who aims at attaining sound doctrine or right practice, more or less looks out of himself; whereas, in labouring after a certain frame of mind, there is an habitual reflex action of the mind upon itself... for, as if it were not enough for a man to look up simply to Christ for salvation, it is declared to be necessary that he should be able to recognize this in himself, that he should define his own state of mind, confess he is justified by faith alone, and explain what is meant by that confession.... He who has learned to give names to his thoughts and deeds, to appraise them as if for the market, to attach to each its due measure of commendation or usefulness, will soon involuntarily corrupt his motives by pride or selfishness. A sort of self-approbation will insinuate itself into his mind: so subtle as not at once to be recognised by himself,—an habitual quiet self-esteem.

The devastating conclusion is contained in the pithy comment "They who make self instead of their Maker the great object of their contemplation will naturally exalt themselves." Alternatively, "a contemplation of self" may lead to the opposite, namely, "a feverish anxiety" about one's "religious state and prospects."[38] Of course, Newman is not suggesting that all Evangelicals are like this, but he is seriously maintaining that such are the spiritual results of an exclusive doctrine of Justification by Faith alone when carried to its logical conclusion.

There was, however, potentially a very positive consequence of the introspection fostered by Evangelicalism as Newman had himself experienced it in his own personal spiritual life, and that was the habit of self-analysis it inevitably also encouraged. Indeed, we can say that this feature of Evangelical religion was significant for the creative achievement of another Victorian ex-Evangelical, the novelist George Eliot, whose subtle probing of intention and motive, and especially of self-delusion, raised the delineation of character in the English novel to an altogether new level. We can say the same about the spirituality of Newman's preaching, where psychological insight is shown to be an important element in progress in the Christian life. In the sense, then, of self-understanding, Newman favours introspection. For he argued that "self-knowledge is at the root of all real religious knowledge," in the sense that "it is in proportion as we search our hearts and understand our own nature, that we understand what is meant by an Infinite Governor and Judge; in proportion as we comprehend the nature of disobedience and our actual sinfulness, that we feel what is the blessing of the removal of sin, redemption, pardon, sanctification, which otherwise are mere words."[39]

It is the lack of this self-knowledge that accounts for the spiritual complacency that is stripped bare of its disguises by the psychological penetration of Newman's preaching. Outward behaviour, however good, for example, is no guarantee of anything.

> It is quite evident that so very much of our apparent obedience to God arises from mere obedience to the world and its fashions.... Let a person merely reflect on the number and variety of bad or foolish thoughts which he suffers, and dwells on in private, which he would be ashamed to put into words, and he will at once see, how very poor a test his outward demeanour in life is of his real holiness in the sight of God.[40]

As for ordinary moral respectability, Newman has no doubt that no credit is due to religious faith: "It is plain, as a matter of fact, that the great mass of men are protected from gross sin by the forms of society. The received laws of propriety and decency, the prospect of a loss of character, stand as sentinels, giving the alarm, long before their *Christian* principles have time to act."[41] People's motives are always suspect: "Do we not support religion for the sake of peace and good order?"[42] The world may praise consistency, but its idea of consistency is hardly very consistent: "A man is conscientious and consistent, who is only inconsistent and goes against conscience in any extremity, when hardly beset, and when he must cut the knot or remain in present difficulties. That is, *he* is thought to obey conscience, who only disobeys it when it is a praise and merit to obey it." The reluctant determination of the world to be inconsistent is analyzed with biting irony:

> This, alas! is the way with some of the most honourable of mere men of the world, nay of the mass of (so-called) respectable men. They never tell untruths, or break their word, or profane the Lord's day, or are dishonest in trade, or falsify their principles, or insult religion, except in very great straits or great emergencies, when driven into a corner; and then perhaps they force themselves ... and (as it were) undergo their

INTRODUCTION

sin as a sort of unpleasant self-denial or penance, being ashamed of it all the while, getting it over as quickly as they can, shutting their eyes and leaping blindfold, and the forgetting it, as something which is bitter to think about.[43]

One psychological lesson the sermons never tire of repeating concerns the part habit plays in our moral and spiritual lives. Newman's great commonsense maxim is that the more we try to be good, the better we become: "We must become what we are not; we must learn to love what we do not love, and practise ourselves in what is difficult."[44] But the difficulty lies precisely in forming new good habits when old bad habits are still dominant. For God's forgiveness does not remove the effects of sin: "God may forgive, but the sin has had its work, and its memento is set up in the soul."[45] And Newman is especially unsentimental about "the sins of our youth," by which "the power of the flesh is exerted against us, as a second creative principle of evil, aiding the malice of the Devil."[46] As a result, those who have various youthful transgressions on their conscience "must not be surprised if obedience is with them a laborious up-hill work all their days."[47] Possession of free will does not remove "the load of corrupt nature and sinful habits which hang upon [the] will and clog it in each particular exercise of it." This is why it is mere "self-deception" to assume that it is possible to delay repentance:

> I do not speak of the dreadful presumption of such a mode of quieting conscience (though many people really use it who do not speak the words out, or are aware that they act upon it), but, merely, of the ignorance it evinces concerning our moral condition, and our power of willing and doing....
>
> So very difficult is obedience, so hardly won is every step in our Christian course, so sluggish and inert our corrupt nature, that I would have a man disbelieve he can do one jot or tittle beyond what he has already done; refrain from borrowing aught on the hope of the future, however good a security for it he seems to be able to show; and never take his good feelings and wishes in pledge for one single untried deed. Nothing but *past* acts are the vouchers for future.[48]

On the other hand, the power of habit ("a permanent power in the mind")[49] is such that "obedience to God's commandments is ever easy, and almost without effort to those who begin to serve Him from the beginning of their days; whereas those who wait a while, find it grievous in proportion to their delay."[50] And without any exaggeration, Newman can say, "Indefinitely great results may follow from one act of obedience."[51] Even so, "no habit is formed at once."[52]

Part of the power of sin over our lives, however, lies in our own self-deception and self-delusion. "Evil thoughts," for example, "do us no harm, if recognized; if repelled, if protested against by the indignation and self-reproach of the mind. It is when we do not discern them, when we admit them, when we cherish them, that they ripen into principles."[53] But then to some extent self-knowledge is impossible because it is not possible to foresee the developments of sin: "When a man begins to do wrong, he cannot answer for himself how far he may be carried on. He does not see beforehand, he cannot know where he shall find himself after the sin is committed. One false step forces him to another, for retreat is impossible."[54] And Newman leaves us in no doubt that there is an ignorance of the implications of sin that is bliss:

> Did we see the complete consequences of any one sin, did we see how it spreads by the contagion of example and influence through the world, how many souls it injures, and what its eternal effects are, doubtless we should become speechless and motionless, as thought we saw the flames of hell fire.[55]

Much less desirable and much more dangerous is that quasi-deliberate amnesia about the sins of our past lives which makes people speak with "sometimes even something of tenderness and affection for their former selves;—or at best they speak of themselves in a sort of moralizing way, as they might of sinners they read of, as if it were not now *their* concern what they then were."[56] But some self-ignorance is quite unconscious, as in someone "who goes on, for years perhaps, and no one ever discovers his particular failings, nor does he know them himself; till at length he is brought into certain circumstances, which bring them out." Sometimes we are not aware of the hidden relation between particular sins, so that "single sins indulged or neglected are often the cause of other defects of character, which seem to have no connexion with them, but which after all are rather symptomatic of the former, than themselves at the bottom of the mischief." Again, a person usually has "some besetting sin or other . . . and this one indulged infirmity may in consequence be producing most distressing effects on his

INTRODUCTION

spiritual state . . . without his being aware of it," which he "gradually" learns "to palliate, or rather account for, on other principles, to refer to other motives, to justify on religious or other grounds."[57]

One common form of self-deception is to try and persuade oneself that one has not sinned—"Sinful feelings and passions generally take upon themselves the semblance of reason, and affect to argue." Accordingly, it is not surprising that "our first parents were as ready with excuses, as their posterity when Christ came."[58] We can even deceive ourselves into thinking that it is possible to stop sinning when it is not in fact possible. For "easy as it is to avoid sin first of all, at length it is (humanly speaking) impossible."[59] Once again, many of our involuntary sins arise out of our past sins:

> We cannot rid ourselves of sin when we would; though we repent, though God forgives us, yet it remains in its power over our souls, in our habits, and in our memories. It has given a colour to our thoughts, words, and works; and though, with many efforts, we would wash it out from us, yet this is not possible except gradually.

Newman does not hesitate to use terrifying images to convey the compulsive nature of such sinning in people who have genuinely repented of previous habits of sin "and would fain be other than they have been, but their former self clings to them, as a poisoned garment, and eats into them." The pain is exacerbated by "those sins which rise from the devil's temptations, inflaming the wounds and scars of past sins healed, or nearly so; exciting the memory, and hurrying us away; and thus making use of our former selves against our present selves contrary to our will."[60]

On the other hand, apparent freedom from temptation can be deceptive. If everything is going well for us, we may think we are better than we actually are—whereas, "Resistance to our acting rightly, whether it proceed from within or without, tries our principle; but when things go smoothly, and we have but to wish, and we can perform, we cannot tell how far we do or do not act from a sense of duty."[61] Another common example of self-deception is for a person to confuse repentance with confession of sins, or to substitute the latter for the former: Such a person "cannot bear to *lose* the love of the world, to part with his present desires and taste; he cannot *consent* to be changed. After all he is well satisfied at the bottom of his heart to remain as he is, only he wants his conscience taken out of the way." Without being necessarily aware of it, most people "go on with a double aim, trying to serve both God and mammon."⁶² This may be possible under ordinary circumstances, but not under trial: "Without self-knowledge you have no root in yourselves personally; you may endure for a time, but under affliction or persecution your faith will not last."⁶³ The Pharisees are thought of as conscious hypocrites, but Newman argues that this was not so: It is true they "said one thing and did another; but they were not aware that they were thus inconsistent; they deceived *themselves* as well as others. Indeed, it is not in human nature to deceive others for any long time, without in a measure deceiving ourselves also."⁶⁴

Newman does not hesitate to employ natural psychology to explain supernatural grace. Thus, for example, educated people are simply not tempted to vulgar forms of self-indulgence if only because they "have too much taste," so that for them "it is more painful to indulge than to abstain," a form of abstinence that may look to poor, uneducated people as remarkable self-denial, whereas it is nothing of the sort. Similarly, the Christian life is not all hard self-abnegation: "Happy he whose way is God's way; when he is used to it, it is as easy as any other way—nay, much easier, for God's service is perfect freedom, whereas Satan is a cruel taskmaster."⁶⁵ Habit and practice actually change our likes and wishes, as Newman never tires of repeating; thus, it is wrong to *force* ourselves to have devout feelings—"but though we cannot at our will thus feel, and at once, we can go the way thus to feel. We can grow in grace till we thus feel."⁶⁶ And yet Newman never underestimates the psychological difficulty for our fallen human nature not to sin: and why? simply because for "those who love sin, and whose very life consists in habits and practices short of religious, what promised prize can reconcile them to the certain destruction of what they delight in, the necessary annihilation of all their most favourite indulgences and enjoyments?"⁶⁷

(iv) *Worldly Religion*

The Evangelical revival had enormous success in Victorian England, especially among the middle classes. It was this very "success" that made Newman suspicious, "when all the rank, and the station, and the intelligence, and the opulence of the country is professedly with religion." For it can "scarcely be denied that attention to their religious duties is becoming a fashion among large portions of the community,—so large, that, to many individuals, these portions are in fact *the world*."

INTRODUCTION

As a result, the danger was "that a man's having a general character for religion, reverencing the Gospel and professing it, and to a certain extent obeying it, so fully promotes his temporal interests, that it is difficult for him to make out for himself whether he really acts on faith, or from a desire of this world's advantages." This is why Newman says that he is "suspicious of any religion that is a people's religion, or an age's religion." And so he warns, "When there is much talk of religion in a country, and much congratulation that there is a general concern for it, a cautious mind will feel anxious lest some counterfeit be, in fact, honoured instead of it." Here, then, is another reason, again involved in his reaction against the influence of Evangelicalism, for the severity of Newman's Anglican spirituality: "If, then, this be a time . . . when a general profession of religion is thought respectable and right in the virtuous and orderly classes of the community, this circumstance should not diminish your anxiety about your own state before God, but rather . . . increase it; for two reasons, first, because you are in danger of doing right from motives of this world; next, because you may . . . be cheated of the Truth, by some ingenuity which the world puts, like counterfeit coin, in the place of the Truth."[68]

Given the comparatively religious tone of Victorian society, Newman emphasises how dangerous a little religion can be, a situation in which people who really love the world think they love God. There was another aspect to this kind of worldly Christianity, and that was the material prosperity of the middle class in the most powerful country in the world, which was busy building up its empire. The same kind of combination of Evangelicalism and power and wealth can, of course, be found today in the United States. Such well-off Evangelicals, comfortably assured of their salvation through Justification by Faith, only too complacently find "their chief and highest *good*, in that state of life to which it has pleased God to call them, resting in it, taking it as their portion." Newman is merciless on this kind of worldly religion: "They do not understand that they are called to be strangers and pilgrims upon the earth, and that their worldly lot and worldly goods are a sort of accident of their existence, and that they really have no property." When church-going is part of social respectability, there is a tendency to associate religious practice with economic success. This, complains Newman, is the "fault" of the Victorian middle class—"an identifying God with this world, and therefore an idolatry towards the world." There is naturally always the danger of "worldly religiousness,"[69] but, even apart from the character of Evangelicalism, it was a special problem when a religious revival had had such a powerful effect on one dominant social class.

THE INFLUENCE OF THE GREEK FATHERS

In the summer and autumn of 1816, apart from the Evangelical authors to which he was introduced by his mentor Walter Mayers, Newman also read Joseph Milner's five-volume *Church History* (1794–1809) and was "nothing short of enamoured of the long extracts" from the Fathers.[70] The "permanent effect" of this reading was that "the first centuries were his beau ideal of Christianity." Not only did this early formative influence not harmonize very well with Evangelicalism, but Newman later wrote that his "imaginative devotion" to the Fathers had "saved him from the danger" of any serious lasting attraction to the theological liberalism he encountered as a young don in the famous Common Room of Oriel College, Oxford.[71] In the summer of 1828 he began to read the Fathers systematically, beginning with the early Apostolic Fathers. The celebrated row between the Provost of Oriel and the Tutors, led by Newman, over changes in the tutorial system, which led in 1830 to Newman's enforced resignation, had the providential effect of releasing him from teaching duties, so that he had the necessary leisure to pursue that profound study of the Fathers that was so important for the spread of the Tractarian (or Oxford) Movement and also so crucial for Newman's eventual conversion to the Roman Catholic Church in 1845. Newman's first published book, *The Arians of the Fourth Century* (1833), reflects his particular interest in the Eastern (and especially the Alexandrian) Fathers. Indeed, this was to be the predominant theological influence on Newman, who owed far more to Athanasius than to Augustine, let alone Aquinas. It was the thought of the Greek Fathers that shaped and guided Newman's reading of Scripture, out of which emerged that great corpus of sermons, the *Parochial and Plain Sermons*, one of the enduring classics of Christian spirituality.

(i) *The Incarnation*

Near the beginning of the *Essay on the Development of Christian Doctrine* (1845), Newman says that if one was looking for the "leading idea ... of Christianity," round which other ideas could be grouped simply "for convenience," then he would "call the Incarnation the central aspect of Christianity, out of which the three main aspects of its teaching

INTRODUCTION

take their rise, the sacramental, the hierarchical, and the ascetic." However, he immediately modifies this by adding, "But one aspect of Revelation must not be allowed to exclude or to obscure another." Later in the book, he writes, cautiously again: "For the convenience of arrangement, I will consider the Incarnation the central truth of the gospel, and the source whence we are to draw out its principles."[72]

This was not the approach of what Newman calls "the popular theology of the day" in Protestant England, which emphasized the Atonement as "the chief doctrine of the Gospel."[73] An emphasis on the crucifixion was very characteristic, of course, both of medieval Catholicism and of Tridentine Catholicism with its stress on the Mass as the sacrifice of Calvary. Newman's own tendency to give priority to the Incarnation sets him apart from what was then at least the predominant tradition of Western Christianity, both Catholic and Protestant, and is to be traced to the profound influence exerted on him by the Greek Fathers.

There has been a tendency in Western theology to view the Incarnation as virtually subordinate to the crucifixion; in other words, Christ came into this world principally in order that he might die for us on the cross. Newman's high doctrine of the Incarnation is the same as the Fathers': God took to himself human nature in order that he might raise it to his own level or "deify" it, "to make us partakers of the Divine nature." God became man so that "men, through brotherhood with Him, might in the end become as gods,"[74] to use the word that the Fathers dared to use. He came, says Newman, "selecting and setting apart for Himself the elements of body and soul; then, uniting them to Himself from their first origin of existence, pervading them, hallowing them by His own Divinity, spiritualizing them, and filling them with light and purity, the while they continued to be human. . . . And as they grew from day to day in their holy union, His Eternal Essence still was one with them, exalting them." And so by "raising human nature with Him . . . He . . . has given us to share His own spiritual nature."[75]

In his Catholic sermons Newman does not hesitate to ally himself with the view of Duns Scotus (as against St. Thomas Aquinas) that even had mankind never sinned, the Son of God would still have "had it in mind to come on earth among innocent creatures . . . to fill them with . . . grace, to receive their worship, to enjoy their company, and to prepare them for . . . heaven." Newman is convinced that there would have been an incarnation, although it would have taken a different form, without the fall: "He once had meant to come on earth in heavenly glory, but we sinned; and then He could not safely visit us, except with a shrouded

INTRODUCTION

radiance and a bedimmed Majesty, for He was God. So He came Himself in weakness, not in power."[76]

(ii) *The Resurrection and Pentecost*

It was not until the second half of the twentieth century that Western theology began to regard the resurrection as more than simply the proof that Christ was divine and that through his crucifixion he had conquered sin and death. Both Catholics and Protestants gave the impression of the resurrection not so much as essential to redemption, as a kind of happy conclusion to the real drama that took place on the cross. More than a century before, however, Newman had discovered what an impoverished version this was of the theology of the New Testament and the Fathers. His scriptural and patristic studies had shown him that "those who omit the resurrection in their view of the divine economy, are as really defective in faith as if they omitted the crucifixion. On the cross He paid the debt of the world, but as He could not have been crucified without first taking flesh, so again He could not . . . apply His Atonement without first rising again."[77] Newman criticised Evangelicals who "think individuals are justified immediately by the great Atonement,—justified by Christ's death, and not, as St. Paul says, by means of His resurrection."[78] The real reason, he says, that the Apostles preached the resurrection "as if it were the main doctrine of the Gospel" is that the resurrection is "the means by which the Atonement is applied to each of us."[79]

Not that Newman ignored the more obvious, external aspects of the resurrection: He preached, for example, that "the very reason *why* Christ showed Himself at all was in order to raise up *witnesses* to His resurrection, ministers of His word, founders of His Church"; for "the real object of His rising again" was "the propagation of His Gospel through the world."[80] But there were deeper reasons, more fundamental to our redemption. Through the Incarnation, human nature was "renewed" in Christ, "glorious and wonderful beyond our thoughts"; as a result of the resurrection this same nature was raised up in glory, so that "henceforth, we dare aspire to enter into the heaven of heavens, and to live for ever in God's presence, because the first-fruits of our race is already there in the Person of His Only-begotten Son."[81]

A sermon for Christmas contains a lyrical, indeed sublime passage where Newman celebrates the great mysteries of the redemption:

INTRODUCTION

> He died, to rise again the third day, the Sun of Righteousness, fully displaying that splendour which had hitherto been concealed by the morning clouds. He rose again, to ascend to the right hand of God, there to plead His sacred wounds in token of our forgiveness, to rule and guide His ransomed people, and from His pierced side to pour forth His choicest blessings upon them. He ascended, thence to descend again in due season to judge the world which He has redeemed.—Great is our Lord, and great is His Power, Jesus the Son of God and Son of man. Ten thousand times more dazzling bright than the highest Archangel, is our Lord and Christ. By birth the Only-begotten and Express image of God; and in taking our flesh, not sullied thereby, but raising human nature with Him, as He rose from the lowly manger to the right hand of power,—raising human nature, for Man has redeemed us, Man is set above all creatures, as one with the Creator, Man shall judge man at the last day.[82]

Three points are worth noticing about this passage. First, the preacher clearly does not envisage Christ's work of redemption as completed on the cross. Second, far from the resurrection merely confirming the victory of the cross, the raising of Christ's body in glory is seen, like his original fleshly Incarnation, as a crucial part of our redemption. Third, Newman, like modern theologians, emphasizes that the crucifixion, resurrection, ascension, and pentecost are to be seen not so much as separate events and actions but as constituting one single divine act unfolding in several closely connected stages.

In a sermon for Easter day Newman shows the close connection between the Incarnation and the resurrection—"Corruption had no power over that Sacred Body, the fruit of a miraculous conception." When Christ was raised from the dead, "the Divine Essence streamed forth (so to say) on every side, and environed His Manhood, as in a cloud of glory. So transfigured was His Sacred Body, that He who had deigned to be born of woman, and to hang upon the cross, had subtle virtue in Him, like a spirit, to pass through the closed doors to His assembled followers."[83] But if the resurrection completes the Incarnation, it also leads directly to the ascension, for when Christ was raised from the dead he was at the same time raised up in glory to the Father. And it was necessary that the post-resurrection appearances should cease and that Christ should leave this world in order that we might receive the Holy

INTRODUCTION

Spirit: "We are able to see that the Saviour, when once He entered into this world, never so departed as to suffer things to be as they were before He came; for He is still with us, not in mere gifts, but by the substitution of His Spirit for Himself, and that, both in the Church, and in the souls of individual Christians."[84]

Pentecost applied the resurrection to our human situation in the sense that the risen and glorified Christ became savingly present to each individual Christian as well as to the whole Church through the Holy Spirit. "Christ's bodily presence, which was limited to place," had to be "exchanged for the manifold spiritual indwelling of the Comforter within us."[85] The Son returned to the Father, and in his place came "the Eternal Love whereby the Father and the Son have dwelt in each other,"[86] the Holy Spirit, the third person of the Trinity. Newman insists that "the Holy Ghost's coming is so really His coming, that we might as well say that He was not here in the days of His flesh, when He was visibly in this world, as deny that He is here now, when He is here by His Divine Spirit."[87] This new Presence was necessary, for "the Spirit came to finish in us, what Christ had finished in Himself, but left unfinished as regards us. To Him it is committed to apply to us severally all that Christ had done for us." Through the Spirit, Christ's redemption comes to each one of us: "What was actually done by Christ in the flesh eighteen hundred years ago, is in type and resemblance really wrought in us one by one even to the end of time."

Newman's theology of the work of the Holy Spirit in Christ's redemption is eloquently comprehensive: Christ

> was born of the Spirit, and we too are born of the Spirit. He was justified by the Spirit, and so are we. He was pronounced the well-beloved Son, when the Holy Ghost descended on Him; and we too cry Abba, Father, through the Spirit sent into our hearts. He was led into the wilderness by the Spirit; He did great works by the Spirit; He offered himself to death by the Eternal Spirit; he was raised from the dead by the Spirit; He was declared to be the Son of God by the Spirit of holiness on His resurrection: We too are led by the same Spirit into and through the world's temptations; we, too, do our works of obedience by the Spirit; we die from sin, we rise again unto righteousness through the Spirit; and we are declared to be God's sons,—declared, pronounced, dealt with as righteous,—through our resurrection unto holiness in the

INTRODUCTION

Spirit.... Christ Himself vouchsafes to repeat in each of us in figure and mystery all that He did and suffered in the flesh. He is formed in us, born in us, suffers in us, rises again in us, lives in us; and this not by a succession of events, but all at once: for he comes to us as a Spirit, all dying, all rising again, all living.[88]

The Holy Spirit unites us not only to the Son but also to the Father, "for He who once was on earth, has now departed from this visible scene of things in a mysterious, twofold way, both to His Father and into our hearts, thus making the Creator and His creatures one." Again Newman insists that the Spirit does not replace or substitute for the Son:

Let us not for a moment suppose that God the Holy Ghost comes in such sense that God the Son remains away. No; He has not so come that Christ does not come, but rather He comes that Christ may come in His coming. Through the Holy Ghost we have communion with Father and Son.... The Holy Spirit causes, faith welcomes, the indwelling of Christ in the heart. Thus the Spirit does not take the place of Christ in the soul, but secures that place to Christ.[89]

Finally, in spite of his emphasis on the concluding acts of the Christian drama of redemption, it should never be thought that Newman ever loses sight of the crucifixion; rather, his spirituality shows a rare balance of cross and resurrection. Faith, he preached, is "always sorrowing" with Christ in His death, "while it rejoices" in His resurrection. "And the same union of opposite thoughts is impressed on us" in the Eucharist, "in which we see Christ's death and resurrection together, at one and the same time."[90] This is why "none rejoice in Easter-tide less than those who have not grieved in Lent." For it is our own "previous humiliation" which "sobers our joy" and "alone secures it to us."[91] And it is the "duty of fearing" that "does but perfect our joy; that joy alone is true Christian joy, which is informed and quickened by fear, and made thereby sober and reverent." The "paradox" of combining two such contradictory emotions is "fulfilled in the case of men of advanced holiness."[92] Again, on the other hand, such a combination of feelings arises out of the twofold effect of the resurrection:

Christ's going to the Father is at once a source of sorrow, because it involves His absence; and of joy, because it involves

INTRODUCTION

> His presence. And out of the doctrine of His resurrection and ascension, spring those Christian paradoxes, often spoken of in Scripture, that we are sorrowing, yet always rejoicing; as having nothing, yet possessing all things.[93]

It is a constant theme of Newman's preaching that "we must fear and be in sorrow, before we can rejoice. The Gospel must be a burden before it comforts and brings us peace."[94] Without severity, love itself is no longer true love: "I wish I saw any prospect of this element of zeal and holy sternness springing up among us, to temper and give character to the languid, unmeaning benevolence which we misname Christian love." To speak only of God's love and never of His justice or wrath is spiritually debilitating. Instead, Newman urges, it is necessary to "condense" one's "feelings by a severe discipline" and to be "loving in the midst of firmness, strictness, and holiness."[95] The problem is that people "find a difficulty in conceiving how Christians can have hope without certainty, sorrow and pain without gloom, suspense with calmness and confidence; how they can believe that in one sense they are in the light of God's countenance, and that in another sense they have forfeited it."[96] So insistent on this is Newman that he is even prepared to say that those "who seem only to fear, or to have very little joy in religion . . . are in a more hopeful state than those who only joy and do not fear at all."[97]

(iii) *The Indwelling of the Holy Spirit*

Newman had discovered for himself in the New Testament and the Fathers the great forgotten doctrine of the indwelling in the soul of the Holy Spirit, and through the Spirit of the Father and the Son as well.[98] It had, after all, been

> the great promise of the Gospel, that the Lord of all, who had hitherto manifested Himself externally to His servants, should take up His abode in their hearts. . . . Though He had come in our flesh, so as to be seen and handled, even this was not enough. Still He was external and separate; but after His ascension He descended again by and in His Spirit, and then at length the promise was fulfilled.[99]

And so Christ came again, but this time in an even more personal and real way, "returning to His redeemed in the power of the Spirit, with a

INTRODUCTION

Presence more pervading because more intimate, and more real because more hidden."[100] Consequently, Christians have "not merely the promise of grace; they have its presence."[101] Indeed, Newman practically defined a Christian as "one who has a ruling sense of God's Presence within him." And it is this very awareness that should be at the heart of the moral and spiritual life of a Christian:

> He alone admits Christ into the shrine of his heart; whereas others wish in some way or other, to be by themselves, to have a home, a chamber, a tribunal, a throne, a self where God is not,—a home within them which is not a temple, a chamber which is not a confessional, a tribunal without a judge, a throne without a king;—that self may be king and judge; and that the Creator may rather be dealt with and approached as though a second party, instead of His being that true and better self, of which self itself should be but an instrument and minister.[102]

Given the sinfulness of Christians, Newman wonders: "How is it that the lamp of God does not go out . . . at once . . . ? Incomprehensible patience in the Holy One, so to dwell, in such a wilderness, with the wild beasts!"[103] In fact, without the presence of God, human life in its fulness is impossible, for

> the contemplation of Him, and nothing but it, is able fully to open and relieve the mind, to unlock, occupy, and fix our affections. We may indeed love things created with great intenseness, but such affection, when disjoined from the love of the Creator, is like a stream running in a narrow channel, impetuous, vehement, turbid. The heart runs out, as it were, only at one door; it is not an expanding of the whole man. Created natures cannot open us, or elicit the ten thousand mental senses which belong to us, and through which we really live. None but the Presence of our Maker can enter us; for to none besides can the whole heart in all its thoughts and feelings be unlocked and subjected. . . . It is this feeling of single and absolute confidence and communion, which soothes and satisfies those to whom it is vouchsafed. We know that even our nearest friends enter into us but partially, and hold intercourse with us only at times; whereas the consciousness of a perfect and enduring Presence, and it alone, keeps the heart open.

INTRODUCTION

Withdraw the Object on which it rests, and it will relapse again into its state of confinement and constraint.

For his cardinalitial motto Newman was to choose the deeply personal words "cor ad cor loquitur," heart speaks to heart. In the remarkable sermon "The Thought of God, the Stay of the Soul," one of his greatest, he makes the heart the focal point of human life and argues that only a personal God can fulfil its longings. Without the possibility of this deepest kind of affectivity, we live and die "with closed heart, with affections undeveloped, unexercised," "with a stone heart." Human affection and love can only center the heart on what is "perishable":

> Life passes, riches fly away, popularity is fickle, the senses decay, the world changes, friends die. One alone is constant; One alone is true to us; One alone can be true; One alone can be all things to us; One alone can supply our needs; One alone can train us up to our full perfection; One alone can give a meaning to our complex and intricate nature; One alone can give us tune and harmony; One alone can form and possess us.[104]

Our redemption, Newman insists, was complete only when the "dreadful reality" of original sin was overtaken by a "new righteousness," a "real righteousness" which "comes from the Holy and Divine Spirit," so that our "works, done in the Spirit of Christ, have a justifying *principle* in them, and that is the Presence of the All-holy Spirit," which "hallows those acts, that life, that obedience of which it is the original cause, and which it orders and fashions."[105] This "gift of the Spirit" is gained by "faith in Christ."

While, then, Newman preaches that without faith there can be no justification of the sinner, he disagrees with Evangelicals who "consider it as a state, not of holiness and righteousness, but merely or mainly of acceptance with God."[106] For him "faith gains the promise, and . . . the promise is the great gift of the Spirit."[107] But while "faith is a condition of Christ's grace," it is not "a token"; and somebody "may have true faith, and still not yet be justified," since having "faith" is not the same as enjoying the "promise." Evangelicals, on the other hand, "consider justification to be nothing more than God's *accounting* them righteous, which is just what justification was to the Jews. Justification *is* God's accounting a man righteous; yes, but it is, in the case of the Christian, something more; it is God's *making* him righteous too." Just as "the presence of a soul is the mode in which God gives man life, so the presence of the Holy Spirit is the mode in which God gives him righteousness."[108] Again, unlike Evangelicals, Catholic Christians agree with pagans and Jews that "works are the means of salvation," only differing "in respect to the quality of these works."[109]

Justification had not been the subject of controversy until the sixteenth century. For the Greek Fathers justifying grace was seen in terms of the deification or divinisation of the Christian by virtue of the indwelling of the Holy Spirit, and through the Spirit of the Father and the Son. This personal union with the Trinity was very different from the Western concept of grace as negatively a remedy for sin and as an abstract quality of the soul. Newman, of course, had found the doctrine of the indwelling of the Spirit in the New Testament as well as in the Fathers: "He pervades us . . . as light pervades a building, or as a sweet perfume the folds of some honourable robe; so that, in Scripture language, we are said to be in Him, and He in us." The Presence of the Holy Spirit necessarily involves the Presence of the other two Persons of the Trinity, and Newman is emphatic that invisible as the "indwelling" is, there is nothing unreal about it—"we are assured of some real though mystical fellowship with the Father, Son, and Holy Spirit . . . so that . . . by a real presence in the soul . . . God is one with every believer, as in a consecrated Temple."[110]

And so the rival sixteenth-century theologies of works and faith, both deeply imbedded in the same late medieval theology of grace, are circumvented by the rediscovery of the central New Testament doctrine of the indwelling of the Holy Spirit, a doctrine that was second nature to the Eastern Fathers who knew nothing of the modern problem of justification: "The presence of the Holy Ghost shed abroad in our hearts, the Author both of faith and of renewal, this is really that which makes us righteous, and . . . our righteousness is the possession of that presence." Justification, then, "is wrought by the power of the Spirit, or rather by His Presence within us," while "faith and renewal are both present also, but as fruits of it."[111] The "connection" between justification and renewal is that they are "both included in that one great gift of God, the indwelling of Christ" through the Holy Spirit "in the Christian soul," which constitutes "our justification and sanctification, as its necessary results."[112]

INTRODUCTION

(iv) *Sacraments*

The great Johannine and Pauline doctrine of the indwelling of the Holy Spirit lies at the heart of Newman's deeply personal spirituality. In his novel *Callista* (1856), the pagan heroine is attracted to Christianity precisely because it is represented to her as a religion of persons rather than abstractions, and made to consist in "the intimate Divine Presence in the heart. It was the friendship or mutual love of person with person."[113] But how do we receive this Presence and enter into this loving relationship? From the Fathers Newman learned that the Sacraments were the concrete means of our union with God: "He inhabits us personally, and His inhabitation is effected by the channel of the Sacraments."[114] For Christ "shines through them, as through transparent bodies, without impediment."[115] In the Sacraments, Newman declares in a magnificently mysterious passage,

> is manifested in greater or less degree, according to the measure of each, that Incarnate Saviour, who is one day to be our Judge, and who is enabling us to bear His presence then, by imparting it to us in measure now. A thick black veil is spread between this world and the next. We mortal men range up and down it, to and fro, and see nothing. There is no access through it into the next world. In the Gospel this veil is not removed; it remains, but every now and then marvellous disclosures are made to us of what is behind it. At times we seem to catch a glimpse of a Form which we shall hereafter see face to face. We approach, and in spite of the darkness, our hands, or our head, or our brow, or our lips become, as it were, sensible of the contact of something more than earthly. We know not where we are, but we have been bathing in water, and a voice tells us that it is blood. Or we have a mark signed upon our foreheads, and it spake of Calvary. Or we recollect a hand laid upon our heads, and surely it had the print of nails in it, and resembled His who with a touch gave sight to the blind and raised the dead. Or we have been eating and drinking; and it was not a dream surely, that One fed us from His wounded side, and renewed our nature by the heavenly meat He gave.[116]

The Sacraments moreover ensure a personal relationship with God the Father in the Son and through the Holy Spirit, since they are both concrete rather than abstract and personal rather than impersonal. A religion that is centered on the doctrine of the Divine indwelling involves "the belief in such sensible tokens of God's favour, as the Sacraments are accounted by the Church," for religion "is of a personal nature, and implies the acknowledgement of a particular providence, of a God speaking, not merely to the world at large, but to this person or that, to one and not to another." The Bible "is a common possession, and speaks to one man as much and as little as to his neighbour," but human nature "requires something special," something of a highly personal character.[117]

And so Baptism not only frees us from original sin and brings us into the Church, but Christ himself personally comes to us in the Spirit: "Did He not in Baptism cast out the evil spirit and enter into thee Himself, and dwell in thee . . . ?" But if so much is given us in this primary sacrament, nothing less is offered in the eucharist—"the Presence of the Lord Incarnate": "He who is at the right hand of God, manifests Himself in that Holy Sacrament as really and fully as if He were visibly there."[118]

(v) *Mystery*

Whereas the Greek Fathers like Athanasius constantly stressed the importance of mystery, it was the lack of this sense that seemed to Newman to characterize a heresy like Arianism. And it was the same loss that he connected with modern unbelief, since "mystery is the necessary note of divine revelation, that is, mystery subjectively to the human mind."[119] A true Christian spirituality for Newman is marked by a due sense of mystery: "There is nothing . . . which will make a greater difference in the temper, character, and habits of an individual, than the circumstance of his holding or not holding the Gospel to be mysterious."[120] It was one of his objections against Evangelicals that they attempted to analyze and explain the doctrine of the Atonement: "One might have thought that here at least somewhat of awful Mystery would have been allowed to hang over it . . . *how* His death expiated our sins, and what satisfaction it was to God's *justice*, are surely subjects quite above us."[121]

The emphasis on mystery was in contrast both to the enthusiasm of Evangelicals and the coldness of other Anglicans, whether of the new liberal or the old high-and-dry school. "Till we understand that the gifts of grace are unseen, supernatural, and mysterious, we have but a choice

INTRODUCTION

between explaining away the high and glowing expressions of Scripture, or giving them that rash, irreverent, and self-exalting interpretation, which is one of the chief errors of this time." The alternative to the assumption that "the gift of the Holy Ghost was almost peculiar to the Apostles' day, that now, at least, it does something more than make us decent and orderly members of society," did not have to be "a sort of religious ecstasy . . . a high-wrought sensibility on second subjects . . . impassioned thoughts, a soft and languid tone of feeling, and an unnatural profession of all this in conversation."[122]

Again, Newman sets both the ordinary kind of English Pelagian Christian and the Evangelical against an altogether different kind of Christianity that he found in the Church of the Fathers. The first two kinds of Christian have a defective or perverted theology, which consequently produces a spirituality devoid of mystery:

> The maintainers of both the one and the other error, whatever their differences in other respects, agree in this,—in depriving a Christian life of its mysteriousness. He who believes that he can please God of himself, or that obedience can be performed by his own powers, of course has nothing more of awe, reverence, and wonder in his personal religion, than when he moves his limbs and uses his reason, though he might well feel awe then also. And in like manner he also who considers that Christ's passion once undergone on the cross absolutely secures his own personal salvation, may see mystery indeed in that cross (as he ought), but he will see no mystery, and feel little solemnity, in prayer, in Ordinances, or in his attempts at obedience. He will be free, familiar, and presuming, in God's Presence. . . . Both the one and the other will be content with a low standard of duty: the one, because he does not believe that God requires much; the other, because he thinks that Christ in His own person has done all. Neither will honour and make much of God's Law: the one, because he brings down the Law to his own power of obeying it; the other because he thinks that Christ has taken away the Law by obeying it in his stead. They only feel awe and true seriousness who think that the Law remains; that it claims to be fulfilled by them; and that it can be fulfilled by them through the power of God's grace.[123]

Here, then is another factor that accounts for the severity of Newman's

INTRODUCTION

preaching, namely, the sense of awe or mystery. And when we remember that for Newman the grace that enables us to keep the commandments of Christ is constituted by the sacramental divinisation of human nature through the indwelling of the Trinity we have another reason for a very demanding spirituality. If believers are really temples of the Holy Spirit, as St. Paul teaches, then it is practically sacrilegious for a baptized Christian not to be living the life of the Spirit.

CHARACTERISTICS OF NEWMAN'S SPIRITUALITY

(i) *Realism*

In considering Newman's reaction against Evangelicalism, we have looked at his own view of what constitutes the *real* Christian, that is to say, the person who *realizes* his or her faith. However, the theme of the real is a much more pervasive and wider theme in Newman's thought,[124] not least in his spirituality.

It is not simply that so many Christians do not realize what it is they profess to believe: There is also the fact that their faith often seems to be so totally unreal because they make so little effort to practise it in fact. Quite apart from normal human weakness of will, much sin, Newman argues, is in effect quite deliberate and voluntary: "After all, nothing perhaps is so rare among those who profess to be Christians, as an assent in practice to the doctrine that they are under a law; nothing so rare as strict obedience, unreserved submission to God's will, uniform conscientiousness in doing their duty." It is not a question of how far people's consciences are enlightened and formed, it is simply that they fail to regard their conscience as in any real sense binding at all: "Most Christians . . . will allow in general terms that they are under a law, but then they admit it with a reserve; they claim for themselves some dispensing power in their observance of the law . . . one and all think it allowable at times to put themselves above the law, even according to their own standard of it; to make exceptions and reserves, as if they were absolute sovereigns of their conscience, and had a dispensing power upon occasions." And it is precisely at times of temptation that Christians are wont to think they have "a leave to dispense with the Law." People dispense with the commandments "at those very times when it is simply the Law of God, without being also the law of self, and of the world." People are happy to do "what is right, while the road of religion runs along the road of the world," but when "they part company awhile," then the choice to follow the world is described as "an exception."[125]

We shall return to the preoccupation with obedience and consistency, but here it is enough to stress the harsh, unflattering light that Newman's realism casts on the complacent self-delusion of so many Christians. If they were honest, they would have to admit that "their real quarrel with religion... is not that it is strict, or engrossing, or imperative, not that it goes too far, but that it *is* religion. It is religion itself which we all by nature dislike, not the excess merely."[126] At a time when respectability and religion were so closely associated and intertwined, there was a particular need for a realism that cut through the appearances and pretences and self-deceptions of the outwardly religious. The figure of Balaam reminds Newman of the typical churchgoing Victorian, anxious "not to please God, but to please self without displeasing God," and for whom this world is really "the first object" and religion merely "a corrective, restraint, upon *too much* attachment to the world."[127] Then there are those who become so obsessed with a particular aspect or part of religion—such as social justice or liturgy or orthodoxy—that "instead of thinking anxiously of God and His law, [they] think only of a portion of it... and make it a sort of idol."[128]

Realism prevented Newman from entertaining any very sanguine ideas about the success of Christianity in the world. In spite of certain external improvements in the moral tone of society, he felt that "on the whole the great multitude of men have to all appearance remained, in a spiritual point of view, no better than before." Most Christian profession as well as practice was fairly superficial: "Human nature remains what it was, though it has been baptized." When all was said and done, Christianity had "not materially changed more than the surface of things; it has made clean the outside; but... it has not acted on a large scale upon the mind within." But then it had never claimed it would have any success on a large scale: "This has been the real triumph of the Gospel, to raise those beyond themselves and beyond human nature... whose wills mysteriously co-operate with God's grace.... It has made men saints, and brought into existence specimens of faith and holiness, which without it are unknown and impossible.... An ordinary kind of religion, praiseworthy and respectable in its way, may exist under many systems; but saints are creations of the Gospel and the Church."[129]

Newman wonders whether Christians, if they had been Christ's contemporaries, would not have thought him "strange, eccentric, extravagant, and fanciful"—hardly more than what we should now call "a

INTRODUCTION

vagrant." And far from "our sinful habits being reformed by the presence of Christ, the chance is, that those same habits would have hindered us from recognizing Him." Indeed, none were closer to Him externally than those who caused His suffering and death—"Oh, dreadful thought, that the nearest approaches man has made to God upon earth have been in blasphemy!"[130] Newman loves to undermine our complacency by challenging our facile assumptions. For example, what "stake" do we really have in the truth of Christianity? Would we be any "the worse off" if it were not true? Would not in fact most people "go on almost as they do . . . if they believed Christianity to be a fable?"[131]

Newman's realism does not allow for any sentimentality about sin. He is as direct about human weakness as he is about the power of evil. Indeed, his acute sense of the dominance of sin involves a genuine understanding of the sheer impotence, and therefore lack of culpability, of the sinner. Thus there are sins that are "humbling and distressing" but that are in fact involuntary because they "arise from our former habits of sin, though now long abandoned." The analysis of this kind of paralysing weakness of will is as pitiless as it is consoling from the point of view of human responsibility:

> We cannot rid ourselves of sin when we would; though we repent, though God forgives us, yet it remains in its power over our souls, in our habits, and in our memories. It has given a colour to our thoughts, words, and works; and though, with many efforts, we would wash it out from us, yet this is not possible except gradually.[132]

Nor are the attractions of sin underestimated, or the lack of appeal of religion. As Newman remarks drily, "most persons called Christians do not go farther than this,—to wish to be religious, and to think it right to be religious, and to feel a respect for religious men; they do not get so far as to have any sort of love for religion." That does not mean that they enjoy sinning exactly, since they know the unhappiness that sin brings: Their unfortunate position is "not to be dead to sin and alive to God, but, while they are alive to sin and the world, to have just so much sense of heaven, as not to be able to enjoy either."[133] The power of habit is such that having once committed a particular sin, we cannot just "continue where we left off," for one sin leads to another until we become enslaved to it. We are able to ignore our conscience because "when we

INTRODUCTION

trifle" with its warnings, "our reason becomes perverted, and comes in aid of our wishes, and deceives us to our ruin."[134]

Scripture has many warnings against the so-called world. Newman refuses in any way to glamorize the temptation, insisting that it is "something wider, and more subtle, and more ordinary" than overt evil—"it is that very world in which we are . . . it is human society itself." For "God would have us live for the world to come, the world would make us live for this life." People do not deny God's existence, but they take it for granted that "religion is not needed for this world, and therefore is of no great importance," refusing to recognize "God's service, as such, as distinct from the service of this world." The world simply takes precedence for no better reason than that "there are so many men in it; they must be right." And as for the scriptural condemnations of the world, "They think that this world is too great an evil for God to punish; or rather that therefore it is not an evil, because it is a great one." Newman sarcastically draws out the logic of the world's reasoning: "They cannot compass the idea that God should allow so great an evil to exist, as the world would be, if it is evil; and therefore, since He does allow it, it is not an evil."[135] As for sin, they "do not believe that the temptations which they themselves experience and to which they yield, can be overcome," so they "reason themselves into the notion that to sin is their very nature, and, therefore, is no fault of theirs; that is, they deny the existence of sin."[136] Nor, on the other hand, should professed Christians think that repentance is easy:

> We do not like to be new-made; we are afraid of it; it is throwing us out of all our natural ways, of all that is familiar to us. We feel as if we should not *be* ourselves any longer, if we do not keep some portion of what we have been hitherto; and much as we prefer in general terms to wish to be changed, when it comes to the point, when particular instances of change are presented to us, we shrink from them, and are content to remain unchanged.

Newman's discomforting realism cuts through the usual bland pieties and informs us very specifically why the Bible tells us we need new hearts: because "you cannot bear to be other than you are. Life would seem a blank to you, were you other."[137]

A characteristic and special mark of the realism of Newman's spirituality is his concern always to be as concrete and specific as possible.

INTRODUCTION

How, for example, do we know that we are at peace with God? Not because of some aspiration or feeling but if "we can point to some occasions on which we have sacrificed anything for God's service, or to any habit of sin or evil tendency of nature which we have more or less overcome, or to any habitual self-denial which we practise, or to any work which we have accomplished to God's honour and glory."[138]

(ii) *Obedience the Means to Holiness*

The title of the first sermon of the first volume of the collected *Parochial and Plain Sermons*, "Holiness Necessary for Future Blessedness," indicates clearly enough the dominant theme of Newman's spirituality: the call to holiness for all Christians. In this sermon Newman exhorts his congregation, "Be you content with nothing short of perfection." But the first thing we notice about this call is that there is nothing vaguely uplifting about it. It is not an invitation to entertain spiritual feelings or thoughts of holiness. There is nothing merely pious about Newman's spirituality: "Is not holiness the result of many patient, repeated efforts after obedience, gradually working on us, and first modifying and then changing our hearts?"[139] The challenge may be a hard one, but Newman assures, or rather warns, us that we have no excuse for failing to meet it if we are Christians:

> We dwell in the full light of the Gospel, and the full grace of the Sacraments. We ought to have the holiness of Apostles. There is no reason except our own wilful corruption, that we are not by this time walking in the steps of St. Paul or St. John, and following them as they followed Christ.[140]

Newman is a preacher not of glowing words but of harsh realities—realities that arise out of the obligation imposed by Baptism to lead the Christian life to the full:

> To love our brethren with a resolution which no obstacles can overcome, so as almost to consent to an anathema on ourselves, if so be we may save those who hate us,—to labour in God's cause against hope, and in the midst of sufferings,—to read the events of life, as they occur, by the interpretation which Scripture gives them, and that, not as if the language were strange to us, but to do it promptly,—to perform all our rela-

INTRODUCTION

tive daily duties most watchfully,—to check every evil thought, and bring the whole mind into captivity to the law of Christ,—to be patient, cheerful, forgiving, meek, honest, and true,—to persevere in this good work till death, making fresh and fresh advances towards perfection—and after all, even to the end, to confess ourselves unprofitable servants, nay, to feel ourselves corrupt and sinful creatures, who (with all our proficiency) would still be lost unless God bestowed on us His mercy in Christ;—these are some of the difficult realities of religious obedience, which we must pursue, and which the Apostles in high measure attained, and which we may well bless God's holy name, if He enables us to make our own.[141]

The trouble with most people is not that they do not "act up to their standard, but it is their standard that is low."[142] And their standard is low because they do not want to be holy. With characteristic psychological realism Newman puts his finger on the central reason why Christians are not better than they are: They do not want to be. In one sermon he exhorts his hearers not to strive for holiness but to strive for the desire for holiness: "Let us strive and pray that the love of holiness may be created within our hearts; and then acts will follow, such as befit us and our circumstances, in due time, without our distressing ourselves to find what they should be."[143]

Nor is there anything unreal about the means to the end that Newman so insistently impresses on his hearers. Indeed, the very practicality often contains a surprise. Thus, we should expect Newman to urge the necessity of prayer, but the actual content of the prayer he recommends is not, perhaps, what we might anticipate: He does not advise his hearers to pray for holiness so much as to "pray for His saving help to change their likings and dislikings, their tastes, their views, their wills, their hearts."[144] For obviously there is little point in praying to be holy if one does not particularly want to be holy and if it is the wish to be holy for which one should in fact be praying.

Again, we might assume from the impassioned language of the preacher and his refusal to be content with anything but the realization of the highest ideals that the means to the end would be correspondingly momentous. But in fact what is so striking about Newman's spirituality is its ordinariness and unpretentiousness. He warns, for example, that "to take up the cross of Christ is no great action done once for all," but "it consists in the continual practice of small duties which are distasteful

INTRODUCTION

to us"; for "the self-denial which is pleasing to Christ consists in little things." A great deal hangs on small acts of apparently little consequence. Thus one "apparently small defect will influence your whole spirit and judgment in all things," since "your judgment of persons, and of events, and of actions, and of doctrines, and your spirit towards God and man, your faith in the high truths of the Gospel, and your knowledge of your duty, all depend in a strange way on this strict endeavour to observe the whole Law, on this self-denial in those little things in which obedience is a self-denial." This emphasis on "daily self-denial"[145] (as opposed to great, occasional self-denials) being the key to true Christian belief and practice is very much in line with Newman's insistence on the connection between moral and intellectual integrity. It is also a great witness to Christianity: "How great a profession, and yet a profession how unconscious and modest, arises from the mere ordinary manner in which any strict Christian lives."[146]

Newman draws our attention to two important psychological truths. First is the aspect of habituation: "There is the most close and remarkable connexion between small observances and the permanence of our chief habits and practices." Second is the peculiar mortification involved in regular discipline: "Nothing is more difficult than to be disciplined and regular in our religion. It is very easy to be religious by fits and starts, and to keep up our feelings by artificial stimulants; but regularity seems to trammel us, and we become impatient."[147] Again, too, it is worth noting "how mysteriously little things are in this world connected with great; how single moments, improved or wasted, are the salvation or ruin of all-important interests."[148] And so "That little deed, suddenly exacted of us, almost suddenly resolved on and executed, may be as though a gate into the second or third heaven."[149] Of this kind of hidden, obscure holiness, in which "the silent duties of every day . . . are blest to the sufficient sanctification of thousands, whom the world knows not of," Mary is herself "a memorial."[150]

As a Catholic, Newman was to observe: "I have ever made consistency the mark of a saint."[151] Already in his Anglican sermons he insists again and again on consistency as the note of authentic Christian faith:

> General conscientiousness is the only assurance we can have
> of possessing it; and at this we must aim, determining to obey
> God consistently, with a jealous carefulness about all things,
> little and great. . . . As far then as a man has reason to hope that

INTRODUCTION

he is *consistent*, so far may he humbly trust that he has true faith.[152]

If we reach heaven through small acts, the opposite is also true for Newman: "Men do not lose their souls by some one extraordinary act, but by a course of acts."[153] In fact, however, the real test lies only in a limited range of actions: "Now let every one consider what his weak point is; in that is his test. His trial is not in those things which are easy to him, but in that one thing, in those several things, whatever they are, in which to do his duty is against his nature."[154] The nature of a person is formed by his or her habits, and Newman warns severely: "Any *one* deliberate habit of sin incapacitates a man for receiving the gifts of the Gospel."[155] Moreover, "sinful habits ... clog" the "exercise" of a person's will.[156] Because "no habit is formed at once ... the flame of religion in the heart" needs to be "purified and strengthened by long practice and experience."[157] By *systematically* trying to be good, we become good.[158]

Holiness is rare simply because it "is hard, indeed, to find a man who gives himself up honestly to his Saviour."[159] There is "nothing so rare as strict obedience, unreserved submission to God's will, uniform conscientiousness in doing [one's] duty."[160] Most Christians "wish to be saved, but in their own way; they wish (as it were) to capitulate upon terms, to carry off their goods with them." It is usual to have "a reserve" in one's "obedience," to keep a "corner" in one's "heart" to oneself; and "a half purpose" is as different from "a whole one" as "ice from the flowing stream."[161] The secret of holiness is rather to depend on Christ: "All of us must rely on something; all must look up to, admire, court, make themselves one with something. Most men cast in their lot with the visible world." Hence holy people seem to the world "like *foreigners*."[162] And the "holier a man is, the less he is understood by men of the world."[163]

Newman agrees with St. Paul that love "is the root of all holy dispositions, and grows and blossoms into them"; it is "the material (so to speak) out of which all graces are made, the quality of mind which is the fruit of regeneration, and in which the Spirit dwells." For "we love for no cause beyond itself: We love, because it is our nature to love; and it is our nature, because God the Holy Ghost has made it our nature." And so love "is the seed of holiness, and grows into all excellences, not indeed destroying their peculiarities, but making them what they are." It is "the first element" of holiness, as faith is of religion. It is "the motion within us of the new spirit, the holy and renewed heart which God the

INTRODUCTION

Holy Ghost gives us." Faith can make "a hero," but "love makes a saint."[164]

But there is a problem about taking love as the measure of holiness. As Newman put it strikingly in a sermon he never published:

> To attempt to be guided by love alone, would be like attempting to walk in a straight line by steadily gazing on some star. It is too high—we must take nearer objects to steady our course.... Love must be wrought out by fear and trembling. It is the offspring of self-abasement and self-discipline.[165]

The ultimate source of holiness is of course for Newman the "indwelling of the Holy Spirit," for "Christ brings us into it by coming to us through His spirit; and, as His Spirit is holy, we are holy, if we are in the state of grace."[166] But if holiness is indistinguishable from His love that God pours into our hearts, it is attainable, humanly speaking, by "nearer objects" than love. And nothing can take "the place of careful obedience, of that *self-denial* which is the very substance of true practical religion."[167] If one had to define the authentic Christian in terms of Newman's spirituality, one would have to say that he or she is characterized by *obedience*. This is not because obedience is more important than faith and love, but because it is the concrete proof and realization of things more important than itself, things only too easily corrupted or counterfeited.

As usual, Newman is realistic about the difficulties of obedience, which "is very grievous to habitual sinners" even after they have been converted. However, distrustful as he is about emotions and feelings, he recognizes that in the early stages after conversion they are very useful in providing "an impulse which may carry us over the first obstacles," leading us "to the more sober and higher comfort resulting from that real *love* for religion, which obedience itself will have by that time begun to form in us, and will gradually go on to perfect." The "excitement of mind" caused by a religious conversion "will wear away," but it "may be made a means of leading [us] into a sound religious course of life." "Therefore," Newman advises, "obey *promptly;* make use of it while it lasts; it waits for no man."[168] And obedience is so difficult precisely because the effects of our past sins form bad habits in us, although a person may not be "conscious of the load of corrupt nature and sinful habits which hang upon his will, and clog it in each particular exercise of it."[169] On the other hand, continual obedience creates good habits, which in turn make obedience easier: "If we strove to obey God's will in all things, we actually should be gradually training our hearts into the fulness of a Christian spirit."[170] Like self-denial, obedience in little things is especially important: "Such creatures are we, there is the most close and remarkable connexion between small observances and the permanence of our chief habits and practices." In the same way disobedience begins in "(apparently) slight omissions" and ends "in open unbelief."[171] But it is "the observance of all lowly deeds of ordinary obedience" that is "the most pleasing sacrifice to God."[172]

Obedience is also the best antidote to religious doubts and problems: "To all those who are perplexed in any way soever, who wish for light but cannot find it, one precept must be given,—*obey*. It is obedience which brings a man into the right path; it is obedience keeps him there and strengthens him in it." Moreover, by setting about "to obey God, in the ordinary businesses of daily life, we are at once interested by realities which withdraw our minds from vague fears and uncertain indefinite surmises about the future."[173] But obedience has a very positive as well as a negative importance, for "it is the rule of God's providence, that those who act up to their light, shall be rewarded with clearer light."[174] It is a spiritual point that Newman never tires of repeating and that is enshrined in his famous hymn "Lead, Kindly Light" in the words "one step enough for me":[175] "Act up to your light, though in the midst of difficulties, and you will be carried on, you do not know how far." For every "truth has its own order; we cannot join the way of life at any point of the course we please; we cannot learn advanced truths before we have learned primary ones . . . but when men refuse to profit by light already granted, their light is turned to darkness."[176] As the Bible constantly teaches, "obedience to the light we possess is the way to gain more light."[177]

Nor must our obedience be anything other than unconditional: "Till we aim at complete, unreserved obedience in all things, we are not really Christians at all."[178] For "it is possible to be *generally* conscientious, or what the world calls honourable and high-principled, yet to be destitute of that religious fear and strictness, which God calls conscientiousness, but which the world calls superstition or narrowness of mind."[179] Thus most so-called conscientious people are concerned "not how to please God, but how to please themselves without displeasing Him." They simply "make this world the first object in their minds, and use religion as a corrective, a restraint, upon *too much* attachment to the world." They "do not take for the object towards which they act, God's

INTRODUCTION

will, but certain maxims, rules, or measures, right perhaps as far as they go, but defective because they admit of being subjected to certain other ultimate ends, which are not religious.... And thus they are what is popularly called moral, without being religious."[180]

So we arrive at the conclusion that true obedience is impossible without faith: "Faith is the element of all perfection; he who begins with faith, will end in unspotted and entire holiness."[181] For "faith is itself of a holy nature, and the first fruits and earnest of holiness to come."[182] The fact is that faith and obedience are the same thing—"They are but one thing viewed differently." This is because to "believe is to look beyond this world to God, and to obey is to look beyond this world to God; to believe is of the heart, and to obey is of the heart; to believe is not a solitary act, but a consistent habit of trust; and to obey is not a solitary act, but a consistent habit of doing our duty in all things." Faith and obedience develop together: "In proportion as a man believes, so he obeys; they come together, and grow together, and last through life."[183]

One of the most consistent themes of Newman's preaching is the difficult of consistency in the Christian life. So bad is "the scandal which a Christian's inconsistency brings upon his cause" that Newman can ask: "The Christian world, so called, what is it practically, but a witness for Satan rather than a witness for Christ? ... is there any *antecedent* prejudice against religion so great as that which is occasioned by the lives of its professors?"[184] Part of the problem lies in the effect of changing circumstances: "We feel variously according to the place, time, and people we are with. We are serious on Sunday, and we sin deliberately on Monday."[185] The truth is, "We can never answer how we shall act under new circumstances."[186] What is especially striking is that "if we look to some of the most eminent Saints of Scripture, we shall find their recorded errors to have occurred in those parts of their duty in which each had had most trial, and generally showed obedience most perfect."[187] And the greatest of Christian Saints "have exhibited inconsistencies such as to surprise and shock their most ardent disciples."[188] As for lesser Christians, "in the heart and life of even the better sort of men, that continual repentance must ever go hand in hand with our endeavours to obey."[189] "In all ages," then, "consistent obedience is a very rare endowment."[190] Much inconsistency is the involuntary result of past sins: "Past years rise up against us in present offences; gross inconsistencies show themselves in our character."[191] It is to "single or forgotten sins" that "are not improbably to be traced the strange inconsistencies of character which we often witness in our experience of life."[192] So

INTRODUCTION

concerned is Newman with the importance of consistency that he even suggests that quantity is better than quality in the sense that someone "serves with a perfect heart, who serves God in all parts of his duty; and, not here and there, but here and there and everywhere; not perfectly indeed as regards the quality of his obedience, but perfectly as regards its extent; not completely, but consistently."[193] And so he can conclude: "The very test of a mature Christian, of a true saint, is consistency in all things."[194]

NOTES

1. *An Essay in Aid of a Grammar of Assent*, ed. 1. T. Ker (Oxford: Clarendon Press, 1985), p. 43.
2. Unpublished letter cit. in Ian Ker, *John Henry Newman: A Biography* (Oxford: Clarendon Press, 1988), p. 3. Hereafter referred to as Ker, *A Biography*.
3. *The Letters and Diaries of John Henry Newman*, ed. Charles Stephen Dessain et al., vols. i–vi (Oxford: Clarendon Press, 1978–1984); xi–xxii (London: Nelson, 1961–1972); xxiii–xxxi (Oxford: Clarendon Press, 1973–1977); vol. xxvi, p. 87. Hereafter *LD*.
4. *Sermon Notes of John Henry Cardinal Newman, 1849–1878*, ed. Fathers of the Birmingham Oratory (London: Longmans, Green, 1913), p. 230.
5. *Parochial and Plain Sermons*, vol. 1, p. 28. Hereafter *PS*. Except where otherwise stated, all references to Newman's writings are to the uniform collected edition (see Select Bibliography).
6. *PS* i.166.
7. *PS* iii.106.
8. *PS* iv.26.
9. *PS* v.230–32.
10. *PS* 244–45.
11. *Sermons Bearing on Subjects of the Day*, pp. 11–12. Hereafter *SD*.
12. *SD* 395–409.
13. James Anthony Froude, *Short Studies on Great Subjects*, 4th series (New York: Charles Scribner's Sons, 1910), p. 188.
14. *PS* vi.73.
15. *John Henry Newman: Autobiographical Writings*, ed. Henry Tristram (New York; Sheed and Ward, 1956), pp. 80, 172. Hereafter *AW*.
16. See Ker, *A Biography*, pp. 21–22.

INTRODUCTION

17. *AW* 79.
18. *PS* i.17, 54, 81; ii.29, 179; v.31; vi.95.
19. *PS* i.17–18.
20. *PS* i.25.
21. *PS* i.126.
22. *PS* vii.136, 138, 140–41.
23. *PS* vi.263.
24. *SD* 278.
25. *LD* v.327.
26. *PS* iii.130–31.
27. *LD* ii.308.
28. *LD* v.14–15, 22.
29. *PS* i.70.
30. *PS* i.117–20.
31. *PS* i.172.
32. *PS* i.188.
33. *PS* ii.371–73, 377.
34. *PS* i.177.
35. *PS* i.178, 185–86.
36. *PS* i.181–82.
37. *PS* i.255.
38. *PS* ii.163–65, 168, 171–73.
39. *PS* i.42–43.
40. *PS* i.73.
41. *PS* i.131.
42. *PS* iii.13.
43. *PS* iv.33.
44. *PS* iv.15.
45. *PS* i.110.
46. *PS* i.90.
47. *PS* i.114.
48. *PS* i.167–68.
49. *PS* v.108.
50. *PS* i.102.
51. *PS* iv.42.
52. *PS* i.142.
53. *PS* iv.72.
54. *PS* iii.67.
55. *PS* iii.295.
56. *PS* iv.95.

INTRODUCTION

57. *PS* iv.44, 45, 47.
58. *PS* v.143, 232.
59. *PS* viii.71.
60. *PS* v.212–13, 217.
61. *PS* i.50.
62. *PS* i.35, 37, 39.
63. *PS* i.55.
64. *PS* i.125.
65. *PS* vi.37.
66. *PS* vi.52.
67. *PS* vii.152.
68. *PS* i.59–63.
69. *PS* iv.326, 329.
70. *Apologia pro Vita Sua*, ed. Martin J. Svaglic (Oxford: Clarendon Press, 1967), p. 20. Hereafter *Apo*.
71. *AW* 83.
72. *An Essay on the Development of Christian Doctrine*, pp. 35–36, 324.
73. *Essays Critical and Historical*, vol. 1, p. 47. Hereafter *Ess*.
74. *PS* v.93, 118.
75. *PS* ii.32, 39–40.
76. *Discourses Addressed to Mixed Congregations*, pp. 321–22, 358. Hereafter *Mix*.
77. *Ess*. i.247.
78. *Lectures on the Doctrine of Justification*, p. 174. Hereafter *Jfc*.
79. *Jfc*. 222.
80. *PS* i.285–86, 290.
81. *PS* i.176.
82. *PS* ii.39.
83. *PS* ii.142–43.
84. *PS* ii.221.
85. *PS* ii.222.
86. *PS* ii.229.
87. *PS* iv.248–49.
88. *PS* v.138–39.
89. *PS* vi.124, 126.
90. *PS* iv.324.
91. *PS* iv.337–38.
92. *PS* v.66–67.
93. *PS* vi.121.

INTRODUCTION

94. *PS* i.24.
95. *PS* ii.286, 289–90.
96. *PS* iv.121.
97. *PS* iv.134.
98. Charles Stephen Dessain, the founder of modern Newman studies, constantly stressed this crucial insight of Newman, especially in his *The Spirituality of John Henry Newman/Newman's Spiritual Themes* (see Select Bibliography), ch. 4, "The Indwelling Spirit."
99. *PS* iv.168.
100. *SD* 141.
101. *PS* iv.145.
102. *PS* v.226–27.
103. *PS* v.216.
104. *PS* v.318, 325–26.
105. *PS* v.156–58.
106. *PS* v.156–58, 161.
107. *PS* v.181.
108. *PS* vi.175–76, 184.
109. *PS* v.171.
110. *PS* ii.222, 35.
111. *Jfc.* 137–38.
112. *Jfc.* 154.
113. *Callista: A Tale of the Third Century*, p. 293.
114. *Select Treatises of St. Athanasius*, vol. 2, p. 193. Hereafter *Ath*.
115. *PS* iii.277.
116. *PS* v.10–11.
117. *Jfc.* 323.
118. *PS* iv.146–48.
119. *Ath.* ii.92.
120. *PS* iv.292.
121. *Ess.* i.66.
122. *PS* iii.267–68.
123. *PS* v.140–41.
124. See Ker, *A Biography, passim.*
125. *PS* iv.5–7.
126. *PS* iv.14.
127. *PS* iv.28–29.
128. *PS* iv.68.
129. *PS* iv.154–57.
130. *PS* iv.245–47; vi.45.

INTRODUCTION

131. *PS* iv.300–01.
132. *PS* v.212–13.
133. *PS* vii.180–82.
134. *PS* viii.65, 67.
135. *SD* 80–81, 90–92.
136. *Mix.* 97.
137. *PS* v.241, 350.
138. *PS* v.220.
139. *PS* i.13, 11.
140. *PS* i.82.
141. *PS* i.344.
142. *PS* iv.165.
143. *PS* vii.100.
144. *PS* iv.17.
145. *PS* i.67, 69.
146. *PS* i.155.
147. *PS* i.252.
148. *PS* ii.114.
149. *PS* viii.29.
150. *PS* ii.136.
151. *LD* xi.191.
152. *PS* ii.159.
153. *PS* iii.217.
154. *PS* i.68.
155. *PS* i.95.
156. *PS* i.167.
157. *PS* i.142.
158. *PS* i.145; iv.15.
159. *PS* iii.238.
160. *PS* iv.5.
161. *PS* v.242, 244, 245, 248.
162. *PS* iv.234, 236.
163. *PS* iv.244.
164. *PS* iv.309–13, 317.
165. *John Henry Newman: Sermons 1824–1843,* vol. 1, ed. Placid Murray, OSB (Clarendon Press: Oxford, 1991), p. 133.
166. *PS* v.179, 181.
167. *PS* i.30.
168. *PS* i.115–17.
169. *PS* i.167.

INTRODUCTION

170. *PS* i.233.
171. *PS* iv.15.
172. *PS* i.349.
173. *PS* i.230, 241.
174. *PS* viii.98.
175. *Verses on Various Occasions*, p. 156.
176. *PS* viii.195–96.
177. *PS* viii.210.
178. *PS* iv.12.
179. *PS* iv.27.
180. *PS* iv.29–30.
181. *PS* v.159.
182. *PS* vi.115.
183. *PS* iii.80–81, 86.
184. *PS* i.136.
185. *PS* i.25.
186. *PS* i.169.
187. *PS* i.46–47.
188. *PS* i.170.
189. *PS* i.71.
190. *PS* ii.272–73.
191. *PS* i.90.
192. *PS* iv.42.
193. *PS* v.239.
194. *PS* vi.186.

Parochial and Plain Sermons

Volume I

SERMON II

The Immortality of the Soul

"What shall a man give in exchange for his soul?"—Mt 16:26

I suppose there is no tolerably informed Christian but considers he has a correct notion of the difference between our religion and the paganism which it supplanted. Every one, if asked what it is we have gained by the Gospel, will promptly answer, that we have gained the knowledge of our immortality, of our having souls which will live for ever; that the heathen did not know this, but that Christ taught it, and that His disciples know it. Every one will say, and say truly, that this was the great and solemn doctrine which gave the Gospel a claim to be heard when first preached, which arrested the thoughtless multitudes, who were busied in the pleasures and pursuits of this life, awed them with the vision of the life to come, and sobered them till they turned to God with a true heart. It will be said, and said truly, that this doctrine of a future life was the doctrine which broke the power and the fascination of paganism. The poor benighted heathen were engaged in all the frivolities and absurdities of a false ritual, which had obscured the light of nature. They knew God, but they forsook Him for the inventions of men; they made protectors and guardians for themselves; and had "gods many and lords many" (1 Cor 8:5). They had their profane worship, their gaudy processions, their indulgent creed, their easy observances, their sensual festivities, their childish extravagances, such as might suitably be the religion of beings who were to live for seventy or eighty years, and then die once for all, never to live again. "Let us eat and drink, for to-morrow we die," was their doctrine and their rule of life. "To-morrow we die";—this the Holy Apostles admitted. They taught so far *as* the heathen; "To-morrow we die"; but then they added, "And after death *the judgment*";—judgment upon the eternal soul, which lives in spite of the death of the body. And this was the truth, which awakened men to the necessity of having a better and deeper religion than that which had spread over the earth, when Christ came,—which so wrought upon them that they left that old false worship of theirs, and it fell. Yes! though throned in all the power of the world, a sight such as eye had never before seen, though supported by the great and the many, the magnificence of kings, and the stubbornness of people, it fell. Its ruins remain scattered over the face of the earth; the shattered works of its great upholder, that fierce enemy of God, the Pagan Roman Empire. Those ruins are found even among themselves, and show how marvellously great was its power, and therefore how much more powerful was that which broke its power; and this was the doctrine of the immortality of the soul. So entire is the revolution which is produced among men, wherever this high truth is really received.

I have said that every one of us is able fluently to speak of this doctrine, and is aware that the knowledge of it forms the fundamental difference between our state and that of the heathen. And yet, in spite of our being able to speak about it and our "form of knowledge" (as St. Paul terms it) (Rom 2:20), there seems scarcely room to doubt, that the greater number of those who are called Christians in no true sense realize it in their own minds at all. Indeed, it is a very difficult thing to bring home to us, and to feel, that we have souls; and there cannot be a more fatal mistake than to suppose we see what the doctrine means, as soon as we can use the words which signify it. So great a thing is it to understand that we have souls, that the knowing it, taken in connexion with its results, is all one with *being serious,* i.e., truly religious. To discern our immortality is necessarily connected with fear and trembling and repentance, in the case of every Christian. Who is there but would be sobered by an actual sight of the flames of hell fire and the souls therein hopelessly enclosed? Would not all his thoughts be drawn to that awful sight, so that he would stand still gazing fixedly upon it, and forgetting every thing else; seeing nothing else, hearing nothing, engrossed with the contemplation of it; and when the sight was withdrawn, still having it fixed in his memory, so that he would be henceforth dead to the pleasures and employments of this world, considered in themselves, thinking of them only in their reference to that fearful vision? This would be the overpowering effect of such a disclosure, whether it actually led a man to repentance or not. And thus absorbed in the thought of the life to come are they who really and heartily receive the words of Christ and His Apostles. Yet to this state of mind, and therefore to this true knowledge, the multitude of men called Christians are certainly strangers; a thick veil is drawn over their eyes; and in spite of their being able to talk of the doctrine, they are as if they never had heard of it. They go on just as the heathen did of old: They eat, they drink; or they amuse themselves in vanities, and live in the world, without fear and without sorrow, just as if God had not declared that their conduct in this life would decide their destiny in the next; just as if they either had no souls, or had nothing or little to do with the saving of them, which was the creed of the heathen.

Now let us consider what it is to bring home to ourselves that we have souls, and in what the especial difficulty of it lies; for this may be of use to us in our attempt to realize that awful truth.

We are from our birth apparently dependent on things about us. We see and feel that we could not live or go forward without the aid of man. To a child this world is every thing: He seems to himself a part of this world,—a part of this world, in the same sense in which a branch is part of a tree; he has little notion of his own separate and independent existence: That is, he has no just idea he has a soul. And if he goes through life with his notions unchanged, he has no just notion, even to the end of life, that he has a soul. He views himself merely in his connexion with this world, which is his all; he looks to this world for his good, as to an idol; and when he tries to look beyond this life, he is able to discern nothing in prospect, because he has no idea of any thing, nor can fancy any thing, *but* this life. And if he is obliged to fancy something, he fancies this life over again; just as the heathen, when they reflected on those traditions of another life, which were floating among them, could but fancy the happiness of the blessed to consist in the enjoyment of the sun, and the sky, and the earth, as before, only as if these were to be more splendid than they are now.

To understand that we have souls, is to feel our separation from things visible, our independence of them, our distinct existence in ourselves, our individuality, our power of acting for ourselves this way or that way, our accountableness for what we do. These are the great truths which lie wrapped up indeed even in a child's mind, and which God's grace can unfold there in spite of the influence of the external world; but at first this outward world prevails. We look off from self to the things around us, and forget ourselves in them. Such is our state,—a depending for support on the reeds which are no stay, and overlooking our real strength,—at the time when God begins His process of reclaiming us to a truer view of our place in His great system of providence. And when

He visits us, then in a little while there is a stirring within us. The unprofitableness and feebleness of the things of this world are forced upon our minds; they promise but cannot perform, they disappoint us. Or, if they do perform what they promise, still (so it is) they do not satisfy us. We still crave for something, we do not well know what; but we are sure it is something which the world has not given us. And then its changes are so many, so sudden, so silent, so continual. It never leaves changing; it goes on to change, till we are quite sick at heart:—then it is that our reliance on it is broken. It is plain we cannot continue to depend upon it, unless we keep pace with it, and go on changing too; but this we cannot do. We feel that, while it changes, we are one and the same; and thus, under God's blessing, we come to have some glimpse of the meaning of our independence of things temporal, and our immortality. And should it so happen that misfortunes come upon us, (as they often do,) then still more are we led to understand the nothingness of this world; then still more are we led to distrust it, and are weaned from the love of it, till at length it floats before our eyes merely as some idle veil, which, notwithstanding its many tints, cannot hide the view of what is beyond it;—and we begin, by degrees, to perceive that there are but two beings in the whole universe, our own soul, and the God who made it.

Sublime, unlooked-for doctrine, yet most true! To every one of us there are but two beings in the whole world, himself and God; for, as to this outward scene, its pleasures and pursuits, its honours and cares, its contrivances, its personages, its kingdoms, its multitude of busy slaves, what are they to us? nothing—no more than a show:—"The world passeth away and the lust thereof." And as to those others nearer to us, who are not to be classed with the vain world, I mean our friends and relations, whom we are right in loving, these, too, after all, are nothing to us here. They cannot really help or profit us; we see them, and they act upon us, only (as it were) at a distance, through the medium of sense; they cannot get at our souls; they cannot enter into our thoughts, or really be companions to us. In the next world it will, through God's mercy, be otherwise; but here we enjoy, not their presence, but the anticipation of what one day shall be; so that, after all, they vanish before the clear vision we have, first, of our own existence, next of the presence of the great God in us, and over us, as our Governor and Judge, who dwells in us by our conscience, which is His representative.

And now consider what a revolution will take place in the mind that is not utterly reprobate, in proportion as it realizes this relation between itself and the most high God. We never in this life can fully understand what is meant by our living for ever, but we can understand what is meant by this world's *not* living for ever, by its dying never to rise again. And learning this, we learn that we owe it no service, no allegiance; it has no claim over us, and can do us no material good nor harm. On the other hand, the law of God written on our hearts bids us serve Him, and partly tells us how to serve Him, and Scripture completes the precepts which nature began. And both Scripture and conscience tell us we are answerable for what we do, and that God is a righteous Judge; and, above all, our Saviour, as our visible Lord God, takes the place of the world as the Only-begotten of the Father, having shown Himself openly, that we may not say that God is hidden. And thus a man is drawn forward by all manner of powerful influences to turn from things temporal to things eternal, to deny himself, to take up his cross and follow Christ. For there are Christ's awful threats and warnings to make him serious, His precepts to attract and elevate him, His promises to cheer him, His gracious deeds and sufferings to humble him to the dust, and to bind his heart once and for ever in gratitude to Him who is so surpassing in mercy. All these things act upon him; and, as truly as St. Matthew rose from the receipt of custom when Christ called, heedless what bystanders would say of him, so they who, through grace, obey the secret voice of God, move onward contrary to the world's way, and careless what mankind may say of them, as understanding that they have souls, which is the one thing they have to care about.

I am well aware that there are indiscreet teachers gone forth into the world, who use language such as I have used, but mean something very different. Such are they who deny the grace of baptism, and think that a man is converted to God all at once. But I have no need now to mention the difference between their teaching and that of Scripture. Whatever their peculiar errors are, so far as they say that we are by nature blind and sinful, and must, through God's grace, and our own endeavours, learn that we have souls and rise to a new life, severing ourselves from the world that is, and walking by faith in what is unseen and future, so far they say true, for they speak the words of Scripture; which says, "Awake thou that sleepest, and arise from the dead, and Christ shall give thee light. See then that ye walk circumspectly, not as fools, but as wise, redeeming the time, because the days are evil; wherefore be ye not unwise, but understanding what the will of the Lord is" (Eph 5:14–17).

Let us, then, seriously question ourselves, and beg of God grace to do so honestly, whether we are loosened from the world; or whether, living as dependent on it, and not on the Eternal Author of our being, we are in fact taking our portion with this perishing outward scene, and ignorant of our having souls. I know very well that such thoughts are distasteful to the minds of men in general. Doubtless many a one there is, who, on hearing doctrines such as I have been insisting on, says in his heart, that religion is thus made gloomy and repulsive; that he would attend to a teacher who spoke in a less severe way; and that in fact Christianity was not intended to be a dark burdensome law, but a religion of cheerfulness and joy. This is what young people think, though they do not express it in this argumentative form. They view a strict life as something offensive and hateful; they turn from the notion of it. And then, as they get older and see more of the world, they learn to defend their opinion, and express it more or less in the way in which I have just put it. They hate and oppose the truth, as it were upon principle; and the more they are told that they have souls, the more resolved they are to live as if they had not souls. But let us take it as a clear point from the first, and not to be disputed, that religion must ever be difficult to those who neglect it. All things that we have to learn are difficult at first; and our duties to God, and to man for His sake, are peculiarly difficult, because they call upon us to take up a new life, and quit the love of this world for the next. It cannot be avoided; we must fear and be in sorrow, before we can rejoice. The Gospel must be a burden before it comforts and brings us peace. No one can have his heart cut away from the natural objects of its love, without pain during the process and throbbings afterwards. This is plain from the nature of the case; and, however true it be, that this or that teacher may be harsh and repulsive, yet he cannot materially alter things. Religion is in itself at first a weariness to the worldly mind, and it requires an effort and a self-denial in every one who honestly determines to be religious.

But there are other persons who are far more hopeful than those I have been speaking of, who, when they hear repentance and newness of life urged on them, are frightened at the thought of the greatness of the work; they are disheartened at being told to do so much. Now let it be well understood, that to realize our own individual accountableness and immortality, of which I have been speaking, is not required of them all at once. I never said a person was not in a hopeful way who did not thus fully discern the world's vanity and the worth of his soul. But a man is truly in a very desperate way who does not wish, who does not try, to discern and feel all this. I want a man on the one hand to confess his immortality with his lips, and on the other, to live as if he tried to understand his own words, and then he is in the way of salvation; he is in the way towards heaven, even though he has not yet fully emancipated himself from the fetters of this world. Indeed none of us (of course) are entirely loosened from this world. We all use words, in speaking of our duties, higher and fuller than we really understand. No one entirely realizes what is meant by his having a soul; even the best of men is but in a state of progress towards the simple truth; and the most weak and ignorant of those who seek after it cannot but be in progress. And therefore no one need be alarmed at hearing that he has much to do before he arrives at a right view of his own condition in God's sight, i.e., at *faith*; for we all have much to do, and the great point is, are we willing to do it?

Oh, that there were such an heart in us, to put aside this visible world, to desire to look at it as a mere screen between us and God, and to think of Him who has entered in beyond the veil, and who is watching us, trying us, yes, and blessing, and influencing, and encouraging us towards good, day by day! Yet, alas, how do we suffer the mere varying circumstances of every day to sway us! How difficult it is to remain firm and in one mind under the seductions or terrors of the world! We feel variously according to the place, time, and people we are with. We are serious on Sunday, and we sin deliberately on Monday. We rise in the morning with remorse at our offences and resolutions of amendment, yet before night we have transgressed again. The mere change of society puts us into a new frame of mind; nor do we sufficiently understand this great weakness of ours, or seek for strength where alone it can be found, in the Unchangeable God. What will be our thoughts in that day, when at length this outward world drops away altogether, and we find ourselves where we ever have been, in His presence, with Christ standing at His right hand!

On the contrary, what a blessed discovery is it to those who make it, that this world is but vanity and without substance; and that really they are ever in their Saviour's presence. This is a thought which it is scarcely right to enlarge upon in a mixed congregation, where there may be some who have not given their hearts to God; for why should the privileges of the true Christian be disclosed to mankind at large, and sacred subjects, which are his peculiar treasure, be made common to the careless liver? He knows his blessedness, and needs not another to tell it him. He knows in whom he has believed; and in the hour of danger or trouble he knows what is meant by that peace, which Christ did not explain when He gave it to His Apostles, but merely said it was not as the world could give.

"Thou wilt keep him in perfect peace whose mind is stayed on Thee, because he trusteth in Thee. Trust ye in the Lord for ever, for in the Lord Jehovah is everlasting strength" (Is 26:3, 4).

SERMON III

Knowledge of God's Will without Obedience

"If ye know these things, happy are ye if ye do them."
—Jn 13:17

There never was a people or an age to which these words could be more suitably addressed than to this country at this time; because we know more of the way to serve God, of our duties, our privileges, and our reward, than any other people hitherto, as far as we have the means of judging. To us then especially our Saviour says, "If ye know these things, happy are ye if ye do them."

Now, doubtless, many of us think we know this very well. It seems a very trite thing to say, that it is nothing to *know* what is right, unless we *do* it; an old subject about which nothing new can be said. When we read such passages in Scripture, we pass over them as admitting them without dispute; and thus we contrive practically to forget them. Knowledge is nothing compared with doing; but the *knowing* that knowledge is nothing, we make to be *something,* we make it count, and thus we cheat ourselves.

This we do in parallel cases also. Many a man instead of *learning* humility in practice, confesses himself a poor sinner, and next *prides* himself upon the confession; he ascribes the glory of his redemption to God, and then becomes in a manner *proud* that he is redeemed. He is proud of his so-called humility.

Doubtless Christ spoke no words in vain. The Eternal Wisdom of God did not utter His voice that we might at once catch up His words in an irreverent manner, think we understand them at a glance, and pass them over. But His word endureth for ever; it has a depth of meaning suited to all times and places, and hardly and painfully to be understood in any. They, who think they enter into it easily, may be quite sure they do not enter into it at all.

Now then let us try, by His grace, to make the text a living word to the benefit of our souls. Our Lord says, "If ye know, happy are ye, if ye do." Let us consider *how* we commonly read Scripture.

We read a passage in the Gospels, for instance, a parable perhaps, or the account of a miracle; or we read a chapter in the Prophets, or a Psalm. Who is not struck with the beauty of what he reads? I do not wish to speak of those who read the Bible only now and then, and who will in consequence generally find its sacred pages dull and uninteresting; but of those who study it. Who of such persons does not see the beauty of it? for instance, take the passage which introduces the text. Christ had been washing His disciples' feet. He did so at a season of great mental suffering; it was just before He was seized by His enemies to be put to death. The traitor, His familiar friend, was in the room. All of His disciples, even the most devoted of them, loved Him much less than they thought they did. In a little while they were all to forsake Him and flee. This He foresaw; yet He calmly washed their feet, and then He told them that He did so by way of an example; that they should be full of lowly services one to the other, as He to them; that he among them was in fact the highest who put himself the lowest. This He had said before; and His disciples must have recollected it. Perhaps they might wonder in their secret hearts *why* He repeated the lesson; they might say to themselves, "We have heard this before." They might be surprised that His significant action, His washing their feet, issued in nothing else than a precept already delivered, the command to be humble. At the same time they would not be able to deny, or rather they would deeply feel, the beauty of His action. Nay, as loving Him (after all) above all things, and reverencing Him as their Lord and Teacher, they would feel an admiration and awe of Him; but their minds would not rest sufficiently on the *practical* direction of the instruction vouchsafed to them. They knew the truth, and they admired it; they did not observe what it was they lacked. Such may be considered their frame of mind; and hence the force of the text, delivered primarily against Judas Iscariot, who knew and sinned deliberately against the truth; secondarily referring to all the Apostles, and St. Peter chiefly, who promised to be faithful, but failed under the trial; lastly, to us all,—all of us here assembled, who hear the word of life continually, know it, admire it, do all but obey it.

Is it not so? is not Scripture altogether pleasant except in its strictness? do not we try to persuade ourselves, that to *feel* religiously, to confess our love of religion, and to be able to talk of religion, will stand in the place of careful obedience, of that *self-denial* which is the very substance of true practical religion? Alas! that religion which is so delightful as a vision, should be so distasteful as a reality. Yet so it is, whether we are aware of the fact or not.

1. The multitude of men even who profess religion are in this state of mind. We will take the case of those who are in better circumstances than the mass of the community. They are well educated and taught; they have few distresses in life, or are able to get over them by the variety of their occupations, by the spirits which attend good health, or at least by the lapse of time. They go on respectably and happily, with the same general tastes and habits which they would have had if the Gospel had not been given them. They have an eye to what the world thinks of them; are charitable when it is expected. They are polished in their manners, kind from natural disposition or a feeling of propriety. Thus their religion is based upon self and the world, a mere *civilization;* the same (I say), as it would have been in the main, (taking the state of society as they find it,) even supposing Christianity were not the religion of the land. But it is; and let us go on to ask, how do they in consequence feel towards it? They accept it, they add it to what they *are,* they ingraft it upon the selfish and worldly habits of an unrenewed heart. They have been taught to revere it, and to believe it to come from God; so they admire it, and accept it as a rule of life, so far forth as it agrees with the carnal principles which govern them. So far as it does *not* agree, they are blind to its excellence and its claims. They overlook or explain away its precepts. They in no sense obey *because* it commands. They do right when they *would* have done right had it not commanded; however, they speak well of it, and think they understand it. Sometimes, if I may continue the description, they adopt it into a certain refined elegance of sentiments and manners, and then the irreligion is all that is graceful, fastidious, and luxurious. They love religious poetry and eloquent preaching. They desire to have their feelings roused and soothed, and to secure a variety and relief in that eternal subject which is unchangeable. They tire of its simplicity, and perhaps seek to keep up their interest in it by means of religious narratives, fictitious or embellished, or of news from foreign countries, or of the history of the prospects or successes of the Gospel; thus perverting what is in itself good and innocent. This is their state of mind at best; for more commonly they think it enough merely to show some slight regard for the subject of religion; to attend its services on the Lord's day, and then only once, and coldly to express an approbation of it. But of course every description of such persons can be but general; for the shades of character are so varied and blended in individuals, as to make it impossible to give an accurate picture, and

often very estimable persons and truly good Christians are partly infected with this bad and earthly spirit.

2. Take again another description of them. They have perhaps turned their attention to the means of promoting the happiness of their fellow-creatures, and have formed a system of morality and religion of their own; then they come to Scripture. They are much struck with the high tone of its precepts, and the beauty of its teaching. It is true, they find many things in it which they do not understand or do not approve; many things they would not have said themselves. But they pass these by; they fancy that these do not apply to the present day, (which is an easy way of removing any thing we do not like,) and *on the whole* they receive the Bible, and they think it highly serviceable for the lower classes. Therefore, they recommend it, and support the institutions which are the channels of teaching it. But as to their own case, it never comes into their minds to apply its precepts seriously to themselves; they *know* them already, they consider. They *know* them and that is enough; but as for *doing* them, by which I mean, going forward to obey them, with an unaffected earnestness and an honest faith *acting upon* them, receiving them as they are, and not as their own previously formed opinions would have them be, they have nothing of this right spirit. They do not contemplate such a mode of acting. To recommend and affect a moral and decent conduct (on *whatever* principles) seems to them to be enough. The spread of knowledge bringing in its train a selfish temperance, a selfish peaceableness, a selfish benevolence, the morality of expedience, this satisfies them. They care for none of the truths of Scripture, *on the ground* of their being in Scripture; these scarcely become more valuable in their eyes for being there written. They do not obey *because* they are told to obey, on faith; and the need of this divine principle of conduct they do not comprehend. Why will it not answer (they seem to say) to make men good in one way as well as another? "Abana and Pharpar, rivers of Damascus, are they not better than all the waters of Israel?" as if all the knowledge and the training that books ever gave had power to unloose one sinner from the bonds of Satan, or to effect more than an outward reformation, an *appearance* of obedience; as if it were not a far different principle, a principle independent of knowledge, above it and before it, which leads to *real* obedience, that principle of divine faith, given from above, which has life in itself, and has power really to use knowledge to the soul's welfare; in the hand of which knowledge is (as it were) the torch lighting us on our way, but not teaching or strengthening us to walk.

3. Or take another view of the subject. Is it not one of the most common excuses made by the poor for being irreligious, that they have had no education? as if to know much was a necessary step for right practice. Again, they are apt to think it *enough* to know and to talk of religion, to make a man religious. Why have you come hither to-day, my brethren?—not as a matter of course, I will hope; not merely because friends or superiors told you to come. I will suppose you have come to church *as a religious act;* but beware of supposing that all is done and over by the act of coming. It is not enough to be *present* here; though many men act as if they forgot they must attend to what is going on, as well as come. It is not enough to listen to what is preached; though many think they have gone a great way when they do this. You *must pray;* now this is very hard in itself to any one who tries (and this is the reason why so many men prefer the sermon to the prayers, because the former is merely the getting *knowledge,* and the latter is to do a *deed* of obedience): you must *pray;* and this I say is very difficult, because our thoughts are so apt to wander. But even this is not all;—you must, as you pray, really intend to *try to practise* what you pray for. When you say, "Lead us not into temptation," you must in good earnest mean to avoid in your daily conduct those temptations which you have already suffered from. When you say, "Deliver us from evil," you must mean to struggle against that evil in your hearts, which you are conscious of, and which you pray to be forgiven. This is difficult; still more is behind. You must actually carry your good intentions into effect during the week, and in truth and reality war against the world, the flesh, and the devil. And any one here present who falls short of this, that is, who thinks it enough to come to church to *learn* God's will, but does not bear in mind to do it in his daily conduct, be he high or be he low, know he mysteries and all knowledge, or be he unlettered and busily occupied in active life, he is a fool in His sight, who maketh the wisdom of this world foolishness. Surely he is but a trifler, as substituting a formal outward service for the religion of the heart; and he reverses our Lord's words in the text, "because he knows these things, most unhappy is he, because he does them not."

4. But some one may say, "It is so very *difficult* to serve God, it is so much against my own mind, such an effort, such a strain upon my strength to bear Christ's yoke, I must give it over, or I must delay it at least. Can nothing be taken instead? I acknowledge His law to be most holy and true, and the accounts I read about good men are most delightful. I wish I were like them with all my heart; and for a little while I feel in a mind to set about imitating them. I have begun several times, I have

had seasons of repentance, and set rules to myself; but for some reason or other, I fell back after a while, and was even worse than before. I know, but I cannot do. Oh, wretched man that I am!"

Now to such an one I say, You are in a much more promising state than if you were contented with yourself, and thought that knowledge was every thing, which is the grievous blindness which I have hitherto been speaking of; that is, you are in a better state, if you do not feel too much comfort or confidence in your confession. For *this* is the fault of many men; they make such an acknowledgment as I have described a *substitute* for real repentance; or allow themselves, after making it, to *put off* repentance, as if they could be suffered to give a word of promise which did not become due (so to say) for many days. You are, I admit, in a better state than if you were satisfied with yourself, *but you are not in a safe state.* If you were now to die, you would have no hope of salvation: no hope, that is, if your own showing be true, for I am taking your own words. Go before God's judgment-seat, and there plead that you know the Truth and have not done it. This is what you frankly own;—how will it there be taken? "Out of thine own mouth will I judge thee," says our Judge Himself, and who shall reverse His judgment? Therefore such an one must make the confession with great and real terror and shame, if it is to be considered a promising sign in him; else it is mere hardness of heart. For instance: I have heard persons say lightly (every one must have heard them) that they own it would be a wretched thing indeed for them or their companions to be taken off suddenly. The young are especially apt to say this; that is, before they have come to an age to be callous, or have formed excuses to overcome the natural true sense of their conscience. They say they hope some day to repent. This is their own witness against themselves, like that bad prophet at Bethel who was constrained with his own mouth to utter God's judgments while he sat at his sinful meat. But let not such an one think that he will receive any thing of the Lord: He does not speak in faith.

When, then, a man complains of his hardness of heart or weakness of purpose, let him see to it whether this complaint is more than a mere pretence to quiet his conscience, which is frightened at his putting off repentance; or, again, more than a mere idle word, said half in jest and half in compunction. But, should he be earnest in his complaint, then let him consider he has no need to complain. Every thing is plain and easy to the earnest; it is the double-minded who find difficulties. If you hate your own corruption in sincerity and truth, if you are really pierced to the heart that you do not do what you know you should do, if you *would* love God if you could, then the Gospel speaks to you words of peace and hope. It is a very different thing indolently to say, "I would I were a different man," and to close with God's offer to make you different, when it is put before you. Here is the test between earnestness and insincerity. You say you wish to be a different man; Christ takes you at your word, so to speak; He offers to make you different. He says, "I will take away from you the heart of stone, the love of this world and its pleasures, if you will submit to My discipline." Here a man draws back. No; he cannot bear to *lose* the love of the world, to part with his present desires and tastes; he cannot *consent* to be changed. After all he is well satisfied at the bottom of his heart to remain as he is, only he wants his conscience taken out of the way. Did Christ offer to do this for him, if He would but make bitter sweet and sweet bitter, darkness light and light darkness, *then* he would hail the glad tidings of peace;—till then he needs Him not.

But if a man is in earnest in wishing to get at the depths of his own heart, to expel the evil, to purify the good, and to gain power over himself, so as to do as well as know the Truth, what is the difficulty?—a matter of time indeed, but not of uncertainty is the recovery of such a man. So simple is the rule which he must follow, and so trite, that at first he will be surprised to hear it. God does great things by plain methods; and men start from them through pride, *because* they are plain. This was the conduct of Naaman the Syrian. Christ says, "Watch and pray"; herein lies our cure. To watch and to pray are surely in our power, and by these means we are certain of getting strength. You feel your weakness; you fear to be overcome by temptation: then keep out of the way of it. This is watching. Avoid society which is likely to mislead you; flee from the very shadow of evil; you cannot be too careful; better be a little too strict than a little too easy,—it is the safer side. Abstain from reading books which are dangerous to you. Turn from bad thoughts when they arise, set about some business, begin conversing with some friend, or say to yourself the Lord's Prayer reverently. When you are urged by temptation, whether it be by the threats of the world, false shame, self-interest, provoking conduct on the part of another, or the world's sinful pleasures, urged to be cowardly, or covetous, or unforgiving, or sensual, shut your eyes and think of Christ's precious blood-shedding. Do not dare to say you cannot help sinning; a little attention to these points will go far (through God's grace) to keep you in the right way. And again, pray as well as watch. You must know that you can do nothing of yourself; your past experience has taught you this; therefore look to God for the will and the power; ask Him earnestly in His Son's name; seek His holy ordinances. Is not *this* in your power? Have you not power at least over the limbs of your body, so as to attend the means of grace constantly? Have you literally not the power to come hither; to observe the Fasts and Festivals of the Church; to come to His Holy Altar and receive the Bread of Life? Get yourself, at least, to do this; to put out the hand, to take His gracious Body and Blood; this is no arduous work;—and you say you really *wish* to gain the blessings He offers. What would you have more than a free gift, vouchsafed "without money and without price"? So, make no more excuses; murmur not about your own bad heart, your knowing and resolving, and not doing. Here is your remedy.

Well were it if men could be persuaded to be in earnest; but few are thus minded. The many go on with a double aim, trying to serve both God and mammon. Few can get themselves to do what is right, *because* God tells them; they have another aim; they desire to please self or men. When they can obey God without offending the bad Master that rules them, then, and then only, they obey. Thus religion, instead of being the *first* thing in their estimation, is but the second. They differ, indeed, one from another what to put foremost: One man loves to be at ease, another to be busy, another to enjoy domestic comfort: but they agree in converting the truth of God, which they know to be Truth, into a mere instrument of secular aims; not discarding the Truth, but degrading it.

When He, the Lord of hosts, comes to shake terribly the earth, what number will He find of the remnant of the true Israel? We live in an educated age. The false gloss of a mere worldly refinement makes us decent and amiable. We all know and profess. We think ourselves wise; we flatter each other; we make excuses for ourselves when we are conscious we sin, and thus we gradually lose the consciousness that we are sinning. We think our own times superior to all others. "Thou blind Pharisee!" This was the fatal charge brought by our blessed Lord against the falsely enlightened teachers of His own day. As then we desire to enter into life, let us come to Christ continually for the two foundations of true Christian faith,—humbleness of mind and earnestness!

SERMON IV

Secret Faults

"Who can understand his errors? Cleanse Thou me from secret faults."—Ps 19:12

Strange as it may seem, multitudes called Christians go through life with no effort to obtain a correct knowledge of themselves. They are contented with general and vague impressions concerning their real state; and, if they have more than this, it is merely such accidental information about themselves as the events of life force upon them. But exact systematic knowledge they have none, and do not aim at it.

When I say this is *strange,* I do not mean to imply that to know ourselves is *easy;* it is very difficult to know ourselves even in part, and so far ignorance of ourselves is not a strange thing. But its strangeness consists in this, viz., that men should profess to receive and act upon the great Christian doctrines, while they are thus ignorant of themselves, considering that self-knowledge is a necessary condition for understanding them. Thus it is not too much to say that all those who neglect the duty of habitual self-examination are using words without meaning. The doctrines of the *forgiveness* of sins, and of a *new birth* from sin, cannot be understood without some right knowledge of the *nature* of sin, that is, of our own heart. We may, indeed, assent to a form of words which declares those doctrines; but if such a mere assent, however sincere, is the same as a real *holding of* them, and belief in them, then it is equally possible to believe in a proposition the terms of which belong to some foreign language, which is obviously absurd. Yet nothing is more common than for men to think that because they are familiar with words, they understand the ideas they stand for. Educated persons despise this fault in illiterate men who use hard words as if they comprehended them. Yet they themselves, as well as others, fall into the same error in a more subtle form, when they think they understand terms used in morals and religion, because such are common words, and have been used by them all their lives.

Now (I repeat) unless we have some just idea of our hearts and of sin, we can have no right idea of a Moral Governor, a Saviour or a Sanctifier, that is, in professing to believe in Them, we shall be using words without attaching distinct meaning to them. Thus self-knowledge is at the root of all real religious knowledge; and it is in vain,—worse than vain,—it is a deceit and a mischief, to think to understand the Christian doctrines as a matter of course, merely by being taught by books, or by attending sermons, or by any outward means, however excellent, taken by themselves. For it is in proportion as we search our hearts and understand our own nature, that we understand what is meant by an Infinite Governor and Judge; in proportion as we comprehend the nature of disobedience and our actual sinfulness, that we feel what is the blessing of the removal of sin, redemption, pardon, sanctification, which otherwise are mere words. God speaks to us primarily in our hearts. Self-knowledge is the key to the precepts and doctrines of Scripture. The very utmost any outward notices of religion can do, is to startle us and make us turn inward and search our hearts; and then, when we have experienced what it is to read ourselves, we shall profit by the doctrines of the Church and the Bible.

Of course self-knowledge admits of degrees. No one perhaps, is *entirely* ignorant of himself; and even the most advanced Christian knows himself only "in part." However, most men are contented with a slight acquaintance with their hearts, and therefore a superficial faith. This is the point which it is my purpose to insist upon. Men are satisfied to have numberless secret faults. They do not think about them, either as sins or as obstacles to strength of faith, and live on as if they had nothing to learn.

Now let us consider attentively the strong presumption that exists, that we all have serious secret faults; a fact which, I believe, all are ready to confess in general terms, though few like calmly and practically to dwell upon it; as I now wish to do.

1. Now the most ready method of convincing ourselves of the existence in us of faults unknown to ourselves, is to consider how plainly we see the secret faults of others. At first sight there is of course no reason for supposing that we differ materially from those around us; and if we see sins in them which *they* do not see, it is a presumption that they have their own discoveries about ourselves, which it would surprise us to hear. For instance: How apt is an angry man to fancy that he has the command of himself! The very charge of being angry, if brought against him, will anger him more; and, in the height of his discomposure, he will profess himself able to reason and judge with clearness and impartiality.

Now, it may be his turn another day, for what we know, to witness the same failing in us; or, if we are not naturally inclined to violent passion, still at least we may be subject to other sins, equally unknown to ourselves, and equally known to him as his anger was to us. For example: There are persons who act mainly from self-interest at times when they conceive they are doing generous or virtuous actions; they give freely, or put themselves to trouble, and are praised by the world, and by themselves, as if acting on high principle; whereas close observers can detect desire of gain, love of applause, shame, or the mere satisfaction of being busy and active, as the principal cause of their good deeds. This may be our condition as well as that of others; or, if it be not, still a parallel infirmity, the bondage of some other sin or sins, which others see, and we do not.

But, say there is no human being sees sin in us, of which we are not aware ourselves, (though this is a bold supposition to make,) yet why should man's accidental knowledge of us limit the extent of our imperfections? Should all the world speak well of us, and good men hail us as brothers, after all there is a Judge who trieth the hearts and the reins. He knows our real state; have we earnestly besought Him to teach us the knowledge of our own hearts? If we have not, that very omission is a presumption against us. Though our praise were throughout the Church, we may be sure He sees sins without number in us, sins deep and heinous, of which we have no idea. If man sees so much evil in human nature, what must God see? "If our heart condemn us, God is greater than our heart, and knoweth all things." Not *acts* alone of sin does He set down against us daily, of which we know nothing, but the thoughts of the heart too. The stirrings of pride, vanity, covetousness, impurity, discontent, resentment, these succeed each other through the day in momentary emotions, and are known to Him. We know them not; but how much does it concern us to know them!

2. This consideration is suggested by the first view of the subject. Now reflect upon the *actual disclosures* of our hidden weakness, which accidents occasion. Peter followed Christ boldly, and suspected not his own heart, till it betrayed him in the hour of temptation, and led him to deny his Lord. David lived years of happy obedience while he was in private life. What calm, clear-sighted faith is manifested in his answer to Saul about Goliath:—"The Lord that delivered me out of the paw of the lion, and out of the paw of the bear, He will deliver me out of the hand of this Philistine" (1 Sm 17:37). Nay, not only in retired life, in severe trial, under ill usage from Saul, he continued faithful to his God;

years and years did he go on, fortifying his heart, and learning the fear of the Lord; yet power and wealth weakened his faith, and for a season overcame him. There was a time when a prophet could retort upon him, "Thou art the man" (2 Sm 12:7) whom thou condemnest. He had kept his principles in words, but lost them in his heart. Hezekiah is another instance of a religious man bearing *trouble* well, but for a season falling back under the temptation of prosperity; and that, after extraordinary mercies had been vouchsafed to him (2 Kgs 20:12–19). And if these things be so in the case of the favoured saints of God, what (may we suppose) is our own real spiritual state in His sight? It is a serious thought. The warning to be deduced from it is this:—Never to think we have a due knowledge of ourselves till we have been exposed to various kinds of temptations, and tried on every side. Integrity on one side of our character is no voucher for integrity on another. We cannot tell how we should act if brought under temptations different from those which we have hitherto experienced. This thought should keep us humble. We are sinners, but we do not know how great. He alone knows who died for our sins.

3. Thus much we cannot but allow; that we do not know ourselves in those respects in which we have not been tried. But farther than this: What if we do not know ourselves even where we *have* been tried, and found faithful? It is a remarkable circumstance which has been often observed, that if we look to some of the most eminent saints of Scripture, we shall find their recorded errors to have occurred in those parts of their duty in which each had had most trial, and generally showed obedience most perfect. *Faithful* Abraham through want of faith denied his wife. Moses, the *meekest* of men, was excluded from the land of promise for a passionate word. The *wisdom* of Solomon was seduced to bow down to idols. Barnabas again, the *son of consolation*, had a sharp contention with St. Paul. If then men, who knew themselves better than we doubtless know ourselves, had so much of hidden infirmity about them, even in those parts of their character which were most free from blame, what are we to think of ourselves? and if our very virtues be so defiled with imperfection, what must be the unknown multiplied circumstances of evil which aggravate the guilt of our sins? This is a third presumption against us.

4. Think of this too. No one begins to examine himself, and to pray to know himself (with David in the text), but he finds within him an abundance of faults which before were either entirely or almost entirely unknown to him. That this is so, we learn from the written lives of good

men, and our own experience of others. And hence it is that the best men are ever the most humble; for, having a higher standard of excellence in their minds than others have, and knowing themselves better, they see somewhat of the breadth and depth of their own sinful nature, and are shocked and frightened at themselves. The generality of men cannot understand this; and if at times the habitual self-condemnation of religious men breaks out into words, they think it arises from affectation, or from a strange distempered state of mind, or from accidental melancholy and disquiet. Whereas the confession of a good man against himself, is really a witness against all thoughtless persons who hear it, and a call on them to examine their own hearts. Doubtless the more we examine ourselves, the more imperfect and ignorant we shall find ourselves to be.

5. But let a man persevere in prayer and watchfulness to the day of his death, yet he will never get to the bottom of his heart. Though he know more and more of himself as he becomes more conscientious and earnest, still the full manifestation of the secrets there lodged, is reserved for another world. And at the last day who can tell the affright and horror of a man who lived to himself on earth, indulging his own evil will, following his own chance notions of truth and falsehood, shunning the cross and the reproach of Christ, when his eyes are at length opened before the throne of God, and all his innumerable sins, his habitual neglect of God, his abuse of his talents, his misapplication and waste of time, and the original unexplored sinfulness of his nature, are brought clearly and fully to his view? Nay, even to the true servants of Christ, the prospect is awful. "The righteous," we are told, "will scarcely be saved" (1 Pt 4:18). Then will the good man undergo the full sight of his sins, which on earth he was labouring to obtain, and partly succeeded in obtaining, though life was not long enough to learn and subdue them all. Doubtless we must all endure that fierce and terrifying vision of our real selves, that last fiery trial of the soul (1 Cor 3:13) before its acceptance, a spiritual agony and second death to all who are not then supported by the strength of Him who died to bring them safe through it, and in whom on earth they have believed.

My brethren, I appeal to your reason whether these presumptions are not in their substance fair and just. And if so, next I appeal to your consciences, whether they are *new* to you; for if you have not even thought about your real state, nor even know how little you know of yourselves, how can you in good earnest be purifying yourselves for the next world, or be walking in the narrow way?

And yet how many are the chances that a number of those who now hear me have no sufficient knowledge of themselves, or sense of their ignorance, and are in peril of their souls! Christ's ministers cannot tell who are, and who are not, the true elect: but when the difficulties in the way of knowing yourselves aright are considered, it becomes a most serious and immediate question for each of you to entertain, whether or not he is living a life of self-deceit, and thinking far more comfortably of his spiritual state than he has any right to do. For call to mind the impediments that are in the way of your knowing yourselves, or feeling your ignorance, and then judge.

1. First of all, self-knowledge does not come as a matter of course; it implies an effort and a work. As well may we suppose, that the knowledge of the languages comes by nature, as that acquaintance with our own heart is natural. Now the very effort of steadily reflecting, is itself painful to many men; not to speak of the difficulty of reflecting correctly. To ask ourselves *why* we do this or that, to take account of the principles which govern us, and see whether we act for conscience' sake or from some lower inducement, is painful. We are busy in the world, and what leisure time we have we readily devote to a less severe and wearisome employment.

2. And then comes in our self-love. We *hope* the best; this saves us the trouble of examining. Self-love answers for our safety. We think it sufficient caution to allow for certain possible unknown faults at the utmost, and to take them *into* the reckoning when we balance our account with our conscience: whereas, if the truth were known to us, we should find we had nothing but debts, and those greater than we can conceive, and ever increasing.

3. And this favourable judgment of ourselves will especially prevail, if we have the misfortune to have uninterrupted health and high spirits, and domestic comfort. Health of body and mind is a great blessing, if we can bear it; but unless chastened by watchings and fastings (2 Cor 11:27), it will commonly seduce a man into the notion that he is much better than he really is. Resistance to our acting rightly, whether it proceed from within or without, tries our principle; but when things go smoothly, and we have but to wish, and we can perform, we cannot tell how far we do or do not act from a sense of duty. When a man's spirits are high, he is pleased with every thing; and with himself especially. He can act with vigour and promptness, and he mistakes this mere constitutional energy for strength of faith. He is cheerful and contented; and he mistakes this for Christian peace. And, if happy in his family,

he mistakes mere natural affection for Christian benevolence, and the confirmed temper of Christian love. In short, he is in a dream, from which nothing could have saved him except deep humility, and nothing will ordinarily rescue him except sharp affliction.

Other accidental circumstances are frequently causes of a similar self-deceit. While we remain in retirement from the world, we do not know ourselves; or after any great mercy or trial, which has affected us much, and given a temporary strong impulse to our obedience; or when we are in keen pursuit of some good object, which excites the mind, and for a time deadens it to temptation. Under such circumstances we are ready to think far too well of ourselves. The world is away; or, at least, we are insensible to its seductions; and we mistake our merely temporary tranquility, or our over-wrought fervour of mind, on the one hand for Christian peace, on the other for Christian zeal.

4. Next we must consider the force of habit. Conscience at first warns us against sin; but if we disregard it, it soon ceases to upbraid us; and thus sins, once known, in time become secret sins. It seems then (and it is a startling reflection), that the more guilty we are, the less we know it; for the oftener we sin, the less we are distressed at it. I think many of us may, on reflection, recollect instances, in our experience of ourselves, of our gradually forgetting things to be wrong which once shocked us. Such is the force of habit. By it (for instance) men contrive to allow themselves in various kinds of dishonesty. They bring themselves to affirm what is untrue, or what they are not sure is true, in the course of business. They overreach and cheat; and still more are they likely to fall into low and selfish ways without their observing it, and all the while to continue careful in their attendance on the Christian ordinances, and bear about them a form of religion. Or, again, they will live in self-indulgent habits; eat and drink more than is right; display a needless pomp and splendour in their domestic arrangements, without any misgiving; much less do they think of simplicity of manners and abstinence as Christian duties. Now we cannot suppose they *always* thought their present mode of living to be justifiable, for *others* are still struck with its impropriety; and what others now feel, doubtless they once felt themselves. But such is the force of habit. So again, to take as a third instance, the duty of stated private prayer; at first it is omitted with compunction, but soon with indifference. But it is not the less a sin because we do not feel it to be such. Habit has made it a secret sin.

5. To the force of habit must be added that of custom. Every age has its own wrong ways; and these have such influence, that even good

men, from living in the world, are unconsciously misled by them. At one time a fierce persecuting hatred of those who erred in Christian doctrine has prevailed; at another, an odious over-estimation of wealth and the means of wealth; at another an irreligious veneration of the mere intellectual powers; at another, a laxity of morals; at another, disregard of the forms and discipline of the Church. The most religious men, unless they are especially watchful, will feel the sway of the fashion of their age; and suffer from it, as Lot in wicked Sodom, though unconsciously. Yet their ignorance of the mischief does not change the nature of their sin;—sin it still is, only custom makes it *secret* sin.

6. Now what is our chief guide amid the evil and seducing customs of the world?—obviously, the Bible. "The world passeth away, but the word of the Lord endureth for ever" (Is 40:8; 1 Pt 1:24, 25; 1 Jn 2:17). How much extended, then, and strengthened, necessarily must be this secret dominion of sin over us, when we consider how little we read Scripture! Our conscience gets corrupted,—true; but the words of truth, though effaced from our minds, remain in Scripture, bright in their eternal youth and purity. Yet, we do not study Scripture to stir up and refresh our minds. Ask yourselves, my brethren, what do you know of the Bible? Is there any one part of it you have read carefully, and as a whole? One of the Gospels, for instance? Do you know very much more of your Saviour's works and words than you have heard read in church? Have you compared His precepts, or St. Paul's, or any other Apostle's, with your own daily conduct, and prayed and endeavoured to act upon them? If you have, so far is well; go on to do so. If you have not, it is plain you do not possess, for you have not sought to possess, an adequate notion of that perfect Christian character which it is your duty to aim at, nor an adequate notion of your actual sinful state; you are in the number of those who "come not to the light, lest their deeds should be reproved."

These remarks may serve to impress upon us the difficulty of knowing ourselves aright, and the consequent danger to which we are exposed, of speaking peace to our souls, when there is no peace.

Many things are against us; this is plain. Yet is not our future prize worth a struggle? Is it not worth present discomfort and pain to accomplish an escape from the fire that never shall be quenched? Can we endure the thought of going down to the grave with a load of sins on our head unknown and unrepented of? Can we content ourselves with such an unreal faith in Christ, as in no sufficient measure includes self-abasement, or thankfulness, or the desire or effort to be holy? For how can we feel our need of His help, or our dependence on Him, or our debt to Him, or the nature of His gift to us, unless we know ourselves? How can we in any sense be said to have that "mind of Christ," to which the Apostle exhorts us, if we cannot follow Him to the height above, or the depth beneath; if we do not in some measure discern the cause and meaning of His sorrows, but regard the world, and man, and the system of Providence, in a light different from that which His words and acts supply? If you receive revealed truth merely through the eyes and ears, you believe words, not things; you deceive yourselves. You may conceive yourselves sound in faith, but you know nothing in any true way. Obedience to God's commandments, which implies knowledge of sin and of holiness, and the desire and endeavour to please Him, this is the only practical interpreter of Scripture doctrine. Without self-knowledge you have no root in yourselves personally; you may endure for a time, but under affliction or persecution your faith will not last. This is why many in this age (and in every age) become infidels, heretics, schismatics, disloyal despisers of the Church. They cast off the form of truth, because it never has been to them more than a form. They endure not, because they never have tasted that the Lord is gracious; and they never have had experience of His power and love, because they have never known their own weakness and need. This *may* be the future condition of some of us, if we harden our hearts to-day,—*apostasy*. Some day, even in this world, we may be found openly among the enemies of God and of His Church.

But, even should we be spared this present shame, what will it ultimately profit a man to profess without understanding? to *say* he has faith, when he has not works (Jas 2:14)? In that case we shall remain in the heavenly vineyard, stunted plants, without the principle of growth in us, barren; and, in the end, we shall be put to shame before Christ and the holy Angels, "as trees of withering fruits, twice dead, plucked up by the roots," even though we die in outward communion with the Church.

To think of these things, and to be alarmed, is the first step towards acceptable obedience; to be at ease, is to be unsafe. We must know what the evil of sin is hereafter, if we do not learn it here. God give us all grace to choose the pain of present repentance before the wrath to come!

SERMON V

Self-Denial the Test of Religious Earnestness

"Now it is high time to awake out of sleep."—Rom 13:2

By "sleep," in this passage, St. Paul means a state of insensibility to things as they really are in God's sight. When we are asleep, we are absent from this world's action, as if we were no longer concerned in it. It goes on without us, or, if our rest be broken, and we have some slight notion of people and occurrences about us, if we hear a voice or a sentence, and see a face, yet we are unable to catch these external objects justly and truly; we make them part of our dreams, and pervert them till they have scarcely a resemblance to what they really are; and such is the state of men as regards religious truth. God is ever Almighty and All-knowing. He is on His throne in heaven, trying the reins and the hearts; and Jesus Christ, our Lord and Saviour, is on His right hand; and ten thousand Angels and Saints are ministering to Him, rapt in the contemplation of Him, or by their errands of mercy connecting this lower world with His courts above; they go to and fro, as though upon the ladder which Jacob saw. And the disclosure of this glorious invisible world is made to us principally by means of the Bible, partly by the course of nature, partly by the floating opinions of mankind, partly by the suggestions of the heart and conscience:—and all these means of information concerning it are collected and combined by the Holy Church, which heralds the news forth to the whole earth, and applies it with power to individual minds, partly by direct instruction, partly by her very form and fashion, which witnesses to them; so that the truths of religion circulate through the world almost as the light of day, every corner and recess having some portion of its blessed rays. Such is the state of a Christian country. Meanwhile, how is it with those who dwell in it? The words of the text remind us of their condition. They are *asleep*. While the Ministers of Christ are using the armour of light, and all things speak of Him, they "walk" not "becomingly, as in the day." Many live altogether as though the day shone not on them, but the shadows still endured; and far the greater part of them are but very faintly sensible of the great truths preached around them. They see and hear as people in a dream; they mix up the Holy Word of God with their own idle imaginings; if startled for a moment, still they soon relapse into slumber; they refuse to be awakened, and think their happiness consists in continuing as they are.

Now I do not for an instant suspect, my brethren, that you are in the sound slumber of sin. This is a miserable state, which I should hope was, on the whole, the condition of few men, at least in a place like this. But, allowing this, yet there is great reason for fearing that very many of you are not wide awake: that though your dreams are disturbed, yet dreams they are; and that the view of religion which you think to be a true one, is not that vision of the Truth which you would see were your eyes open, but such a vague, defective, extravagant picture of it as a man sees when he is asleep. At all events, however this may be, it will be useful (please God) if you ask yourselves, one by one, the question, "*How do I know* I am in the right way? *How do I know* that I have real faith, and am not in a dream?"

The circumstances of these times render it very difficult to answer this question. When the world was against Christianity it was comparatively easy. But (in one sense) the world is now *for it*. I do not mean there are not turbulent lawless men, who would bring all things into confusion, if they could; who hate religion, and would overturn every established institution which proceeds from, or is connected with it. Doubtless there are very many such, but from such men religion has nothing to fear. The truth has ever flourished and strengthened under persecution. But what we have to fear is the opposite fact, that all the rank, and the station, and the intelligence, and the opulence of the country is professedly with religion. We have cause to fear from the very circumstance that the institutions of the country are based upon the acknowledgment of religion as true. Worthy of all honour are they who so based them! Miserable is the guilt which lies upon those who have attempted, and partly succeeded, in shaking that holy foundation! But it often happens that our most bitter are not our most dangerous enemies; on the other hand, greatest blessings are the most serious temptations to the unwary. And our danger, at present, is this, that a man's having a general character for religion, reverencing the Gospel and professing it, and to a certain point obeying it, so fully promotes his temporal interests, that it is difficult for him to make out for himself whether he really acts on faith, or from a desire of this world's advantages. It is difficult to find *tests* which may bring home the truth to his mind, and probe his heart after the manner of Him who, from His throne above, tries it with an Almighty Wisdom. It can scarcely be denied that attention to their religious duties is becoming a fashion among large portions of the community,—so large, that, to many individuals, these portions are in fact *the world*. We are, every now and then, surprised to find persons to be in the observance of family prayer, of reading Scripture, or of Holy Communion, of whom we should not have expected beforehand such a profession of faith; or we hear them avowing the high evangelical truths of the New Testament, and countenancing those who maintain them. All this brings it about, that it is our interest in this world to profess to be Christ's disciples.

And further than this, it is necessary to remark, that, in spite of this general profession of zeal for the Gospel among all respectable persons at this day, nevertheless there is reason for fearing, that it is not altogether the real Gospel that they are zealous for. Doubtless we have cause to be thankful whenever we see persons earnest in the various ways I have mentioned. Yet, somehow, after all, there is reason for being dissatisfied with the character of the religion of the day; dissatisfied, first, because oftentimes these same persons are very inconsistent;—often, for instance, talk irreverently and profanely, ridicule or slight things sacred, speak against the Holy Church, or against the blessed Saints of early times, or even against the favoured servants of God, set before us in Scripture; or *act* with the world and the worse sort of men, even when they do not speak like them; attend to them more than to the Ministers of God, or are very lukewarm, lax, and unscrupulous in matters of conduct, so much so, that they seem hardly to go by principle, but by what is merely expedient and convenient. And then again, putting aside our judgment of these men as individuals, and thinking of them as well as we can (which of course it is our duty to do), yet, after all, taking merely the multitude of them as a symptom of a state of things, I own I am suspicious of any religion that is a people's religion, or an age's religion. Our Saviour says, "Narrow is the way." This, of course, must not be interpreted without great caution; yet surely the whole tenor of the Inspired Volume leads us to believe that His Truth will not be heartily received by the many, that it is against the current of human feeling and opinion, and the course of the world, and so far forth as it *is* received by a man, will be opposed by himself, i.e., by his old nature which remains about him, next by all others, so far forth as they have not received it.

"The light shining in darkness" is the token of true religion; and, though doubtless there are seasons when a sudden enthusiasm arises in favour of the Truth (as in the history of St. John the Baptist, in whose "light" the Jews "were willing for a season to rejoice" [Jn 5:35] so as even "to be baptized of him, confessing their sins" [Mt 3:6]), yet such a popularity of the Truth is *but* sudden, comes at once and goes at once, has no regular growth, no abiding stay. It is error alone which grows and is received heartily on a large scale. St. Paul has set up his warning against our supposing Truth will ever be heartily accepted, whatever show there may be of a general profession of it, in his last Epistle, where he tells Timothy, among other sad prophecies, that "evil men and seducers shall wax worse and worse" (2 Tm 3:13). Truth, indeed, has that power in it, that it forces men to profess it in words; but when they go on to act, instead of obeying *it*, they substitute some idol in the place of it. On these accounts, when there is much talk of religion in a country, and much congratulation that there is a general concern for it, a cautious mind will feel anxious lest some counterfeit be, in fact, honoured instead of it: lest it be the dream of man rather than the verities of God's word, which has become popular, and lest the received form have no more of truth in it than is just necessary to recommend it to the reason and conscience:—lest, in short, it be Satan transformed into an angel of light, rather than the Light itself, which is attracting followers.

If, then, this be a time (which I suppose it is) when a general profession of religion is thought respectable and right in the virtuous and orderly classes of the community, this circumstance should not diminish your anxiety about your own state before God, but rather (I may say) increase it; for two reasons, first, because you are in danger of doing right from motives of this world; next, because you may, perchance, be cheated of the Truth, by some ingenuity which the world puts, like counterfeit coin, in the place of the Truth.

Some, indeed, of those who now hear me, are in situations where they are almost shielded from the world's influence, whatever it is. There are persons so happily placed as to have religious superiors, who direct them to what is good only, and who are kind to them, as well as pious towards God. This is their happiness, and they must thank God for the gift; but it is their temptation too. At least they are under one of the two temptations just mentioned; good behaviour is, in their case, not only a matter of duty, but of interest. If they obey God, they gain praise from men as well as from Him; so that it is very difficult for them to know whether they do right for conscience' sake, or for the world's sake. Thus, whether in private families, or in the world, in all the ranks of middle life, men lie under a considerable danger at this day, a more than ordinary danger, of self-deception, of being asleep while they think themselves awake.

How then shall we try ourselves? Can any tests be named which will bring certainty to our minds on the subject? No indisputable tests can be given. We cannot know for certain. We must beware of an impatience about knowing what our real state is. St. Paul himself did not know till the last days of his life (as far as we know), that he was one of God's elect who shall never perish. He said, "I know nothing by myself, yet am I not hereby justified" (1 Cor 4:4); i.e., though I am not conscious to myself of neglect of duty, yet am I not therefore confident of my acceptance? Judge nothing before the time. Accordingly he says in another place, "I keep under my body, and bring it into subjection, lest that by any means, when I have preached to others, I myself should be a castaway" (1 Cor 9:27). And yet though this absolute certainty of our election unto glory be unattainable, and the desire to obtain it an impatience which ill befits sinners, nevertheless a comfortable hope, a sober and subdued belief that God has pardoned and justified us for Christ's sake (blessed be His name!), is attainable, according to St. John's words, "If our heart condemn us not, then have we confidence toward God" (1 Jn 3:21). And the question is, how are we to attain to this, under the circumstances in which we are placed? In what does it consist?

Were we in a heathen land (as I said just now) it were easy to answer. The very profession of the Gospel would almost bring evidence of true faith, as far as we could have evidence; for such profession among Pagans is almost sure to involve persecution. Hence it is that the Epistles are so full of expressions of joy in the Lord Jesus, and in the exulting hope of salvation. Well might they be confident who had suffered for Christ. "Tribulation worketh patience, and patience experience, and experience hope" (Rom 5:3, 4). "Henceforth let no man trouble me, for I bear in my body the marks of the Lord Jesus" (Gal 6:17). "Always bearing about in the body the dying of the Lord Jesus; that the life also of Jesus might be made manifest in our body" (2 Cor 4:10). "Our hope of you is steadfast, knowing that as ye are partakers of the suffering, so shall ye be also of the consolation" (2 Cor 1:7). These and such like texts belong to those only who have witnessed for the truth like the early Christians. They are beyond *us*.

This is certain; yet since the nature of Christian obedience is the same in every age, it still brings with it, as it did then, an evidence of

God's favour. We cannot indeed make ourselves as sure of our being in the number of God's true servants as the early Christians were, yet we may possess our degree of certainty, and by the same kind of evidence, the evidence of *self-denial*. This was the great evidence which the first disciples gave, and which we can give still. Reflect upon our Saviour's plain declarations, "Whosoever will come after Me, let him deny himself, and take up his cross and follow Me" (Mk 8:34). "If any man come to Me, and hate not his father and mother, and wife, and children, and brethren, and sisters, yea, and his own life also, he cannot be My disciple. And whosoever doth not bear his cross and come after Me, he cannot be My disciple" (Lk 14:26, 27). "If thy hand offend thee, cut it off . . . if thy foot offend thee, cut it off . . . if thine eye offend thee, pluck it out: . . . it is better for thee to enter into life maimed . . . halt . . . with one eye than to be cast into hell" (Mk 9:43–47).

Now without attempting to explain perfectly such passages as these, which doubtless cannot be understood without a fulness of grace which is possessed by very few men, yet at least we learn thus much from them, that a rigorous self-denial is a chief duty, nay, that it may be considered the test whether we are Christ's disciples, whether we are living in a mere dream, which we mistake for Christian faith and obedience, or are really and truly awake, alive, living in the day, on our road heavenwards. The early Christians went through self-denials in their very profession of the Gospel; *what are our self-denials*, now that the profession of the Gospel is not a self-denial? In what sense do *we* fulfil the words of Christ? Have we any distinct notion what is meant by the words "taking up our cross?" In what way are we acting, in which we should not act, supposing the Bible and the Church were unknown to this country, and religion, as existing among us, was *merely* a fashion of this world? What are we doing, which we have reason to trust is done for Christ's sake who bought us?

You know well enough that works are said to be the fruits and evidence of faith. That faith is said to be dead which has them not. Now what works have we to show of such a kind as to give us "confidence," so that we may "not be ashamed before Him at His coming" (1 Jn 2:28)?

In answering this question I observe, first of all, that, according to Scripture, the self-denial which is the test of our faith must be daily. "If any man will come after Me, let him deny himself, and take up his cross *daily*, and follow Me" (Lk 9:23). It is thus St. Luke records our Saviour's words. Accordingly, it seems that Christian obedience does not consist merely in a few occasional efforts, a few accidental good deeds, or certain seasons of repentance, prayer, and activity; a mistake, which minds of a certain class are very apt to fall into. This is the kind of obedience which constitutes what the world calls a great man, i.e., a man who has some noble points, and every now and then acts heroically, so as to astonish and subdue the minds of beholders, but who in private life has no abiding personal religion, who does not regulate his thoughts, words, and deeds, according to the Law of God. Again, the word *daily* implies, that the self-denial which is pleasing to Christ consists in little things. This is plain, for opportunity for great self-denials does not come every day. Thus to take up the cross of Christ is no great action done once for all, it consists in the continual practice of small duties which are distasteful to us.

If, then, a person asks how he is to know whether he is dreaming on in the world's slumber, or is really awake and alive unto God, let him first fix his mind upon some one or other of his besetting infirmities. Every one who is at all in the habit of examining himself, must be conscious of such within him. Many men have more than one, all of us have some one or other; and in resisting and overcoming such, self-denial has its first employment. One man is indolent and fond of amusement, another man is passionate or ill-tempered, another is vain, another has little control over his tongue; others are weak, and cannot resist the ridicule of thoughtless companions; others are tormented with bad passions, of which they are ashamed, yet are overcome. Now let every one consider what his weak point is; in that is his trial. His trial is not in those things which are easy to him, but in that one thing, in those several things, whatever they are, in which to do his duty is against his nature. Never think yourself safe because you do your duty in ninety-nine points; it is the hundredth which is to be the ground of your self-denial, which must evidence, or rather instance and realize your faith. It is in reference to this you must watch and pray; pray continually for God's grace to help you, and watch with fear and trembling lest you fall. Other men may not know what these weak points of your character are, they may mistake them. But you may know them; you may know them by *their* guesses and hints, and your own observation, and the light of the Spirit of God. And oh, that you may have strength to wrestle with them and overcome them! Oh, that you may have the wisdom to care little for the world's religion, or the praise you get from the world, and your agreement with what clever men, or powerful men, or many men, make the standard of religion, compared with the secret consciousness that you are obeying God in little things as well as great, in the hundredth duty as well as in the ninety-nine! Oh, that you may (as it were) sweep the house diligently to discover what you lack of the *full* measure of obedience! For be quite sure, that this apparently small defect will influence your whole spirit and judgment in all things. Be quite sure that your judgment of persons, and of events, and of actions, and of doctrines, and your spirit towards God and man, your faith in the high truths of the Gospel, and your knowledge of your duty, all depend in a strange way on this strict endeavour to observe the whole law, on this self-denial in those little things in which obedience *is* a self-denial. Be not content with a warmth of faith carrying you over many obstacles even in your obedience, forcing you past the fear of men, and the usages of society, and the persuasions of interest; exult not in your experience of God's past mercies, and your assurance of what He has already done for your soul, if you are conscious you have neglected the one thing needful, the "one thing" which "thou lackest,"—daily self-denial.

But, besides this, there are other modes of self-denial to try your faith and sincerity, which it may be right just to mention. It may so happen that the sin you are most liable to, is not called forth every day. For instance: Anger and passion are irresistible perhaps when they come upon you, but it is only at times that you are provoked, and then you are off your guard; so that the occasion is over, and you have failed, before you were well aware of its coming. It is right then almost to *find out* for yourself daily self-denials; and this because our Lord bids you take up your cross daily, and because it proves your earnestness, and because by doing so you strengthen your general power of self-mastery, and come to have such an habitual command of yourself, as will be a defense ready prepared when the season of temptation comes. Rise up then in the morning with the purpose that (please God) the day shall not pass without its self-denial, with a self-denial in innocent pleasures and tastes, if none occurs to mortify sin. Let your very rising from your bed be a self-denial; let your meals be self-denials. Determine to yield to others in things indifferent, to go out of your way in small matters, to inconvenience yourself (so that no direct duty suffers by it), rather than you should not meet with your daily discipline. This was the Psalmist's method, who was, as it were, "punished all day long, and chastened every morning" (Ps 73:14). It was St. Paul's method, who "kept under," or bruised "his body, and brought it into subjection" (1 Cor 9:27). This is one great end of fasting. A man says to himself, "How am I to know I am in earnest?" I would suggest to him, Make some sacrifice, do some distasteful thing, which you are not actually obliged to do (so that it be lawful), to bring home to your mind that in fact you do love your Saviour, that you do hate sin, that you do hate your sinful nature, that you have put aside the present world. Thus you will have an evidence (to a certain point) that you are not using mere words. It is easy to make professions, easy to say fine things in speech or in writing, easy to astonish men with truths which they do not know, and sentiments which rise above human nature. "But thou, O servant of God, flee these things, and follow after righteousness, godliness, faith, love, patience, meekness." Let not your words run on; force every one of them into action as it goes, and thus, cleansing yourself from all pollution of the flesh and spirit, perfect holiness in the fear of God. In dreams we sometimes move our arms to see if we are awake or not, and so we are awakened. This is the way to keep your heart awake also. Try yourself daily in little deeds, to prove that your faith is more than a deceit.

I am aware all this is a hard doctrine; hard to those even who assent to it, and can describe it most accurately. There are such imperfections, such inconsistencies in the heart and life of even the better sort of men, that continual repentance must ever go hand in hand with our endeavours to obey. Much we need the grace of Christ's blood to wash us from the guilt we daily incur; much we need the aid of His promised Spirit! And surely He will grant all the riches of His mercy to His true servants; but as surely He will vouchsafe to none of us the power to believe in Him, and the blessedness of being one with Him, who are not as earnest in obeying Him as if salvation depended on themselves.

SERMON VII

Sins of Ignorance and Weakness

"Let us draw near with a true heart in full assurance of faith, having our hearts sprinkled from an evil conscience, and our bodies washed with pure water."—Heb 10:22

Among the reasons which may be assigned for the observance of prayer at stated times, there is one which is very obvious, and yet perhaps is not so carefully remembered and acted upon as it should be. I mean the necessity of sinners cleansing themselves from time to time of the ever-accumulating guilt which loads their consciences. We are ever sinning; and though Christ has died once for all to release us from our penalty, yet we are not pardoned once for all, but according as, and whenever each of us supplicates for the gift. By the prayer of faith we appropriate it; but only for the time, not for ever. Guilt is again contracted, and must be again repented of and washed away. We cannot by one act of faith establish ourselves for ever after in the favour of God. It is going beyond His will to be impatient for a final acquittal, when we are bid ask only for our *daily* bread. We are still so far in the condition of the Israelites; and though we do not offer sacrifice, or observe the literal washings of the Law, yet we still require the periodical renewal of those blessings which were formerly conveyed in their degree by the Mosaic rites; and though we gain far more excellent gifts from God than the Jews did, and by more spiritual ordinances, yet means of approaching Him we still need, and continual means to keep us in the justification in which baptism first placed us. Of this the text reminds us. It is addressed to Christians, to the regenerate; yet so far from their regeneration having cleansed them once for all, they are bid ever to sprinkle the blood of Christ upon their consciences, and renew (as it were) their baptism, and so continually appear before the presence of Almighty God.

Let us now endeavour to realize a truth, which few of us will be disposed to dispute as far as words go.

1. First consider our present condition, as shown us in Scripture. Christ has not changed this, though He has died; it is as it was from the

beginning,—I mean our actual state as men. We have Adam's nature in the same sense as if redemption had not come to the world. It *has* come to all the world, but the world is not changed thereby as a whole,—that change is not a work done and over in Christ. We are changed *one by one;* the race of man is what it ever was, guilty;—what it was before Christ came; with the same evil passions, the same slavish will. The history of redemption, if it is to be effectual, must begin from the beginning with every individual of us, and be carried on through our own life. It is not a work done ages before we were born. We cannot profit by the work of a Saviour, though He be the Blessed Son of God, so as to be saved thereby without our own working; for we are moral agents, we have a will of our own, and Christ must be formed in us, and turn us from darkness to light, if God's gracious purpose, fulfilled upon the cross, is to be in our case more than a name, an abused, wasted privilege. Thus the world, viewed as in God's sight, can never become wiser or more enlightened than it has been. We cannot mount upon the labours of our forefathers. We have the same nature that man ever had, and we must begin from the point man ever began from, and work out our salvation in the same slow, persevering manner.

(1.) When this is borne in mind, how important the Jewish Law becomes to us Christians! important in itself, over and above all references contained in it to that Gospel which it introduced. To this day it fulfils its original purpose of impressing upon man his great guilt and feebleness. Those legal sacrifices and purifications which are now all done away, are still evidence to us of a fact which the Gospel has not annulled,—our corruption. Let no one lightly pass over the Book of Leviticus, and say it only contains the ceremonial of a national law. Let no one study it merely with a critic's eye, satisfied with connecting it in a nicely arranged system with the Gospel, as though it contained prophecy only. No; it speaks to us. Are we better than the Jews? is our nature less unbelieving, sensual, or proud, than theirs? Surely man is at all times the same being, as even the philosophers tell us. And if so, that minute ceremonial of the Law presents us with a picture of *our* daily life. It impressively testifies to our continual sinning, by suggesting that an expiation is needful in all the most trivial circumstances of our conduct; and that it is at our peril if we go on carelessly and thoughtlessly, trusting to our having been once accepted,—whether in Baptism,—or (as we think) at a certain season of repentance, or (as we may fancy) at the very time of the death of Christ (as if then the whole race of man were really and at once pardoned and exalted),—or (worse still) if we profanely doubt that man has ever fallen under a curse, and trust idly in the mercy of God, without a feeling of the true misery and infinite danger of sin.

Consider the ceremony observed on the great day of atonement, and you will see what was the sinfulness of the Israelites, and therefore of all mankind, in God's sight. The High Priest was taken to represent the holiest person of the whole world. The nation itself was holy above the rest of the world; from it a holy tribe was selected; from the holy tribe, a holy family; and from that family, a holy person. This was the High Priest, who was thus set apart as the choice specimen of the whole human race; yet even he was not allowed, under pain of death, to approach even the mercy-seat of God, except once a year: nor then in his splendid robes, nor without sacrifices for the sins of himself and the people, the blood of which he carried with him into the holy place.

Or consider the sacrifices necessary according to the Law for sins of ignorance (Lv 5); or again, for the mere touching any thing which the Law pronounced unclean, or for bodily disease (Lv 5:2, 6; 14:1–32), and hence learn how sinful our ordinary thoughts and deeds must be, represented to us as they are by these outward ceremonial transgressions. Not even their thanksgiving might the Israelites offer without an offering of blood to cleanse it; for our corruption is not merely in this act or that, but in our *nature*.

(2.) Next, to pass from the Jewish Law, you will observe that God tells us expressly in the history of the fall of Adam, what the legal ceremonies implied; that it *is* our very nature which is sinful. Herein is the importance of the doctrine of original sin. It is very humbling, and as such the only true introduction to the preaching of the Gospel. Men can without trouble be brought to confess that they sin, i.e., that they commit sins. They know well enough they are not perfect; nay, that they do nothing in the best manner. But they do not like to be told that the race from which they proceed is degenerate. Even the indolent have pride here. They think they *can* do their duty, *only do not choose to do it;* they like to believe (though strangely indeed, for they condemn themselves while they believe it), they like to believe that they do not want assistance. A man must be far gone in degradation, and has lost even that false independence of mind which is often a substitute for real religion in leading to exertion, who, while living in sin, steadily and contentedly holds the opinion that he is born *for* sin. And much more do the industrious and active dislike to have it forced upon their minds, that, do what they will, they have the taint of corruption about all their doings and imaginings. We know how ashamed men are of being low born, or discreditably connected. This is the sort of shame forced upon every son of Adam. "Thy first father hath sinned": this is the legend on our forehead which even the sign of the cross does no more than blot out, leaving the mark of it. This is our shame; but I notice it here, not so much as a humbling thought, as with a view of pressing upon your consciences the necessity of appearing before God at stated seasons, in order to put aside the continually renewed guilt of your nature. Who will dare go on day after day in neglect of earnest prayer, and the Holy Communion, while each day brings its own fearful burden, coming as if spontaneously, springing from our very nature, but not got rid of without deliberate and direct acts of faith in the Great Sacrifice which has been set forth for its removal?

(3.) Further, look into your own souls, my brethren, and see if you cannot discern some part of the truth of the Scripture statement, which I have been trying to set before you. Recollect the bad thoughts of various kinds which come into your minds like darts; for these will be some evidence to you of the pollution and odiousness of your nature. True, they proceed from your adversary, the Devil; and the very circumstance of your experiencing them is in itself no proof of your being sinful, for even the Son of God, your Saviour, suffered from the temptation of them. But you will scarcely deny that they are received by you so freely and heartily, as to show that Satan tempts you through your nature, not against it. Again, let them be ever so external in their first coming, do you not make them your own? Do you not detain them? or do you impatiently and indignantly shake them off? Even if you reject them, still do they not answer Satan's purpose in inflaming your mind at the instant, and so evidence that the matter of which it is composed is corruptible? Do you not, for instance, dwell on the thought of wealth and splendour till you covet these temporal blessings? or do you not suffer yourselves, though for a while, to be envious, or discontented, or angry, or vain, or impure, or proud? Ah! who can estimate the pollution hence, of one single day; the pollution of touching merely that dead body of sin which we put off indeed at our baptism, but which is tied about us while we live here, and is the means of our Enemy's assaults upon us! The taint of death is upon us, and surely we shall be stifled by the encompassing plague, unless God from day to day vouchsafes to make us clean.

2. Again, reflect on the *habits* of sin which we superadded to our evil nature before we turned to God. Here is another source of continual defilement. Instead of checking the bad elements within us, perhaps we indulged them for years; and they truly had their fruit unto death. Then

Adam's sin increased, and multiplied itself within us; there was a change, but it was for the worse, not for the better; and the new nature we gained, far from being spiritual, was twofold more the child of hell than that with which we were born. So when, at length, we turned back into a better course, what a complicated work lay before us, to unmake ourselves! And however long we have laboured at it, still how much unconscious, unavoidable sin, the result of past transgression, is thrown out from our hearts day by day in the energy of our thinking and acting! Thus, through the sins of our youth, the power of the flesh is exerted against us, as a second creative principle of evil, aiding the malice of the Devil; Satan from without,—and our hearts from within, not passive merely and kindled by temptation, but *devising* evil, and speaking hard things against God with articulate voice, whether we will or not! Thus do past years rise up against us in present offences; gross inconsistencies show themselves in our character; and much need have we continually to implore God to forgive us our past transgressions, which still live in spite of our repentance, and act of themselves vigorously against our better mind, feebly influenced by that younger principle of faith, by which we fight against them.

3. Further, consider how many sins are involved in our obedience, I may say from the mere necessity of the case; that is, from not having that more vigorous and clear-sighted faith which would enable us accurately to discern and closely to follow the way of life. The case of the Jews will exemplify what I mean. There were points of God's perfect Law which were not urged upon their acceptance, because it was foreseen that they would not be able to receive them as they really should be received, or to bring them home practically to their minds, and obey them simply and truly. We, Christians, with the same evil hearts as the Jews had, and most of us as unformed in holy practice, have, nevertheless, a perfect Law. We are bound to take and use all the precepts of the New Testament, though it stands to reason that many of them are, in matter of fact, quite above the comprehension of most of us. I am speaking of the actual state of the case, and will not go aside to ask why, or under what circumstances God was pleased to change His mode of dealing with man. But so it is; the Minister of Christ has to teach His sinful people a perfect obedience, and does not know how to set about it, or how to insist on any precept, so as to secure it from being misunderstood and misapplied. He sees men are acting upon low motives and views, and finds it impossible to raise their minds all at once, however clear his statements of the Truth. He feels that their good deeds might be done in

a much better manner. There are numberless small circumstances about their mode of doing things, which offend him, as implying poverty of faith, superstition, and contracted carnal notions. He is obliged to leave them to themselves with the hope that they may improve generally, and outgrow their present feebleness; and is often perplexed whether to praise or blame them. So is it with all of us, Ministers as well as people; it is so with the most advanced of Christians while in the body, and God sees it. What a source of continual defilement is here; not an omission merely of what might be added to our obedience, but a cause of positive offence in the Eyes of Eternal Purity! Who is not displeased when a man attempts some great work which is above his powers? and is it an excuse for his miserable performance that the work is above him? Now this is our case; we are bound to serve God with a perfect heart; an exalted work, a work for which our sins disable us. And when we attempt it, necessary as is our endeavour, how miserable must it appear in the eyes of the Angels! how pitiful our exhibition of ourselves; and, withal, how sinful! since did we love God more from the heart, and had we served Him from our youth up, it would not have been with us as it is. Thus our very calling, as creatures, and again as elect children of God, and freemen in the Gospel, is by our sinfulness made our shame; for it puts us upon duties, and again upon the use of privileges, which are above us. We attempt great things with the certainty of failing, and yet the necessity of attempting; and so *while* we attempt, need continual forgiveness for the *failure* of the attempt. We stand before God as the Israelites at the passover of Hezekiah, who *desired* to serve God according to the Law, but could not do so accurately from lack of knowledge; and we can but offer, through our Great High Priest, our sincerity and earnestness instead of exact obedience, as Hezekiah did for them. "The good Lord pardon every one, that *prepareth his heart* to seek God, the Lord God of his fathers, though he be not cleansed according to the purification of the sanctuary" (2 Chr 30:18, 19); not performing, that is, the full duties of his calling.

And if such be the deficiencies, even of the established Christian, in his ordinary state, how great must be those of the penitent, who has but lately begun the service of God? or of the young, who are still within the influence of some unbridled imagination, or some domineering passion? or of the heavily depressed spirit, whom Satan binds with the bonds of bodily ailment, or tosses to and fro in the tumult of doubt and indecision? Alas! how is their conscience defiled with the thoughts, nay the words of every hour! and how inexpressibly needful for them to relieve themselves of the evil that weighs upon their heart, by drawing near to God in full assurance of faith, and washing away their guilt in the Expiation which He has appointed!

What I have said is a call upon you, my brethren, in the first place, to daily private prayer. Next, it is a call upon you to join the public services of the Church, not only once a week, but whenever you have the opportunity; knowing well that your Redeemer is especially present where two or three are gathered together. And, further, it is an especial call upon you to attend upon the celebration of the Lord's Supper, in which blessed ordinance we really and truly gain that spiritual life which is the object of our daily prayers. The Body and Blood of Christ give power and efficacy to our daily faith and repentance. Take this view of the Lord's Supper; as the appointed means of obtaining the great blessings you need. The daily prayers of the Christian do but spring from, and are referred back to, his attendance on it. Christ died once, long since: by communicating in His Sacrament, you renew the Lord's death; you bring into the midst of you that Sacrifice which took away the sins of the world; you appropriate the benefit of it, while you eat it under the elements of bread and wine. These outward signs are simply the means of an hidden grace. You do not expect to sustain your animal life without food; be but as rational in spiritual concerns as you are in temporal. Look upon the consecrated elements as *necessary*, under God's blessing, to your continual sanctification; approach them as the salvation of your souls. Why is it more strange that God should work through means for the health of the soul, than that He should ordain them for the preservation of bodily life, as He certainly has done? It is unbelief to think it matters not to your spiritual welfare whether you communicate or not. And it is worse than unbelief, it is utter insensibility and obduracy, not to discern the state of death and corruption into which, when left to yourselves, you are continually falling back. Rather thank God, that whereas you are sinners, instead of His leaving you the mere general promise of life through His Son, which is addressed to all men, He has allowed you to take that promise to yourselves one by one, and thus gives you a humble hope that He has chosen you out of the world unto salvation.

Lastly, I have all along spoken as addressing true Christians, who are walking in the narrow way, and have hope of heaven. But these are the "few." Are there none here present of the "many" who walk in the broad way, and have upon their heads all their sins, from their baptism upwards? Rather, is it not probable that there are persons in this congregation, who, though mixed with the people of God, are really unforgiven, and if they now died, would die in their sins? First, let those who neglect the Holy Communion ask themselves whether this is not their condition; let them reflect whether among the signs by which it is given us to ascertain our state, there can be, to a man's own conscience, a more fearful one than this, that he is omitting what is appointed, as the ordinary means of his salvation. This is a plain test, about which no one can deceive himself. But next, let him have recourse to a more accurate search into his conscience; and ask himself whether (in the words of the text) he "draws near to God with a true heart," i.e., whether in spite of his prayers and religious services, there be not some secret, unresisted lusts within him, which make his devotion a mockery in the sight of God, and leave him in his sins; whether he be not in truth thoughtless, and religious only as far as his friends make him seem so,—or lightminded and shallow in his religion, being ignorant of the depths of his guilt, and resting presumptuously on his own innocence (as he thinks it) and God's mercy;—whether he be not set upon gain, obeying God only so far as *His* service does not interfere with the service of mammon;—whether he be not harsh, evil-tempered,—unforgiving, unpitiful, or high-minded,—self-confident, and secure;—or whether he be not fond of the fashions of this world, which pass away, desirous of the friendship of the great, and of sharing in the refinements of society;—or whether he be not given up to some engrossing pursuit, which indisposes him to the thought of his God and Saviour.

Any *one* deliberate habit of sin incapacitates a man for receiving the gifts of the Gospel. All such states of mind as these are fearful symptoms of the *existence* of some such wilful sin in our hearts; and in proportion as we trace these symptoms in our conduct, so much we dread, lest we be reprobate.

Let us then approach God, all of us, confessing that we do not know ourselves; that we are more guilty than we can possibly understand, and can but timidly hope, not confidently determine, that we have true faith. Let us take comfort in our being still in a state of grace, though we have no certain pledge of salvation. Let us beg Him to enlighten us, and comfort us; to forgive us all our sins, teaching us those we do not see, and enabling us to overcome them.

SERMON XIII

Promising without Doing

"A certain man had two sons; and he came to the first, and said, Son, go work to-day in my vineyard. He answered and said, I will not; but afterward he repented, and went. And he came to the second, and said likewise. And he answered and said, I go, Sir; and went not."—Mt 21:28–30

Our religious professions are at a far greater distance from our acting upon them, than we ourselves are aware. We know generally that it is our duty to serve God, and we resolve we will do so faithfully. We are sincere in thus generally desiring and purposing to be obedient, and we think we are in earnest; yet we go away, and presently, without any struggle of mind or apparent change of purpose, almost without knowing ourselves what we do,—we go away and do the very contrary to the resolution we have expressed. This inconsistency is exposed by our Blessed Lord in the second part of the parable which I have taken for my text. You will observe, that in the case of the first son, who said he would not go work, and yet did go, it is said, "afterward he repented"; he underwent a positive change of purpose. But in the case of the second, it is merely said, "He answered, I go, Sir, and went not";—for here there was *no* revolution of sentiment, nothing deliberate; he merely acted according to his habitual frame of mind; he did *not* go work, because it was contrary to his general character to work; only he did not know this. He said, "I go, Sir," sincerely, from the feeling of the moment; but when the words were out of his mouth, then they were forgotten. It was like the wind blowing against a stream, which seems for a moment to change its course in consequence, but in fact flows down as before.

To this subject I shall now call your attention, as drawn from the latter part of this parable, passing over the case of the repentant son, which would form a distinct subject in itself. "He answered and said, I go, Sir; and went not." We promise to serve God: We do not perform; and that not from deliberate faithlessness in the particular case, but because it is our nature, our *way* not to obey, and *we* do not know this; we do not know ourselves, or what we are promising. I will give several instances of this kind of weakness.

1. For instance, that of mistaking good feelings for real religious principle. Consider how often this takes place. It is the case with the young necessarily, who have not been exposed to temptation. They have (we will say) been brought up religiously, they wish to be religious, and so are objects of our love and interest; but they think themselves far more religious than they really are. They suppose they hate sin, and understand the Truth, and can resist the world, when they hardly know the meaning of the words they use. Again, how often is a man incited by circumstances to utter a virtuous wish, or propose a generous or valiant deed, and perhaps applauds himself for his own good feeling, and has no suspicion that he is not able to act upon it! In truth, he does not understand where the real difficulty of his duty lies. He thinks that the characteristic of a religious man is his having correct notions. It escapes him that there is a great interval between feeling and acting. He takes it for granted he can do what he wishes. He knows he is a free agent, and can on the whole do what he will; but he is not conscious of the load of corrupt nature and sinful habits which hang upon his will, and clog it in each particular exercise of it. He has borne these so long, that he is insensible to their existence. He knows that in little things, where passion and inclination are excluded, he can perform as soon as he resolves. Should he meet in his walk two paths, to the right and left, he is sure he can take which he will at once, without any difficulty; and he fancies that obedience to God is not much more difficult than to turn to the right instead of the left.

2. One especial case of this self-deception is seen in delaying repentance. A man says to himself, "Of course, if the worst comes to the worst, if illness comes, or at least old age, I can repent." I do not speak of the dreadful presumption of such a mode of quieting conscience (though many persons really use it who do not speak the words out, or are aware that they act upon it), but, merely, of the ignorance it evidences concerning our moral condition, and our power of willing and doing. If men can repent, why do they not do so at once? They answer, that "they intend to do so hereafter"; i.e., they do *not* repent because they *can*. Such is their argument; whereas, the very fact that they do not now, should make them suspect that there is a greater difference between intending and doing than they know of.

So very difficult is obedience, so hardly won is every step in our Christian course, so sluggish and inert our corrupt nature, that I would have a man disbelieve he can do one jot or tittle beyond what he has already done; refrain from borrowing aught on the hope of the future, however good a security for it he seems to be able to show; and never take his good feelings and wishes in pledge for one single untried deed. Nothing but *past* acts are the vouchers for *future*. Past sacrifices, past labours, past victories over yourselves,—these, my brethren, are the tokens of the like in store, and doubtless of greater in store; for the path of the just is as the shining, growing light (Prv 4:18). But trust nothing short of these. "Deeds, not words and wishes," this must be the watchword of your warfare and the ground of your assurance. But if you have done nothing firm and manly hitherto, if you are as yet the coward slave of Satan, and the poor creature of your lusts and passions, never suppose you will one day rouse yourselves from your indolence. Alas! there are men who walk the road to hell, always the while looking back at heaven, and trembling as they pace forward towards their place of doom. They hasten on as under a spell, shrinking from the consequences of their own deliberate doings. Such was Balaam. What would he have given if words and feelings might have passed for deeds! See how religious he was so far as profession goes! How did he revere God in speech! How piously express a desire to die the death of the righteous! Yet he died in battle among God's *enemies;* not suddenly overcome by temptation, only on the other hand, not suddenly turned to God by his good thoughts and fair purposes. But in this respect the power of sin differs from any literal spell or fascination, that we are, after all, willing slaves of it, and shall answer for following it. If "our iniquities, like the wind, take us away" (Is 64:6), yet we can help this.

Nor is it only among beginners in religious obedience that there is this great interval between promising and performing. We can never answer how we shall act under new circumstances. A very little knowledge of life and of our own hearts will teach us this. Men whom we meet in the world turn out, in the course of their trial, so differently from what their former conduct promised, they view things so differently *before* they were tempted and *after,* that we, who see and wonder at it, have abundant cause to look to ourselves, not to be "high-minded," but to "fear." Even the most matured Saints, those who imbibed in largest measure the power and fulness of Christ's Spirit, and worked righteousness most diligently in their day, could they have been thoroughly scanned even by man, would (I am persuaded) have exhibited inconsistencies such as to surprise and shock their most ardent disciples. After all, one good deed is scarcely the pledge of another, though I just now said it was. The best men are uncertain; they are great, and they are little again; they stand firm, and then fall. Such is human virtue;—reminding us to call no one master on earth, but to look up to our sinless and perfect Lord; reminding us to humble ourselves, each within himself, and to reflect what we must appear to God, if even to ourselves and each other we seem so base and worthless; and showing clearly that all who are saved, even the least inconsistent of us, can be saved only by faith, not by works.

3. Here I am reminded of another plausible form of the same error. It is a mistake concerning what is meant by faith. We know Scripture tells us that God accepts those who have faith in Him. Now the question is, What *is* faith, and how can a man tell that he *has* faith? Some persons answer at once and without hesitation, that "to have faith is to feel oneself to be nothing, and God every thing; it is to be convinced of sin, to be conscious one cannot save oneself, and to wish to be saved by Christ our Lord; and that it is, moreover, to have the love of Him warm in one's heart, and to rejoice in Him, to desire His glory, and to resolve to live to Him and not to the world." But I will answer, with all due seriousness, as speaking on a serious subject, that this is *not* faith. Not that it is not necessary (it is very necessary) to be convinced that we are laden with infirmity and sin, and without health in us, and to look for salvation solely to Christ's blessed sacrifice on the cross; and we may well be thankful if we are thus minded; but that a man may feel all this that I have described, vividly, and still not yet possess one particle of true religious faith. Why? Because there is an immeasurable distance between feeling right and doing right. A man may have all these good thoughts and emotions, yet (if he has not yet hazarded them to the experiment of practice) he cannot promise himself that he has any sound and permanent principle at all. If he has not yet acted upon them, we have no voucher, barely on *account* of them, to believe that they are any thing but words. Though a man spoke like an angel, I would not believe him, on the mere ground of his speaking. Nay, till he acts upon them, he has not even evidence to himself that he has true living faith. Dead faith (as St. James says) profits no man. Of course; the Devils have it. What, on the other hand is *living* faith? Do fervent thoughts make faith *living?* St. James tells us otherwise. He tells us *works,* deeds of obedience, are the life of faith. "As the body without the spirit is dead, so faith without works is dead also" (Jas 2:26). So that those who think they really believe, because they have in word and thought surrendered themselves to God, are much too hasty in their judgment. They have done something, indeed, but not at all the

most difficult part of their duty, which is to surrender themselves to God in deed and act. They have as yet done nothing to show they will not, after saying "I go," the next moment "go not"; nothing to show they will not act the part of the self-deceiving disciple, who said, "Though I die with Thee, I will not deny Thee," yet straightway went and denied Christ thrice. As far as we know any thing of the matter, justifying faith has no existence independent of its particular definite acts. It may be described to be the temper under which men obey; the humble and earnest desire to please Christ which causes and attends on actual services. He who does one little deed of obedience, whether he denies himself some comfort to relieve the sick and needy, or curbs his temper, or forgives an enemy, or asks forgiveness for an offence committed by him, or resists the clamour or ridicule of the world—such an one (as far as we are given to judge) evinces more true faith than could be shown by the most fluent religious conversation, the most intimate knowledge of Scripture doctrine, or the most remarkable agitation and change of religious sentiments. Yet how many are there who sit still with folded hands, dreaming, doing nothing at all, thinking they have done every thing, or need do nothing, when they merely have had these good *thoughts*, which will save no one!

My object has been, as far as a few words can do it, to lead you to some true notion of the depths and deceitfulness of the heart, which we do not really know. It is easy to speak of human nature as corrupt in the general, to admit it in the general, and then get quit of the subject; as if the doctrine being once admitted, there was nothing more to be done with it. But in truth we can have no real apprehension of the doctrine of our corruption, till we view the structure of our minds, part by part; and dwell upon and draw out the signs of our weakness, inconsistency, and ungodliness, which are such as can arise from nothing else than some strange original defect in our moral nature.

1. Now it will be well if such self-examination as I have suggested leads us to the habit of constant dependence upon the Unseen God, in whom "we live and move and have our being." We are in the dark about ourselves. When we act, we are groping in the dark, and may meet with a fall any moment. Here and there, perhaps, we see a little; or, in our attempts to influence and move our minds, we are making experiments (as it were) with some delicate and dangerous instrument, which works we do not know how, and may produce unexpected and disastrous effects. The management of our hearts is quite above us. Under these circumstances it becomes our comfort to look up to God. "Thou, God,

seest me!" Such was the consolation of the forlorn Hagar in the wilderness. He knoweth whereof we are made, and He alone can uphold us. He sees with most appalling distinctness all our sins, all the windings and recesses of evil within us; yet it is our only comfort to know this, and to trust Him for help against ourselves. To those who have a right notion of their weakness, the thought of their Almighty Sanctifier and Guide is continually present. They believe in the necessity of a spiritual influence to change and strengthen them, not as a mere abstract doctrine, but as a practical and most consolatory truth, daily to be fulfilled in their warfare with sin and Satan.

2. And this conviction of our excessive weakness must further lead us to try ourselves continually in little things, in order to prove our own earnestness; ever to be suspicious of ourselves, and not only to refrain from promising much, but actually to put ourselves to the test in order to keep ourselves wakeful. A sober mind never enjoys God's blessings to the full; it draws back and refuses a portion to show its command over itself. It denies itself in trivial circumstances, even if nothing is gained by denying, but an evidence of its own sincerity. It makes trial of its own professions; and if it has been tempted to say any thing noble and great, or to blame another for sloth or cowardice, it takes itself at its word, and resolves to make some sacrifice (if possible) in little things, as a price for the indulgence of fine speaking, or as a penalty on its censoriousness. Much would be gained if we adopted this rule even in our professions of friendship and service one towards another; and never said a thing which we were not willing to do.

There is only one place where the Christian allows himself to profess openly, and that is in Church. Here, under the guidance of Apostles and Prophets, he says many things boldly, as speaking after them, and as before Him who searcheth the reins. There can be no harm in professing much directly to God, because, *while* we speak, we know He sees through our professions, and takes them for what they really are, *prayers*. How much, for instance, do we profess when we say the Creed! and in the Collects we put on the full character of a Christian. We desire and seek the best gifts, and declare our strong purpose to serve God with our whole hearts. By doing this, we remind ourselves of our duty; and withal, we humble ourselves by the taunt (so to call it) of putting upon our dwindled and unhealthy forms those ample and glorious garments which befit the upright and full-grown believer.

Lastly, we see from the parable, what is the course and character of human obedience on the whole. There are two sides of it. I have taken the darker side; the case of profession without practice, of saying "I go, Sir," and of not going. But what is the brighter side? Nothing better than to say, "I go not," and to repent and go. The more *common* condition of men is, not to know their inability to serve God, and readily to answer for themselves; and so they quietly pass through life, as if they had nothing to fear. Their best estate, what is it, but to rise more or less in rebellion against God, to resist His commandments and ordinances, and then poorly to make up for the mischief they have done, by repenting and obeying? Alas! to be alive as a Christian, is nothing better than to struggle against sin, to disobey and repent. There has been but One amongst the sons of men who has said and done *consistently;* who said, "I come to do Thy will, O God," and without delay or hindrance did it. He came to show us what human nature might become, if carried on to its perfection. Thus He teaches us to think highly of our nature as viewed in Him; not (as some do) to speak evil of our nature and exalt ourselves personally, but while we acknowledge *our own* distance from heaven, to view our *nature* as renewed in Him, as glorious and wonderful beyond our thoughts. Thus He teaches us to be hopeful; and encourages us while conscience abases us. Angels seem little in honour and dignity, compared with that nature which the Eternal Word has purified by His own union with it. Henceforth, we dare aspire to enter into the heaven of heavens, and to live for ever in God's presence, because the first-fruits of our race is already there in the Person of His Only-begotten Son.

SERMON XXIV

The Religion of the Day

"Let us have grace, whereby we may serve God acceptably with reverence and godly fear. For our God is a consuming fire."—Heb 12:28, 29

In every age of Christianity, since it was first preached, there has been what may be called a *religion of the world*, which so far imitates the one true religion, as to deceive the unstable and unwary. The world does not oppose religion *as such*. I may say, it never has opposed it. In particular, it has, in all ages, acknowledged in one sense or other the Gospel of Christ, fastened on one or other of its characteristics, and professed to embody this in its practice; while by neglecting the other parts of the holy doctrine, it has, in fact, distorted and corrupted even that portion of it which it has exclusively put forward, and so has contrived to explain away the whole;—for he who cultivates only one precept of the Gospel to the exclusion of the rest, in reality attends to no part at all. Our duties *balance* each other; and though we are too sinful to perform them all perfectly, yet we may in some measure be performing them all, and preserving the balance on the whole; whereas, to give ourselves only to this or that commandment, is to incline our minds in a wrong direction, and at length to pull them down to the earth, which is the aim of our adversary, the Devil.

It is his *aim* to break our strength; to force us down to the earth,—to bind us there. The world is his instrument for this purpose; but he is too wise to set it in open opposition to the Word of God. No! he affects to be a prophet like the prophets of God. He calls his servants also prophets; and they mix with the scattered remnant of the true Church, with the solitary Micaiahs who are left upon the earth, and speak in the name of the Lord. And in one sense they speak the truth; but it is not the whole truth; and we know, even from the common experience of life, that half the truth is often the most gross and mischievous of falsehoods.

Even in the first age of the Church, while persecution still raged, he set up a counter religion among the philosophers of the day, partly like Christianity, but in truth a bitter foe to it; and it deceived and made shipwreck of the faith of those who had not the love of God in their hearts.

Time went on, and he devised a second idol of the true Christ, and it remained in the temple of God for many a year. The age was rude and fierce. Satan took the darker side of the Gospel: its awful mysteriousness, its fearful glory, its sovereign inflexible justice; and here *his* picture of the truth ended, "God is a consuming fire"; so declares the text, and we know it. But we know more, viz., that God is love also; but Satan did not add this to his religion, which became one of *fear*. The religion of the world was then a fearful religion. Superstitions abounded, and cruelties. The noble firmness, the graceful austerity of the true Christian were superseded by forbidding spectres, harsh of eye, and haughty of brow; and these were the patterns or the tyrants of a beguiled people.

What is Satan's device in this day? a far different one; but perhaps a more pernicious. I will attempt to expose it, or rather to suggest some remarks towards its exposure, by those who think it worth while to attempt it; for the subject is too great and too difficult for an occasion such as the present, and, after all, no one can detect falsehood for another;—every man must do it for himself; we can but *help* each other.

What is the world's religion now? It has taken the brighter side of the Gospel,—its tidings of comfort, its precepts of love; all darker, deeper views of man's condition and prospects being comparatively forgotten. This is the religion *natural* to a civilized age, and well has Satan dressed and completed it into an idol of the Truth. As the reason is cultivated, the taste formed, the affections and sentiments refined, a general decency and grace will of course spread over the face of society, quite independently of the influence of Revelation. That beauty and delicacy of thought, which is so attractive in books, then extends to the conduct of life, to all we have, all we do, all we are. Our manners are courteous; we avoid giving pain or offence; our words become correct; our relative duties are carefully performed. Our sense of propriety shows itself even in our domestic arrangements, in the embellishments of our houses, in our amusements, and so also in our religious profession. Vice now becomes unseemly and hideous to the imagination, or, as it is sometimes familiarly said, "out of taste." Thus elegance is gradually made the test and standard of virtue, which is no longer thought to possess an intrinsic claim on our hearts, or to exist, *further than* it leads to the quiet and comfort of others. Conscience is no longer recognized as an independent arbiter of actions, its authority is explained away; partly it is superseded in the minds of men by the so-called moral sense, which is regarded merely as the love of the beautiful; partly by the rule of expediency, which is forthwith substituted for it in the details of conduct. Now conscience is a stern, gloomy principle; it tells us of guilt and of prospective punishment. Accordingly, when its terrors disappear, then disappear also, in the creed of the day, those fearful images of Divine wrath with which the Scriptures abound. They are explained away. Every thing is bright and cheerful. Religion is pleasant and easy; benevolence is the chief virtue; intolerance, bigotry, excess of zeal, are the first of sins. Austerity is an absurdity;—even firmness is looked on with an unfriendly, suspicious eye. On the other hand, all open profligacy is discountenanced; drunkenness is accounted a disgrace; cursing and swearing are vulgarities. Moreover, to a cultivated mind, which recreates itself in the varieties of literature and knowledge, and is interested in the ever-accumulating discoveries of science, and the ever-fresh accessions of information, political or otherwise, from foreign countries, religion will commonly seem to be dull, from want of novelty. Hence excitements are eagerly sought out and rewarded. New objects in religion, new systems and plans, new doctrines, new preachers, are necessary to satisfy that craving which the so-called spread of knowledge has created. The mind becomes morbidly sensitive and fastidious; dissatisfied with things as they are, desirous of a change *as such*, as if alteration must of itself be a relief.

    Now I would have you put Christianity for an instant out of your thoughts; and consider whether such a state of refinement as I have attempted to describe, is not that to which men might be brought, quite independent of religion, by the mere influence of education and civilization; and then again, whether, nevertheless, this mere refinement of mind is not more or less all that is called religion at this day. In other words, is it not the case, that Satan has so composed and dressed out what is the mere natural produce of the human heart under certain circumstances, as to serve his purposes as the counterfeit of the Truth? I do not at all deny that this spirit of the world uses words, and makes professions, which it would not adopt except for the suggestions of Scripture; nor do I deny that it takes a general colouring from Christianity, so as really to be modified by it, nay, in a measure enlightened and exalted by it. Again, I fully grant that many persons in whom this bad spirit shows itself, are but partially infected by it, and at bottom, good Christians, though imperfect. Still, after all, here is an existing teaching, only partially evangelical, built upon worldly principle, yet pretending to be the Gospel, dropping one whole side of the Gospel, its austere character, and considering it enough to be benevolent, courteous, candid, correct in conduct, delicate,—though it includes no true fear of God, no fervent zeal for His honour, no deep hatred of sin, no horror at the sight of sinners, no indignation and compassion at the blasphemies of heretics, no jealous adherence to doctrinal truth, no especial sensitiveness about the particular means of gaining ends, provided the ends be good, no loyalty to the Holy Apostolic Church, of which the Creed speaks, no sense of the authority of religion as external to the mind: in a word, no seriousness,—and therefore is neither hot nor cold, but (in Scripture language) *lukewarm*. Thus the present age is the very contrary to what are commonly called the dark ages; and together with the faults of those ages we have lost their virtues. I say their virtues; for even the errors then prevalent, a persecuting spirit, for instance, fear of religious inquiry, bigotry, these were, after all, but perversions and excesses of *real virtues*, such as zeal and reverence; and we, instead of limiting and purifying them, have taken them away root and branch. Why? because we have not acted from a love of the Truth, but from the influence of the Age. The old generation has passed, and its character with it; a new order of things has arisen. Human society has a new framework, and fosters and develops a new character of mind; and this new character is made by the enemy of our souls, to resemble the Christian's obedience as near as it may, its likeness all the time being but accidental. Meanwhile, the Holy Church of God, as from the beginning, continues her course heavenward; despised by the world, yet influencing it, partly correcting it, partly restraining it, and in some happy cases reclaiming its victims, and fixing them firmly and for ever within the lines of the faithful host militant here on earth, which journeys towards the City of the Great King. God give us grace to search our hearts, lest we be blinded by the deceitfulness of sin! lest we serve Satan transformed into an Angel of light, while we think we are pursuing true knowledge; lest, overlooking and ill-treating the elect of Christ here, we have to ask that awful question at the last day, while the truth is bursting upon us, "Lord, *when* saw we Thee a stranger and a prisoner?" when saw we Thy sacred Word and Servants despised and oppressed, "and did not minister unto Thee" (Mt 25:44).

Nothing shows more strikingly the power of the world's religion, as now described, than to consider the very different classes of men whom it influences. It will be found to extend its sway and its teaching both over the professedly religious and the irreligious.

PAROCHIAL AND PLAIN SERMONS

1. Many religious men, rightly or not, have long been expecting a millennium of purity and peace for the Church. I will not say, whether or not with reason, for good men may well differ on such a subject. But, any how, in the case of those who have expected it, it has become a temptation to take up and recognize the world's religion as I have already delineated it. They have more or less identified their vision of Christ's kingdom with the elegance and refinement of mere human civilization; and have hailed every evidence of improved decency, every wholesome civil regulation, every beneficent and enlightened act of state policy, as signs of their coming Lord. Bent upon achieving their object, an extensive and glorious diffusion and profession of the Gospel, they have been little solicitous about the *means* employed. They have countenanced and acted with men who openly professed unchristian principles. They have accepted and defended what they considered to be reformations and ameliorations of the existing state of things, though injustice must be perpetrated in order to effect them, or long-cherished rules of conduct, indifferent perhaps in their origin but consecrated by long usage, must be violated. They have sacrificed Truth to expedience. They have strangely imagined that bad men are to be the immediate instruments of the approaching advent of Christ; and (like the deluded Jews not many years since in a foreign country) they have taken, if not for their Messiah (as the Jews did), at least for their Elijah, their reforming Baptist, the Herald of the Christ, children of this world, and sons of Belial, on whom the anathema of the Apostle lies from the beginning, declaring, "If any man love not the Lord Jesus Christ, let him be Anathema Maran-atha" (1 Cor 16:22).

2. On the other hand, the form of doctrine, which I have called the religion of the day, is especially adapted to please men of sceptical minds, the opposite extreme to those just mentioned, who have never been careful to obey their conscience, who cultivate the intellect without disciplining the heart, and who allow themselves to speculate freely about what religion *ought to be*, without going to Scripture to discover what it really is. Some persons of this character almost consider religion itself to be an obstacle in the advance of our social and political well-being. But they know human nature requires it; therefore they select the most *rational* form of religion (so they call it) which they can find. Others are far more seriously disposed, but are corrupted by bad example or other cause. But they *all* discard (what they call) gloomy views of religion; they all trust themselves more than God's word, and thus may be classed together; and are ready to embrace the pleasant consoling religion natu-

ral to a polished age. They lay much stress on works on *Natural Theology,* and think that all religion is contained in these; whereas, in truth, there is no greater fallacy than to suppose such works to be in themselves in any true sense religious at all. Religion, it has been well observed, is something *relative to us;* a system of commands and promises from God *towards* us. But how are we concerned with the sun, moon, and stars? or with the laws of the universe? how will they teach us our *duty?* how will they speak to *sinners?* They do not speak to sinners at all. They were created *before* Adam fell. They "declare the *glory* of God," but not His *will.* They are all perfect, all harmonious; but that brightness and excellence which they exhibit in their own creation, and the Divine benevolence therein seen, are of little moment to fallen man. We see nothing there of God's *wrath,* of which the conscience of a sinner loudly speaks. So that there cannot be a more dangerous (though a common) device of Satan, than to carry us off from our own secret thoughts, to make us forget our own hearts, which tell us of a God of justice and holiness, and to fix our attention merely on the God who made the heavens; who is *our* God indeed, but not God as manifested to us sinners, but as He shines forth to His Angels, and to His elect hereafter.

When a man has so far deceived himself as to trust his destiny to what the heavens tell him of it, instead of consulting and obeying his conscience, what is the consequence? that at once he misinterprets and perverts the whole tenor of Scripture. It cannot be denied that, pleasant as religious observances are declared in Scripture to be to the holy, yet to men in general they are said to be difficult and distasteful; to all men *naturally* impossible, and by few fulfilled even with the assistances of grace, on account of their wilful corruption. Religion is pronounced to be against nature, to be against our original will, to require God's aid to make us love and obey it, and to be commonly refused and opposed in spite of that aid. We are expressly told, that "strait is the gate and narrow the way that leads to life, and few there be that find it"; that we must "*strive*" or struggle "to enter in at the strait gate," for that "many shall *seek* to enter in," but that is not enough, they merely seek and therefore do not find; and further, that they who do not obtain everlasting life, "shall go into everlasting punishment" (Mt 7:14; Lk 13:24; Mt 25:46). This is the dark side of religion; and the men I have been describing cannot bear to think of it. They shrink from it as too terrible. They easily get themselves to believe that those strong declarations of Scripture do not belong to the present day, or that they are figurative. They have no language within their heart responding to them. Conscience has been silenced. The only information they have received concerning God has been from Natural Theology, and that speaks only of benevolence and harmony; so they will not credit the plain word of Scripture. They seize on such parts of Scripture as seem to countenance their own opinions; they insist on its being commanded us to "rejoice evermore"; and they argue that it is our duty to solace ourselves here (in moderation, of course) with the goods of this life,—that we have only to be thankful while we use them,—that we need not alarm ourselves,—that God is a merciful God,—that amendment is quite sufficient to atone for our offences,—that though we have been irregular in our youth, yet that is a thing gone by,—that we forget it, and therefore God forgets it,—that the world is, on the whole, very well disposed towards religion,—that we should avoid enthusiasm,—that we should not be over serious,—that we should have large views on the subject of human nature,—and that we should love all men. This indeed is the creed of shallow men, in *every* age, who reason a little, and feel not at all, and who think themselves enlightened and philosophical. Part of what they say is false, part is true, but misapplied; but why I have noticed it here, is to show how exactly it fits in with what I have already described as the peculiar religion of a civilized age; it fits in with it equally well as does that of the (so called) religious world, which is the opposite extreme.

One further remark I will make about these professedly rational Christians; who, be it observed, often go on to deny the mysteries of the Gospel. Let us take the text:—"Our God is a consuming fire." Now supposing these persons fell upon these words, or heard them urged as an argument against their own doctrine of the unmixed satisfactory character of our prospects in the world to come, and supposing they did not know what part of the Bible they occurred in, what would they say? Doubtless they would confidently say that they applied only to the Jews and not to Christians; that they only described the Divine Author of the Mosaic Law (Dt 4:24); that God formerly spoke in terrors to the Jews, because they were a gross and brutish people, but that civilization has made us quite other men; that our *reason*, not our *fears*, is appealed to, and that the Gospel is love. And yet, in spite of all this argument, the text occurs in the Epistle to the Hebrews, written by an Apostle of Christ.

I shall conclude with stating more fully what I mean by the dark side of religion; and what judgment ought to be passed on the superstitious and gloomy.

Here I will not shrink from uttering my firm conviction, that it would be a gain to this country, were it vastly more superstitious, more bigoted, more gloomy, more fierce in its religion, than at present it shows itself to be. Not, of course, that I think the tempers of mind herein implied desirable, which would be an evident absurdity; but I think them infinitely more desirable and more promising than a heathen obduracy, and a cold, self-sufficient, self-wise tranquility. Doubtless, peace of mind, a quiet conscience, and a cheerful countenance are the gift of the Gospel, and the sign of a Christian; but the same effects (or, rather, what appear to be the same) may arise from very different causes. Jonah slept in the storm,—so did our Blessed Lord. The one slept in an evil security: the Other in the "peace of God which passeth all understanding." The two states cannot be confounded together, they are perfectly distinct; and as distinct is the calm of the man of the world from that of the Christian. Now take the case of the sailors on board the vessel; they cried to Jonah, "What meanest thou, O sleeper?"—so the Apostles said to Christ, "Lord, we perish." This is the case of the superstitious; they stand between the false peace of Jonah and the true peace of Christ; they are better than the one, though far below the other. Applying this to the present religion of the educated world, full as it is of security and cheerfulness, and decorum, and benevolence, I observe that these appearances may arise either from a great deal of religion, or from the absence of it; they may be the fruits of shallowness of mind and a blinded conscience, or of that faith which has peace with God through our Lord Jesus Christ. And if this alternative be proposed, I might leave it to the common sense of men to decide (if they could get themselves to think seriously) to which of the two the temper of the age is to be referred. For myself I cannot doubt, seeing what I see of the world, that it arises from the sleep of Jonah; and it is therefore but a dream of religion, far inferior in worth to the well-grounded alarm of the superstitious, who are awakened and see their danger, though they do not attain so far in faith as to embrace the remedy of it.

Think of this, I beseech you, my brethren, and lay it to heart, as far as you go with me, as you will answer for having heard it at the last day. I would not willingly be harsh; but knowing "that the world lieth in wickedness," I think it highly probable that you, so far as you are in it (as you must be, and we all must be in our degree), are, most of you, partially infected with its existing error, that shallowness of religion, which is the result of a blinded conscience; and, therefore, I speak earnestly to you. Believing in the existence of a general plague in the land, I judge that you probably have your share in the sufferings, the voluntary sufferings, which it is spreading among us. The fear of

God is the beginning of wisdom; till you see Him to be a consuming fire, and approach Him with reverence and godly fear, as being sinners, you are not even in sight of the strait gate. I do not wish you to be able to point to any particular time when you renounced the world (as it is called), and were converted; this is a deceit. Fear and love must go together; always fear, always love, to your dying day. Doubtless;—still you must know what it is to sow in tears here, if you would reap in joy hereafter. Till you know the weight of your sins, and that not in mere imagination, but in practice, not so as merely to confess it in a formal phrase of lamentation, but daily and in your heart in secret, you cannot embrace the offer of mercy held out to you in the Gospel, through the death of Christ. Till you know what it is to fear with the terrified sailors or the Apostles, you cannot sleep with Christ at your Heavenly Father's feet. Miserable as were the superstitions of the dark ages, revolting as are the tortures now in use among the heathen of the East, better, far better is it, to torture the body all one's days, and to make this life a hell upon earth, than to remain in a brief tranquility here, till the pit at length opens under us, and awakens us to an eternal fruitless consciousness and remorse. Think of Christ's own words: "What shall a man give in exchange for his soul?" Again, He says, "Fear Him, who after He hath killed, hath power to cast into hell; yea, I say unto you, fear Him." Dare not to think you have got to the bottom of your hearts; you do not know what evil lies there. How long and earnestly must you pray, how many years must you pass in careful obedience, before you have any right to lay aside sorrow, and to rejoice in the Lord? In one sense, indeed, you may take comfort from the first; for, though you dare not yet anticipate you are in the number of Christ's true elect, yet from the first you know He desires your salvation, has died for you, has washed away your sins by baptism, and will ever help you; and this thought must cheer you while you go on to examine and review your lives, and to turn to God in self-denial. But, at the same time, you never can be sure of salvation, while you are here; and therefore you must always fear while you hope. Your knowledge of your sins increases with your view of God's mercy in Christ. And this is the true Christian state, and the nearest approach to Christ's calm and placid sleep in the tempest;—not perfect joy and certainty in heaven, but a deep resignation to God's will, a surrender of ourselves, soul and body, to Him; hoping indeed, that we shall be saved, but fixing our eyes more earnestly on Him than on ourselves; that is, acting for His glory, seeking to please Him, devoting ourselves to Him in all manly obedience and strenuous good works; and, when we do look within, thinking of ourselves with a certain abhorrence and contempt as being sinners, mortifying our flesh, scourging our appetites, and composedly awaiting that time when, if we be worthy, we shall be stripped of our present selves, and new made in the kingdom of Christ.

Volume II

SERMON XV

Self-Contemplation

(TUESDAY IN EASTER WEEK)

"Looking unto Jesus, the Author and Finisher of our faith."
—Heb 12:2

Surely it is our duty ever to look off ourselves, and to look unto Jesus, that is, to shun the contemplation of our own feelings, emotions, frame and state of mind, as if that were the main business of religion, and to leave these mainly to be secured in their fruits. Some remarks were made yesterday upon this "more excellent" and Scriptural way of conducting ourselves, as it has ever been received in the Church; now let us consider the merits of the rule for holy living, which the fashion of this day would substitute for it.

Instead of looking off to Jesus, and thinking little of ourselves, it is at present thought necessary, among the mixed multitude of religionists, to examine the heart with a view of ascertaining whether it is in a spiritual state or no. A spiritual frame of mind is considered to be one in which the heinousness of sin is perceived, our utter worthlessness, the impossibility of our saving ourselves, the necessity of some Saviour, the sufficiency of our Lord Jesus Christ to be that Saviour, the unbounded riches of His love, the excellence and glory of His work of Atonement, the freeness and fulness of His grace, the high privilege of communion with Him in prayer, and the desirableness of walking with Him in all holy and loving obedience; all of them solemn truths, too solemn to be lightly mentioned, but our hearty reception of which is scarcely ascertainable by a direct inspection of our feelings. Moreover, if one doctrine must be selected above the rest as containing the essence of the truths, which (according to this system) are thus vividly understood by the spiritual Christian, it is that of the necessity of renouncing our own righteousness for the righteousness provided by our Lord and Saviour; which is considered, not as an elementary and simple principle (as it really is), but as rarely and hardly acknowledged by any man, especially repugnant to a certain (so-called) pride of heart, which is supposed to run through the whole race of Adam, and to lead every man instinctively to insist even before God on the proper merit of his good deeds; so that, to trust in Christ, is not merely the work of the Holy Spirit (as all good in our souls is), but is the especial and critical event which marks a man, as issuing from darkness, and sealed unto the privileges and inheritance of the sons of God. In other words, the doctrine of Justification by Faith is accounted to be the one cardinal point of the Gospel; and it is in vain to admit it readily as a clear Scripture truth (which it is), and to attempt to go on unto perfection; the very wish to pass forward is interpreted into a wish to pass over it, and the test of believing it at all, is in fact to insist upon no doctrine but it. And this peculiar mode of inculcating that great doctrine of the Gospel is a proof (if proof were wanting) that the persons who adopt it are not solicitous even about *it* on its own score merely, considered as (what is called) a dogma, but as ascertaining and securing (as they hope) a certain state of heart. For, not content with the simple admission of it on the part of another, they proceed to divide faith into its kinds, living and dead, and to urge against him, that the Truth may be held in a carnal and unrenewed mind, and that men may speak without real feelings and convictions. Thus it is clear they do not contend for the doctrine of Justification as a truth external to the mind, or article of faith, any more than for the doctrine of the Trinity. On the other hand, since they use the same language about dead and living faith, however exemplary the life and conduct be of the individual under their review, they as plainly show that neither are the fruits of righteousness in their system an evidence of spiritual-mindedness, but that a something is to be sought for in the frame of mind itself. All this is not stated at present by way of objection, but in order to settle accurately what they mean to maintain. So now we have the two views of doctrine clearly before us:—the ancient and universal teaching of the Church, which insists on the Objects and fruits of faith, and considers the spiritual character of that faith itself sufficiently secured, if these are as they should be; and the method, now in esteem, of attempting instead to secure directly and primarily that "mind of the Spirit," which may savingly receive the truths, and fulfil the obedience of the Gospel. That such a spiritual temper is indispensable, is agreed on all hands. The simple question is, whether it is formed by the Holy Spirit immediately acting upon our minds, or, on the other hand, by our own particular acts (whether of faith or obedience), prompted, guided, and prospered by Him; whether it is ascertainable otherwise than by its fruits; whether such frames of mind as *are* directly ascertainable and profess to be spiritual, are not rather a delusion, a mere excitement, capricious feeling, fanatic fancy, and the like.—So much then by way of explanation.

1. Now, in the first place, this modern system certainly does disparage the revealed doctrines of the Gospel, however its more moderate advocates may shrink from admitting it. Considering a certain state of heart to be the main thing to be aimed at, they avowedly make the "truth as it is in Jesus," the definite Creed of the Church, secondary in their teaching and profession. They will defend themselves indeed from the appearance of undervaluing it, by maintaining that the existence of right religious affections is a security for sound views of doctrine. And this is abstractedly true;—but not true in the use they make of it: for they unhappily conceive that they can ascertain in each other the presence of these affections; and when they find men possessed of them (as they conceive), yet not altogether orthodox in their belief, then they relax a little, and argue that an admission of (what they call) the strict and technical niceties of doctrine, whether about the Consubstantiality of the Son or the Hypostatic Union, is scarcely part of the definition of a spiritual believer. In order to support this position, they lay it down as self-evident, that the main purpose of revealed doctrine is to affect the heart,—that which does not seem to affect it does not affect it,—that what does not affect it, is unnecessary,—and that the circumstance that this or that person's heart seems rightly affected, is a sufficient warrant that such Articles as he may happen to reject, may safely be universally rejected, or at least are only accidentally important. Such principles, when once become familiar to the mind, induce a certain disproportionate attention to the doctrines connected with the work of Christ, in comparison of those which relate to His Person, from their more immediately interesting and exciting character; and carry on the more speculative and philosophical class to view the doctrines of Atonement and Sanctification as the essence of the Gospel, and to advocate them in the place of those "Heavenly Things" altogether, which, as theologically expressed, they have already assailed; and of which they now openly complain as mysteries for bondsmen, not Gospel consolations. The last and most miserable stage of this false wisdom is, to deny that in matters of doctrine there is any one sense of Scripture such, that it is true and all

others false; to make the Gospel of Truth (so far) a revelation of words and a dead letter; to consider that inspiration speaks merely of divine operations, not of Persons; and that that is truth to each, which each man thinks to be true, so that one man may say that Christ is God, another deny His pre-existence, yet each have received the Truth according to the peculiar constitution of his own mind, the Scripture doctrine having no real independent substantive meaning. Thus the system under consideration tends legitimately to obliterate the great Objects brought to light in the Gospel, and to darken what I called yesterday the eye of faith,—to throw us back into the vagueness of Heathenism, when men only felt after the Divine Presence, and thus to frustrate the design of Christ's Incarnation, so far as it is a manifestation of the Unseen Creator.

2. On the other hand, the necessity of obedience in order to salvation does not suffer less from the upholders of this modern system than the articles of the Creed. They argue, and truly, that if faith is living, works must follow; but mistaking a following *in order of conception* for a following *in order of time*, they conclude that faith ever comes first, and works afterwards; and therefore, that faith must first be secured, and that, by some means in which works have no share. Thus, instead of viewing works as the concomitant development and evidence, and instrumental cause, as well as the subsequent result of faith, they lay all the stress upon the direct creation, in their minds, of faith and spiritual-mindedness, which they consider to consist in certain emotions and desires, because they can form abstractedly no better or truer notion of those qualities. Then, instead of being "careful to maintain good works," they proceed to take it for granted, that since they have attained faith (as they consider), works will follow without their trouble as a matter of course. Thus the wise are taken in their own craftiness; they attempt to reason, and are overcome by sophisms. Had they kept to the Inspired Record, instead of reasoning, their way would have been clear; and, considering the serious exhortations to keeping God's commandments, with which all Scripture abounds, from Genesis to the Apocalypse, is it not a very grave question, which the most charitable among Churchmen must put to himself, whether these random expounders of the Blessed Gospel are not risking a participation in the woe denounced against those who preach any other doctrine besides that delivered unto us, or who "take away from the words of the Book" of revealed Truth?

3. But still more evidently do they fall into this last imputation, when we consider how they are obliged to treat the Sacred Volume al-

together, in order to support the system they have adopted. Is it too much to say that, instead of attempting to harmonize Scripture with Scripture, much less referring to Antiquity to enable them to do so, they either drop altogether, or explain away, whole portions of the Bible, and those most sacred ones? How does the authority of the Psalms stand with their opinions, except at best by a forced figurative interpretation? And our Lord's discourses in the Gospels, especially the Sermon on the Mount, are they not virtually considered as chiefly important to the persons immediately addressed, and of inferior instructiveness to us now that the Spirit (as it is profanely said) is come? In short, is not the rich and varied Revelation of our merciful Lord practically reduced to a few chapters of St. Paul's Epistles, whether rightly (as they maintain) or (as we should say) perversely understood? If then the Romanists have added to the Word of God, is it not undeniable that there is a school of religionists among us who have taken from it?

4. I would remark, that the immediate tendency of these opinions is to undervalue ordinances as well as doctrines. The same argument evidently applies; for, if the renewed state of heart is (as it is supposed) attained, what matter whether Sacraments have or have not been administered? The notion of invisible grace and invisible privileges is, on this supposition, altogether superseded; that of communion with Christ is limited to the mere exercise of the affections in prayer and meditation,—to sensible effects; and he who considers he has already gained this one essential gift of grace (as he calls it), may plausibly inquire, after the fashion of the day, why he need wait upon ordinances which he has anticipated in his religious attainments,—which are but means to an end, which *he* has not to seek, even if they be not outward forms altogether,—and whether Christ will not accept at the last day all who believe, without inquiring if they were members of the Church, or were confirmed, or were baptized, or received the blessing of mere men who are "earthen vessels."

5. The foregoing remarks go to show the utterly unevangelical character of the system in question; unevangelic in the full sense of the word, whether by the Gospel be meant the inspired document of it, or the doctrines brought to light through it, or the Sacramental Institutions which are the gift of it, or the theology which interprets it, or the Covenant which is the basis of it. A few words shall now be added, to show the inherent mischief of the system as such; which I conceive to lie in its necessarily involving a continual self-contemplation and reference to self, in all departments of conduct. He who aims at attaining sound doc-

trine or right practice, more or less looks out of himself; whereas, in labouring after a certain frame of mind, there is an habitual reflex action of the mind upon itself. That this is really involved in the modern system, is evident from the very doctrine principally insisted on by it; for, as if it were not enough for a man to look up simply to Christ for salvation, it is declared to be necessary that he should be able to recognise this in himself, that he should define his own state of mind, confess he is justified by faith alone, and explain what is meant by that confession. Now, the truest obedience is indisputably that which is done from love of God, without narrowly measuring the magnitude or nature of the sacrifice involved in it. He who has learned to give names to his thoughts and deeds, to appraise them as if for the market, to attach to each its due measure of commendation or usefulness, will soon involuntarily corrupt his motives by pride or selfishness. A sort of self-approbation will insinuate itself into his mind: so subtle as not at once to be recognised by himself,—an habitual quiet self-esteem, leading him to prefer his own views to those of others, and a secret, if not avowed persuasion, that he is in a different state from the generality of those around him. This is an incidental, though of course not a necessary evil of religious journals; nay, of such compositions as Ministerial duties involve. They lead those who write them, in some respect or other, to a contemplation of self. Moreover, as to religious journals, useful as they often are, at the same time I believe persons find great difficulty, while recording their feelings, in banishing the thought that one day these good feelings will be known to the world, and are thus insensibly led to modify and prepare their language as if for a representation. Seldom indeed is any one in the *practice* of contemplating his better thoughts or doings without proceeding to display them to others; and hence it is that it is so easy to discover a conceited man. When this is encouraged in the sacred province of religion, it produces a certain unnatural solemnity of manner, arising from a wish to be, nay, to appear spiritual, which is at once very painful to beholders, and surely quite at variance with our Saviour's rule of anointing our head and washing our face, even when we are most self-abased in heart. Another mischief arising from this self-contemplation is the peculiar kind of selfishness (if I may use so harsh a term) which it will be found to foster. They who make self instead of their Maker the great object of their contemplation will naturally exalt themselves. Without denying that the glory of God is the great end to which all things are to be referred, they will be led to connect indisolubly His glory with their own certainty of salvation; and this partly accounts for its being so common to find rigid predestinarian views, and the exclusive maintenance of Justification by Faith in the same persons. And for the same reason, the Scripture doctrines relative to the Church and its offices will be unpalatable to such persons; no one thing being so irreconcilable with another, as the system which makes a man's thoughts centre in himself, with that which directs them to a fountain of grace and truth, on which God has made him dependent.

And as self-confidence and spiritual pride are the legitimate results of these opinions in one set of persons, so in another they lead to a feverish anxiety about their religious state and prospects, and fears lest they are under the reprobation of their All-merciful Saviour. It need scarcely be said that a contemplation of self is a frequent attendant, and a frequent precursor of a deranged state of the mental powers.

To conclude. It must not be supposed from the foregoing remarks that I am imputing all the consequences enumerated to every one who holds the main doctrine from which they legitimately follow. Many men zealously maintain principles which they never follow out in their own minds, or after a time silently discard, except as far as words go, but which are sure to receive a full development in the history of any school or party of men which adopts them. Considered thus, as the characteristics of a school, the principles in question are doubtless antichristian; for they destroy all positive doctrine, all ordinances, all good works; they foster pride, invite hypocrisy, discourage the weak, and deceive most fatally, while they profess to be the especial antidotes to self-deception. We have seen these effects of them two centuries since in the history of the English Branch of the Church; for what we know, a more fearful triumph is still in store for them. But, however that may be, let not the watchmen of Jerusalem fail to give timely warning of the approaching enemy, or to acquit themselves of all cowardice or compliance as regards it. Let them prefer the Old Commandment, as it has been from the beginning, to any novelties of man, recollecting Christ's words, "Blessed is he that watcheth, and keepeth his garments, lest he walk naked, and they see his shame." (Rv 16:15).

SERMON XIX

The Indwelling Spirit

(THE FEAST OF PENTECOST)

"Ye are not in the flesh, but in the Spirit, if so be that the Spirit of God dwell in you."—Rom 8:9

God the Son has graciously vouchsafed to reveal the Father to His creatures from without; God the Holy Ghost, by inward communications. Who can compare these separate works of condescension, either of them being beyond our understanding? We can but silently adore the Infinite Love which encompasses us on every side. The Son of God is called the Word, as declaring His glory throughout created nature, and impressing the evidence of it on every part of it. He has given us to read it in His works of goodness, holiness, and wisdom. He is the Living and Eternal Law of Truth and Perfection, that Image of God's unapproachable Attributes, which men have ever seen by glimpses on the face of the world, felt that it was sovereign, but knew not whether to say it was a fundamental Rule and self-existing Destiny, or the Offspring and Mirror of the Divine Will. Such has He been from the beginning, graciously sent forth from the Father to reflect His glory upon all things, distinct from Him, while mysteriously one with Him; and in due time visiting us with an infinitely deeper mercy, when for our redemption He humbled Himself to take upon Him that fallen nature which He had originally created after His own image.

The condescension of the Blessed Spirit is as incomprehensible as that of the Son. He has ever been the secret Presence of God within the Creation: a source of life amid the chaos, bringing out into form and order what was at first shapeless and void, and the voice of Truth in the hearts of all rational beings, tuning them into harmony with the intimations of God's Law, which were externally made to them. Hence He is especially called the "life-giving" Spirit; being (as it were) the Soul of universal nature, the Strength of man and beast, the Guide of faith, the Witness against sin, the inward Light of patriarchs and prophets, the

Grace abiding in the Christian soul, and the Lord and Ruler of the Church. Therefore let us ever praise the Father Almighty, who is the first Source of all perfection, in and together with His Coequal Son and Spirit, through whose gracious ministrations we have been given to see "what manner of love" it is wherewith the Father has loved us.

On this Festival I propose, as is suitable, to describe as scripturally as I can, the merciful office of God the Holy Ghost, towards us Christians; and I trust I may do so, with the sobriety and reverence which the subject demands.

The Holy Spirit has from the beginning pleaded with man. We read in the Book of Genesis, that, when evil began to prevail all over the earth before the flood, the Lord said, "My Spirit shall not always strive with man" (Gn 6:3); implying that He had hitherto striven with his corruption. Again, when God took to Him a peculiar people, the Holy Spirit was pleased to be especially present with them. Nehemiah says, "Thou gavest also Thy Good Spirit to instruct them" (Neh 9:20), and Isaiah, "They rebelled and vexed His Holy Spirit" (Is 63:10). Further, He manifested Himself as the source of various gifts, intellectual and extraordinary, in the Prophets, and others. Thus at the time the Tabernacle was constructed, the Lord filled Bezaleel "with the Spirit of God, in wisdom, and in understanding, and in knowledge, and in all manner of workmanship, to devise cunning works" (Ex 31:3, 4) in metal, stone, and timber. At another time, when Moses was oppressed with his labours, Almighty God vouchsafed to "take of the Spirit" which was upon him, and to put it on seventy of the elders of Israel, that they might share the burden with him. "And it came to pass, that, when the Spirit rested upon them, they prophesied, and did not cease" (Nm 11:17, 25). These texts will be sufficient to remind you of many others, in which the gifts of the Holy Ghost are spoken of under the Jewish covenant. These were great mercies; yet, great as they were, they are as nothing compared with that surpassing grace with which we Christians are honoured; that great privilege of receiving into our hearts, not the mere gifts of the Spirit, but His very presence, Himself, by a real not a figurative indwelling.

When our Lord entered upon His Ministry, He acted as though He were a mere man, needing grace, and received the consecration of the Holy Spirit for our sakes. He became the Christ, or Anointed, that the Spirit might be seen to come from God, and to pass from Him to us. And, therefore, the heavenly Gift is not simply called the Holy Ghost, or the Spirit of God, but the Spirit of Christ, that we might clearly understand, that He comes to us from and instead of Christ. Thus St. Paul says, "God hath sent forth the Spirit of His Son into your hearts"; and our Lord breathed on His Apostles, saying, "Receive ye the Holy Ghost"; and He says elsewhere to them, "If I depart, I will send Him unto you" (Gal 4:6; Jn 20:22, 16:7). Accordingly this "Holy Spirit of promise" is called "the earnest of our inheritance," "the seal and earnest of an Unseen Saviour" (Eph 1:14; 2 Cor 1:22, 5:5); being the present pledge of Him who is absent,—or rather more than a pledge, for an earnest is not a mere token which will be taken from us when it is fulfilled, as a pledge might be, but a something in advance of what is one day to be given in full.

This must be clearly understood; for it would seem to follow, that if so, the Comforter who has come instead of Christ, must have vouchsafed to come in the same sense in which Christ came; I mean, that He has come, not merely in the way of gifts, or of influences, or of operations, as He came to the Prophets, for then Christ's going away would be a loss, and not a gain, and the Spirit's presence would be a mere pledge, not an earnest; but He comes to us as Christ came, by a real and personal visitation. I do not say we could have inferred this thus clearly by the mere force of the above cited texts; but it being actually so revealed to us in other texts of Scripture, we are able to see that it may be legitimately deduced from these. We are able to see that the Saviour, when once He entered into this world, never so departed as to suffer things to be as before He came; for He still is with us, not in mere gifts, but by the substitution of His Spirit for Himself, and that, both in the Church and in the souls of individual Christians.

For instance, St. Paul says in the text, "Ye are not in the flesh, but in the Spirit, if so be that the Spirit of God *dwell in you*." Again, "He shall quicken even your mortal bodies by His Spirit that *dwelleth* in you." "Know ye not that your body is the Temple of the Holy Ghost which is in you?" "Ye are the Temple of the Living God, as God hath said, I will dwell in them, and walk in them." The same Apostle clearly distinguishes between the indwelling of the Spirit, and His actual operations within us, when he says, "The love of God is shed abroad in our hearts by the Holy Ghost which is given unto us"; and again, "The Spirit Himself beareth witness with our spirit that we are the children of God" (Rom 8:9, 11; 1 Cor 6:19; 2 Cor 6:16; Rom 5:5, 8:16).

Here let us observe, before proceeding, what indirect evidence is afforded us in these texts of the Divinity of the Holy Spirit. Who can be personally present at once with every Christian, but God Himself? Who but He, not merely ruling in the midst of the Church invisibly, as Michael might keep watch over Israel, or another Angel might be "the Prince of Persia,"—but really taking up His abode as one and the same in many separate hearts, so as to fulfil our Lord's words, that it was expedient that He should depart; Christ's bodily presence, which was limited to place, being exchanged for the manifold spiritual indwelling of the Comforter within us? This consideration suggests both the dignity of our Sanctifier, and the infinite preciousness of His Office towards us.

To proceed: The Holy Ghost, I have said, dwells in body and soul, as in a temple. Evil spirits indeed have power to possess sinners, but His indwelling is far more perfect; for He is all-knowing and omnipresent, He is able to search into all our thoughts, and penetrate into every motive of the heart. Therefore, He pervades us (if it may be so said) as light pervades a building, or as a sweet perfume the folds of some honourable robe; so that, in Scripture language, we are said to be in Him, and He in us. It is plain that such an inhabitation brings the Christian into a state altogether new and marvellous, far above the possession of mere gifts, exalts him inconceivably in the scale of beings, and gives him a place and an office which he had not before. In St. Peter's forcible language, he becomes "partaker of the Divine Nature," and has "power" or authority, as St. John says, "to become the son of God." Or, to use the words of St. Paul, "he is a new creation; old things are passed away, behold all things are become new." His rank is new; his parentage and service new. He is "of God," and "is not his own," "a vessel unto honour, sanctified and meet for the Master's use, and prepared unto every good work." (2 Pt 1:4; Jn 1:12; 2 Cor 5:17; 1 Jn 4:4; 1 Cor 6:19, 20; 2 Tm 2:21).

This wonderful change from darkness to light, through the entrance of the Spirit into the soul, is called Regeneration, or the New Birth; a blessing which, before Christ's coming, not even prophets and righteous men possessed, but which is now conveyed to all men freely through the Sacrament of Baptism. By nature we are children of wrath; the heart is sold under sin, possessed by evil spirits; and inherits death as its eternal portion. But by the coming of the Holy Ghost, all guilt and pollution are burned away as by fire, the Devil is driven forth, sin, original and actual, is forgiven, and the whole man is consecrated to God. And this is the reason why He is called "the earnest" of that Saviour who died for us, and will one day give us the fulness of His own presence in heaven. Hence, too, He is our "seal unto the day of redemption"; for as the potter moulds the clay, so He impresses the Divine image on us members of the household of God. And His work may truly be called

Regeneration; for though the original nature of the soul is not destroyed, yet its past transgressions are pardoned once and for ever, and its source of evil staunched and gradually dried up by the pervading health and purity which has set up its abode in it. Instead of its own bitter waters, a spring of health and salvation is brought within it; not the mere streams of that fountain, "clear as crystal," which is before the Throne of God (Rv 4:6; Ps 46:4), but, as our Lord says, "a well of water *in him*," in a man's heart, "springing up into everlasting life." Hence He elsewhere describes the heart as giving forth, not receiving, the streams of grace: "Out of his belly shall flow rivers of Living Water." St. John adds, "this spake He of the Spirit" (Jn 4:14, 7:38, 39).

Such is the inhabitation of the Holy Ghost within us, applying to us individually the precious cleansing of Christ's blood in all its manifold benefits. Such is the great doctrine, which we hold as a matter of faith and without actual experience to verify it to us. Next I must speak briefly concerning the manner in which the Gift of grace manifests itself in the regenerate soul; a subject which I do not willingly take up, and which no Christian perhaps is ever able to consider without some effort, feeling that he thereby endangers either his reverence towards God, or his humility, but which the errors of this day, and the confident tone of their advocates, oblige us to dwell upon, lest truth should suffer by our silence.

1. The heavenly gift of the Spirit fixes the eyes of our mind upon the Divine Author of our salvation. By nature we are blind and carnal; but the Holy Ghost by whom we are new-born, reveals to us the God of mercies, and bids us recognise and adore Him as our Father with a true heart. He impresses on us our Heavenly Father's image, which we lost when Adam fell, and disposes us to seek His presence by the very instinct of our new nature. He gives us back a portion of that freedom in willing and doing, of that uprightness and innocence, in which Adam was created. He unites us to all holy beings, as before we had relationship with evil. He restores for us that broken bond, which, proceeding from above, connects together into one blessed family all that is anywhere holy and eternal, and separates it off from the rebel world which comes to nought. Being then the sons of God, and one with Him, our souls mount up and cry to Him continually. This special characteristic of the regenerate soul is spoken of by St. Paul soon after the text "Ye have received the Spirit of adoption, whereby we cry, Abba, Father." Nor are we left to utter these cries to Him, in any vague uncertain way of our own; but He who sent the Spirit to dwell in us habitually, gave us also a form of words to sanctify the separate acts of our minds. Christ left His

sacred Prayer to be the peculiar possession of His people, and the voice of the Spirit. If we examine it, we shall find in it the substance of that doctrine, to which St. Paul has given a name in the passage just quoted. We begin it by using our privilege of calling on Almighty God in express words as "Our Father." We proceed, according to this beginning, in that waiting, trusting, adoring, resigned temper, which children ought to feel; looking towards Him, rather than thinking of ourselves; zealous for His honour rather than fearful about our safety; resting in His present help, not with eyes timorously glancing towards the future. His name, His kingdom, His will, are the great objects for the Christian to contemplate and make his portion, being stable and serene, and "complete in Him," as beseems one who has the gracious presence of His Spirit within him. And, when he goes on to think of himself, he prays, that he may be enabled to have towards others what God has shown towards himself, a spirit of forgiveness and loving-kindness. Thus he pours himself out on all sides, first looking up to catch the heavenly gift, but, when he gains it, not keeping it to himself, but diffusing "rivers of living water" to the whole race of man, thinking of self as little as may be, and desiring ill and destruction to nothing but that principle of temptation and evil, which is rebellion against God;—lastly, ending, as he began, with the contemplation of His kingdom, power, and glory everlasting. This is the true "Abba, Father," which the Spirit of adoption utters within the Christian's heart, the infallible voice of Him who "maketh intercession for the Saints in God's way." And if he has at times, for instance, amid trial or affliction, special visitations and comfortings from the Spirit, "plaints unutterable" within him, yearnings after the life to come, or bright and passing gleams of God's eternal election, and deep stirrings of wonder and thankfulness thence following, he thinks too reverently of "the secret of the Lord," to betray (as it were) His confidence, and, by vaunting it to the world, to exaggerate it perchance into more than it was meant to convey: but he is silent, and ponders it as choice encouragement to his soul, meaning something, but he knows not how much.

2. The indwelling of the Holy Ghost raises the soul, not only to the thought of God, but of Christ also. St. John says, "Truly our fellowship is with the Father, and with His Son Jesus Christ." And our Lord Himself, "If a man love Me, he will keep My words; and My Father will love him, and We will come unto him, and make our abode with him" (1 Jn 1:3; Jn 14:23). Now, not to speak of other and higher ways in which these texts are fulfilled, one surely consists in that exercise of

faith and love in the thought of the Father and Son, which the Gospel, and the Spirit revealing it, furnish to the Christian. The Spirit came especially to "glorify" Christ; and vouchsafes to be a shining light within the Church and the individual Christian, reflecting the Saviour of the world in all His perfections, all His offices, all His works. He came for the purpose of unfolding what was yet hidden, whilst Christ was on earth; and speaks on the house-tops what was delivered in closets, disclosing Him in the glories of His transfiguration, who once had no comeliness in His outward form, and was but a man of sorrows and acquainted with grief. First, He inspired the Holy Evangelists to record the life of Christ, and directed them which of His words and works to select, which to omit; next, He commented (as it were) upon these, and unfolded their meaning in the Apostolic Epistles. The birth, the life, the death and resurrection of Christ, has been the text which He has illuminated. He has made history to be doctrine; telling us plainly, whether by St. John or St. Paul, that Christ's conception and birth was the real Incarnation of the Eternal Word,—His life, "God manifest in the Flesh,"—His death and resurrection, the Atonement for sin, and the Justification of all believers. Nor was this all: He continued His sacred comment in the formation of the Church, superintending and overruling its human instruments, and bringing out our Saviour's words and works, and the Apostles' illustrations of them, into acts of obedience and permanent Ordinances, by the ministry of Saints and Martyrs. Lastly, He completes His gracious work by conveying this system of Truth, thus varied and expanded, to the heart of each individual Christian in whom He dwells. Thus He vouchsafes to edify the whole man in faith and holiness: "casting down imaginations and every high thing that exalteth itself against the knowledge of God, and bringing into captivity every thought to the obedience of Christ" (2 Cor 10:5). By His wonder-working grace all things tend to perfection. Every faculty of the mind, every design, pursuit, subject of thought, is hallowed in its degree by the abiding vision of Christ, as Lord, Saviour, and Judge. All solemn, reverent, thankful, and devoted feelings, all that is noble, all that is choice in the regenerate soul, all that is self-denying in conduct, and zealous in action, is drawn forth and offered up by the Spirit as a living sacrifice to the Son of God. And, though the Christian is taught not to think of himself above his measure, and dare not boast, yet he is also taught that the consciousness of the sin which remains in him, and infects his best services, should not separate him from God, but lead him to Him who can save. He reasons with St. Peter, "To whom should he go?" and, without daring to decide, or being impatient to be told how far he is able to consider as his own every Gospel privilege in its fulness, he gazes on them all with deep thought as the Church's possession, joins her triumphant hymns in honour of Christ, and listens wistfully to her voice in inspired Scripture, the voice of the Bride calling upon and blest in the Beloved.

3. St. John adds, after speaking of "our fellowship with the Father and His Son": "These things write we unto you, that your joy may be full." What is fulness of joy but *peace?* Joy is tumultuous only when it is not full; but peace is the privilege of those who are "filled with the knowledge of the glory of the Lord, as the waters cover the sea." "Thou wilt keep him in perfect peace, whose mind is stayed on Thee, because he trusteth in Thee" (Is 26:3). It is peace, springing from trust and innocence, and then overflowing in love towards all around him. What is the effect of mere animal ease and enjoyment, but to make a man pleased with everything which happens? "A merry heart is a perpetual feast"; and such is peculiarly the blessing of a soul rejoicing in the faith and fear of God. He who is anxious, thinks of himself, is suspicious of danger, speaks hurriedly, and has no time for the interests of others; he who lives in peace is at leisure, wherever his lot is cast. Such is the work of the Holy Spirit in the heart, whether in Jew or Greek, bond or free. He Himself perchance in His mysterious nature, is the Eternal Love whereby the Father and the Son have dwelt in each other, as ancient writers have believed; and what He is in heaven, that He is abundantly on earth. He lives in the Christian's heart, as the never-failing fount of charity, which is the very sweetness of the living waters. For where He is, "there is liberty" from the tyranny of sin, from the dread, which the natural man feels, of an offended, unreconciled Creator. Doubt, gloom, impatience have been expelled; joy in the Gospel has taken their place, the hope of heaven and the harmony of a pure heart, the triumph of self-mastery, sober thoughts, and a contented mind. How can charity towards all men fail to follow, being the mere affectionateness of innocence and peace? Thus the Spirit of God creates in us the simplicity and warmth of heart which children have, nay, rather the perfections of His heavenly hosts, high and low being joined together in His mysterious work; for what are implicit trust, ardent love, abiding purity, but the mind both of little children and of the adoring Seraphim!

Thoughts, such as these, will affect us rightly, if they make us fear and be watchful, while we rejoice. They cannot surely do otherwise; for the mind of a Christian, as I have been attempting to describe it, is not so much what we have, as what we ought to have. To look, indeed, after dwelling on it, upon the multitude of men who have been baptized in Christ's name, is too serious a matter, and we need not force ourselves to do so. We need not do so, further than to pray for them, and to protest and strive against what is evil among them; for as to the higher and more solemn thought, how persons, set apart individually and collectively, as temples of Truth and Holiness, should become what they seem to be, and what their state is in consequence in God's sight, is a question which it is a great blessing to be allowed to put from us as not our concern. It is our concern only to look to ourselves, and to see that, as we have received the gift, we "grieve not the Holy Spirit of God, whereby we are sealed unto the day of redemption"; remembering that "if any man destroy the temple of God, him shall God destroy." This reflection and the recollection of our many backslidings, will ever keep us, please God, from judging others, or from priding ourselves on our privileges. Let us but consider how we have fallen from the light and grace of our Baptism. Were we now what that Holy Sacrament made us, we might ever "go on our way rejoicing"; but having sullied our heavenly garments, in one way or other, in a greater or less degree (God knoweth! and our own consciences too in a measure), alas! the Spirit of adoption has in part receded from us, and the sense of guilt, remorse, sorrow, and penitence must take His place. We must renew our confession, and seek afresh our absolution day by day, before we dare call upon God as "our Father," or offer up Psalms and Intercessions to Him. And, whatever pain and affliction meets us through life, we must take it as a merciful penance imposed by a Father upon erring children, to be borne meekly and thankfully, and as intended to remind us of the weight of that infinitely greater punishment, which was our desert by nature, and which Christ bore for us on the cross.

SERMON XXIII

Tolerance of Religious Error

(THE FEAST OF ST. BARNABAS
THE APOSTLE)

"He was a good man, and full of the Holy Ghost and of faith."—Acts 11:24

When Christ came to form a people unto Himself to show forth His praise, He took of every kind. Highways and hedges, the streets and lanes of the city, furnished guests for His supper, as well as the wilderness of Judea, or the courts of the Temple. His first followers are a sort of type of the general Church, in which many and various minds are as one. And this is one use, if we duly improve it, of our Festivals; which set before us specimens of the Divine Life under the same diversity of outward circumstances, advantages, and dispositions, which we discern around us. The especial grace poured upon the Apostles and their associates, whether miraculous or moral, had no tendency to destroy their respective peculiarities of temper and character, to invest them with a sanctity beyond our imitation, or to preclude failings and errors which may be our warning. It left them, as it found them, men. Peter and John, for instance, the simple fishers on the lake of Gennesareth, Simon the Zealot, Matthew the busy tax-gatherer, and the ascetic Baptist, how different are these,—first, from each other,—then, from Apollos the eloquent Alexandrian, Paul the learned Pharisee, Luke the physician, or the Eastern Sages, whom we celebrate at the Feast of the Epiphany; and these again how different from the Blessed Virgin Mary, or the Innocents, or Simeon and Anna, who are brought before us at the Feast of the Purification, or the women who ministered to our Lord, Mary the wife of Cleophas, the Mother of James and John, Mary Magdalene, Martha and Mary, sisters of Lazarus; or again, from the widow with her two mites, the woman whose issue of blood was staunched, from her who poured forth tears of penitence upon His feet, and the ignorant Samaritan at the well! Moreover, the definiteness and evident truth of many of the pictures presented to us in the Gospels serve to realize to us the history, and to help our faith, while at the same time they afford us abundant instruction. Such, for instance, is the immature ardour of James and John, the sudden fall of Peter, the obstinacy of Thomas, and the cowardice of Mark. St. Barnabas furnishes us with a lesson in his own way; nor shall I be wanting in piety towards that Holy Apostle, if on this his day I hold him forth, not only in the peculiar graces of his character, but in those parts of it in which he becomes our warning, not our example.

The text says, that "he was a good man, full of the Holy Ghost and of faith." This praise of goodness is explained by his very name, Barnabas, "the Son of Consolation," which was given him, as it appears, to mark his character of kindness, gentleness, considerateness, warmth of heart, compassion, and munificence.

His acts answer to this account of him. The first we hear of him is his selling some land which was his, and giving the proceeds to the Apostles, to distribute to his poorer brethren. The next notice of him sets before us a second deed of kindness, of as amiable, though of a more private character. "When Saul was come to Jerusalem, he assayed to join himself to the disciples; but they were all afraid of him, and believed not that he was a disciple. But Barnabas took him and brought him to the Apostles, and declared how he had seen the Lord in the way, and that He had spoken to him, and how he had preached boldly at Damascus, in the name of Jesus" (Acts 9:26, 27). Next, he is mentioned in the text, and still with commendation of the same kind. How had he shown that "he was a good man"? by going on a mission of love to the first converts at Antioch. Barnabas, above the rest, was honoured by the Church with this work, which had in view the encouraging and binding together in unity and strength this incipient fruit of God's grace. "When he came, and had seen the grace of God, he was glad" (surely this circumstance itself is mentioned by way of showing his character); "and exhorted them all that with purpose of heart they would cleave unto the Lord." Thus he may even be accounted the founder of the Church of Antioch, being aided by St. Paul, whom he was successful in bringing thither. Next, on occasion of an approaching famine, he is joined with St. Paul in being the minister of the Gentiles' bounty towards the poor saints of Judea. Afterwards, when the Judaizing Christians troubled the Gentile converts with the Mosaic ordinances, Barnabas was sent with the same Apostle and others from the Church of Jerusalem to relieve their perplexity. Thus the Scripture history of him does but answer to his name, and is scarcely more than a continued exemplification of his characteristic grace. Moreover, let the particular force of his name be observed. The Holy Ghost is called our Paraclete, as assisting, advocating, encouraging, comforting us; now, as if to put the highest honour upon the Apostle, the same term is applied to him. He is called "the Son of Consolation," or the Paraclete; and in accordance with this honourable title, we are told, that when the Gentile converts of Antioch had received from his and St. Paul's hands the Apostles' decision against the Judaizers, "they rejoiced for the *consolation*."

On the other hand, on two occasions his conduct is scarcely becoming an Apostle, as instancing somewhat of that infirmity which uninspired persons of his peculiar character frequently exhibit. Both are cases of indulgence towards the faults of others, yet in a different way; the one, an over-easiness in a matter of doctrine, the other, in a matter of conduct. With all his tenderness for the Gentiles, yet on one occasion he could not resist indulging the prejudices of some Judaizing brethren, who came from Jerusalem to Antioch. Peter first was carried away; before they came, "he did eat with the Gentiles, but when they were come, he withdrew, and separated himself, fearing them which were of the circumcision. And the other Jews dissembled likewise with him; insomuch, that Barnabas also was carried away with their dissimulation." The other instance was his indulgent treatment of Mark, his sister's son, which occasioned the quarrel between him and St. Paul. "Barnabas determined to take with them," (Gal 2:12, 13) on their Apostolic journey, "John, whose surname was Mark. But Paul thought not good to take him with them, who departed from them from Pamphylia, and went not with them to the work" (Acts 15:37, 38).

Now it is very plain what description of character, and what kind of lesson, is brought before us in the history of this Holy Apostle. Holy he was, full of the Holy Ghost and of faith; still the characteristics and the infirmities of man remained in him, and thus he is "unto us for an ensample," consistently with the reverence we feel towards him as one of the foundations of the Christian Church. He is an ensample and warning to us, not only as showing us what we ought to be, but as evidencing how the highest gifts and graces are corrupted in our sinful nature, if we are not diligent to walk step by step, according to the light of God's commandments. Be our mind as heavenly as it may be, most loving, most holy, most zealous, most energetic, most peaceful, yet if we look off from Him for a moment, and look towards ourselves, at once these excellent tempers fall into some extreme or mistake. Charity becomes over-easiness, holiness is tainted with spiritual pride, zeal degenerates into fierceness, activity eats up the spirit of prayer, hope is heightened into presumption. We cannot guide ourselves. God's revealed word is our sovereign rule of conduct; and therefore, among other reasons, is faith so principal a grace, for it is the directing power which receives the commands of Christ, and applies them to the heart.

And there is particular reason for dwelling upon the character of St. Barnabas in this age, because he may be considered as the type of the better sort of men among us, and those who are most in esteem. The world itself indeed is what it ever has been, ungodly; but in every age it chooses some one or other peculiarity of the Gospel as the badge of its particular fashion for the time being, and sets up as objects of admiration those who eminently possess it. Without asking, therefore, how far men act from Christian principle, or only from the imitation of it, or from some mere secular or selfish motive, yet, certainly, this age, as far as appearance goes, may be accounted in its character not unlike Barnabas, as being considerate, delicate, courteous, and generous-minded in all that concerns the intercourse of man with man. There is a great deal of thoughtful kindness among us, of conceding in little matters, of scrupulous propriety of words, and a sort of code of liberal and honourable dealing in the conduct of society. There is a steady regard for the rights of individuals, nay, as one would fain hope in spite of misgivings, for the interest of the poorer classes, the stranger, the fatherless, and the widow. In such a country as ours, there must always be numberless instances of distress after all; yet the anxiety to relieve it existing among the more wealthy classes is unquestionable. And it is an unquestionable that we are somewhat disposed to regard ourselves favourably in consequence; and in the midst of our national trials and fears, to say (nay, sometimes with real humility and piety) that we do trust that these characteristic virtues of the age may be allowed to come up as a memorial before God, and to plead for us. When we think of the commandments, we know Charity to be the first and greatest; and we are tempted to ask with the young ruler, "What lack we yet?"

I ask, then, by way of reply, does not our kindness too often degenerate into weakness, and thus become not Christian Charity, but lack of Charity, as regards the objects of it? Are we sufficiently careful to do what is right and just, rather than what is pleasant? Do we clearly understand our professed principles, and do we keep to them under temptation?

The history of St. Barnabas will help us to answer this question honestly. Now I fear we lack altogether, what he lacked in certain occurrences in it, firmness, manliness, godly severity. I fear it must be confessed, that our kindness, instead of being directed and braced by principle, too often becomes languid and unmeaning; that it is exerted on improper objects, and out of season, and thereby is uncharitable in two ways, indulging those who should be chastised, and preferring their comfort to those who are really deserving. We are over-tender in dealing with sin and sinners. We are deficient in jealous custody of the revealed Truths which Christ has left us. We allow men to speak against the Church, its ordinances, or its teaching, without remonstrating with them. We do not separate from heretics, nay, we object to the word as if uncharitable; and when such texts are brought against us as St. John's command, not to show hospitality towards them, we are not slow to answer that they do not apply to us. Now I scarcely can suppose any one really means to say for certain, that these commands are superseded in the present day, and is quite satisfied upon the point; it will rather be found that men who so speak, merely wish to put the subject from them. For a long while they have forgotten that there were any such commands in Scripture; they have lived as though there were not, and not being in circumstances which immediately called for the consideration of them, they have familiarized their minds to a contrary view of the matter, and built their opinions upon it. When reminded of the fact, they are sorry to have to consider it, as they perhaps avow. They perceive that it interferes with the line of conduct to which they are accustomed. They are vexed, not as if allowing themselves to be wrong, but as feeling conscious that a plausible argument (to say the least) may be maintained against them. And instead of daring to give this argument fair play, as in honesty they ought, they hastily satisfy themselves that objections may be taken against it, use some vague terms of disapprobation against those who use it, recur to, and dwell upon, their own habitual view of the benevolent and indulgent spirit of the Gospel, and then dismiss the subject altogether, as if it had never been brought before them.

Observe *how* they rid themselves of it; it is by confronting it with other views of Christianity, which they consider incompatible with it: whereas the very problem which Christian duty requires us to accomplish, is the reconciling in our conduct opposite virtues. It is not difficult (comparatively speaking) to cultivate single virtues. A man takes some one partial view of his duty, whether severe or kindly, whether of action or of meditation: He enters into it with all his might, he opens his heart to its influence, and allows himself to be sent forward on its current.

PAROCHIAL AND PLAIN SERMONS

This is not difficult: There is no anxious vigilance or self-denial in it. On the contrary, there is a pleasure often in thus sweeping along in one way; and especially in matters of giving and conceding. Liberality is always popular, whatever be the subject of it, and excites a glow of pleasure and self-approbation in the giver, even though it involves no sacrifice, nay, is exercised upon the property of others. Thus in the sacred province of religion, men are led on,—without any bad principle, without that utter dislike or ignorance of the Truth, or that self-conceit, which are chief instruments of Satan at this day, nor again from mere cowardice or worldliness, but from thoughtlessness, a sanguine temper, the excitement of the moment, the love of making others happy, susceptibility of flattery, and the habit of looking only one way,—led on to give up Gospel Truths, to consent to open the Church to the various denominations of error which abound among us, or to alter our Services so as to please the scoffer, the lukewarm, or the vicious. To be kind is their one principle of action; and, when they find offence taken at the Church's creed, they begin to think how they may modify or curtail it, under the same sort of feeling as would lead them to be generous in a money transaction, or to accommodate another at the price of personal inconvenience. Not understanding that their religious privileges are a trust to be handed on to posterity, a sacred property entailed upon the Christian family, and their own in enjoyment rather than in possession, they act the spendthrift, and are lavish of the goods of others. Thus, for instance, they speak against the Anathemas of the Athanasian Creed, or of the Commination Service, or of certain of the Psalms, and wish to rid themselves of them.

Undoubtedly, even the best specimens of these men are deficient in a due appreciation of the Christian Mysteries, and of their own responsibility in preserving and transmitting them; yet, some of them are such truly "good" men, so amiable and feeling, so benevolent to the poor, and of such repute among all classes, in short, fulfil so excellently the office of shining like lights in the world, and witnesses of Him "who went about doing good," that those who most deplore their failing, will still be most desirous of excusing them personally, while they feel it a duty to withstand them. Sometimes it may be, that these persons cannot bring themselves to think evil of others; and harbour men of heretical opinions or immoral life from the same easiness of temper which makes them fit subjects for the practices of the cunning and selfish in worldly matters. And sometimes they fasten on certain favourable points of character in the person they should discountenance, and cannot get themselves to attend to any but these; arguing that he is certainly pious and well-meaning, and that his errors plainly do himself no harm;—whereas the question is not about their effects on this or that individual, but simply whether they *are* errors; and again, whether they are not certain to be injurious to the mass of men, or on the long run, as it is called. Or they cannot bear to hurt another by the expression of their disapprobation, though it be that "his soul may be saved in the day of the Lord." Or perhaps they are deficient in keenness of intellectual perception as to the moral mischief of certain speculative opinions, as they consider them; and not knowing their ignorance enough to forbear the use of private judgment, nor having faith enough to acquiesce in God's word, or the decision of His Church, they incur the responsibility of serious changes. Or, perhaps they shelter themselves behind some confused notion, which they have taken up, of the peculiar character of our own Church, arguing that they belong to a tolerant Church, that it is but consistent as well as right in her members to be tolerant, and that they are but exemplifying tolerance in their own conduct, when they treat with indulgence those who are lax in creed or conduct. Now, if by the tolerance of our Church, it be meant that she does not countenance the use of fire and sword against those who separate from her, so far she is truly called a tolerant Church; but she is not tolerant of error, as those very formularies, which these men wish to remove, testify; and if she retains within her bosom proud intellects, and cold hearts, and unclean hands, and dispenses her blessings to those who disbelieve or are unworthy of them, this arises from other causes, certainly not from her principles; else were she guilty of Eli's sin, which may not be imagined.

Such is the defect of mind suggested to us by the instances of imperfection recorded of St. Barnabas; it will be more clearly understood by contrasting him with St. John. We cannot compare good men together in their points of excellence; but whether the one or the other of these Apostles had the greater share of the spirit of love, we all know that anyhow the Beloved Disciple abounded in it. His General Epistle is full of exhortations to cherish that blessed temper, and his name is associated in our minds with such heavenly dispositions as are more immediately connected with it,—contemplativeness, serenity of soul, clearness of faith. Now see in what he differed from Barnabas; in uniting charity with a firm maintenance of "the Truth as it is in Jesus." So far were his fervour and exuberance of charity from interfering with his zeal for God, that rather, the more he loved men, the more he desired to bring before them the great unchangeable Verities to which they must submit, if they would see life, and on which a weak indulgence suffers them to shut their eyes. He loved the brethren, but he "loved them in the Truth" (3 Jn 1). He loved them for the Living Truth's sake which had redeemed them, for the Truth which was in them, for the Truth which was the measure of their spiritual attainments. He loved the Church so honestly, that he was stern towards those who troubled her. He loved the world so wisely, that he preached the Truth in it; yet, if men rejected it, he did not love them so inordinately as to forget the supremacy of the Truth, as the Word of Him who is above all. Let it never be forgotten then, when we picture to ourselves this saintly Apostle, this unearthly Prophet, who fed upon the sights and voices of the world of spirits, and looked out heavenwards day by day for Him whom he had once seen in the flesh, that this is he who gives us that command about shunning heretics, which whether of force in this age or not, still certainly in any age is (what men now call) severe; and that this command of his is but in unison with the fearful descriptions he gives in other parts of his inspired writings of the Presence, the Law, and the Judgments of Almighty God. Who can deny that the Apocalypse from beginning to end is a very fearful book; I may say, the most fearful book in Scripture, full of accounts of the wrath of God? Yet, it is written by the Apostle of love. It is possible, then, for a man to be at once kind as Barnabas, yet zealous as Paul. Strictness and tenderness had no "sharp contention" in the breast of the Beloved Disciple; they found their perfect union, yet distinct exercise, in the grace of charity, which is the fulfilling of the whole Law.

 I wish I saw any prospect of this element of zeal and holy sternness springing up among us, to temper and give character to the languid, unmeaning benevolence which we misname Christian love. I have no hope of my country till I see it. Many schools of Religion and Ethics are to be found among us, and they all profess to magnify, in one shape or other, what they consider the principle of love; but what they lack is, a firm maintenance of that characteristic of the Divine Nature, which, in accommodation to our infirmity, is named by St. John and his brethren, the wrath of God. Let this be well observed. There are men who are advocates of Expedience; these, as far as they are religious at all, resolve conscience into an instinct of mere benevolence, and refer all the dealings of Providence with His creatures to the same one Attribute. Hence, they consider all punishment to be remedial, a means to an end, deny that the woe threatened against sinners is of eternal duration, and explain away the doctrine of the Atonement. There are others, who place religion in the mere exercise of the excited feelings; and these too, look upon their God and Saviour, as far (that is) as they themselves are concerned, solely as a God of love. They believe themselves to be converted from sin to righteousness by the mere manifestation of that love to their souls, drawing them on to Him; and they imagine that that same love, untired by any possible transgressions on their part, will surely carry forward every individual so chosen to final triumph. Moreover, as accounting that Christ has already done everything for their salvation, they do not feel that a moral change is necessary on their part, or rather they consider that the Vision of revealed love works it in them spontaneously; in either case dispensing with all laborious efforts, all "fear and trembling," all self-denial in "working out their salvation," nay, looking upon such qualifications with suspicion, as leading to a supposed self-confidence and spiritual pride. Once more, there are others of a mystical turn of mind, with untutored imaginations and subtle intellects, who follow the theories of the old Gentile philosophy. These, too, are accustomed to make love the one principle of life and providence in heaven and earth, as if it were a pervading Spirit of the world, finding a sympathy in every heart, absorbing all things into itself, and kindling a rapturous enjoyment in all who contemplate it. They sit at home speculating, and separate moral perfection from action. These men either hold, or are in the way to hold, that the human soul is pure by nature; sin an external principle corrupting it; evil, destined to final annihilation; Truth attained by means of the imagination; conscience, a taste; holiness, a passive contemplation of God; and obedience, a mere pleasurable work. It is difficult to discriminate accurately between these three schools of opinion, without using words of unseemly familiarity; yet I have said enough for those who wish to pursue the subject. Let it be observed then, that these three systems, however different from each other in their principles and spirit, yet all agree in this one respect, viz., in overlooking that the Christian's God is represented in Scripture, not only as a God of Love, but also as "a consuming fire." Rejecting the testimony of Scripture, no wonder they also reject that of conscience, which assuredly forebodes ill to the sinner, but which, as the narrow religionist maintains, is not the voice of God at all,—or is a mere benevolence, according to the disciple of Utility,—or, in the judgment of the more mystical sort, a kind of passion for the beautiful and sublime. Regarding thus "the goodness" only, and not "the severity of God," no wonder that they ungird their loins and become effeminate; no wonder that their ideal notion of a perfect Church, is a Church which lets every one go on his way, and disclaims any right to pronounce an opinion, much less inflict a censure on religious error.

But those who think themselves and others in risk of an eternal curse, dare not be thus indulgent. Here then lies our want at the present day, for this we must pray,—that a reform may come in the spirit and power of Elias. We must pray God thus "to revive His work in the midst of the years"; to send us a severe discipline, the Order of St. Paul and St. John, "speaking the Truth in love," and "loving in the Truth,"— a Witness of Christ, "knowing the terror of the Lord," fresh from the presence of Him "whose head and hairs are white like wool, as white as snow, and whose eyes are as a flame of fire, and out of His mouth a sharp sword,"—a Witness not shrinking from proclaiming His wrath, as a real characteristic of His glorious nature, though expressed in human language for our sakes, proclaiming the narrowness of the way of life, the difficulty of attaining heaven, the danger of riches, the necessity of taking up our cross, the excellence and beauty of self-denial and austerity, the hazard of disbelieving the Catholic Faith, and the duty of zealously contending for it. Thus only will the tidings of mercy come with force to the souls of men, with a constraining power and with an abiding impress, when hope and fear go together. Then only will Christians be successful in fight, "quitting themselves like men," conquering and ruling the fury of the world, and maintaining the Church in purity and power, when they condense their feelings by a severe discipline, and are loving in the midst of firmness, strictness, and holiness. Then only can we prosper (under the blessing and grace of Him who is the Spirit both of love and of truth), when the heart of Paul is vouchsafed to us, to withstand even Peter and Barnabas, if ever they are overcome by mere human feelings, to "know henceforth no man after the flesh," to put away from us sister's son, or nearer relative, to relinquish the sight of them, the hope of them, and the desire of them, when He commands, who raises up friends even to the lonely, if they trust in Him, and will give us "within His walls a name better than of sons and of daughters, an everlasting name that shall not be cut off" (Is 56:4, 5).

SERMON XXIX

The Powers of Nature

(THE FEAST OF ST. MICHAEL AND ALL ANGELS)

"Who maketh His Angels spirits, His ministers a flaming fire."—Ps 104:4

On to-day's Festival it well becomes us to direct our minds to the thought of those Blessed Servants of God, who have never tasted of sin; who are among us, though unseen, ever serving God joyfully on earth as well as in heaven; who minister, through their Maker's condescending will, to the redeemed in Christ, the heirs of salvation.

There have been ages of the world, in which men have thought too much of Angels, and paid them excessive honour; honoured them so perversely as to forget the supreme worship due to Almighty God. This is the sin of a dark age. But the sin of what is called an educated age, such as our own, is just the reverse: to account slightly of them, or not at all; to ascribe all we see around us, not to their agency, but to certain assumed laws of nature. This, I say, is likely to be our sin, in proportion as we are initiated into the learning of this world;—and this is the danger of many (so called) philosophical pursuits, now in fashion, and recommended zealously to the notice of large portions of the community, hitherto strangers to them,—chemistry, geology, and the like; the danger, that is, of resting in things seen, and forgetting unseen things, and our ignorance about them.

I will attempt to say what I mean more at length. The text informs us that Almighty God makes His Angels spirits or winds, and His Ministers a flame of fire. Let us consider what is implied in this.

1. What a number of beautiful and wonderful objects does nature present on every side of us! and how little we know concerning them! In some indeed we see symptoms of intelligence, and we get to form some idea of what they are. For instance, about brute animals we know little,

but still we see they have sense, and we understand that their bodily form which meets the eye is but the index, the outside token of something we do not see. Much more in the case of men: We see them move, speak, and act, and we know that all we see takes place in consequence of their will, because they have a spirit within them, though we do not see it. But why do rivers flow? Why does rain fall? Why does the sun warm us? And the wind, why does it blow? Here our natural reason is at fault; we know, I say, that it is the *spirit* in man and in beast that makes man and beast move, but reason tells us of no spirit abiding in what is commonly called the natural world, to make it perform its ordinary duties. Of course, it is *God's* will which *sustains* it all; so does God's will enable *us* to move also, yet this does not hinder, but, in one sense we may be truly said to move ourselves: but how do the wind and water, earth and fire, move? Now here Scripture interposes, and seems to tell us, that all this wonderful harmony is the work of Angels. Those events which we ascribe to chance as the weather, or to nature as the seasons, are duties done to that God who maketh His Angels to be winds, and His Ministers a flame of fire. For example, it was an Angel which gave to the pool at Bethesda its medicinal quality; and there is no reason why we should doubt that other health-springs in this and other countries are made such by a like unseen ministry. The fires on Mount Sinai, the thunders and lightnings, were the work of Angels; and in the Apocalypse we read of the Angels restraining the four winds. Works of vengeance are likewise attributed to them. The fiery lava of the volcanoes, which (as it appears) was the cause of Sodom and Gomorrah's ruin, was caused by the two Angels who rescued Lot. The hosts of Sennacherib were destroyed by an Angel, by means (it is supposed) of a suffocating wind. The pestilence in Israel when David numbered the people, was the work of an Angel. The earthquake at the resurrection was the work of an Angel. And in the Apocalypse the earth is smitten in various ways by Angels of vengeance (Jn 5:4; Ex 19:16–18; Gal 3:19; Acts 7:53; Rv 7:1; Gn 19:13; 2 Kgs 19: 35; 2 Sm 24:15–17; Mt 28:2; Rv 8, 9, 16).

Thus, as far as the Scripture communications go, we learn that the course of nature, which is so wonderful, so beautiful, and so fearful, is effected by the ministry of those unseen beings. Nature is not inanimate; its daily toil is intelligent; its works are *duties*. Accordingly, the Psalmist says, "The heavens declare the glory of God, and the firmament showeth His handy-work." "O Lord, Thy word endureth for ever in heaven. Thy truth also remaineth from one generation to another; Thou hast laid the foundation of the earth, and it abideth. They continue this day according to Thine ordinance, for *all things serve thee*" (Ps 19:1, 119:89–91).

I do not pretend to say, that we are told in Scripture what matter is; but I affirm, that as our souls move our bodies, be our bodies what they may, so there are Spiritual Intelligences which move those wonderful and vast portions of the natural world which seem to be inanimate; and as the gestures, speech, and expressive countenances of our friends around us enable us to hold intercourse with them, so in the motions of universal nature, in the interchange of day and night, summer and winter, wind and storm, fulfilling His word, we are reminded of the blessed and dutiful Angels. Well then, on this day's Festival, may we sing the hymn of those Three Holy Children whom Nebuchadnezzar cast into the fiery furnace. The Angels were bid to change the nature of the flame, and make it harmless to them; and they in turn called on all the creatures of God, on the Angels especially, to glorify Him. Though many hundreds of years have passed since that time, and the world now vainly thinks it knows more than it did, and that it has found the real causes of the things it sees, still may we say, with grateful and simple hearts, "O all ye works of the Lord, O ye Angels of the Lord, O ye sun and moon, stars of heaven, showers and dew, winds of God, light and darkness, mountains and hills, green things upon the earth, bless ye the Lord, praise Him, and magnify Him for ever." Thus, whenever we look abroad, we are reminded of those most gracious and holy Beings, the servants of the Holiest, who deign to minister to the heirs of salvation. Every breath of air and ray of light and heat, every beautiful prospect, is, as it were, the skirts of their garments, the waving of the robes of those whose faces see God in heaven. And I put it to any one, whether it is not as philosophical, and as full of intellectual enjoyment, to refer the movements of the natural world to them, as to attempt to explain them by certain theories of science; useful as these theories certainly are for particular purposes, and capable (in subordination to that higher view) of a religious application.

2. And thus I am led to another use of the doctrine under consideration. While it raises the mind, and gives it a matter of thought, it is also profitable as a humbling doctrine, as indeed I have already shown. Vain man would be wise, and he curiously examines the works of nature, as if they were lifeless and senseless; as if he alone had intelligence, and they were base inert matter, however curiously contrived at the first. So he goes on, tracing the order of things, seeking for Causes in that order, giving names to the wonders he meets with, and thinking he understands

what he has given a name to. At length he forms a theory, and recommends it in writing, and calls himself a philosopher. Now all these theories of science, which I speak of, are useful, as classifying, and so assisting us to *recollect*, the works and ways of God and of His ministering Angels. And again, they are ever most useful, in enabling us to *apply* the course of His Providence, and the ordinances of His will, to the benefit of man. Thus we are enabled to enjoy God's gifts; and let us thank Him for the knowledge which enables us to do so, and honour those who are His instruments in communicating it. But if such an one proceeds to imagine that, because he knows something of this world's wonderful order, he therefore knows *how* things really go on, if he treats the miracles of nature (so to call them) as mere mechanical processes, continuing their course by themselves,—as works of man's contriving (a clock, for instance) are set in motion, and go on, as it were, of themselves,—if in consequences he is, what may be called, irreverent in his conduct towards nature, thinking (if I may so speak) that it does not hear him, and see how he is bearing himself towards it; and if, moreover, he conceives that the Order of Nature, which he partially discerns, will stand in the place of the God who made it, and that all things continue and move on, not by His will and power, and the agency of the thousands and ten thousands of His unseen Servants, but by fixed laws, self-caused and self-sustained, what a poor weak worm and miserable sinner he becomes! Yet such, I fear, is the condition of many men nowadays, who talk loudly, and appear to themselves and others to be oracles of science, and, as far as the detail of facts goes, do know much more about the operations of Nature than any of us.

Now let us consider what the real state of the case is. Supposing the inquirer I have been describing, when examining a flower, or a herb, or a pebble, or a ray of light, which he treats as something so beneath him in the scale of existence, suddenly discovered that he was in the presence of some powerful being who was hidden behind the visible things he was inspecting, who, though concealing his wise hand, was giving them their beauty, grace, and perfection, as being God's instrument for the purpose, nay whose robe and ornaments those wondrous objects were, which he was so eager to analyse, what would be his thoughts? Should we but accidentally show a rudeness of manner towards our fellow-man, tread on the hem of his garment, or brush roughly against him, are we not vexed, not as if we had hurt him, but from the fear we may have been disrespectful? David had watched the awful pestilence three days, doubtless not with curious eyes, but with indescribable terror and remorse; but when at length he "lifted up his eyes and saw the *Angel* of the Lord" (who caused the pestilence) "stand between the earth and the heaven, having a drawn sword in his hand stretched out over Jerusalem, *then* David and the elders, who were clothed in sackcloth, *fell* upon their faces" (1 Chr 21:16). The mysterious, irresistible pestilence became still more fearful when the cause was known;—and what is true of the terrible, is true on the other hand of the pleasant and attractive operations of nature. When then we walk abroad, and "meditate in the field at the eventide," how much has every herb and flower in it to surprise and overwhelm us! For, even did we know as much about them as the wisest of men, yet there are those around us, though unseen, to whom our greatest knowledge is as ignorance; and, when we converse on subjects of nature scientifically, repeating the names of plants and earths, and describing their properties, we should do so religiously, as in the hearing of the great Servants of God, with the sort of diffidence which we always feel when speaking before the learned and wise of our own mortal race, as poor beginners in intellectual knowledge, as well as in moral attainments.

Now I can conceive persons saying all this is fanciful; but if it appears so, it is only because we are not accustomed to such thoughts. Surely we are not told in Scripture about the Angels for nothing, but for practical purposes; nor can I conceive a use of our knowledge more practical than to make it connect the sight of this world with the thought of another. Nor one more consolatory; for surely it is a great comfort to reflect that, wherever we go, we have those about us, who are ministering to all the heirs of salvation, though we see them not. Nor one more easily to be understood and felt by all men; for we know that at one time the doctrine of Angels was received even too readily. And if any one would argue hence against it as dangerous, let him recollect the great principle of our Church, that the abuse of a thing does not supersede the use of it; and let him explain, if he can, St. Paul's exhorting Timothy not only as "before God and Christ," but before "the elect Angels" also. Hence, in the Communion Service, our Church teaches us to join our praises with that of "Angels and Archangels, and all the Company of heaven"; and the early Christians even hoped that they waited on the Church's seasons of worship, and glorified God with her. Nor are these thoughts without their direct influence on our faith in God and His Son; for the more we can enlarge our view of the next world, the better. When we survey Almighty God surrounded by His Holy Angels, His thousand thousands of ministering Spirits, and ten thousand times ten thousand standing before Him, the idea of His awful Majesty rises before us more powerfully and impressively. We begin to see how little we are, how altogether mean and worthless in ourselves, and how high He is, and fearful. The very lowest of His Angels is indefinitely above us in this our present state; how high then must be the Lord of Angels! The very Seraphim hide their faces before His glory, while they praise Him; how shamefaced then should sinners be, when they come into His presence!

Lastly, it is a motive to our exertions in doing the will of God, to think that, if we attain to heaven, we shall become the fellows of the blessed Angels. Indeed, what do we know of the courts of heaven, but as peopled by them? and therefore doubtless they are revealed to us, that we may have something to fix our thoughts on, when we look heavenwards. Heaven indeed is the palace of Almighty God, and of Him doubtless we must think in the first place; and again of His Son our Saviour, who died for us, and who is manifested in the Gospels, in order that we may have something definite to look forward to: for the same cause, surely, the Angels also are revealed to us, that heaven may be as little as possible an unknown place in our imaginations.

Let us then entertain such thoughts as these of the Angels of God; and while we try to think of them worthily, let us beware lest we make the contemplation of them a mere feeling, and a sort of luxury of the imagination. This world is to be a world of practice and labour; God reveals to us glimpses of the Third Heaven for our comfort; but if we indulge in these as the end of our present being, not trying day by day to purify ourselves for the future enjoyment of the fulness of them, they become but a snare of our enemy. The Services of religion, day by day, obedience to God in our calling and in ordinary matters, endeavours to imitate our Saviour Christ in word and deed, constant prayer to Him, and dependence on Him, these are the due preparation for receiving and profiting by His revelations; whereas many a man can write and talk beautifully about them, who is not at all better or nearer heaven for all his excellent words.

SERMON XXX

The Danger of Accomplishments

(THE FEAST OF ST. LUKE
THE EVANGELIST)

"In the hearts of all that are wise hearted, I have put wisdom."—Ex 31:6

St. Luke differed from his fellow-evangelists and fellow-disciples in having received the advantages of (what is called) a liberal education. In this respect he resembled St. Paul, who, with equal accomplishments appears to have possessed even more learning. He is said to have been a native of Antioch, a city celebrated for the refined habits and cultivated intellect of its inhabitants; and his profession was that of a physician or surgeon, which of itself evidences him to have been in point of education something above the generality of men. This is confirmed by the character of his writings, which are superior in composition to any part of the New Testament, excepting some of St. Paul's Epistles.

There are persons who doubt whether what are called "accomplishments," whether in literature or in the fine arts, can be consistent with deep and practical seriousness of mind. They think that attention to these argues a lightness of mind, and, at least, takes up time which might be better employed; and, I confess, at first sight they seem to be able to say much in defence of their opinion. Yet, notwithstanding, St. Luke and St. Paul were accomplished men, and evidently took pleasure in their accomplishments.

I am not speaking of human *learning;* this also many men think inconsistent with simple uncorrupted faith. They suppose that learning must make a man proud. This is of course a great mistake; but of it I am not speaking, but of an over-jealousy of *accomplishments*, the elegant arts and studies, such as poetry, literary composition, painting, music, and the like; which are considered (not indeed to make a man *proud*, but) to make him *trifling*. Of this opinion, how far it is true, and how far not true, I am going to speak: being led to the consideration of it by the known fact, that St. Luke was a polished writer, and yet an Evangelist.

Now, that the accomplishments I speak of have a *tendency* to make us trifling and unmanly, and therefore are to be viewed by each of us with suspicion as far as regards himself, I am ready to admit, and shall presently make clear. I allow, that in matter of fact, refinement and luxury, elegance and effeminacy, go together. Antioch, the most polished, was the most voluptuous city of Asia. But the *abuse* of good things is no argument against the things themselves; mental cultivation *may* be a divine gift, though it is abused. All God's gifts are perverted by man; health, strength, intellectual power, are all turned by sinners to bad purposes, yet they are not evil in themselves: therefore an acquaintance with the elegant arts may be a gift and a good, and intended to be an instrument of God's glory, though numbers who have it are rendered thereby indolent, luxurious, and feeble-minded.

But the account of the building of the Tabernacle in the wilderness, from which the text is taken, is decisive on this point. It is too long to read to you, but a few verses will remind you of the nature of it. "Thou shalt speak unto all that are wise hearted, whom I have filled with the spirit of wisdom, that they may make Aaron's garments to consecrate him, that he may minister unto me in the priest's office." "See I have called by name Bezaleel . . . and have filled him with the Spirit of God, in wisdom and in understanding, and in knowledge, and in all manner of workmanship, to devise cunning works, to work in gold, and in silver, and in brass, and in cutting of stones, to set them, and in carving of timber, to work all manner of workmanship." "Take ye from among you an offering unto the Lord; whosoever is of a willing heart let him bring it, an offering of the Lord, gold, and silver, and brass, and blue, and purple, and scarlet and fine linen, and goats' hair, and rams' skins dyed red, and badgers' skins, and shittim wood, and oil for the light, and spices for anointing oil, and for the sweet incense, and onyx stones, and stones to be set for the ephod, and for the breast-plate. And every wise hearted among you shall come and make all that the Lord hath commanded" (Ex 28:3, 31:2–5, 35:5–10).

How then is it, that what in itself is of so excellent, and (I may say) divine a nature, is yet so commonly perverted? I proceed to state what is the danger, as it appears to me, of being accomplished, with a view to answer this question.

Now the *danger* of an elegant and polite education is, that it separates feeling and acting; it teaches us to think, speak, and be affected aright, without forcing us to practise what is right. I will take an illustration of this, though somewhat a familiar one, from the effect produced upon the mind by reading what is commonly called a romance or novel, which comes under the description of polite literature, of which I am speaking. Such works contain many good sentiments (I am taking the better sort of them): Characters too are introduced, virtuous, noble, patient under suffering, and triumphing at length over misfortune. The great truths of religion are upheld, we will suppose, and enforced; and our affections excited and interested in what is good and true. But it is all fiction; it does not exist out of a book which contains the beginning and end of it. *We* have nothing *to do;* we read, are affected, softened or roused, and that is all; we cool again—nothing comes of it. Now observe the effect of this. God has made us feel in order that we may *go on to act* in consequence of feeling; if then we allow our feelings to be excited without acting upon them, we do mischief to the moral system within us, just as we might spoil a watch, or other piece of mechanism, by playing with the wheels of it. We weaken its springs, and they cease to act truly. Accordingly, when we have got into the habit of amusing ourselves with these works of fiction, we come at length to feel the excitement without the slightest thought or tendency to act upon it; and, since it is very difficult to begin any duty *without* some emotion or other (that is, to begin on mere principles of dry reasoning), a grave question arises, how, after destroying the connexion between feeling and acting, how shall we get ourselves to act when circumstances make it our duty to do so? For instance, we will say we have read again and again, of the heroism of facing danger, and we have glowed with the thought of its nobleness. We have felt how great it is to bear pain, and submit to indignities, rather than wound our conscience; and all this, again and again, when we had no opportunity of carrying our good feelings into practice. Now, suppose at length we actually come into trial, and let us say, our feelings become roused, as often before, at the thought of boldly resisting temptations to cowardice, shall we therefore do our duty, quitting ourselves like men? rather, we are likely to talk loudly, and then run from the danger. Why?—rather let us ask, why *not?* what is to keep us from yielding? Because we *feel* aright? nay, we have again and again felt aright, and thought aright, without accustoming ourselves to act aright, and, though there was an original connexion in our minds between feeling and acting, there is none now; the wires within us, as they may be called, are loosened and powerless.

And what is here instanced of fortitude, is true in all cases of duty.

The refinement which literature gives, is that of thinking, feeling, knowing, and speaking right, not of acting right; and thus, while it makes the manners amiable, and the conversation decorous and agreeable, it has no tendency to make the conduct, the practice of the man *virtuous*.

Observe, I have supposed the works of fiction I speak of to inculcate right sentiments; though such works (play-books for example) are often vicious and immoral. But even at best, supposing them well principled, still after all, at best, they are, I say, dangerous, in themselves;—that is, if we allow refinement to stand in the place of hardy, rough-handed obedience. It follows, that I am much opposed to certain *religious* novels, which some persons think so useful: that they sometimes do good, I am far from denying;—but they do more harm than good. They do harm on the whole; they lead men to cultivate the religious affections separate from religious practice. And here I might speak of that entire religious system (miscalled religious) which makes Christian faith consist, not in the honest and plain practice of what is right, but in the luxury of excited religious feeling, in a mere mediating on our Blessed Lord, and dwelling as in a reverie on what He has done for us;—for such indolent contemplation will no more sanctify a man *in fact*, than reading a poem or listening to a chant or psalm-tune.

The case is the same with the arts last alluded to, poetry and music. These are especially likely to make us unmanly, if we are not on our guard, as exciting emotions without insuring correspondent practice, and so destroying the connexion between feeling and acting; for I here mean by unmanliness the inability to do with ourselves what we wish,—the saying fine things and yet lying slothfully on our couch, as if we could not get up, though we ever so much wished it.

And here I must notice something besides in elegant accomplishments, which goes to make us over-refined and fastidious, and falsely delicate. In books, everything is made beautiful in its way. Pictures are drawn of *complete* virtue; little is said about failures, and little or nothing of the drudgery of ordinary, every-day obedience, which is neither poetical nor interesting. True faith teaches us to do numberless disagreeable things for Christ's sake, to bear petty annoyances, which we find written down in no book. In most books Christian conduct is made grand, elevated, and splendid; so that any one, who only knows of true religion from books, and not from actual endeavours to be religious, is sure to be offended at religion when he actually comes upon it, from the roughness and humbleness of his duties, and his necessary deficiencies in doing them. It is beautiful in a picture to wash the disciples' feet; but the sands of the real desert have no lustre in them to compensate for the servile nature of the occupation.

And further still, it must be observed, that the art of composing, which is a chief accomplishment, has in itself a tendency to make us artificial and insincere. For to be ever attending to the fitness and propriety of our words, is (or at least there is the risk of its being) a kind of acting; and knowing what can be said on both sides of a subject, is a main step towards thinking the one side as good as the other. Hence men in ancient times, who cultivated polite literature, went by the name of "Sophists"; that is, men who wrote elegantly, and talked eloquently, on any subject whatever, right or wrong. St. Luke perchance might have been such a Sophist, had he not been a Christian.

Such are some of the dangers of elegant accomplishments; and they beset more or less all educated persons; and of these perhaps not the least such females as happen to have no very direct duties, and are above the drudgery of common life, and hence are apt to become fastidious and fine,—to love a luxurious ease, and to amuse themselves in mere elegant pursuits, the while they admire and profess what is religious and virtuous, and think that they really possess the character of mind which they esteem.

With these thoughts before us, it is necessary to look back to the Scripture instances which I began by adducing, to avoid the conclusion that accomplishments are positively dangerous, and unworthy a Christian. But St. Luke and St. Paul show us, that we may be sturdy workers in the Lord's service, and bear our cross manfully, though we be adorned with all the learning of the Egyptians; or rather, that the resources of literature, and the graces of a cultivated mind, may be made both a lawful source of enjoyment to the possessor, and a means of introducing and recommending the Truth to others; while the history of the Tabernacle shows that all the cunning arts and precious possessions of this world may be consecrated to a religious service, and be made to speak of the world to come.

I conclude then with the following cautions, to which the foregoing remarks lead. First, we must avoid giving too much time to lighter occupations; and next, we must never allow ourselves to read works of fiction or poetry, or to interest ourselves in the fine arts for the mere sake of the things themselves: but keep in mind all along that we are Christians and accountable beings, who have fixed principles of right and wrong, by which all things must be tried, and have religious habits to be matured within them, towards which all things are to be made subservient. Nothing is more common among accomplished people than the habit of reading books so entirely for reading's sake, as to praise and blame the actions and persons described in a random way, according to their fancy, not considering whether they are really good or bad according to the standard of moral truth. I would not be austere; but when this is done habitually, surely it is dangerous. Such too is the abuse of poetical talent, that sacred gift. Nothing is more common than to fall into the practice of uttering fine sentiments, particularly in letter writing, as a matter of course, or a kind of elegant display. Nothing more common in singing than to use words which have a light meaning, or a bad one. All these things are hurtful to seriousness of character. It is for this reason (to put aside others) that the profession of stage-players, and again of orators, is a dangerous one. They learn to say good things, and to excite in themselves vehement feelings, about nothing at all.

If we are in earnest, we shall let nothing lightly pass by which may do us good, nor shall we dare to trifle with such sacred subjects as morality and religious duty. We shall apply all we read to ourselves; and this almost without intending to do so, from the mere sincerity and honesty of our desire to please God. We shall be suspicious of all such good thoughts and wishes, and we shall shrink from all such exhibitions of our principles, as fall short of action. We shall aim at doing right, and so glorifying our Father, and shall exhort and constrain others to do so also; but as for talking on the appropriate subjects of religious meditation, and *trying* to show piety, and to excite corresponding feelings in another, even though our nearest friend, far from doing this, we shall account it a snare and a mischief. Yet this is what many persons consider the highest part of religion, and call it spiritual conversation, the test of a spiritual mind; whereas, putting aside the incipient and occasional hypocrisy, and again the immodesty of it, I call all formal and intentional expression of religious emotions, all studied passionate discourse, *dissipation,*—dissipation the same in nature, though different in subject, as what is commonly so called; for it is a drain and a waste of our religious and moral strength, a general weakening of our spiritual powers (as I have already shown); and all for what?—for the pleasure of the immediate excitement. Who can deny that this religious disorder is a parallel case to that of the sensualist? Nay, precisely the same as theirs, from whom the religionists in question think themselves very far removed, of the fashionable world, I mean, who read works of fiction, frequent the public shows, are ever on the watch for novelties, and affect a pride of manners and a "mincing" (Is 3:16) deportment, and are ready with all kinds of good thoughts and keen emotions on all occasions.

Of all such as abuse the decencies and elegancies of moral truth into a means of luxurious enjoyment, what would a prophet of God say? Hear the words of the holy Ezekiel, that stern rough man of God, a true Saint in the midst of a self-indulgent, high-professing people: "Thou son of man, the children of thy people still are talking against thee by the walls and in the doors of the houses, and speak one to another, every one to his brother, saying, Come, I pray you, and hear what is the word that cometh forth from the Lord. And they come unto thee as the people cometh, and they sit before thee as My people, and they hear thy words, but they will not do them: for with their mouth they show much love, but their heart goeth after their covetousness. And, lo, thou art unto them as a very lovely song of one that hath a pleasant voice, and can play well on an instrument: for they hear they words, but they do them not" (Ez 33:30–32).

Or, consider St. Paul's words; which are still more impressive, because he was himself a man of learning and accomplishments, and took pleasure, in due place, in the pursuits to which these give rise:

"Preach the word; be instant in season, out of season; reprove, rebuke, exhort, with all long-suffering and doctrine. For the time will come when they will not endure sound doctrine; but after their own lusts shall they heap to themselves teachers, having itching ears. And they shall turn away their ears from the Truth, and shall be turned unto fables." "Watch ye, stand fast in the faith, quit you like men, be strong" (2 Tm 4:2–4; 1 Cor 16:13).

Volume III

SERMON VIII

Contracted Views in Religion

"Lo, these many years do I serve thee, neither transgressed I at any time they commandment; and yet thou never gavest me a kid, that I might make merry with my friends."—Lk 15:29

There is a general correspondence between this parable, and that in St. Matthew's gospel of the two sons whom their father bade go work in his vineyard; but they differ as regards the character of the professedly obedient son: In St. Matthew he says, "I go, sir, and went not"; in the parable before us he is of a far different class of Christians, though not without his faults. There is nothing to show that he is insincere in his profession, though in the text he complains in a very unseemly and foolish way. He bears a considerable resemblance to the labourers in the vineyard, who complained of their master; though they are treated with greater severity. The elder brother of the prodigal complained of his father's kindness towards the penitent; the labourers of the vineyard murmured against the good-man of the house for receiving and rewarding those who came late to his service as liberally as themselves. They, however, spoke in selfishness and presumption; but he in perplexity, as it would appear, and distress of mind. Accordingly, he was comforted by his father, who graciously informed him of the reason of his acting as he had done. "Son, *thou* art ever with me," he says, "and all that I have is thine. It was meet that we should make merry and be glad; for this thy brother was dead and is alive again, and was lost and is found."

Now let us try to understand the feelings of the elder brother, and to apply the picture to the circumstances in which we find ourselves at present.

First, then, in the conduct of the father, there seemed, at first sight, an evident departure from the rules of fairness and justice. Here was a reprobate son received into his favour on the first stirrings of repentance. What was the use of serving him dutifully, if there were no difference in the end between the righteous and the wicked? This is what we feel and act upon in life constantly. In doing good to the poor, for instance, a chief object is to encourage industrious and provident habits; and it is evident we should hurt and disappoint the better sort, and defeat our object, if, after all, we did not take into account the difference of their conduct, though we promised to do so, but gave those who did not work nor save all the benefits granted to those who did. The elder brother's case, then, seemed a hard one; and that, even without supposing him to feel jealous, or to have unsuitable notions of his own importance and usefulness. Apply this to the case of religion, and it still holds good. At first sight, the reception of the penitent sinner seems to interfere with the reward of the faithful servant of God. Just as the promise of pardon is abused by bad men to encourage themselves in sinning on, that grace may abound; so, on the other hand, it is misapprehended by the good, so as to dispirit them. For what is our great stay and consolation amid the perturbations of this world? The truth and justice of God. This is our one light in the midst of darkness. "He loveth righteousness, and hateth iniquity"; "just and right is He." Where else should we find rest for our foot all over the world? Consider in how mysterious a state all things are placed; the wicked are uppermost in power and name, and the righteous are subjected to bodily pain and mental suffering, as if they did not serve God. What a temptation is this to unbelief! The Psalmist felt it when he spoke of the prosperity of the wicked. "Behold, these are the ungodly, who prosper in the world; they increase in riches. Verily I have cleansed my heart in vain, and washed my hands in innocency" (Ps 73:12, 13). It is to meet this difficulty that Almighty God has vouchsafed again and again to declare the unswerving rule of His government—favour to the obedient, punishment to the sinner; that there is "no respect of persons with Him"; that "the righteousness of the righteous shall be upon him, and the wickedness of the wicked shall be upon him" (Rom 2:11; Ez 18:20). Recollect how often this is declared in the book of Psalms. "The Lord knoweth the way of the righteous: but the way of the ungodly shall perish." "The righteous Lord loveth righteousness; His countenance doth behold the upright." "With the merciful Thou wilt show Thyself merciful; with an upright man Thou wilt show Thyself upright. With the pure Thou wilt show Thyself pure; and with the forward Thou wilt show Thyself froward. For Thou wilt save the afflicted people; but wilt bring down high looks."

"Many sorrows shall be to the wicked; but he that trusteth in the Lord, mercy shall compass him about." "Do good, O Lord, unto those that be good" (Ps 1:6, 11:7, 18:25-27, 32:10, 125:4). These declarations, and numberless others like them, are familiar to us all; and why, I say, so often made, except to give us that one fixed point for faith to rest upon, while all around us is changing and disappointing us? viz., that we are quite sure of peace in the end, bad as things may now look, if we do but follow the rule of conscience, avoid sin, and obey God. Hence, St. Paul tells us that "he that cometh to God, must believe that He is a *rewarder* of them that diligently seek Him" (Heb 11:6). Accordingly, when we witness the inequalities of the present world, we comfort ourselves by reflecting that they will be put right in another.

Now the restoration of sinners seems to interfere with this confidence; it seems, at first sight, to put bad and good on a level. And the feeling it excites in the mind is expressed in the parable by the words of the text: "These many years do I serve Thee, neither transgressed I at any time Thy commandment," yet I never have been welcomed and honoured with that peculiar joy which Thou showest towards the repentant sinner. This is the expression of an agitated mind, that fears lest it be cast back upon the wide world, to grope in the dark without a God to guide and encourage it in its course.

The condescending answer of the Father in the parable is most instructive. It sanctions the great truth, which seemed in jeopardy, that is *not* the same thing in the end to obey or disobey, expressly telling us that the Christian penitent is not placed on a footing with those who have consistently served God from the first. "Son, *thou* art ever with Me, and all that I have is thine": that is, why this sudden fear and distrust? can there be any misconception on thy part because I welcome thy brother? dost thou not yet understand Me? Surely thou hast known Me too long to suppose that *thou* canst lose by his gain. *Thou* art in My confidence. I do not make any outward display of kindness towards *thee*, for it is a thing to be taken for granted. We give praise and make professions to strangers, not to friends. Thou art My heir, all that I have is thine. "O thou of little faith, wherefore didst thou doubt?" Who could have thought that it were needful to tell to thee truths which thou hast heard all thy life long? Thou art *ever* with Me; and canst thou really grudge that I should, by one mere *act* of rejoicing, show My satisfaction at the sinner's recovery, and should console him with a promise of mercy, who, before he heard of it, was sinking down under the dread of deserved punishment? "It was *meet* that we should make merry and be glad," thou as well as thy Father.—Such is our merciful God's answer to His suspicious servants, who think He cannot pardon the sinner without withdrawing His favour from them; and it contains in it both a consolation for the perplexed believer not to distrust Him; and again, a warning to the disobedient, not to suppose that repentance makes all straight and even, and puts a man in the same place as if he had never departed from grace given.

But let us now notice the unworthy feeling which appears in the conduct of the elder brother. "He was angry, and would not go" into the house. How may this be fulfilled in our own case?

There exists a great deal of infirmity and foolishness even in the better sort of men. This is not to be wondered at, considering the original corrupt state of their nature; however it is to be deplored, repented of, and corrected. Good men are, like Elijah, "jealous for the Lord God of hosts," and rightly solicitous to see His tokens around them, the pledges of His unchangeable just government; but then they mix with such good feelings undue notions of self-importance, of which they are not aware. This seemingly was the state of mind which dictated the complaint of the elder brother.

This will especially happen in the case of those who are in the most favoured situations in the Church. All places possess their peculiar temptation. Quietness and peace, those greatest of blessings, constitute the trial of the Christians who enjoy them. To be cast on the world, and to see life (as it is called) is a vanity, and "drowns" the unstable "in destruction and perdition"; but while, on the one hand, a religious man may thrive even in the world's pestilent air and on unwholesome food, so, on the other hand, he may become sickly, unless he guards against it, from the very abundance of privileges vouchsafed to him in a peaceful lot. The elder brother had always lived at home; he had seen things go on one way, and, as was natural and right, got attached to them in that one way. But then he could not conceive that they possibly could go on in any other way; he thought he understood his father's ways and principles far more than he did, and when an occurrence took place, for which he had hitherto met with no precedent, he lost himself, as being suddenly thrust aside out of the contracted circle in which he had hitherto walked. He was disconcerted, and angry with his father. And so in religion, we have need to watch against that narrowness of mind, to which we are tempted by the uniformity and tranquility of God's providence towards us. We should be on our guard lest we suppose ourselves to have such a clear knowledge of God's ways, as to rely implicitly on our own notions and feelings. Men attach an undue importance to this or that point in received opinions or practices, and cannot understand how God's blessing can be given to modes of acting to which they themselves are unaccustomed. Thus the Jews thought religion would come to an end, if the Temple were destroyed, whereas, in fact, it has spread abroad and flourished more marvellously since than ever it did before. In this perplexity of mind the Church Catholic is our divinely intended guide, which keeps us from a narrow interpretation of Scripture, from local prejudices and excitements of the day; and by its clear-sighted and consolatory teaching scatters those frightful self-formed visions which scare us.

But I have not described the extreme state of the infirmity into which the blessing of peace leads unwary Christians. They become not only over-confident of their knowledge of God's ways, but positive in their over-confidence. They do not like to be contradicted in their opinions, and are generally most attached to the very points which are most especially of their own devising. They forget that all men are at best but learners in the school of Divine Truth, and that they themselves ought to be *ever* learning, and that they may be sure of the truth of their creed, without a like assurance in the details of religious opinion. They find it a much more comfortable view, much more agreeable to the indolence of human nature, to give over seeking, and to believe they had nothing more to find. A right faith is ever eager and on the watch, with quick eyes and ears, for tokens of God's will, whether He speak in the way of nature or of grace. "I will stand upon my watch, and set me upon the tower, and will watch to see what He will say unto me, and what I shall answer when I am reproved" (Heb 2:1). This is that faith by which (as the Prophet continues) "the just shall live." The Psalmist also expresses this expectant temper. "Unto Thee lift I up mine eyes, O Thou that dwellest in the heavens. Behold, as the eyes of servants look unto the hand of their masters, and as the eyes of a maiden unto the hand of her mistress" (Ps 123:1, 2). But as for those who have long had God's favour without cloud or storm, so it is, they grow secure. They do not feel the great gift. They are apt to presume, and so to become irreverent. The elder brother was too familiar with his father. Irreverence is the very opposite temper to faith. "Son, thou art ever with Me, and all that I have is thine." This most gracious truth was the very cause of his murmuring. When Christians have but a little, they are thankful; they gladly pick up the crumbs from under the table. Give them much, they soon forget it is much; and when they find it is not all, and that for other men, too, even for penitents, God has some good in store, straightway they are offended. Without denying in words their own natural unworthiness, and still having real convictions of it to a certain point, nevertheless, somehow, they have a certain secret over-regard for themselves; at least they *act* as if they thought that the Christian privileges belonged to them over others, by a sort of fitness. And they like respect to be shown them by the world, and are jealous of anything which is likely to interfere with the continuance of their credit and authority. Perhaps, too, they have pledged themselves to certain received opinions, and this is an additional reason for their being suspicious of what to them is a novelty. Hence such persons are least fitted to deal with difficult times. God works wondrously in the world; and at certain eras His providence puts on a new aspect. Religion seems to be failing, when it is merely changing its form. God seems for an instant to desert His own appointed instruments, and to be putting honour upon such as have been framed in express disobedience to His commands. For instance, sometimes He brings about good by means of wicked men, or seems to bless the efforts of those who have separated from His Holy Church more than those of His true labourers. Here is the trial of the Christian's faith, who, if the fact is so, must not resist it, lest haply he be found fighting against God, nor must he quarrel with it after the manner of the elder brother. But he must take everything as God's gift, hold fast his *principles*, not give *them* up because appearances are for the moment against them, but believe all things will come round at length. On the other hand, he must not cease to beg of God, and try to gain, the spirit of a sound mind, the power to separate truth from falsehood, and to try the spirits, the disposition to submit to God's teaching, and the wisdom to act as the varied course of affairs requires; in a word, a portion of that spirit which rested on the great Apostle, St. Paul.

I have thought it right to enlarge upon the conduct of the elder brother in the parable, because something of his character may perchance be found among ourselves. We have long had the inestimable blessings of peace and quiet. We are unworthy of the least of God's mercies, much more of the greatest. But with the blessing we have the trial. Let us then guard against abusing our happy lot, while we have it, or we may lose it for having abused it. Let us guard against discontent in any shape; and as we cannot help hearing what goes on in the world, let us guard, on hearing it, against all intemperate, uncharitable feelings towards those who differ from us, or oppose us. Let us pray for our enemies; let us try to make out men to be as good as they can fairly and safely be considered; let us rejoice at any symptoms of repentance, or any marks of good principle in those who are on the side of error. Let us be forgiving. Let us try to be very humble, to understand our ignorance, and to rely constantly on the enlightening grace of our Great Teacher. Let us be "slow to speak, slow to wrath";—not abandoning our principles, or shrinking from the avowal of them when seasonable, or going over to the cause of error, or fearing consequences, but acting ever from a sense of duty, not from passion, pride, jealousy, or an unbelieving dread of the future; feeling gently, even when we have reason to act severely. "Son, thou art ever with Me, and all that I have is thine." What a gracious announcement, if we could realize it! and how consolatory, so far as we have reason to hope that we are following on to know God's will, and living in His faith and fear! What should alarm those who have Christ's power, or make them envious who have Christ's fulness? How ought we calmly to regard, and resolutely endure, the petty workings of an evil world, thinking seriously of nothing but of the souls that are perishing in it!

"I, even I, am He that comforteth you," says Almighty God: "Who art thou, that thou shouldest be afraid of a man that shall die, and of the son of man which shall be made as grass; and forgettest the Lord thy Maker; and hast feared continually every day because of the fury of the oppressor, as if he were ready to destroy? And where is the fury of the oppressor? I am the Lord thy God; and I have put My words in thy mouth, and have covered thee in the shadow of Mine hand, that I may plant the heavens, and lay the foundations of the earth, and say unto Zion, Thou art My people" (Is 51:12, 13, 15, 16).

SERMON XI

Bodily Suffering

"I fill up that which is behind of the afflictions of Christ in my flesh for His body's sake, which is the Church."—Col 1:24

Our Lord and Saviour Jesus Christ came by blood as well as by water, not only as a Fount of grace and truth—the source of spiritual light, joy, and salvation—but as a combatant with Sin and Satan, who was "consecrated through suffering." He was, as prophecy had marked Him out, "red in His apparel, and His garments like Him that treadeth in the wine-vat"; or, in the words of the Apostle, "He was clothed with a vesture dipped in blood." It was the untold sufferings of the Eternal Word in our nature, His body dislocated and torn, His blood poured out, His soul violently separated by a painful death, which has put away from us the wrath of Him whose love sent Him for that very purpose. This only was our Atonement; no one shared in the work. He "trod the wine-press alone, and of the people there was none with Him." When lifted up upon the cursed tree, He fought with all the hosts of evil, and conquered by suffering.

Thus, in a most mysterious way, all that is needful for this sinful world, the life of our souls, the regeneration of our nature, all that is most joyful and glorious, hope, light, peace, spiritual freedom, holy influences, religious knowledge and strength, all flow from a fount of blood. A work of blood is our salvation; and we, as we would be saved, must draw near and gaze upon it in faith, and accept it as the way to heaven. We must take Him, who thus suffered, as our guide; we must embrace His sacred feet, and follow Him. No wonder, then, should we receive on ourselves some drops of the sacred agony which bedewed His garments; no wonder, should we be sprinkled with the sorrows which He bore in expiation of our sins!

And so it has ever been in very deed; to approach Him has been, from the first, to be partaker, more or less, in His sufferings; I do not say in the case of every individual who believes in Him, but as regards the more conspicuous, the more favoured, His choice instruments, and His most active servants; that is, it has been the lot of the Church, on the whole, and of those, on the whole, who had been most like Him, as Rulers, Intercessors, and Teachers of the Church. He, indeed, alone meritoriously; they, because they have been near Him. Thus, immediately upon His birth, He brought the sword upon the infants of His own age at Bethlehem. His very shadow, cast upon a city, where He did not abide, was stained with blood. His Blessed Mother had not clasped Him to her breast for many weeks, ere she was warned of the penalty of that fearful privilege: "Yea, a sword shall pierce through thy own soul also" (Lk 2:35). Virtue went out of Him; but the water and the blood flowed together as afterwards from His pierced side. From among the infants He took up in His arms to bless, is said to have gone forth a chief martyr of the generation after Him. Most of His Apostles passed through life-long sufferings to a violent death. In particular, when the favoured brothers, James and John, came to Him with a request that they might sit beside Him in His kingdom, He plainly stated this connection between nearness to Him and affliction. "Are ye able," He said, "to drink of the cup that I shall drink of, and to be baptized with the baptism that I am baptized with?" (Mt 20:22). As if He said, "Ye cannot have the sacraments of grace without the painful figures of them. The Cross, when imprinted on your foreheads, will draw blood. You shall receive, indeed, the baptism of the Spirit, and the cup of My communion, but it shall be with the attendant pledges of My cup of agony, and My baptism of blood." Elsewhere He speaks the same language to all who would partake the benefits of His death and passion: "Whosoever doth not bear his cross, and come after Me, cannot be My disciple" (Lk 14:27).

Accordingly, His Apostles frequently remind us of this necessary, though mysterious appointment, and bid us "think it not strange concerning the fiery trial which is to try us, as though some strange thing happened unto us, but to rejoice in having communion with the sufferings of Christ" (1 Pt 4:12, 13). St. Paul teaches us the same lesson in the text, in which he speaks of taking up the remnant of Christ's sorrows, as some precious mantle dropt from the cross, and wearing it for His sake. "I rejoice in my sufferings for you, and fill up in my flesh what remains of the afflictions of Christ for His body's sake, that is, the Church" (see also 2 Cor 4:10). And though he is speaking especially of persecution and other sufferings borne in the cause of the Gospel, yet it is our great privilege, as Scripture tells us, that all pain and trouble, borne in faith and patience, will be accounted as marks of Christ, grace-tokens from the absent Saviour, and will be accepted and rewarded for His sake at the last day. It declares generally, "When thou passest through the waters, I will be with thee; and through the rivers, they shall not overflow thee: when thou walkest through the fire, thou shalt not be burned; neither shall the flame kindle upon thee." "Our light affliction, which is but for a moment, worketh for us a far more exceeding and eternal weight of glory (Is 43:2; 2 Cor 4:17).

Thus the Gospel, which has shed light in so many ways upon the state of this world, has aided especially our view of the *sufferings* to which human nature is subjected; turning a punishment into a privilege, in the case of all pain, and especially of bodily pain, which is the most mysterious of all. Sorrow, anxiety, and disappointment are more or less connected with sin and sinners; but bodily pain is involuntary for the most part, stretching over the world by some external irresistible law, reaching to children who have never actually sinned, and to the brute animals, who are strangers to Adam's nature, while in its manifestations it is far more piteous and distressing than any other suffering. It is the lot of all of us, sooner or later; and that, perhaps in a measure which it would be appalling and wrong to anticipate, whether from disease, or from the casualties of life. And all of us at length must die; and death is generally ushered in by disease, and ends in that separation of soul and body, which itself may, in some cases, involve peculiar pain.

Worldly men put such thoughts aside as gloomy; they can neither deny nor avert the prospect before them; and they are wise, on their own principles, not to embitter the present by anticipating it. But Christians may bear to look at it without undue apprehension; for this very infliction, which most touches the heart and imagination, has (as I have said) been invested by Almighty God with a new and comfortable light, as being the medium of His choicest mercies towards us. Pain is no longer a curse, a necessary evil to be undergone with a dry submission or passive endurance—it may be considered even as a blessing of the Gospel, and being a blessing, admits of being met well or ill. In the way of nature, indeed, it seems to shut out the notion of duty, as if so masterful a discipline from without superseded the necessity or opportunity of self-mastery; but now that "Christ hath suffered in the flesh," we are bound "to arm ourselves with the same mind," and to obey, as He did, amid suffering.

In what follows, I shall remark briefly, first, on the natural effect of pain upon the mind; and next, upon the remedies and correctives of that effect which the knowledge of the Gospel supplies.

1. Now, as to its effect upon the mind, let it be well understood

that it has no sanctifying influence in itself. Bad men are made worse by it. This should be borne in mind, lest we deceive ourselves; for sometimes we speak (at least the poor often so speak) as though present hardship and suffering were in some sense a ground of confidence in themselves as to our future prospects, whether as expiating our sins or bringing our hearts nearer to God. Nay, even the more religious among us may be misled to think that pain makes them better than it really does; for the effect of it at length, on any but very proud or ungovernable tempers, is to cause a languor and composure of mind, which looks like resignation, while it necessarily throws our reason upon the especial *thought* of God, our only stay in such times of trial. Doubtless it does really benefit the Christian, and in no scanty measure; and he may thank God who thus blesses it; only let him be cautious of *measuring* his spiritual state by the particular exercise of faith and love in his heart at the time, especially if that exercise be limited to the affections themselves, and have no opportunity of showing itself in works. St. Paul speaks of chastisement "yielding *afterwards* the peaceable fruit of righteousness" (Heb 12:11), formed indeed and ripened at the moment, but manifested in due season. This may be the real fruit of the suffering of a death-bed, even though it may not have time to show itself to others before the Christian departs hence. Surely we may humbly hope that it perfects habits hitherto but partially formed, and blends the several graces of the Spirit more entirely. Such is the issue of it in *established* Christians;— but it *may* possibly effect nothing so blessed. Nay, in the case of those who have followed Christ with but a half heart, it may be a trial too strong for their feebleness, and may overpower them. This is a dreadful reflection for those who put off the day of repentance. Well does our Church pray for us: "Suffer us not, at our last hour, for any pains of death to fall from Thee!" As for unbelievers, we know how it affects them, from such serious passages of Scripture as the following: "They gnawed their tongues for pain, and blasphemed the God of heaven because of their pains and their sores, and repented not of their deeds (Rv 16:10, 11).

Nay, I would go so far as to say, not only that pain does not commonly improve us, but that without care it has a strong tendency to do our souls harm, viz., by making us selfish; an effect produced, even when it does us good in other ways. Weak health, for instance, instead of opening the heart, often makes a man supremely careful of his bodily ease and well-being. Men find an excuse in their infirmities for some extraordinary attention to their comforts; they consider they may fairly consult, on all occasions, their own convenience rather than that of another. They indulge their wayward wishes, allow themselves in indolence when they really might exert themselves, and think they may be fretful because they are weak. They become querulous, self-willed, fastidious, and egotistical. Bystanders, indeed, should be very cautions of thinking any particular sufferer to be thus minded, because, after all, sick people have a multitude of feelings which they cannot explain to any one else, and are often in the right in those matters in which they appear to others most fanciful or unreasonable. Yet this does not interfere with the correctness of my remark on the whole.

Take another instance under very different circumstances. If bodily suffering can be presented under distinct aspects, it is in the lassitude of a sick-bed and in the hardships of the soldier's life. Yet of the latter we find selfishness almost a proverbial characteristic. Surely the life of soldiers on service is a very school of generosity and self-neglect, if rightly understood, and is used as such by the noble and high-principled; yet here, a low and carnal mind, instead of profiting by its advantages, will yield to the temptation of referring everything that befalls it to its own comfort and profit. To secure its own interests, will become enshrined within it as its main duty, and with the greater plausibility, inasmuch as there is a sense in which it may really be so accounted. Others (it will suggest) must take care of themselves; it is a folly and weakness to think of them; there are but few chances of safety; the many must suffer, some unto death; it is wisdom to struggle for life and comfort, and to dismiss the thought of others. Alas! instances occur, every now and then, in the experience of life, which show that such thoughts and feelings are not peculiar to any one class of men, but are the actuating principles of the multitude. If an alarm of danger be given amid a crowd, the general eagerness for safety leads men to act towards each other with utter unconcern, if not with frantic cruelty. There are stories told of companies of men finding themselves at sea with scanty provisions, and of the shocking deeds which followed, when each was struggling to preserve his own life.

The natural effect, then, of pain and fear, is to individualize us in our own minds, to fix our thoughts on ourselves, to make us selfish. It is through pain, chiefly, that we realize to ourselves even our bodily organs; a frame entirely without painful sensations is (as it were) one whole without parts, and prefigures that future spiritual body which shall be the portion of the Saints. And to this we most approximate in our youth, when we are not sensible that we are compacted of gross terrestrial matter, as advancing years convince us. The young reflect little upon themselves; they gaze around them, and live out of doors, and say they have souls, little understanding their words. "They rejoice in their youth." This, then, is the effect of suffering, that it arrests us: that it puts, as it were, a finger upon us to ascertain for us our own individuality. But it does no more than this; if such a warning does not lead us through the stirrings of our conscience heavenwards, it does but imprison us in ourselves and make us selfish.

2. Here, then, it is that the Gospel finds us; heirs to a visitation, which, sooner or later, comes upon us, turning our thoughts from outward objects, and so tempting us to idolize self, to the dishonour of that God whom we ought to worship, and the neglect of man whom we should love as ourselves. Thus it finds us, and it obviates this danger, not by removing pain, but by giving it new associations. Pain, which by nature leads us only to ourselves, carries on the Christian mind from the thought of self to the contemplation of Christ, His passion, His merits, and His pattern; and, thence, further to that united company of sufferers who follow Him and "are what He is in this world." He is the great Object of our faith; and, while we gaze upon Him, we learn to forget ourselves.

Surely that is not the most fearful and hateful of evils, here below, however trying to the flesh, which Christ underwent voluntarily. No one chooses evil for its own sake, but for the greater good wrought out through it. He underwent it as for ends greater than the immediate removal of it, "not grudgingly or of necessity," but cheerfully doing God's will, as the Gospel history sets before us. When His time was come, we are told, "He steadfastly set His face to go to Jerusalem." His disciples said, "Master, the Jews of late sought to stone Thee, and goest Thou thither again?" but He persisted. Again, He said to Judas, "That thou doest, do quickly." He proceeded to the garden beyond Cedron, though Judas knew the place; and when the band of officers came to seize Him, "He went forth, and said unto them, I am He" (Lk 9:51; Jn 11:8, 13:27, 18:2, 4, 5). And with what calmness and majesty did He bear His sufferings, when they came upon Him, though by His agony in the garden He showed He fully felt their keenness! The Psalmist, in his prediction of them, says, "I am poured out like water, and all my bones are out of joint; my heart is like wax, it is melted" (Ps 22:14); describing, as it would seem, that sinking of spirit and enfeebling of nerve which severe pain causes. Yet, in the midst of distress which seemed to preclude the opportunity of obedience, He was "about His Father's business," even more diligently than when in His childhood He asked questions of the doctors in the Temple; not thinking to be merely passive under the trial, but accounting it as if a great occasion for a noble and severe surrender of Himself to His Father's will. Thus He "learned obedience by the things that He suffered." Consider the deep and serene compassion which led Him to pray for those who crucified Him; His solicitous care of His Mother; and His pardoning words addressed to the robber who suffered with Him. And so, when He said, "It is finished," He showed that He was still contemplating, with a clear intellect, "the travail of His soul, and was satisfied"; and in the solemn surrender of Himself into His Father's hand, He showed where His mind rested in the midst of its darkness. Even when He seemed to be thinking of Himself, and said, "I thirst," He really was regarding the words of prophecy, and was bent on vindicating, to the very letter, the divine announcements concerning Him. Thus, upon the cross itself, we discern in Him the mercy of a Messenger from heaven, the love and grace of a Saviour, the dutifulness of a Son, the faith of a created nature, and the zeal of a servant of God. His mind was stayed upon His Father's sovereign will and infinite perfections, yet could pass, without effort, to the claim of filial duty, or the need of an individual sinner. Six out of His seven last words were words of faith and love. For one instant a horrible dread overwhelmed Him, when He seemed to ask why God had forsaken Him. Doubtless "that voice was for our sakes"; as when He made mention of His thirst; and, like the other, was taken from inspired prophecy. Perhaps it was intended to set before us an example of a special trial to which human nature is subject, whatever was the real and inscrutable manner of it in Him, who was all along supported by an inherent Divinity; I mean the trial of sharp agony, hurrying the mind on to vague terrors and strange inexplicable thoughts; and is, therefore, graciously recorded for our benefit, in the history of His death, "who was tempted, in all points, like as we are, yet without sin (Heb 4:15).

Such, then, were our Lord's sufferings, voluntarily undergone, and ennobled by an active obedience; themselves the centre of our hopes and worship, yet borne without thought of self, towards God and for man. And who, among us, habitually dwells upon them, but is led, without deliberate purpose, by the very warmth of gratitude and adoring love, to attempt bearing his own inferior trials in the same heavenly mind? Who does not see that to bear pain well is to meet it courageously, not to shrink or waver, but to pray for God's help, then to look at it steadfastly, to summon what never we have of mind and body, to receive its attack, and to bear up against it (while strength is given us) as against some visible enemy in close combat? Who will not acknowledge that, when sent to us, we must make its presence (as it were) our own voluntary act, by the cheerful and ready concurrence of our own will with the will of God? Nay, who is there but must own that with Christ's sufferings before us, pain and tribulation are, after all, not only the most blessed, but even the most congruous attendants upon those who are called to inherit the benefit of them? Most congruous, I say, not as though necessary, but as most natural and befitting, harmonizing most fully, with the main Object in the group of sacred wonders on which the Church is called to gaze. Who, on the other hand, does not at least perceive that all the glare and gaudiness of this world, its excitements, its keenly pursued goods, its successes and its transports, its pomps and its luxuries, are not in character with that pale and solemn scene which faith must ever have in its eye? What Christian will not own that to "reign as kings," and to be "full," is not his calling; so as to derive comfort in the hour of sickness, or bereavement, or other affliction, from the thought that he is now in his own place, if he be Christ's, in his true home, the sepulchre in which his Lord was laid? So deeply have His Saints felt this, that when times were peaceful, and the Church was in safety, they could not rest in the lap of ease, and have secured to themselves hardnesses, lest the world should corrupt them. They could not bear to see the much-enduring Paul adding to his necessary tribulations a self-inflicted chastisement of the flesh, and yet allow themselves to live delicately, and fare sumptuously every day. They saw the image of Christ reflected in tears and blood, in the glorious company of the Apostles, the goodly fellowship of the Prophets, and the noble army of Martyrs; they read in prophecy of the doom of the Church, as "a woman fed by God in the wilderness" (see Rv 12:6, 11:3), and her witnesses as "clothed in sackcloth"; and they could not believe that they were meant for nothing more than to enjoy the pleasures of this life, however innocent and moderate might be their use of them. Without deciding about their neighbours, they felt themselves called to higher things; their own sense of the duty became the sanction and witness of it. They considered that God, at least, would afflict them in His love, if they spared themselves ever so much. The thorn in the flesh, the buffetings of Satan, the bereavement of their eyes, these were their portion; and, in common prudence, were there no higher thought, they could not live out of time and measure with these expected visitations. With no superstitious alarms, or cowardly imaginations, or senseless hurrying into difficulty or trial, but calmly and in faith, they surrendered themselves into His hands, who had told them in His inspired word that affliction was to be their familiar food; till at length they gained such distaste for the luxuries of life as to be impatient of them from their very fulness of grace.

Even in these days, when the "fine gold has become dim," such has been the mind of those we most revere.* But such was it especially in primitive times. It was the temper, too, of those Apostles who were removed, more than their brethren, from the world's buffetings; as if the prospect of suffering afterwards were no ground of dispensation for a present self-inflicted discipline, but rather demanded it. St. James the Less was Bishop of Jerusalem, and was highly venerated for his uprightness by the unbelieving Jews among whom he lived unmolested. We are told that he drank no wine nor strong drink, nor did he eat any animal food, nor indulge in the luxury of the bath. "So often was he in the Temple on his knees, that they were thin and hard by his continual supplication."† Thus he kept his "loins girded about, and his lamp burning," for the blessed martyrdom which was to end his course. Could it be otherwise? How could the great Apostle, sitting at home by his Lord's decree, "nourish his heart," as he calls it, "as for the slaughter?" How could he eat, and drink, and live as other men, when "the Ark, and Israel, and Judah were in tents," encamped in the open fields, and one by one, God's chosen warriors were falling before the brief triumph of Satan! How could he be "delicate on the earth, and wanton," when Paul and Barnabas, Peter, too, and John were in stripes and prisons, in labours and perils, in hunger and thirst, in cold and nakedness! Stephen had led the army of Martyrs in Jerusalem itself, which was his own post of service. James, the brother of John, had followed him in the same city; he first of the Apostles tasting our Lord's cup, who had unwittingly asked to drink it. And if this was the feeling of the Apostles, when in temporary safety, why is it not ours, who altogether live at ease, except that we have not faith enough to realize what is past? Could we see the cross upon Calvary, and the list of sufferers who resisted unto blood in the times that followed it, is it possible that we should feel surprise when pain overtook us, or impatience at its continuance? Is it strange though we are smitten by ever so new a plague? Is it grievous that the cross presses

---

* "It is a most miserable state for a man to have everything according to his desire, and quietly to enjoy the pleasures of life. There needs no more to expose him to eternal misery" (Bishop Wilson, *Sacra Privata, Wednesday*).

† *Euseb. Hist.* 2:23.

on one nerve or limb ever so many years till hope of relief is gone? Is it, indeed, not possible with the Apostle to rejoice in "bearing in our body the marks of the Lord Jesus?" And much more, can we, for very shame's sake, suffer ourselves to be troubled at what is but ordinary pain, to be irritated or saddened, made gloomy or anxious by inconveniences which never could surprise or unsettle those who had studied and understood their place as servants of a crucified Lord?

Let us, then, determine with cheerful hearts to sacrifice unto the Lord our God our comforts and pleasures, however innocent, when He calls for them, whether for the purposes of His Church, or in His own inscrutable providence. Let us lend to Him a few short hours of present ease, and we shall receive our own with abundant usury in the day of His coming. There is a Treasury in heaven stored with such offerings as the natural man abhors; with sighs and tears, wounds and blood, torture and death. The Martyrs first began the contribution, and we all may follow them; all of us, for every suffering, great or little, may, like the widow's mite, be sacrificed in faith to Him who sent it. Christ gave us the words of consecration, when He for an ensample said, "Thy will be done." Henceforth, as the Apostle speaks, we may "glory in tribulation," as the seed of future glory.

Meanwhile, let us never forget in all we suffer, that, properly speaking, our own sin is the cause of it, and it is only by Christ's mercy that we are allowed to range ourselves at His side. We who are children of wrath, are made through Him children of grace; and our pains—which are in themselves but foretastes of hell—are changed by the sprinkling of His blood into a preparation for heaven.

SERMON XXIV

Intercession

"Praying always with all prayer and supplication in the Spirit, and watching thereunto with all perseverance and supplication for all saints."—Eph 6:18

Every one knows, who has any knowledge of the Gospel, that Prayer is one of its especial ordinances; but not every one, perhaps, has noticed what kind of prayer its inspired teachers most carefully enjoin. Prayer for self is the most obvious of duties, as soon as leave is given us to pray at all, which Christ distinctly and mercifully accorded, when He came. This is plain from the nature of the case; but He Himself has given us also an express command and promise about ourselves, to "ask and it shall be given to us." Yet it is observable, that though prayer for self is the first and plainest of Christian duties, the Apostles especially insist on another kind of prayer; prayer for others, for ourselves with others, for the Church, and for the world, that it may be brought into the Church. Intercession is the characteristic of Christian worship, the privilege of the heavenly adoption, the exercise of the perfect and spiritual mind. This is the subject to which I shall now direct your attention.

1. First, let us turn to the express injunctions of Scripture. For instance, the text itself: "Praying in every season with all prayer and supplication in the Spirit, and abstaining from sleep for the purpose, with all perseverance and supplication for all saints." Observe the earnestness of the intercession here inculcated; "in every season," "with all supplication," and "to the loss of sleep." Again, in the Epistle to the Colossians; "Persevere in prayer, watching in it with thanksgiving, withal praying for us also." Again, "Brethren, pray for us." And again in detail, "I exhort that, first of all, supplications, prayers, intercessions, and giving of thanks, be made for all men; for kings, and all that are in authority. I will therefore that men pray in every place." On the other hand, go through the Epistles, and reckon up how many exhortations occur therein to pray merely for self. You will find there are few, or rather none at all. Even those which seem at first sight to be such, will

be found really to have in view the good of the Church. Thus, to take the words following the text, St. Paul, in asking his brethren's prayers, seems to pray for himself: but he goes on to explain why—"that he might make known the Gospel": or elsewhere—that "the word of the Lord might have free course and be glorified"; or, as where he says—"Let him that speaketh in an unknown tongue, pray that he may interpret" (Col 4:2; 1 Thes 5:25; 1 Tm 2:1, 2, 8; 2 Thes 3:1; 1 Cor 14:3), for this, too, was a petition in order to the edification of the Church.

Next, consider St. Paul's own example, which is quite in accordance with his exhortations: "I cease not to give thanks for you, making mention of you in my prayers, that the God of our Lord Jesus Christ, the Father of Glory, may give unto you the Spirit of wisdom and revelation in the knowledge of Him." "I thank my God upon every remembrance of you, always in every prayer of mine for you all, making request with joy." "We give thanks to God, the Father of our Lord Jesus Christ, praying always for you." "We give thanks to God always for you all, making mention of you in our prayers" (Eph 1:16, 17; Phil 1:3, 4; Col 1:3; 1 Thes 1:2).

The instances of prayer, recorded in the book of Acts, are of the same kind, being almost entirely of an intercessory nature, as offered at ordinations, confirmations, cures, missions, and the like. For instance, "As they interceded before the Lord, and fasted, the Holy Ghost said, Separate Me Barnabas and Saul for the work whereunto I have called them; and when they had fasted and prayed, and laid their hands on them, they sent them away." Again, "And Peter put them all forth, and kneeled down, and prayed: and turning him to the body, said, Tabitha, arise" (Acts 13:2, 3; 9:40).

2. Such is the lesson taught us by the words and deeds of the Apostles and their brethren. Nor could it be otherwise, if Christianity be a social religion, as it is pre-eminently. If Christians are to live together, they will pray together; and united prayer is necessarily of an intercessory character, as being offered for each other and for the whole, and for self as one of the whole. In proportion, then, as unity is an especial Gospel-duty, so does Gospel-prayer partake of a social character; and Intercession becomes a token of the existence of a Church Catholic.

Accordingly, the foregoing instances of intercessory prayer are supplied by *Christians*. On the other hand, contrast with these the recorded instances of prayer in men who were *not* Christians, and you will find they are not intercessory. For instance: St. Peter's prayer on the house-top was, we know, answered by the revelation of the call of the

Gentiles: viewing it then by the light of the texts already quoted, we may conclude, that, as was the answer, such was the prayer—that it had reference to others. On the other hand, Cornelius, not yet a Christian, was also rewarded with an answer to his prayer. "Thy prayer is heard; call for Simon, whose surname is Peter; *he shall tell thee what thou oughtest to do.*" Can we doubt, from these words of the Angel, that his prayers had been offered for himself especially? Again, on St. Paul's conversion, we are told, "Behold, he prayeth." It is plain he was praying for himself; and observe, it was before he was a Christian. Thus, if we are to judge of the relative prominence of religious duties by the recorded instances of the performance of them, we should say that Intercession is the kind of prayer distinguishing a Christian from such as are not Christians.

3. But the instance of St. Paul opens upon us a second reason for this distinction. Intercession is the especial observance of the Christian, because he alone is in a condition to offer it. It is the function of the justified and obedient, of the sons of God, "who walk not after the flesh but after the spirit"; not of the carnal and unregenerate. This is plain even to natural reason. The blind man, who was cured, said of Christ, "We know that God heareth not sinners; but, if any man *be a worshiper of God and doeth His will,* him He heareth (Jn 9:31). Saul the persecutor obviously could not intercede like St. Paul the Apostle. He had yet to be baptized and forgiven. It would be a presumption and an extravagance in a penitent, before his regeneration, to do aught but confess his sins and deprecate wrath. He has not yet proceeded, he has had no leave to proceed, out of himself; and has enough to do within. His conscience weighs heavy on him, nor has he "the wings of a dove to flee away and be at rest." We need not, I say, go to Scripture for information on so plain a point. Our first prayers ever must be for ourselves. Our own salvation is our personal concern; till we labour to secure it, till we try to live religiously, and pray to be enabled to do so, nay, and have made progress, it is but hypocrisy, or at best it is overbold, to busy ourselves with others. I do not mean that prayer for self always comes first in order of time, and Intercession second. Blessed be God, we were all made His children before we had actually sinned; we began life in purity and innocence. Intercession is never more appropriate than when sin had been utterly abolished, and the heart was most affectionate and least selfish. Nor would I deny, that a care for the souls of other men may be the first symptom of a man's beginning to think about his own; or that persons, who are conscious to themselves of much guilt, often pray for those whom they revere and love, when under the influence of fear, or

in agony, or other strong emotion, and, perhaps, at other times. Still it is true, that there is something incongruous and inconsistent in a man's presuming to intercede, who is an habitual and deliberate sinner. Also it is true, that most men do, more or less, fall away from God, sully their baptismal robe, need the grace of repentance, and have to be awakened to the necessity of prayer for self, as the first step in observing prayer of any kind.

"God heareth not sinners"; nature tells us this; but none but God Himself could tell us that He will hear and answer those who are not sinners; for "when we have done all, we are unprofitable servants, and can claim no reward for our services." But He has graciously promised us this mercy, in Scripture, as the following texts will show.

For instance, St. James says, "The effectual fervent prayer of a *righteous* man availeth much." St. John, "Whatsoever we ask, we receive of Him, *because we keep* His commandments, and do those things that are pleasing in His sight" (Jas 5:16; 1 Jn 3:22). Next let us weigh carefully our Lord's solemn announcements uttered shortly before His crucifixion, and, though addressed primarily to His Apostles, yet, surely, in their degree belonging to all who "believe on Him through their word." We shall find that consistent obedience, mature, habitual, lifelong holiness, is therein made the condition of His intimate favour, and of power in Intercession. "If ye abide in Me," He says, "and My words abide in you, ye shall ask what ye will, and it shall be done unto you. Herein is my Father glorified, that ye bear much fruit; so shall ye be My disciples. As the Father hath loved Me, so have I loved you; abide ye in My love. If ye keep my commandments, ye shall abide in My love. Ye are My friends, if ye do whatsoever I command you. Henceforth I call you not servants; for the servant knoweth not what his lord doeth; but I have called you friends, for all that I have heard of My Father, I have made known unto you" (Jn 15:7–15). From this solemn grant of the peculiarly Gospel privilege of being the "friends" of Christ, it is certain, that as the prayer of repentance gains for us sinners Baptism and justification, so our higher gift of having power with Him and prevailing, depends on our "adding to our faith virtue."

Let us turn to the examples given us of holy men under former dispensations, whose obedience and privileges were anticipations of the evangelical. St. James, after the passage already cited from his Epistle, speaks of Elijah thus: "Elias was a man subject to like passions as we are, yet he prayed earnestly that it might not rain, and it rained not on the earth by the space of three years and six months." Righteous Job was appointed by Almighty God to be the effectual intercessor for his erring friends. Moses, who was "faithful in all the house" of God, affords us another eminent instance of intercessory power; as in the Mount, and on other occasions, when he pleaded for his rebellious people, or in the battle with Amalek, when Israel continued conquering as long as his hands remained lifted up in prayer. Here we have a striking emblem of that continued, earnest, unwearied prayer of men "lifting up *holy* hands," which, under the Gospel, prevails with Almighty God. Again, in the book of Jeremiah, Moses and Samuel are spoken of as mediators so powerful, that only the sins of the Jews were too great for the success of their prayers. In like manner it is implied, in the book of Ezekiel, that three such as Noah, Daniel, and Job, would suffice, in some cases, to save guilty nations from judgment. Sodom might have been rescued by ten. Abraham, though he could not save the abandoned city just mentioned, yet was able to save Lot from the overthrow; as at another time he interceded successfully for Abimelech. The very intimation given him of God's purpose towards Sodom was of course an especial honour, and marked him as the friend of God. "Shall I hide from Abraham that thing which I do, seeing that Abraham shall surely become a great and mighty nation; and all the nations of the world shall be blessed in him?" The reason follows, "*for I know him*, that he will command his children and his household after him, and they shall keep the way of the Lord to do justice and judgment, that the Lord may bring upon Abraham that which He hath spoken of him" (Gn 18:17–19).

4. The history of God's dealings with Abraham will afford us an additional lesson, which must be ever borne in mind in speaking of the privilege of the saints on earth as intercessors between God and man. I can fancy a person, from apprehension lest the belief in it should interfere with the true reception of the doctrine of the cross, perplexed at finding it in the foregoing texts so distinctly connected with obedience: I say *perplexed*, for I will not contemplate the case of those, though there are such, who, when the text of Scripture seems to them to be at variance with itself, and one portion to diverge from another, will not allow themselves to be perplexed, will not suspend their minds and humbly wait for light, will not believe that the Divine Scheme is larger and deeper than their own capacities, but boldly wrest into a factitious agreement what is already harmonious in God's infinite counsels, though not to them. I speak to perplexed persons; and would have them observe that Almighty God has, in this very instance of Abraham our spiritual father, been mindful of that other aspect under which the most

highly exalted among the children of flesh must ever stand in His presence. It is elsewhere said of him, "Abraham *believed* in the Lord, and He counted it to Him for righteousness" (Gn 15:6), as St. Paul points out, when he is discoursing upon the free grace of God in our redemption. Even Abraham was justified by faith, though he was perfected by works; and this being told us in the book of Genesis, seems as if an intimation to the perplexed inquirer that his difficulty can be but an apparent one—that, while God reveals the one doctrine, He is not the less careful of the other also, nor rewards His servants (though He rewards them) for works done by their own strength. On the other hand, it is a caution to us, who rightly insist on the prerogatives imparted by his grace, ever to remember that it is grace only that ennobles and exalts us in His sight. Abraham is our spiritual father; and as he is, so are his children. In us, as in him, faith must be the foundation of all that is acceptable with God. "By faith we stand," by faith we are justified, by faith we obey, by faith our works are sanctified. Faith applies to us again and again the grace of our Baptism; faith opens upon us the virtue of all other ordinances of the Gospel—of the Holy Communion, which is the highest. By faith we prevail "in the hour of death and in the day of judgment." And the distinctness and force with which this is told us in the Epistles, and its obviousness, even to our natural reason, may be the cause why less stress is laid in them on the duty of prayer for self. The very instinct of faith will lead a man to do this without set command, and the Sacraments secure its observance.—So much then, by way of caution, on the influence of faith upon our salvation, furthering it, yet not interfering with the distinct office of works in giving virtue to our Intercession.

And here let me observe on a peculiarity of Scripture, its speaking as if separate rewards attended on separate graces, according to our Lord's words, "To him that hath more shall be given"; so that what has been said in contrasting faith and works, is but one instance under a general rule. Thus, in the Sermon on the Mount, the beatitudes are pronounced on separate virtues respectively. "Blessed are the meek, for they shall inherit the earth"; "Blessed are the pure in heart, for they shall see God"; and the rest in like manner. I am not attempting to determine what these particular graces are, what the rewards, what the aptitude of the one to the other, what the real connection between the reward and the grace, or how far one grace can be separated from another in fact. We know that all depend on one root, faith, and are but differently developed in different persons. Again, we see in Scripture that the same reward is not invariably assigned to the same grace, as if, from the intimate union between all graces, their rewards might (as it were) be lent and interchanged one with another; yet enough is said there to direct our minds to the existence of the principle itself, though we be unable to fathom its meaning and consequences. It is somewhat upon this principle that our Articles ascribe justification to faith *only,* as a symbol of the free grace of our redemption; just as in the parable of the Pharisee and Publican, our Lord would seem to impute it to self-abasement, and in His words to the "woman which was a sinner," to love as well as to faith, while St. James connects it with works. In other instances the reward follows in the course of nature. Thus the gift of wisdom is the ordinary result of trial borne religiously; courage, of endurance. In this way St. Paul draws out a series of spiritual gifts one from another, experience from patience, hope from experience, boldness and confidence from hope. I will add but two instances from the Old Testament. The commandment says, "Honour thy father and thy mother, that thy days may be long"; a promise which was signally fulfilled in the case even of the Rechabites, who were not of Israel. Again, from Daniel's history we learn that illumination, or other miraculous power, is the reward of fasting and prayer. "In those days I, Daniel, was mourning three full weeks. I ate no pleasant bread, neither came flesh nor wine in my mouth, neither did I anoint myself at all, till three whole weeks were fulfilled. . . . And he said unto me, Fear not, Daniel; for from the first day that thou didst set thine heart *to understand and to chasten thyself before thy God,* thy words were heard, and I am come for thy words. . . . Now I am come to make thee understand what shall befall thy people in the latter days." With this passage compare St. Peter's vision about the Gentiles while he prayed and fasted; and, again, our Lord's words about casting out the "dumb and deaf spirit,"—"This kind can come forth by nothing but by prayer and fasting" (Ex 20:12; Jer 35:18, 19; Dn 10:2–14; Mk 9:29). It is then by a similar appointment that Intercession is the prerogative and gift of the obedient and holy.

5. Why should we be unwilling to admit what it is so great a consolation to know? Why should we refuse to credit the transforming power and efficacy of our Lord's Sacrifice? Surely He did not die for any common end, but in order to exalt man, who was of the dust of the field, into "heavenly places." He did not die to leave him as he was, sinful, ignorant, and miserable. He did not die to see His purchased possession, as feeble in good works, as corrupt, as poor-spirited, and as desponding as before He came. Rather, He died to renew him after His own image, to make him a being He might delight and rejoice in, to make him "par-

taker of the divine nature," to fill him within and without with a flood of grace and glory, to pour out upon him gift upon gift, and virtue upon virtue, and power upon power, each acting upon each, and working together one and all, till he becomes an angel upon earth, instead of a rebel and an outcast. He died to bestow upon him that privilege which implies or involves all others, and brings him into nearest resemblance to Himself, the privilege of Intercession. This, I say, is the Christian's especial prerogative; and if he does not exercise it, certainly he has not risen to the conception of his real place among created beings. Say not he is a son of Adam, and has to undergo a future judgment; I know it; but he is something besides. How far he is advanced into that higher state of being, how far he still languishes in his first condition, is, in the case of individuals, a secret with God. Still every Christian is in a certain sense both in the one and in the other: viewed in himself he ever prays for pardon, and confesses sin; but viewed in Christ, he "has access into this grace wherein we stand, and rejoices in hope of the glory of God" (Rom 5:2). Viewed in his place in "the Church of the First-born enrolled in heaven," with his original debt cancelled in Baptism, and all subsequent penalties put aside by Absolution, standing in God's presence upright and irreprovable, accepted in the Beloved, clad in the garments of righteousness, anointed with oil, and with a crown upon his head, in royal and priestly garb, as an heir of eternity, full of grace and good works, as walking in all the commandments of the Lord blameless, such an one, I repeat it, is plainly in his fitting place when he intercedes. He is made after the pattern and in the fulness of Christ—he is what Christ is. Christ intercedes above, and he intercedes below. Why should he linger in the doorway, praying for pardon, who has been allowed to share in the grace of the Lord's passion, to die with Him and rise again? He is already in a capacity for higher things. His prayer thenceforth takes a higher range, and contemplates not himself merely, but others also. He is taken into the confidence and counsels of his Lord and Saviour. He reads in Scripture what the many cannot see there, the course of His providence, and the rules of His government in this world. He views the events of history with a divinely enlightened eye. He sees that a great contest is going on among us between good and evil. He recognizes in statesmen, and warriors, and kings, and people, in revolutions and changes, in trouble and prosperity, not merely casual matters, but instruments and tokens of heaven and of hell. Thus he is in some sense a prophet; not a servant, who obeys without knowing his Lord's plans and purposes, but even a confidential "familiar friend" of the Only-begotten

Son of God, calm, collected, prepared, resolved, serene, amid this restless and unhappy world. O mystery of blessedness, too great to think of steadily, lest we grow dizzy! Well is it for those who are so gifted, that they do not for certain know their privilege; well is it for them that they can but timidly guess at it, or rather, I should say, are used, as well as bound, to contemplate it as external to themselves, lodged in the Church of which they are but members, and the gift of all Saints in every time and place, without curiously inquiring whether it is theirs peculiarly above others, or doing more than availing themselves of it as any how a trust committed to them (with whatever success) to use. Well is it for them; for what mortal heart could bear to know that it is brought so near to God Incarnate, as to be one of those who are perfecting holiness, and stand on the very steps of the throne of Christ?

To conclude. If any one asks, "How am I to know whether I am advanced enough in holiness to intercede?" he has plainly mistaken the doctrine under consideration. The privilege of Intercession is a trust committed to all Christians who have a clear conscience and are in full communion with the Church. We leave secret things to God—what each man's real advancement is in holy things, and what his real power in the unseen world. Two things alone concern us, to exercise our gift and make ourselves more and more worthy of it. The slothful and unprofitable servant hid his Lord's talent in a napkin. This sin be far from us as regards one of the greatest of our gifts! By words and works we can but teach or influence a few; by our prayers we may benefit the whole world, and every individual of it, high and low, friend, stranger, and enemy. Is it not fearful then to look back on our past lives even in this one respect? How can we tell but that our king, our country, our Church, our institutions, and our own respective circles, would be in far happier circumstances than they are, had we been in the practice of more earnest and serious prayer for them? How can we complain of difficulties, national or personal, how can we justly blame and denounce evil-minded and powerful men, if we have but lightly used the intercessions offered up in the Litany, the Psalms, and in the Holy Communion? How can we answer to ourselves for the souls who have, in our time, lived and died in sin; the souls that have been lost and are now waiting for judgment, the infidel, the blasphemer, the profligate, the covetous, the extortioner; or those again who have died with but doubtful signs of faith, the death-bed penitent, the worldly, the double-minded, the ambitious, the unruly, the trifling, the self-willed, seeing that, for what we know, we were ordained to influence or reverse their present destiny and have not done it?

Secondly and lastly, If so much depend on us, "What manner of persons ought we to be, in all holy conversation and godliness!" Oh, that we may henceforth be more diligent than heretofore, in keeping the mirror of our hearts unsullied and bright, so as to reflect the image of the Son of God in the Father's presence, clean from the dust and stains of this world, from envies and jealousies, strife and debate, bitterness and harshness, indolence and impurity, care and discontent, deceit and meanness, arrogance and boasting! Oh, that we may labour, not in our own strength, but in the power of God the Holy Spirit, to be sober, chaste, temperate, meek, affectionate, good, faithful, firm, humble, patient, cheerful, resigned, under all circumstances, at all times, among all people, amid all trials and sorrows of this mortal life! May God grant us the power, according to His promise, through His Son our Saviour Jesus Christ!

Volume IV

SERMON I

The Strictness of the Law of Christ

"Being then made free from sin, ye became the servants of righteousness."—Rom 6:18

In the passage of which these words form a part, St. Paul insists again and again on the great truth which they declare, that Christians are not their own, but bought with a price, and, as being so, are become the servants or rather the slaves of God and His righteousness; and this, upon their being rescued from the state of nature. The great Apostle is not content with speaking half the truth; he does not merely say that we are set free from guilt and misery, but he adds, that we have become the servants of Christ; nay, he uses a word which properly means *slaves*. Slaves are bought and sold; we were by nature slaves to sin and Satan; we are bought by the blood of Christ; we do not cease to be slaves. We no longer indeed belong to our old master; but a master we have, unless slaves on being bought become freemen. We are still slaves, but to a new master, and that master is Christ. He has not bought us, and then set us loose upon the world; but He has done for us what alone could complete His first benefit, bought us to be His servants or slaves. He has given us that only liberty which is really such, bond-service to Himself; lest if left to ourselves, we should fall back again, as we certainly should, to the cruel bondage from which He redeemed us. But anyhow, whatever be the consequences it involves, whatever the advantage, whatever the trial, we did not cease to be slaves on being set free from Satan; but we became subject to a new Master, to Him who bought us.

This needs insisting on; for a number of persons who are not unwilling to confess that they are slaves by nature, from some cause or other have learned to think that they are not bound to any real service at all, now that Christ has set them free. Now if by the word *slavery*, some cruel and miserable state of suffering is meant, such as human masters often inflict on their slaves, in that sense indeed Christians are not slaves, and the word is improper to apply to them; but if by being slaves, is meant that we cannot throw up our service, change our place, and do as we will, in that sense it is literally true, that we are more than servants to Christ, we are, as the text really words it, slaves. Men often speak as if the perfection of human happiness lay in our being free to do or not to do, to choose and to reject. Now we are indeed thus free, as far as this,—that if we do not choose to be Christ's servants, we can go back to that old bondage from which He rescued us, and be slaves again to the powers of evil. But though we are free to make our situation worse, we are not free to be without service or post of any kind. It is not in man's nature to be out of all service and to be self-dependent. We may choose our master, but God or mammon we must serve. We cannot possibly be in a neutral or intermediate state. Such a state does not exist. If we will not be Christ's servants, we are forthwith Satan's; and Christ set us free from Satan only by making us His servants. Satan's kingdom touches upon Christ's, the world touches on the Church; and we cease to be Satan's property by becoming Christ's. We cannot be without a master, such is the law of our nature; yet a number of persons, as I have said, overlook it, and think their Christian liberty lies in being free from all law, even from the law of God. Such an error seems to have obtained even in St. Paul's time, and is noticed in the chapter before us. Men seem to have thought that, since the law of sin was annulled, and the terrors of the law of nature removed, that therefore they were under no law at all; that their own will was their law, and that faith stood instead of obedience. In opposition to this great mistake, St. Paul reminds his brethren in the text, that when they were "made free from *sin*," they "became the servants of *righteousness*." And again, "Sin shall not have dominion over you; for ye are not under the law," that is, the law of nature, "but under grace," or (as he elsewhere expresses it), "the law of faith," or, "the law of the Spirit of life." They were not without a master, but they had a gracious and bountiful one.

He says the same in other Epistles. For instance, "He that is called, being free" (that is, free as regards this world), "is Christ's servant" or slave. "Ye are bought with a price: be not ye slaves of *men*," but, that is, be slaves of Christ. Again, after saying, "Slaves obey in all things your masters according to the flesh," he adds, "for ye are slaves to the Lord Christ." Elsewhere he speaks of himself as "Paul a servant," or slave, as the word really means, "of Jesus Christ"; and again, as "not without law to God, but under the law to Christ" (1 Cor 7:22, 23; Col 3:22, 24; Rom 1:1; 1 Cor 9:21).

Religion then is a necessary service; of course it is a privilege too, but it becomes more and more of a privilege, the more we exercise ourselves in it. The perfect Christian state is that in which our duty and our pleasure are the same, when what is right and true is natural to us, and in which God's "service is perfect freedom." And this is the state towards which all true Christians are tending; it is the state in which the Angels stand; entire subjection to God in thought and deed is their happiness; an utter and absolute captivity of their will to His will, is their fulness of joy and everlasting life. But it is not so with the best of us, except in part. Upon our regeneration indeed, we have a seed of truth and holiness planted within us, a new law introduced into our nature; but still we have that old nature to subdue, "the old man, which is corrupt according to the deceitful lusts" (Eph 4:22). That is, we have a work, a conflict all through life. We have to master and bring under all we are, all we do, expelling all disorder and insubordination, and teaching and impressing on every part of us, of soul and body, its due place and duty, till we are wholly Christ's in will, affections, and reason, as we are by profession; in St. Paul's words, "casting down imaginations and every high thing that exalteth itself against the knowledge of God, and bringing into captivity every thought to the obedience of Christ" (2 Cor 10:5).

Now I may seem to have been saying what every one will at once confess. And yet, after all, nothing perhaps is so rare among those who profess to be Christians, as an assent in practice to the doctrine that they are under a law; nothing so rare as strict obedience, unreserved submission to God's will, uniform conscientiousness in doing their duty,—as a few instances will at once show.

Most Christians then will allow in general terms that they are under a law, but then they admit it with a reserve; they claim for themselves some dispensing power in their observance of the law. What I am saying is quite independent of the question, what is the *standard* of obedience which each man proposes to himself? One man puts the line of his duty higher than another; some men take a low view of it, confining it to mere personal morality; others confine it to their social obligations; others limit it by some conventional law, which is received in particular classes or circles; others include religious observances. But whether men view the law of conscience as high or low, as broad or narrow, few indeed there are who make it a rule to themselves; few there are who make their own notion of it, whatever that be, binding on themselves; few who even profess to act up to it uniformly and consistently. Inquire of the multitude of men, as you meet them in the world, and you will find that one and all think it allowable at times to put themselves above the law, even according to their own standard of it; to make exceptions and reserves, as if they were absolute sovereigns of their conscience, and had a dispensing power upon occasions.

What is the sort of man whom the world accounts respectable and religious, in a high rank or a lower? At best he is such as this. He has a number of good points in his character; but some of these he has by nature, and if others have been acquired by trouble, it is either because outward circumstances compelled him to acquire them, or that he has from nature some active principle within him, of one kind or another, which has exerted itself, and brought other principles under, and rules him. He has acquired a certain self-command, because no one is respected without it. He has been forced into habits of diligence, punctuality, precision, and honesty. He is courteous and obliging; and has learned not to say all he thinks and feels, or to do all he wishes to do, on all occasions. The great mass of men of course are far from having in them so much that is really praise-worthy as this; but I am supposing the best. I am supposing then, that a man's character and station are such, that only now and then he will feel his inclinations or his interest to run counter to his duty. Such times constitute his trial; there is nothing to hinder him serving God in the ordinary course, but the proof of his sincerity lies in his conduct on these extraordinary occasions. Now this is the point to which I wish to draw attention; for these very occasions, which alone are his times of trial, are just the times on which he is apt to consider that he has a leave to dispense with the law. He dispenses with it at those very times when it is simply the law of God, without being also the law of self, and of the world. He does what is right, while the road of religion runs along the road of the world; when they part company awhile, he chooses the world, and calls his choice an exception. He does right for ninety-nine days, but on the hundredth he knowingly and wilfully does wrong; and if he does not justify, at least he absolves himself in doing it.

For instance; he *generally* comes to church, it is his *practice;* but some urgent business at a certain time presses on him, or some scheme of pleasure tempts him:—he omits his attendance; he knows this is wrong, and says so, but it is only once in a way.

Again; he is strictly honest in his dealings; he speaks the truth, that is, it is his rule to do so; but if hard pressed, he allows himself now and then in a falsehood, particularly if it is a slight one. He knows he should not lie; he confesses it; but he thinks it cannot be helped; it is unavoidable from circumstances, as being his only way of escaping some great difficulty. In *such* a case it is, as he says, all fair, and so he gets over it; that is, in a case where he must either disobey God, or incur some temporal disadvantage.

Again; he has learned to curb his temper and his tongue; but on some unusual provocation they get the better of him. He becomes angry, says what he should not, perhaps curses and swears. Are not all men subject to be overtaken with anger or ill temper? That is not the point: The point is this,—that he does not feel compunction afterwards, he does not feel he has done any thing which needs forgiveness. On the contrary, he defends himself to himself, on the plea that such language is very *unusual* with him; he does not understand that he is under a law, which he may not put himself above, which he may not dispense with.

Once more; he is in general sober and temperate; but he joins a party of friends and makes merry; he is tempted to exceed. Next day he says that it is a long time since such a thing happened to him; it is not at all his way; he hardly touches wine or the like in common. He does not understand he has any sin to repent of, because it is but once in a way.

And now, I suppose, you quite understand what I mean, and I need not say more in explanation. Such men, being thus indulgent to themselves, are indulgent to each other; they make allowance for all around them, as taking what they give freely. This is the secret of being friends with the world, to have a sympathy and a share in its sins. They who are strict with themselves are strict with the world; but where men grant themselves a certain licence of disobedience, they do not draw the line very rigidly as regards others. Conscious of what might be said against themselves, they are cautious what they say against others; and they meet them on the understanding of a mutual sufferance. They learn to say, that the private habits of their neighbours are nothing to them; and they hold intercourse with them only as public men, or members of society, or in the way of business, not at all as with responsible beings having immortal souls. They desire to see and know nothing but what is on the surface; and they call a man's personal history sacred, because it is sinful. In their eyes, their sole duty to their neighbour is, not to offend him; whatever his morals, whatever his creed, is nothing to them. Such are they in mature and advanced life; in youth, they are pliable as well as indulgent, they readily fall in with the ways of the world, as they come across them. They are, and have the praise of being, pleasant, good-tempered, and companionable. They are not bad-principled, or evilly disposed, or flagrantly irregular, but they are lax. They in no sense live by rule. They have high spirits, and all the natural amiableness which youth has to show, and they generally go right; but, since they have no root in themselves, an accident from within or without, the stirring of a passion, or the incitement of a friend, makes them swerve at once. They swerve, and they have little compunction afterwards; they forget it. They shrink from the notion of being under a law, and think religion gloomy as imposing it. They like their own way, and without any great extreme of sin, or at least any habits of sin, follow it. They are orderly and well-conducted, when among well-conducted people,—at home, for instance; but they indulge themselves abroad, when temptation comes in their way. They have the world at will; they are free; alas! what a melancholy freedom! yet in one sense a freedom it is. A religious man must withdraw his eyes from sights which inflame his heart, recollecting our Saviour's caution; but a man of the world thinks it no harm to gaze where he should not, because he goes no further. A religious man watches his words; but the other utters whatever his heart prompts, and excuses himself for profane language, on the plea that he means nothing by it. A religious man will scruple about his society; but the other takes part in jests and excesses, though he condemns while he shares them, but not himself for sharing, and despises those with whom he shares them. He can see life, as it is called. He can go among all sorts of people, for he has no troublesome ceremonial, no rule of religion to shackle him. Perhaps he goes abroad, and then for a time he considers himself to be in disguise, as an unknown person in unknown countries, permitted to fall in with all things bad and good, as they come. Or again, he may be so circumstanced, whatever his station, as to find himself engaged in what are called politics; and then he thinks that though truth and religion are certainly all-commanding and all-important, yet still the world could not go on, public business would be at a stand, political parties would be unable to act, all that he really loves and reveres would become but of secondary concern, if religion refused at all times to give way ever so little. Again; a religious man carries his religion into his conduct throughout the day; but lax persons will do many things in private, which they would not like to be known. They will overreach, if they can do it without noise. They will break promises when made to an inferior. Or, if they have time on their hands, they will be curious and meddlesome; they will speak against others and spread scandals. They will pry into things which do not concern them, according to their station in life. They will listen where they have no right to listen; they will read what they have no right to read. Or they will allow themselves in petty thefts, where they think they do no injury, excusing themselves on the plea that what they take will never be missed. Or in matters of trade, they think a certain sort and degree of double-dealing allowable, and no dishonesty. They argue with themselves as if it were not their business to be true and just, but of others to find them out; and as if fraud and cheating did not imply sin in the one party, but dulness in the other. If in humble life, they think it no harm to put on an appearance; to profess what is not strictly true, if they are to gain by it; to colour a story; or to affect to be more religious than they are; or to pretend to agree in religion with persons from whom they hope something; or to take up a religion if it is their interest to do so; or to profess two or three religions at once, when any alms or other benefit is to be given away.

These are a few out of a multitude of traits which mark an easy religion,—the religion of the world; which would cast in its lot with Christian truth, were not that truth so very strict, and quarrels with it and its upholders, not as if it were not good and right, but because it is so unbending,—because it will not suit itself to times and emergencies, and to the private and occasional likings and tastes of individuals. This is the kind of religion which St. Paul virtually warns us against, as often as he speaks of the Gospel as really being a law and a servitude. He indeed glories in its being such; for, as the happiness of all creatures lies in their performing their parts well, where God has placed them, so man's greatest good lies in obedience to God's law and in imitation of God's perfections. But the Apostle knew that the world would not think so, and therefore he insists on it. Therefore it is that he insists on the necessity of Christians "*fulfilling* the righteousness of the law"; fulfilling it, because till we aim at complete, unreserved obedience in all things, we are not really Christians at all. Hence St. James says, "Whosoever shall keep the whole law, and yet offend in one point, he is guilty of all." And our Saviour assures us that "Whosoever shall break one of these least commandments, and shall teach men so, he shall be called least in the kingdom of heaven"; and that "Except our righteousness shall exceed the righteousness of the Scribes and Pharisees," which was thus partial and circumscribed, "we shall in no case enter into the kingdom of heaven." And when the young man came to Him, saying that he had kept all the commandments, and asking what he lacked, He pointed out the "one thing" wanting in him; and when he would not complete his obedience by that one thing, but went away sorrowful, then, as if all his obedience in other points availed him nothing, Christ added, "Children, how hard is it for them that trust in riches to enter into the Kingdom of God?" (Rom 8:1-4; Jas 2:10; Mt 5:19, 20; Mk 10:21, 24). Let us not then deceive ourselves; what God demands of us is to fulfil His law, or at least to aim at fulfilling it; to be content with nothing short of perfect obedience,—to attempt every thing,—to avail ourselves of the aids given us, and throw ourselves, not first, but afterwards on God's mercy for our short-comings. This is, I know, at first hearing a startling doctrine; and so averse are our hearts to it, that some men even attempt to maintain that it is an unchristian doctrine. A forlorn expedient indeed, with the Bible to refer to, and its statements about the strait gate and the narrow way. Still men would fain avail themselves of it, if they could; they argue that all enforcement of religion as a service or duty is erroneous, or what they call legal, and that no observance is right but what proceeds from impulse, or what they call the heart. They would fain prove that the law is not binding on us, because Christ has fulfilled it; or because, as is the case, faith would be accepted instead of obedience in those who had not yet had time to begin fulfilling it.

Such persons appeal to Scripture, and they must be refuted, as is not difficult, from Scripture; but the multitude of men do not take so much trouble about the matter. Instead of even professing to discover what God has said, they take what they call a common-sense view of it. They maintain it is impossible that religion should really be so strict according to God's design. They condemn the notion as over-strained and morose. They profess to admire and take pleasure in religion as a whole, but think that it should not be needlessly pressed in details, or, as they express it, carried too far. They complain only of its particularity, if I may use the term, or its want of indulgence and consideration in little things; that is, in other words, they like religion before they have experience of it,—in prospect,—at a distance,—*till* they have to be religious. They like to talk of it, they like to see men religious; they think it commendable and highly important; but directly religion comes home to them in real particulars of whatever kind, they like it not. It suffices them to have seen and praised it; they feel it a burden whenever they feel it at all, whenever it calls upon them to do what otherwise they would not do. In a word, the state of the multitude of men is this,—their hearts are going the wrong way; and their real quarrel with religion, if they know themselves, is not that it is strict, or engrossing, or imperative, not that it goes too far, but that it *is* religion. It is religion itself which we all by nature dislike, not the excess merely.

Nature tends towards the earth, and God is in heaven. If I want to travel north, and all the roads are cut to the east, of course I shall complain of the roads. I shall find nothing but obstacles; I shall have to surmount walls, and cross rivers, and go round about, and after all fail of my end. Such is the conduct of those who are not bold enough to give up a profession of religion, yet wish to serve the world. They try to reach Babylon by roads which run to Mount Sion. Do you not see that they necessarily must meet with thwartings, crossings, disappointments, and failure? They go mile after mile, watching in vain for the turrets of the city of Vanity, because they are on the wrong road; and, unwilling to own what they are really seeking, they find fault with the road as circuitous and wearisome. They accuse religion of interfering with what they consider their innocent pleasures and wishes. But religion is a bondage only to those who have not the heart to like it, who are not cast into its mould. Accordingly, in the verse before the text, St. Paul thanks God that his brethren had "obeyed from the *heart* that *form* of teaching, into which they had been delivered." We Christians are cast into a certain mould. So far as we keep within it, we are not sensible that it is a mould, or has an outline. It is when our hearts would overflow in some evil direction, then we discover that we are confined, and consider ourselves in prison. It is the law in our members warring against the law of the Spirit which brings us into a distressing bondage. Let us then see where we stand, and what we must do. Heaven cannot change; God is "without variableness or shadow of turning." His "word endureth for ever in heaven." His law is from everlasting to everlasting. *We* must change. We must go over to the side of heaven. Never had a soul true happiness but in conformity to God, in obedience to His will. We must become what we are not; we must learn to love what we do not love, and practise ourselves in what is difficult. We must have the law of the Spirit of life written and set up in our hearts, "that the righteousness of the law may be fulfilled in us," and that we may learn to please and to love God.

    Lastly, as some men defend their want of strictness on what they consider the authority of Scripture, and others, that is, the majority, try to persuade themselves that religion cannot really be strict, whatever strong expressions or statements may be found in Scripture, others again there are, who take a more candid, but a more daring course. Instead of making excuses, such as I have been considering, they frankly admit the fact, and then go on to urge it as a valid argument against religion altogether. Instead of professing to like religion, *all but* its service, they boldly object that religion is altogether unnatural, and therefore cannot be incumbent on us. They say that it is very well for its ministers and teachers to set up a high doctrine, but that men are men, and the world is the world, and that life was not meant to be a burden, and that God sent us here for enjoyment, and that He will never punish us hereafter for following the law of our nature. I answer, doubtless this life was meant to be enjoyment; but why not a rejoicing in the Lord? We were meant to follow the law of our nature; but why of our old nature, why not of our new? Were we indeed in the state of our first nature, under the guilt and defilement of our birth-sin, then this argument might be urged speciously, though not conclusively of course then; but how does it apply to Christians? Now that God has opened the doors of our prison-house, and brought us into the kingdom of His Son, if men are still carnal men, and the world a sinful world, and the life of Angels a burden, and the law of our nature not the law of God, whose fault is it?

We Christians are indeed under the law as other men, but, as I have already said, it is the new law, the law of the Spirit of Christ. We are under grace. That law, which to nature is a grievous bondage, is to those who live under the power of God's presence, what it was meant to be, a rejoicing. When then we feel reluctant to serve God, when thoughts rise within us as if He were a hard Master, and that His promises are not attractive enough to balance the strictness of His commandments, let us recollect that we, as being Christians, are not in the flesh, but in the Spirit, and let us act upon the conviction of it. Let us go to Him for grace. Let us seek His face. Let us come where He gives grace. Let us come to the ordinances of grace, in which Christ gives His Holy Spirit, to enable us to do that which by nature we cannot do, and to be "the servants of righteousness." They who pray for His saving help to change their likings and dislikings, their tastes, their views, their wills, their hearts, do not indeed all at once gain what they seek;—they do not gain it at once asking;—they do not *perceive* they gain it while they gain it,—but if they come continually day by day to Him,—if they come humbly,—if they come in faith,—if they come, not as a trial how they shall like God's service, but throwing (as far as may be) their whole hearts and souls into their duty as a sacrifice to Him,—if they come, not seeking a sign, but determined to go on seeking Him, honouring Him, serving Him, trusting Him, whether they see light, or feel comfort, or discern their growth, or no,—such men *will* gain, though they know it not; they will find, even while they are still seeking; before they call,

He will answer them and they will in the end find themselves saved wondrously, to their surprise, how they know not, and when their crown seemed at a distance. "They that wait on the Lord," says the Prophet, "shall renew their strength; they shall mount up with wings as eagles; they shall run and not be weary, and they shall walk and not faint" (Is 40:31).

SERMON II

Obedience without Love, as instanced in the Character of Balaam

"The word that God putteth in my mouth, that shall I speak."—Nm 22:38

When we consider the Old Testament as written by divine inspiration, and preserved, beyond the time of its own Dispensation, for us Christians,—as acknowledged and delivered over to us by Christ Himself, and pronounced by St. Paul to be "profitable for doctrine, reproof, correction, and instruction in righteousness" (2 Tm 3:16)—we ought not surely to read any portion of it with indifference, nay, without great and anxious interest. "Lord, what wilt Thou have me to do?" is the sort of inquiry which spontaneously arises in the serious mind. Christ and His Apostle cannot have put the Law and the Prophets into our hands for nothing. I would this thought were more carefully weighed than it commonly is. We profess indeed to revere the Old Testament; yet, for some reason or other, at least one considerable part of it, the historical, is regarded by the mass, even of men who think about religion, as merely historical, as a relation of facts, as antiquities; not in its divine characters, not in its practical bearings, not in reference to themselves. The notion that God speaks in it to them personally, the question, "*What* does He say?" "What must I *do?*" does not occur to them. They consider that the Old Testament concerns them only as far as it can be made typical of one or two of the great Christian doctrines; they do not consider it in its fulness, and in its literal sense, as a collection of deep moral lessons, such as are not vouchsafed in the New, though St. Paul expressly says that it is "profitable for instruction in righteousness."

If the Old Testament history generally be intended as a permanent instruction to the Church, much more, one would think, must such prominent and remarkable passages in it as the history of Balaam. Yet I suspect a very great number of readers carry off little more from it than the impression of the miracle which occurs in it, the speaking of his ass. And not unfrequently they talk more lightly on the subject than is expedient. Yet I think some very solemn and startling lessons may be drawn from the history, some of which I shall now attempt to set before you.

What is it which the chapters in question present to us? The first and most general account of Balaam would be this;—that he was a very eminent person in his age and country, that he was courted and gained by the enemies of Israel, and that he promoted a wicked cause in a very wicked way; that, when he could do nothing else for it, he counselled the Moabites to employ their women as means of seducing the chosen people into idolatry; and that he fell in battle in the war which ensued. These are the chief points, the prominent features of his history as viewed at a distance;—and repulsive indeed they are. He took on him the office of a tempter, which is especially the Devil's office. But Satan himself does not seem so hateful near as at a distance; and when we look into Balaam's history closely, we shall find points of character which may well interest those who do not consider his beginning and his end. Let us then approach him more nearly, and forget for a moment the summary account of him, which I have just been giving.

Now first he was blessed with God's especial favour. You will ask at once, How could so bad a man be in God's favour? but I wish you to put aside reasonings, and contemplate facts. I say he was especially favoured by God; God has a store of favours in His treasure-house, and of various kinds,—some for a time, some for ever,—some implying His approbation, others not. He showers favours even on the bad. He makes His sun to rise on the unjust as well as on the just. He willeth not the death of a sinner. He is said to have loved the young ruler, whose heart, notwithstanding, was upon the world. His loving-mercy extends over all His works. How He separates in His own divine thought, kindness from approbation, time from eternity, what He does from what He foresees, we know not and need not inquire. At present He is loving to all men, as if He did not foresee that some are to be saints, others reprobates to all eternity. He dispenses His favours variously,—gifts, graces, rewards, faculties, circumstances being indefinitely diversified, nor admitting of discrimination or numbering on our part. Balaam, I say, was in His favour; not indeed for his holiness' sake, not for ever; but in a certain sense, according to His inscrutable purpose,—who chooses whom He will choose, and exalts whom He will exalt, without destroying man's secret responsibilities or His own governance, and the triumph of truth and holiness, and His own strict impartiality in the end. Balaam was favoured in an especial way above the mere heathen. Not only had he the grant of inspiration, and the knowledge of God's will, an insight into the truths of morality, clear and enlarged, such as even we Christians cannot surpass; but he was even admitted to conscious intercourse with God, such as we Christians have not. In our Sunday Services, you may recollect, we read the chapters which relate to this intercourse; and we do not read those which record the darker passages of his history. Now, do you not think that most persons, who know only so much of him as our Sunday lessons contain, form a very mild judgment about him? They see him indeed to be on the wrong side, but still view him as a prophet of God. Such a judgment is not incorrect as far as it goes; and I appeal to it, if it be what I think it is, as a testimony how highly Balaam was in God's favour.

But again, Balaam was, in the ordinary and commonly received sense of the word, without straining its meaning at all, a very *conscientious* man. That this is so, will be plain from some parts of his conduct and some speeches of his, of which I proceed to remind you; and which will show also his enlightened and admirable view of moral and religious obligation. When Balak sent to him to call him to curse Israel, he did not make up his mind for himself, as many a man might do, or according to the suggestions of avarice and ambition. No, he brought the matter before God in prayer. He *prayed* before he did what he did, as a religious man ought to do. Next, when God forbade his going, he at once, as he ought, positively refused to go. "Get you into your land," he said, "for the Lord refuseth to give me leave to go with you." Balak sent again a more pressing message and more lucrative offers, and Balaam was even more decided than before. "If Balak," he said, "would give me his house full of silver and gold, I cannot go beyond the word of the Lord my God, to do less or more." Afterwards God gave him leave to go. "If the men come to call thee, rise up, and go with them" (Nm 22). Then, and not till then, he went.

Almighty God added, "Yet the word which I shall say unto thee, that shalt thou do." Now, in the next place, observe how strictly he obeyed this command. When he first met Balak, he said, in the words of the text, "Lo I am come unto thee; have I now any power at all to say any thing? the word that God putteth in my mouth, that shall I speak." Again, when he was about to prophesy, he said, "Whatsoever He showeth me I will tell thee" (Nm 23); and he did so, in spite of Balak's disappointment and mortification to hear him bless Israel. When Balak showed his impatience, he only replied calmly, "Must I not take heed to speak that which the Lord hath put in my mouth?" Again he prophesied, and again it was a blessing; again Balak was angered, and again the prophet firmly and serenely answered, "Told not I thee, saying, All that the Lord speaketh, that I must do?" A third time he prophesied blessing; and now Balak's anger was kindled, and he smote his hands together, and bade him depart to his place. But Balaam was not thereby moved from his duty. "The wrath of a king is as messengers of death" (Prv 16:14). Balak might have instantly revenged himself upon the prophet; but Balaam, not satisfied with blessing Israel, proceeded, as a prophet should, to deliver himself of what remained of the prophetic burden, by foretelling more pointedly than before, destruction to Moab and the other enemies of the chosen people. He prefaced his prophecy with these unacceptable words,—"Spake I not also unto thy messengers which thou sentest unto me, saying, If Balak would give me his house full of silver and gold, I cannot go beyond the commandment of the Lord, to do either good or bad of mine own mind? But what the Lord saith, that will I speak. And now behold, I go unto my people; come, therefore, and I will advertise thee what this people shall do to thy people in the latter days." After delivering his conscience, he "rose up, and went and returned to his place."

All this surely expresses the conduct and the feelings of a high-principled, honourable, conscientious man. Balaam, I say, was certainly such, in that very sense in which we commonly use those words. He said, and he did; he professed, and he acted according to his professions. There is no inconsistency in word and deed. He obeys as well as talks about religion; and this being the case, we shall feel more intimately the value of the following noble sentiments which he lets drop from time to time, and which, if he had shown less firmness in his conduct, might have passed for mere words, the words of a maker of speeches, a sophist, moralist, or orator. "Let me die the death of the righteous, and let my last end be like his." "God is not a man that He should lie; neither the son of man, that He should repent.... Behold, I have received commandment to bless; and He hath blessed, and I cannot reverse it." "I shall see Him, but not now; I shall behold Him, but not nigh." It is remarkable that these declarations are great and lofty in their mode of expression; and the saying of his recorded by the prophet Micah is of the same kind. Balak asked what sacrifices were acceptable to God. Balaam answered, "He hath showed thee, O man, what is good; and what doth the Lord require of thee, but to do justly, and to love mercy, and to walk humbly with thy God?" (Mi 6:8).

Viewing then the inspired notices concerning Balaam in all their parts, we cannot deny to him the praise which, if those notices have a plain meaning, they certainly do convey, that he was an honourable and religious man, with a great deal of what was great and noble about him; a man whom any one of us at first sight would have trusted, sought out in our difficulties, perhaps made the head of a party, and anyhow spoken of with great respect. We may indeed, if we please, say that he fell away afterwards from all this excellence: though, after all, there is something shocking in such a notion. Nay, it is not natural even that ordinarily honourable men should suddenly change; but however this *may* be said,—it may be said he fell away; but, I presume, it *cannot* be said that he was other than a high-principled man (in the language of the world) *when* he so spoke and acted.

But now the strange thing is, that at this very time, *while* he so spoke and acted, he seems, as in one sense to be in God's favour, so in another and higher to be under His displeasure. If this be so, the supposition that he fell away will not be in point; the difficulty it proposes to solve will remain; for it will turn out that he was displeasing to God *amid* his many excellences. The passage I have in mind is this, as you will easily suppose. "God's anger was kindled, because he went" with the princes of Moab, "and the Angel of the Lord stood in the way for an adversary against him." Afterwards, when God opened his eyes, "he saw the Angel of the Lord standing in the way, and his sword drawn in his hand"; "And Balaam said, I have *sinned*, for I knew not that thou stoodest in the way against me; now, therefore, if it displease thee, I will get me back again." You observe Balaam said, "I have sinned," *though* he avers he did not *know* that God was his adversary. What makes the whole transaction the more strange is this,—that Almighty God had said before, "If the men come to call thee, rise up, and go with them"; and that when Balaam offered to go back again, the Angel repeated, "Go with the men." And afterwards we find in the midst of his heathen enchantments "God met Balaam," and "put a word in his mouth"; and afterwards "the Spirit of God came unto him."

Summing up then what has been said, we seem, in Balaam's history, to have the following remarkable case, that is, remarkable according to our customary judgment of things: a man divinely favoured, visited, influenced, guided, protected, eminently honoured, illuminated,—a man possessed of an enlightened sense of duty, and of moral and religious acquirements, educated, high-minded, conscientious, honourable, firm; and yet on the side of God's enemies, personally under God's displeasure, and in the end (if we go on to that) the direct instrument of Satan, and having his portion with the unbelievers. I do not think I have materially overstated any part of this description; but if it be correct only in substance, it certainly is most fearful, after allowing for incidental exaggeration,—most fearful to every one of us, the more fearful the more we are conscious to ourselves in the main of purity of intention in what we do, and conscientious adherence to our sense of duty.

And now it is natural to ask, what is the *meaning* of this startling exhibition of God's ways? Is it really possible that a conscientious and religious man should be found among the enemies of God, nay, should be personally displeasing to Him, and that at the very time God was visiting him with extraordinary favour? What a mystery is this! Surely, if this be so, Revelation has added to our perplexities, not relieved them! What instruction, what profit, what correction, what doctrine is there in such portions of inspired Scripture?

In answering this difficulty, I observe in the first place, that it certainly is impossible, quite impossible, that a really conscientious man should be displeasing to God; at the same time it is possible to be *generally* conscientious, or what the world calls honourable and high-principled, yet to be destitute of that religious fear and strictness, which God calls conscientiousness, but which the world calls superstition or narrowness of mind. And bearing this in mind, we shall, perhaps, have a solution of our perplexities concerning Balaam.

And here I would make a remark: that when a passage of Scripture, descriptive of God's dealings with man, is obscure or perplexing, it is as well to ask ourselves whether this may not be owing to some insensibility, in ourselves or in our age, to certain peculiarities of the Divine Law or government therein involved. Thus, to those who do not understand the nature and history of religious truth, our Lord's assertion about sending a sword on earth is an obscurity. To those who consider sin a light evil, the doctrine of eternal punishment is a difficulty. In like manner the history of the flood, of the call of Abraham, of the plagues of Egypt, of the wandering in the desert, of the judgment on Korah, Dathan, and Abiram, and a multitude of other occurrences, may be insuperable difficulties, except to certain states and tempers of mind, to which, on the contrary, they will seem quite natural and obvious. I consider that the history of Balaam is a striking illustration of this remark. Those whose hearts, like Josiah's, are "tender," scrupulous, sensitive in religious matters, will see with clearness and certainty what the real state of the case was as regards him; on the other hand, our difficulties about it, if we have them, are a presumption that the age we live in has not the key to a certain class of Divine providences, is deficient in a certain class of religious principles, ideas, and sensibilities. Let it be considered then whether the following remarks may not tend to lessen our perplexity.

Balaam obeyed God from a sense of its being right to do so, but not from a *desire to please Him,* not from *fear and love.* He had other ends, aims, wishes of his own, distinct from God's will and purpose, and he would have effected these if he could. His endeavour was, not to please God, but to please self without displeasing God; to pursue his own ends *as far* as was consistent with his duty. In a word, he did not give his heart to God, but obeyed Him, as a man may obey human law, or observe the usages of society or his country, as something external to himself, because he knows he ought to do so, from a sort of rational good sense, a conviction of its propriety, expediency, or comfort, as the case may be.

You will observe he *wished* to go with Balak's messengers, only he felt he *ought not* to go; and the problem which he attempted to solve was *how* to go and yet not offend God. He was quite resolved he *would* anyhow act religiously and conscientiously; he was too honourable a man to break any of his engagements; if he had given his word, it was sacred; if he had duties, they were imperative: He had a character to maintain, and an inward sense of propriety to satisfy; but he would have given the world to have got rid of his duties; and the question was, *how* to do so without violence; and he did not care about walking on the very brink of transgression, so that he could keep from falling over. Accordingly he was not content with *ascertaining* God's will, but he attempted to *change* it. He inquired of Him a *second time,* and this was to tempt Him. Hence, while God bade him go, His anger was kindled against him because he went.

This surely is no uncommon character; rather, it is the common case even with the more respectable and praiseworthy portion of the community. I say plainly, and without fear of contradiction, though it is a serious thing to say, that the aim of most men esteemed conscientious and religious, or who are what is called honourable, upright men, is, to all appearance, not how to please God, but how to please themselves without displeasing Him. I say confidently,—that is, if we may judge of men in general by what we see,—that they make this world the first object in their minds, and use religion as a corrective, a restraint, upon *too much* attachment to the world. They think that religion is a negative thing, a sort of moderate love of the world, a moderate luxury, a moderate avarice, a moderate ambition, and a moderate selfishness. You see this in numberless ways. You see it in the course of trade, of public life, of literature, in all matters where men have objects to pursue. Nay you see it in religious exertions; of which it too commonly happens that the chief aim is, to attain *anyhow* a certain definite end, religious indeed, but of man's own choosing; not, to please God, and *next*, if possible, to attain it; not, to attain it religiously, or not at all.

This surely is so plain that it is scarcely necessary to enlarge upon it. Men do not take for the object towards which they act, God's will, but certain maxims, rules, or measures, right perhaps as far as they go, but defective because they admit of being subjected to certain other ultimate ends, which are not religious. Men are just, honest, upright, trustworthy; but all this not from the love and fear of God, but from a mere feeling of obligation to be so, and in subjection to certain worldly objects. And thus they are what is popularly called moral, without being religious. Such was Balaam. He was in a popular sense a strictly moral, honourable, conscientious man; that he was not so in a heavenly and true sense is plain, if not from the considerations here insisted on, at least from his after history, which (we may presume) brought to light his secret defect, in whatever it consisted.

And here we see why he spoke so much and so vauntingly of his determination to follow God's direction. He made a great *point* of following it; his end was not to please God, but to keep straight with Him. He who loves does not act from calculation or reasoning; he does not in his cool moments reflect upon or talk of what he is doing, as if it were a great sacrifice. Much less does he pride himself on it; but this is what Balaam seems to have done.

I have been observing that his defect lay in this, that he had not a single eye towards God's will, but was ruled by other objects. But moreover, this evil heart of unbelief showed itself in a peculiar way, to which it is necessary to draw your attention, and to which I alluded just now in saying that the difficulties of Scripture often arose from the defective moral condition of our hearts.

Why did Almighty God give Balaam leave to go to Balak, and then was angry with him for going? I suppose for this reason, because his asking twice was tempting God. God is a jealous God. Sinners as we are, nay as creatures of His hands, we may not safely intrude upon Him, and make free with Him. We may not dare to do that, which we should not dare to do with an earthly superior, which we should be punished, for instance, for attempting in the case of a king or noble of this world. To rush into His presence, to address Him familiarly, to urge Him, to strive to make our duty lie in one direction when it lies in another, to handle rudely and practise upon His holy word, to trifle with truth, to treat conscience lightly, to take liberties (as it may be called) with any thing that is God's, all irreverence, profaneness, unscrupulousness, wantonness, is represented in Scripture not only as a sin, but as felt, noticed, quickly returned on God's part (if I may dare use such human words of the Almighty and All-holy God, without transgressing the rule I am myself laying down,—but He vouchsafes in Scripture to represent Himself to us in that only way in which we can attain to the knowledge of Him), I say all irreverence towards God is represented as being jealously and instantly and fearfully noticed and visited, as friend or stranger among men might resent an insult shown him. This should be carefully considered; we are apt to act towards God and the things of God as towards a mere system, a law, a name, a religion, a principle, not as against a Person, a living, watchful, present, prompt, and powerful Eye and Arm. That all this is a great error, is plain to all who study Scripture; as is sufficiently shown by the death of that multitude of persons for looking into the ark—the death of the Prophet by the lion, who was sent to Jeroboam from Judah, and did not minutely obey the instructions given him—the slaughter of the children at Bethel by the bears, for mocking Elisha—the exclusion of Moses from the promised land, for smiting the rock twice—and the judgment on Ananias and Sapphira. Now Balaam's fault seems to have been of this nature. God told him distinctly not to go to Balak. He was rash enough to ask a second time, and God as a punishment gave him leave to ally himself with His enemies, and to take part against His people. With this presumptuousness and love of self in his innermost heart, his prudence, firmness, wisdom, illumination, and general conscientiousness, availed him nothing.

A number of reflections crowd upon the mind on the review of this awful history, as I may well call it; and with a brief notice of some of these I shall conclude.

1. First, we see how little we can depend, in judging of right and wrong, on the apparent excellence and high character of individuals. There *is* a right and a wrong in matters of conduct, in spite of the world; but it is the world's aim and Satan's aim to take our minds off from the indelible distinctions of things, and to fix our thoughts upon man, to make us the slaves of man, to make us dependent on his opinion, his patronage, his honour, his smiles, and his frowns. But if Scripture is to be our guide, it is quite plain that the most conscientious, religious, high-principled, honourable men (I use the words in their ordinary, not in

their Scripture sense), may be on the side of evil, may be Satan's instruments in cursing, if that were possible, and at least in seducing and enfeebling the people of God. For in the world's judgment, even when most refined, a person is conscientious and consistent, who acts up to his standard, *whatever that is*, not he only who aims at taking the highest standard. This is the world's highest flight; but in its ordinary judgment, a man is conscientious and consistent, who is only inconsistent and goes against conscience in any extremity, when hardly beset, and when he must cut the knot or remain in present difficulties. That is, *he* is thought to obey conscience, who only disobeys it when it is a praise and merit to obey it. This, alas! is the way with some of the most honourable of mere men of the world, nay of the mass of (so-called) respectable men. They never tell untruths, or break their word, or profane the Lord's day, or are dishonest in trade, or falsify their principles, or insult religion, except in very great straits or great emergencies, when driven into a corner; and then perhaps they force themselves, as Saul did when he offered sacrifice instead of Samuel;—they force themselves, and (as it were) undergo their sin as a sort of unpleasant self-denial or penance, being ashamed of it all the while, getting it over as quickly as they can, shutting their eyes and leaping blindfold, and then forgetting it, as something which is bitter to think about. And if memory is ever roused and annoys them, they console themselves that after all they have only gone against their conscience now and then. This is their view of themselves and of each other, taken at advantage; and if any one come across them who has lived more out of the world than themselves, and has a truer sense of right and wrong, and who fastens on some one point in them, which to his mind is a token and warning to himself against them, such an one seems of course narrow-minded and overstrict in his notions. For instance; supposing some such man had fallen in with Balaam, and had been privy to the history of his tempting God, it is clear that Balaam's general correctness, his nobleness of demeanour, and his enlightened view of duty, would not have availed one jot or tittle to overcome such a man's repugnance to him. He would have been startled and alarmed, and would have kept at a distance, and in consequence he would have been called by the world uncharitable and bigoted.

2. A second reflection which rises in the mind has relation to the wonderful secret providence of God, while all things seem to go on according to the course of this world. Balaam did not see the Angel, yet the Angel went out against him as an adversary. He had no open denunciation of God's wrath directed against him. He had sinned, and

nothing happened outwardly, but wrath was abroad and in his path. *This* again is a very serious and awful thought. God's arm is not shortened. What happened to Balaam is as if it took place yesterday. God is what He ever was; we sin as man has ever sinned. We sin without being aware of it. God is our enemy without our being aware of it; and when the blow falls, we turn our thoughts to the creature, we ill-treat our ass, we lay the blame on circumstances of this world, instead of turning to Him. "Lord, when Thy hand is lifted up, they will not see; but they shall see," in the next world if not here, "and be ashamed for their envy at the people; yea the fire of Thine enemies shall devour them" (Is 26:11).

3. Here too is a serious reflection, if we had time to pursue it, that when we have begun an evil course, we cannot retrace our steps. Balaam was forced to go with the men; he offered to draw back—he was not allowed—yet God's wrath followed him. This is what comes of committing ourselves to an evil line of conduct; and we see daily instances of it in our experience of life. Men get entangled, and are bound hand and foot in unadvisable courses. They make imprudent marriages or connexions; they place themselves in dangerous situations; they engage in unprofitable or harmful undertakings. Too often indeed they do not discern their evil plight; but when they do, they cannot draw back. God seems to say, "Go with the men." They are in bondage, and they must make the best of it; being the slave of the creature, without ceasing to be the responsible servants of God; under His displeasure, yet bound to act as if they could please Him. All this is very fearful.

4. Lastly, I will but say this in addition,—God gives us warnings now and then, but does not repeat them. Balaam's sin consisted in not acting upon what was told him *once for all*. In like manner, you, my brethren, now hear what you may never hear again, and what perchance in its substance is the Word of God. You may never hear it again, though with your outward ears you hear it a hundred times, because you may be impressed with it now, but never may again. You may be impressed with it now, and the impression may die away; and some time hence, if you ever think about it, you may then speak of it thus,—that the view struck you at the time, but somehow the more you thought about it, the less you liked or valued it. True; this *may* be so, and it *may* also arise, as you think, from the doctrine I have been setting before you not being true and scriptural; but it *may* also arise from your having heard God's voice and not obeyed it. It may be that you have become blind, not the doctrine been disproved. Beware of trifling with your conscience. It is often said that second thoughts are best; so they are in matters of judgment, but not

in matters of conscience. In matters of duty first thoughts are commonly best—they have more in them of the voice of God. May He give you grace so to hear what has been said, as you will wish to have heard, when life is over; to hear in a practical way, with a desire to profit by it, to learn God's will, and to do it!

SERMON IX

The State of Grace

"Being justified by faith we have peace with God through our Lord Jesus Christ; by whom also we have access by faith into this grace wherein we stand, and rejoice in hope of the glory of God."—Rom 5:1, 2

There are many men, nay the greater part of a Christian country, who have neither hope nor fear about futurity or the unseen world; they do not think of it at all, or bring the idea of it home to them in any shape. They do not really understand, or try to understand, that they are in God's presence, and must one day be judged for what they are now doing, any more than they see what is going on in another quarter of the world, or concern themselves about what is to happen to them ten years hence. The next world is far more distant from them than any future period of this life or any other country; and consequently, they have neither hope nor fear about it, for they have no thought about it of any kind.

There are others who feel no fear whatever, though they profess to feel much joy and transport. I cannot sympathize with such, nor do I think St. Paul would, for he bids us "work out our own salvation with fear and trembling"; nor St. Peter, who bids us "pass the time of our sojourning here in fear" (Phil 2:12; 1 Pt 1:17).

But there are others who seem only to fear, or to have very little joy in religion. These are in a more hopeful state than those who only joy and do not fear at all; yet they are not altogether in a right state. However, they are in an interesting state. I purpose to describe it now, and to make some remarks upon it.

It is certainly the duty, as it is the privilege, of every Christian to have his heart so fixed on Christ as to desire His coming; yet alas! it too often happens that when we say, "Thy kingdom come," our sins rise up before our minds, and make our words falter. Now the persons I speak of are in so sad and uncomfortable a state of mind, as to be distressed whenever they think of the next world. They may be well-living, serious persons, and have ever been such from their youth; yet they have an indefinite sense of guilt on their minds, a consciousness of their own miserable failings and continual transgressions, such as annoys and distresses them, as a wound or sore might, when they think of Christ's coming in judgment. A sense of guilt, indeed, every one, the best of us, must have. I am not blaming *that*, but I speak of *such* a sense as hinders those who feel it from rejoicing in the Lord. They have one thought alone before their minds, the great irregularity of their lives; they come to Church, and try to attend, but their thoughts wander; the day passes, and it seems to them unprofitable. They have done God no service. Or again, they have some natural failing which breaks out from time to time, and grievously afflicts them on recollection. Perhaps they are passionate, and are ever saying what they are sorry for afterwards; or they are ill-tempered, and from time to time put every thing about them into confusion, and make every one unhappy by their gloomy looks and sullen words; or they are slothful, and with difficulty moved to do any thing, and they are ever lamenting wasted hours, and opportunities lost. The consequence is, that their religion is a course of sorrowful attempting and failing, self-reproach, and dryness of spirits. They are deeply sensible how good God is, and how wonderful His providence; they really feel very grateful, and they really put their trust where it should be put. But their faith only leads them to see that judgment is a fearful thing, and their sense of God's mercies to say, "How little grateful am I." They hear of the blessings promised to God's true servants after death, and they say, "Oh, how unprepared am I to receive them."

Now no one will fancy, I should trust, that I am saying any thing in disparagement of such feelings; they are very right and true. I only say they should not be the whole of a man's religion. He ought to have other and more cheerful feelings too. No one on earth is free from imperfection and sin, no one but has much continually to repent of; yet St. Paul bids us "rejoice in the Lord alway"; and in the text, he describes Christians as having peace with God and rejoicing in hope of His glory. Sins of infirmity, then, such as arise from the infection of our original nature, and not from deliberation and wilfulness, have no divine warrant to keep us from joy and peace in believing.

Now, then, the question is, *how* the persons in question come to have this defective kind of religion.

1. In the first place, of course, we must take into account bodily disorder, which is not unfrequently the cause of the perplexity of mind I have been describing. Many persons have an anxious self-tormenting

disposition, or depression of spirits, or deadness of the affections, in consequence of continued or peculiar ill-health; and though it is their study, as it is their duty, to strive against this evil as much as they can, yet it often may be impossible to be rid of it. Of course, in such cases we can impute no fault to them. It is God's will; He has willed in His inscrutable purpose that they should not be able to rejoice in the Gospel, doubtless for their ultimate good, to try and prove them; as any thing else may be a trial, as ill-health itself is such. They should not repine. It is an undeserved mercy that they have the Gospel brought near to them at all, that they have the prospect of heaven, be it faint or distinct; and they must be patient under their fears, and try to serve God more strictly.

2. But, again, the uncomfortable state of mind I have described, sometimes, it is to be feared, arises, I will not say from wilful sin, but from some habitual deficiency which might be corrected, but is not. It is very difficult of course to draw the line between sins which are (as it were) the direct consequences of our old nature, and those which are more strictly and entirely our own, yet there is a class which rises above the former, though it would be harsh to call them wilful. The sins I speak of arise partly through frailty, partly through want of love; and they seem just to have this effect, of dimming or quenching our peace and joy. Such, for instance, are recurring and stated acts of sin, such as might be foreseen and provided against. Anger, on the contrary, may overtake a man when he least expects it. Indolence may show itself in a difficulty or inability to fix his mind on the subject which ought to occupy it, so that time goes and nothing is done. Ill-temper may fall upon him like a spell, and bind his faculties, so that his very attempts to break it may make him seem more gloomy, untoward, and disagreeable, from the appearance of an effort and struggle. Such need not be more than sins of infirmity. But there are sins which happen at certain times or places, and which a man ought to prepare for and overcome. I do not say that he must overcome them this time or that, but he must be in a state of warfare against them, and must be tending to overcome them. Such, for instance, is indolence in rising from his bed. Such, again, is a careless, irregular, or hurried way of saying private prayer. Such is any habitual excess in eating or drinking. Such is running into temptation,—going again and again to places, or among people, who will induce him to do what he should not, to idle, or to jest, or to talk much. Such is extravagance in spending money. All these laxities of conduct impress upon our conscience a vague sense of irregularity and guilt. The absence of a vigilant walk, of exact conscientiousness in all things, of an earnest and vigorous warfare against our

spiritual enemies, in a word, of strictness, this is what obscures our peace and joy. Strictness is the condition of rejoicing. The Christian is a soldier; he may have many falls; these need not hinder his joy in the Gospel; he must be humbled indeed, but not downcast; it does not prove he is not fighting; he has enemies within and without him; he has the remains of a fallen nature. But wilful sin in any shape proves that he is not an honest soldier of Christ. If it is habitual and deliberate, of course it destroys his hope; but if it be less than deliberate, and yet of the nature of wilful sin, it is sufficient, though not (we trust) to separate him at once from Christ, yet to separate him from the inward vision of Him. The same result will follow, perhaps irremediably, where men have been in past life open or habitual sinners, though they may now have repented. Penitents cannot hope to be as cheerful and joyful in faith as those who have never fallen away from God; perhaps it is not desirable they should be, and is a bad sign if they are. I do not mean to say that in the course of years, and after severe humiliation, it is not possible for a repentant sinner to feel a well-grounded peace and comfort, but he must not expect it. He must expect to be haunted with the ghosts of past sins, rising from the charnel-house, courting him to sin again, yet filling him the while with remorse; he must expect "a trembling heart, and failing of eyes, and sorrow of mind" (Dt 28:65), misgivings about his safety, misgivings about the truth of religion, and about particular doctrines, painful doubts and difficulties, so that he is forced to grope in darkness or in cold and dreary twilight. I do not say there are not ways of escaping all this misery at a moment, but they are false ways; but if he continues in the true and narrow way, he will find it rough and painful; and this is his fit correction.

3. Again, where there is no room for supposing the existence of wilful sins, past or present, this fearful anxious state of mind arises very commonly from another cause in one shape or other—from not having a lively sense of our present privileges; and this is the subject to which I shall call your attention. Many indeed, finding that Scripture says great things about the joy which true Christians have in the Gospel, think it consists in their having personally and individually an assurance of their absolute predestination to eternal life; or at least of their being now in a state of salvation, such that, were they at once to die, they would be sure of heaven. Such a knowledge of course would inspire great joy if they had it; and they fancy that the joy of the Christian does arise from it. But since they have it not, and only think they have it, it is obvious what extravagances will follow from the notion instead of real benefit; what

perversion of the Gospel, what rashness, presumption, self-exaltation, and intemperate conduct. Such persons of course claim the more consolatory parts of Scripture, such as the text, for themselves. They forcibly take them from more sober Christians, as if they were their own, and others had no right to them, nay, as if others had no right to explain them, to comment on them, or to have an opinion about them; as if they alone could understand them, or feel them, or appreciate them, or use them. What is the consequence? Better men are robbed of their portion; their comfortable texts are gone, they acquiesce in the notion (too readily) that these texts are *not* theirs; not that they exactly allow that they belong to the enthusiastic persons who claim them, but they think they belong to no one at all, that they belonged indeed to St. Paul, and to inspired or highly gifted men, but to no one now.

And this conclusion is strengthened by the circumstance, that men of duller and less sensitive minds are willing to give them up. There are persons highly respectable indeed, and serious, but whose religion is of a dry and cold character, with little heart or insight into the next world. They have strong sense and regular habits; their passions are not violent, their feelings not quick, and they have no imagination or restless reason to run away with their thoughts or to perplex them. They do not grieve much or joy much. They do joy and grieve, but it is in a way, in a certain line, and not the highest. They are most excellent men in their line, but they do not walk in a lofty path. There is nothing unearthly about them; they cannot be said to be worldly, yet they do not walk by things unseen; they do not discern and contemplate the next world. They are not on the alert to detect, patient in watching, keen-sighted in tracing the movements of God's secret providence. They do not feel they are in an immense unbounded system, with a height above and a depth beneath. They think every thing is plain and easy, they have no difficulties in religion, they see no recondite and believe in no hidden meanings in Scripture, and discern no hints there sympathetic with guesses within them. Such men are used to explain away such passages as the text; to be "at peace with God," to "have access into the grace in which we stand," to "rejoice in hope of the glory of God,"—to them have little or no meaning. Their joy does not rise higher than what they call a "rational faith and hope, a satisfaction in religion, a cheerfulness, a well-ordered mind, and the like,"—all very good words, if properly used, but shallow to express the fulness of the Gospel privileges.

What with the enthusiastic, then, on the one hand, who pervert the texts in question, and with the barren-minded on the other, who explain them away, Christians are commonly left without the texts at all, and so have nothing to contemplate but their own failings; and these surely are numerous enough, and fit to make them dejected.

Observe, then, what religion becomes to them—a system of duties with little of privilege or comfort. Not that any one would have cause to complain (God forbid!) though it had no privilege; for what can sinners claim to whom it is a great gain to be respited from hell? Not that religion can really be without privilege; for the very leave to serve God is a privilege, the very thought of God is a privilege, the very knowledge that Christ has so loved the world as to die for it is an inestimable privilege. Religion is full of privileges, involved in the very notion of it, and drawn out on the right hand and on the left, as a man walks along the path of duty. He cannot stir this way or that, but he awakens some blessed and consoling thought which cheers and strengthens him insensibly, even if it does not so present itself to him, that he can contemplate and feed upon it. However, in the religious system I speak of, the privilege of obedience *is* concealed, and the bare duty prominently put forward; the privileges are made vague and general rather than personal; and thus a man is almost reduced to the state of natural religion, in which God's Law is known without His Gospel. Under such circumstances, religion becomes little more than a code of morals, the word and will of an absent God, who will one day come to judge and recompense, not the voice of a present and bountiful Saviour.

And this may in one sense be called a bondage,—a bondage, yet without thereby disparaging the excellence and perfection of God's Law. Men at this day so boldly talk of the bondage of the Law, that if you heard them, you would think that the being under that Law was in itself a misery or an inferior state, as if obedience to God's commandments were something low and second best. But is it really so? Then are the Angels in a very low state. The highest blessedness of any creature is to be under the Law, the highest glory is obedience. It is our shame, not our privilege, that we do not obey as the Angels do. Men speak as if the Gospel were glorious, because it destroyed the Law of obedience. No; it destroyed the Jewish Law, but not the holy Law of God therein contained and manifested. And if that Holy Word, which "endureth for ever in heaven," which is co-eternal with God, is a bondage to us, as it is by nature, so much the more shame for us. It is our great sinfulness, not any inherent defect in the Law, which makes it a bondage; and the message of the Gospel is glorious, not because it releases us from the Law, but because it enables us to fulfil it,—fulfil it (I do not say wholly and perfectly), but with a continual approximation to perfect obedience, with an obedience running on into perfection, and which in the next world will rise into and result in perfection. This is St. Paul's account of it, "Being not without law to God," he says, "but under the law to Christ" (1 Cor 9:21). Again, "Not having mine own righteousness, which is of the law," that is, that kind of obedience to the Law to which he *by himself* attained, "but that which is through the faith of Christ" (Phil 3:9), that high and spiritual obedience which faith in Christ, aided by the grace of Christ, enabled him to accomplish. And in another place, "The commandment which was ordained to life, I found to be unto death.... The Law is holy, and the commandment holy, and just, and good. Was then that which is good made death unto me? God forbid. But sin, that it might appear sin, working death in me by that which is good, that sin by the commandment might become exceeding sinful.... The law is spiritual, but *I* am carnal, sold under sin." And again, "What the law could not do, in that it was weak through the flesh, God sending His own Son in the likeness of sinful flesh, and for sin, condemned sin in the flesh; that the righteousness of the law might be fulfilled in us, who walk not after the flesh but after the Spirit" (Rom 8:3, 4).

When then I say that religion, considered as a law or code of morals, is a bondage, let no one suppose me to countenance that presumptuous and unchristian spirit, which seems to exult in being through Christ free (as it thinks) from the Law, instead of being bound and able through Christ to obey it more perfectly. The glory of the Gospel is, not that it *destroys* the Law, but that it makes it *cease* to *be* a bondage; not that it gives us freedom *from* it, but *in* it; and the notion of the Gospel which I have been describing as cold and narrow is, not that of supposing Christianity a law, but of supposing it to be scarcely more than a law, and thus leaving us where it found us. He who thinks it but a law, will of course be fearful and miserable. The commandment of God will seem true, but to him, a helpless sinner, hard and uninviting; and though it is still his duty to try to obey, and he will do so, if he be Christ's in heart, yet he will do so sadly and sorrowfully, his memory continually embittered, and his conscience laden with fresh and fresh sins. Two thoughts alone will be before him, God's perfections and his own sinfulness; and he will feel love and gratitude indeed to his Almighty Lord and Saviour, but not joy. He will look upon the message of the Gospel as a series of *conditions*. He will consider the Gospel as a *covenant*, in which he must do his part, and God will assuredly do His. Now, salvation, doubtless, *is* conditional, and the Gospel *is* a covenant. These words are as good and as true as the word "law"; but then salvation is not *merely* conditional, nor the Gospel *merely* a covenant; and those who think so, unless they have peculiarly happy minds, will obey in a certain dry, dull, heavy way, without spring, animation, life, vigour, and nobleness. And if possessed of sensitive, gentle, affectionate minds, they will be very likely to sink into despondency and fear. And they are the prey or the mockery of every proud, self-confident boaster, who passes by on the other side, boldly proclaiming himself to be elect and safe and possessed of a joyful assurance, and that every one else, who does not make as venturesome a profession as he, is carnal and a slave of Satan, or at least in a state far, far below himself.

What then is it, that these little ones of Christ lack, who, without wilful sin, past or present, on their consciences, are in gloom and sorrow? What is the doctrine that will quicken them, and make their devotion healthy? What will brace them and nerve them, and make them lift up their heads, and will pour light and joy upon their countenance till it shines like the face of Moses when he came down from the Mount? What but the great and high doctrines connected with the Church? They are not merely taken into covenant with God; they are taken into His Church. They have not merely the promise of grace; they have its presence. They have not merely the conditional prospect of a reward; for a blessing, nay, unspeakable, fathomless, illimitable, infinite, eternal blessings are poured into their very hearts, even as a first step and an earnest from God our Saviour, of what He will do for those who love Him. They "are passed from death unto life," and are the children of God and heirs of heaven. Let us steadily contemplate this comfortable view, and we shall gain strength, and feel cheerful and joyful in spite of our sins. O fearful follower of Christ, how is it thou hast never thought of what thou art and what is in thee? Art thou not Christ's purchased possession? Has He not rescued thee from the Devil, and put a new nature within thee? Did He not in Baptism cast out the evil spirit and enter into thee Himself, and dwell in thee as if thou hadst been an Archangel, or one of the Seraphim who worship before Him continually? Much and rightly as thou thinkest of thy sins, hast thou no thought, I do not say of gratitude, but of wonder, of admiration, of amazement, of awful and overpowering transport, at what thou art through grace? When Jacob woke in the morning, his first thought was not about his sins or his danger, though he rightly felt both, but about God;—he said, "How dreadful is this place! this is none other but the house of God, and this is the gate of heaven" (Gn 28:17). Contemplate then thyself, not in thyself, but as thou art in the Eternal God. Fall down in astonishment at the glories which are around thee and in thee, poured to and fro in such a wonderful way that thou art (as it were) dissolved into the kingdom of God, as though thou hadst nought to do but to contemplate and feed upon that great vision. This surely is the state of mind the Apostle speaks of in the text when he reminds us who are justified and at peace with God, that we have the access to His royal courts, and stand in His grace, and rejoice in hope of His glory. All the trouble which the world inflicts upon us, and which flesh cannot but feel, sorrow, pain, care, bereavement, these avail not to disturb the tranquility and the intensity with which faith gazes upon the Divine Majesty. All the necessary exactness of our obedience, the anxiety about failing, the pain of self-denial, the watchfulness, the zeal, the self-chastisements which are required of us, as little interfere with this vision of faith, as if they were practised by another, not by ourselves. We are two or three selves at once, in the wonderful structure of our minds, and can weep while we smile, and labour while we meditate.

And if so much is given us by the first Sacrament of the Church, what, think we, is given us in the second? O my brethren, let us raise and enlarge our notions of Christ's Presence in that mysterious Ordinance, and we shall understand how it is that the Christian, in spite of his infirmities, and not forgetting them, still may rejoice "with joy unspeakable and full of glory." For what is it that is vouchsafed to us at the Holy Table, when we commemorate the Lord's death? It is, "Jesus Christ before our eyes evidently set forth, crucified among us" (Gal 3: 1). Not before our bodily eyes; so far, every thing remains at the end of that Heavenly Communion as it did at the beginning. What was bread remains bread, and what was wine remains wine. We need no carnal, earthly, visible miracle to convince us of the Presence of the Lord Incarnate. We have, we trust, more faith than to need to see the heavens open, or the Holy Ghost descend in bodily shape,—more faith than to attempt, in default of sight, to indulge our reason, and to confine our notion of the Sacrament to some clear assemblage of words of our own framing. We have faith and love enough, in St. Paul's words, to *discern* the Lord's Body." He who is at the right hand of God, manifests Himself in that Holy Sacrament as really and fully as if He were visibly there. We are allowed to draw near, to "give, take, and eat" His sacred Body and Blood, as truly as though like Thomas we could touch His hands and thrust our hand into His side. When He ascended into the Mount, "His face did shine as the sun, and His raiment was white as the light" (Mt

17:2). Such is the glorious presence which faith sees in the Holy Communion, though every thing looks as usual to the natural man. Not gold or precious stones, pearls of great price or gold of Ophir, are to the eye of faith so radiant as those lowly elements which He, the Highest, is pleased to make the means of conveying to our hearts and bodies His own gracious self. Not the light of the sun sevenfold is so awfully bright and overpowering, if we could see as the Angels do, as that seed of eternal life, which by eating and drinking we lay up in our hearts against the day of His coming. In spite then of all recollections of the past or fear for the future, we have a present source of rejoicing; whatever comes, weal or woe, however stands our account as yet in the books against the Last Day, this we have and this we may glory in, the present power and grace of God in us and over us, and the means thereby given us of victory in the end.

Such are the thoughts which fill the heart with joy, yet without tending in consequence to relax our obedience, for a reason already mentioned, viz., that *strictness* of life, exact conscientiousness, is the tenure of our privileges. They are ours to possess, that is our glory; they are ours to lose, that is our solicitude. We can keep them, we have not to gain them,—but we shall not keep them without fear and trembling; still we *have* them, and there is nothing to hinder our rejoicing in them while we have them. For fear has reference to the future; and that we *may* lose them to-morrow (which God forbid), but supposing it, is no reason why we should not rejoice in them to-day.

SERMON X

The Visible Church for the Sake of the Elect

"I endure all things for the elect's sakes; that they may also obtain the salvation which is in Christ Jesus with eternal glory."—2 Tm 2:10

If we were asked what was the object of Christian preaching, teaching, and instruction, what the office of the Church, considered as the dispenser of the Word of God, I suppose we should not all return the same answer. Perhaps we might say that the object of Revelation was to enlighten and enlarge the mind, to make us act by reason, and to expand and strengthen our powers;—or to impart knowledge about religious truth, knowledge being power directly it is given, and enabling us forthwith to think, judge, and act for ourselves;—or to make us good members of the community, loyal subjects, orderly and useful in our station, whatever it be;—or to secure, what otherwise would be hopeless, our leading a religious life; the reason why persons go wrong, throw themselves away, follow bad courses and lose their character being, that they have had no education, and that they are ignorant. These and other answers might be given; some beside, and some short of the mark. It may be useful then to consider with what end, with what expectation, we preach, teach, instruct, discuss, bear witness, praise, and blame; what fruit the Church is right in anticipating as the result of her ministerial labours.

St. Paul gives us a reason in the text different from any of those which I have mentioned. He laboured more than all the Apostles; and why? not to civilize the world, not to smooth the face of society, not to facilitate the movements of civil government, not to spread abroad knowledge, not to cultivate the reason, not for any great worldly object, but "for the elect's sake." He "endured all things," all pain, all sorrow, all solitariness; many a tear, many a pang, many a fear, many a disappointment, many a heartache, many a strife, many a wound; he was "five times scourged, thrice beaten with rods, once stoned, thrice in shipwreck, in journeys often, in perils of waters, of robbers, of his own countrymen, of the heathen, of the city, of the wilderness, of the sea, of false brethren, in weariness and painfulness, in watchings often, in hunger and thirst, in fastings often, in cold and nakedness" (2 Cor 11:24–27); and some men could have even been content so to have suffered, had they by these voluntary acts of suffering, been buying as by a price first one and then another triumph of the Gospel. If every stripe was a sinner's ransom, and every tear restored a backslider, and every disappointment was balanced with a joy, and every privation was a brother's edification, then he might have gladly endured all things, knowing that the more he suffered the more he did. And to a certain degree this effect certainly followed; the jailor after his scourging at Philippi, was converted, and washed his stripes; and his "bonds in Christ" were "manifest" at Rome, "in all the palace, and in all other places" (Phil 1:13). In spite, however, of such gracious compensations vouchsafed to the Apostle from time to time, still great visible effects, adequate to the extent of his suffering, were neither its result nor its motive. He sowed in abundance that he might reap in measure; he spoke to the many that he might gain the few; he mixed with the world that he might build up the Church; he "endured all things," not for the sake of all men, but "for the elect's sake," that he might be the means of bringing them to glory. This is instanced of him and the other Apostles in the book of Acts. Thus when St. Peter first preached the Gospel, on the day of Pentecost, "they were all amazed," some "mocked," but "they that gladly received the word were baptized." And when St. Paul and St. Barnabas preached at Antioch to the Gentiles, "As many as were ordained to eternal life, believed" (Acts 2:12, 13; 13:48; 17:32–34). When St. Paul preached at Athens, "some mocked," others said, "We will hear thee again," but "certain men clave unto him." And when he addressed the Jews at Rome, "some believed the things which were spoken, and some believed not." Such was the view, which animated, first Christ Himself, then all His Apostles, and St. Paul in particular, to preach to all, in order to succeed with some. Our Lord "saw of the travail of His soul, and was satisfied." St. Paul, as His servant and instrument, was satisfied in like manner to endure all things for the elect's sake; or, as he says in another place, "I am made all things to all men, that I might by all means save some" (1 Cor 9:22). And such is the office of the Church in every nation where she sojourns; she attempts much, she expects and promises little.

This is a great Scripture truth, which in this busy and sanguine day needs insisting upon. There are in every age a certain number of souls in the world, known to God, unknown to us, who will obey the Truth when offered to them, whatever be the mysterious reason that they do and others do not. These we must contemplate, for these we must labour, these are God's special care, for these are all things; of these and among these we must pray to be, and our friends with us, at the Last Day. They are the true Church, ever increasing in number, ever gathering in, as time goes on; with them lies the Communion of Saints; they have power with God; they are His armies who follow the Lamb, who overcome princes of the earth, and who shall hereafter judge Angels. These are that multitude which took its beginning in St. Paul's day, for which he laboured, having his portion in it himself; for which we in our day must labour too, that, if so be, we too may have a place in it: according to the text, "He that receiveth a prophet in the name of a prophet shall receive a prophet's reward; and he that receiveth a righteous man in the name of a righteous man shall receive a righteous man's reward. And whosoever shall give to drink unto one of these little ones a cup of cold water only in the name of a disciple, verily I say unto you, he shall in no wise lose his reward" (Mt 10:41, 42).

God is neither "without witness" nor without fruit, even in a heathen country:—"In every nation," says St. Peter, "he that feareth God and worketh righteousness is accepted with Him" (Acts 10:35). In every nation, among many bad, there are some good; and, as nations are before the Gospel is offered to them, such they seem to remain on the whole after the offer; "many are called, few are chosen." And to spend and be spent upon the many called for the sake of the chosen few, is the office of Christian teachers and witnesses.

That their office is such seems to be evident from the existing state of Christian countries from the first. Unless it be maintained that the Church has never done her duty towards the nations where she has sojourned, it must be granted that success in the hearts of the many is not promised her. Christianity has raised the tone of morals, has restrained the passions, and enforced external decency and good conduct in the world at large; it has advanced certain persons in virtuous or religious habits, who otherwise might have been imbued with the mere rudiments of truth and holiness; it has given a firmness and consistency to religious profession in numbers, and perhaps has extended the range of really religious practice. Still on the whole the great multitude of men have to all appearance remained, in a spiritual point of view, no better than before. The state of great cities now is not so very different from what it was of old; or at least not so different as to make it appear that the main work of Christianity has lain with the face of society, or what is called the world. Again, the highest class in the community and the lowest, are not so different from what they would be respectively without the knowledge of the Gospel, as to allow it to be said that Christianity has succeeded with the world, *as* the world, in its several ranks and classes. And so of its pursuits and professions; they are in character what they were, softened or restrained in their worst consequences, but still with the same substantial fruits. Trade is still avaricious, not in tendency only but in fact, though it has heard the Gospel; physical science is still sceptical as it was when heathen. Lawyers, soldiers, farmers, politicians, courtiers, nay, shame to say, the priesthood, still savour of the old Adam. Christian states move forward upon the same laws as before, and rise and fall as time goes on, upon the same internal principles. Human nature remains what it was, though it has been baptized; the proverbs, the satires, the pictures, of which it was the subject in heathen times, have their point still. In a word, taking religion to mean as it well may, the being bound by God's law, the acting under God's will instead of our own, how few are there in a country called Christian who even profess religion in this sense! how few there are who live by any other rule than that of their own ease, habit, inclination, as the case may be, on the one hand, and of external circumstances on the other! with how few is the will of God an habitual object of thought, or search, or love, or obedience! All this is so notorious that unbelievers taunt us with it. They see, and scoff at seeing, that Christians, whether the many or the educated or the old, nay, or the sacred ministry, are open to the motives, and unequal to the temptations, which prevail with human nature generally.

The knowledge of the Gospel then has not materially changed more than the surface of things; it has made clean the outside; but as far as we have the means of judging, it has not acted on a large scale upon the mind within, upon that "heart" out of which proceed the evil things "which defile a man." Nor did it ever promise it would do so. Our Saviour's words, spoken of the Apostles in the first instance, relate to the Church at large,—"I pray not for the world, but for them which Thou hast given Me, for they are Thine." In like manner St. Paul says that Christ came, not to convert the world, but "to purify unto Himself a *peculiar people,* zealous of good works"; not to sanctify this evil world, but to "deliver us *out of* this present evil world according to the will of God and our Father" (Jn 17:9; Ti 2:14; Gal 1:4); not to turn the whole earth into a heaven, but to bring down a heaven upon earth. This has been the real triumph of the Gospel, to raise those beyond themselves and beyond human nature, in whatever rank and condition of life, whose wills mysteriously co-operate with God's grace, who, while God visits them, really fear and really obey God, whatever be the unknown reason why one man obeys Him and another not. It has made men saints, and brought into existence specimens of faith and holiness, which without it are unknown and impossible. It has laboured for the elect, and it has succeeded with them. This is, as it were, its token. An ordinary kind of religion, praiseworthy and respectable in its way, may exist under many systems; but Saints are creations of the Gospel and the Church. Not that such an one need in his lifetime seem to be more than other well-living men, for his graces lie deep, and are not known and understood till after his death, even if then. But then, it may be, he "shines forth as the sun in the kingdom of his Father," figuring in his memory on earth what will be fulfilled in soul and body in heaven. And hence we are not accustomed to give to living men the *title* of saints, since *we* cannot well know, while they are among us, who have lived up to their calling and who have not. But in process of time, after death, their excellence perhaps gets abroad; and then they become a witness, a specimen of what the Gospel can do, and a sample and a pledge of all those other high creations of God, His Saints in full number, who die and are never known.

There are many reasons why God's Saints cannot be known all at once;—first, as I have said, their good deeds are done in secret. Next, good men are often slandered, ridiculed, ill-treated in their lifetime; they are mistaken by those, whom they offend by their holiness and strictness, and perhaps they are obliged to withstand sin in their day, and this raises about them a cloud of prejudice and dislike, which in time indeed, but not till after a time, goes off. Then again their intentions and aims are misunderstood; and some of their excellent deeds or noble traits of character are known to some men, others to others, not all to all. This is the case in their lifetime; but after their death, when envy and anger have died away, and men talk together about them, and compare what each knows, their good and holy deeds are added up; and while they evidence their fruitfulness, also clear up or vindicate their motives, and strike the mind of survivors with astonishment and fear; and the Church honours them, thanks God for them, and "glorifies God in" (Gal 1:24) them. This is why the Saints of God are commonly honoured, not while they live, but in their death; and if I am asked to state plainly how such an one differs from an ordinary religious man, I say in this,—that he sets before him as the one object of life, to please and obey God; that he ever aims to submit his will to God's will; that he earnestly follows after holiness; and that he is habitually striving to have a closer resemblance to Christ in all things. He exercises himself, not only in social duties, but in Christian graces; he is not only kind, but meek; not only generous, but humble; not only persevering, but patient; not only upright, but forgiving; not only bountiful, but self-denying; not only contented, but meditative and devotional. An ordinary man thinks it enough to do as he is done by; he will think it fair to resent insults, to repay injuries, to show a becoming pride, to insist on his rights, to be jealous of his honour, when in the wrong to refuse to confess it, to seek to be rich, to desire to be well with the world, to fear what his neighbours will say. He seldom thinks of the Day of Judgment, seldom thinks of sins past, says few prayers, cares little for the Church, has no zeal for God's truth, spends his money on himself. Such is an ordinary Christian, and such is not one of God's elect. For the latter is more than just, temperate, and kind; he has a devoted love of God, high faith, holy hope, over-flowing charity, a noble self-command, a strict conscientiousness, humility never absent, gentleness in speech, simplicity, modesty, and unaffectedness, an unconsciousness of what his endowments are, and what they make him in God's sight. This is what Christianity has done in the world; such is the result of Christian teaching; viz., to elicit, foster, mature the seeds of heaven which lie hid in the earth, to multiply (if it may be said) images of Christ, which, though they be few, are worth all else that is among men, and are an ample recompense and "a crown of rejoicing" for Apostles and Evangelists "in the presence of our Lord Jesus Christ at His coming" (1 Thes 2:19).

It is no triumph then for unbelievers that the Gospel has not done what it never attempted. From the first it announced what was to be the condition of the many who heard and professed it. "Many are called, few are chosen." "Broad is the way that leadeth to destruction, and many there be which go in thereat. Strait is the gate and narrow is the way which leadeth unto life, and few there be that find it." Though we laboured ever so much, with the hope of satisfying the objector, we could not reverse our Saviour's witness, and make the many religious and the bad few. We can but do what is to be done. With our utmost toil we do but reach those for whom crowns are prepared in heaven. "Whom He did foreknow, them did He predestinate." "He that is unjust, let him be unjust still; and he that is filthy, let him be filthy still; and he that is righteous, let him be righteous still; and he that is holy, let him be holy still" (Rom 8:29; Rv 22:11). We cannot destroy the personal differences which separate man and man; and to lay it as a fault to baptism, teaching, and other ministrations, that they cannot pass the bounds predicted in God's word, is as little reasonable as attempting to make one mind the same as another.

And if this be the case, how mistaken is the notion of the day, that the main undertaking of a Christian Church is to make men good members of society, honest, upright, industrious, and well-conducted; and that it fails of its duty, and has cause of shame unless it succeeds in doing so; and that of two religious communities, that must be the more scriptural in its tenets, of which the members are more decent and orderly!—whereas it may easily happen that a corruption of the Gospel, which sacrifices the better fruit, may produce the more abundant, men being not unwilling to compound for neglect of a strict rule by submitting to an easy one. How common is it, at this time, to debate the question, whether the plans of education pursued for the last fifty years have diminished crime or not; whether those who are convicted of offences against the law have for the most part been at school or not! Such inquiries surely are out of place, if Christian education is in question. If the Church set out by engaging to make men good members of the state, they would be very much in place; but if the great object of her Sacraments, preaching, Scriptures, and instructions, is to save the elect of God, to foster into life and rear up into perfection what is really good, not in the sight of man merely, but in the sight of God; not what is useful merely, but what is true and holy; and if to influence those who act on secondary motives require a lowering of the Christian standard, and if an exhibition of the truth makes a man worse unless it makes him better, then she has fulfilled her calling if she has saved the few; and she has done more than her calling, so far as by God's grace she has, consistently with the higher object, restrained, softened, or sobered the many. Much doubtless she will do in this way, but what she does must not be by compromise or unfaithfulness. The Church and the world cannot meet without either the world rising or the Church falling; and the world forsooth pleads necessity, and says it cannot rise to the Church, and deems the Church unreasonable when she will not descend instead.

The Gospel then has come to us, not merely to make us good subjects, good citizens, good members of society, but to make us members of the New Jerusalem, and "fellow-citizens with the saints and of the household of God." Certainly no one is a true Christian who is not a good subject and member of society; but neither is he a true Christian if he is nothing more than this. If he is not aiming at something beyond the power of the natural man, he is not really a Christian, or one of the elect. The Gospel offers to us things supernatural. "Call unto Me," says Almighty God by His prophet, "and I will answer thee, and show thee great and mighty things which thou knowest not" (Jer 33:3). But, alas! the multitude of men do not enter into the force of such an invitation, or feel its graciousness or desirableness. They are satisfied to remain where they find themselves by nature, to be what the world makes them, to bound their conceptions of things by sight and touch, and to conceive of the Gospel according to the thoughts, motives, and feelings which spring up spontaneously within them. They form their religion for themselves from what they are, and live and die in the ordinary and common-place round of hopes and fears, pleasures and pains. In the ordinary common-place round of *duties* indeed, they ought to be engaged, and are bound to find satisfaction. To be out of conceit with our lot in life, is no high feeling,—it is discontent or ambition; but to be out of conceit with the ordinary way of *viewing* our lot, with the ordinary thoughts and feelings of mankind, is nothing but to be a Christian. This is the difference between worldly ambition and heavenly. It is a heavenly ambition which prompts us to soar above the vulgar and ordinary *motives* and *tastes* of the world, the while we abide *in* our calling; like our Saviour who, though the Son of God and partaking of His Father's fulness, yet all His youth long was obedient to His earthly parents, and learned a humble trade. But it is a sordid, narrow, miserable ambition to attempt to *leave* our earthly lot; to be wearied or ashamed of what we are, to hanker after greatness of station, or novelty of life. However, the multitude of men go neither in the one way nor the other; they neither have the high ambition nor the low ambition. It is well they have not the low, certainly; it is well they do not aim at being great men, or heroes; but they have no temptation to do so. What they are tempted to, is to settle down in a satisfied way in the world as they find it, to sit down in the "mire and dirt" of their natural state, to immerse themselves and be absorbed in the unhealthy marsh which is under them. They tend to become part of the world, and be sucked in by it, and (as it were) changed into it; and so to lose all aspirations and thoughts, whether good or bad, after any thing higher than what they are. I do not know whether rich or poor are in greater temptation this way. Poor people, having daily wants, having their bread to earn, and raiment and shelter to provide, being keenly and earnestly and day by day pressed with the realities of pain and anxiety, seem cut off from all high thoughts. To call on a poor man to live a Seraph's life, to live above the world, and to be ambitious of perfection, seems at first sight, as things go, all one with bidding him be a man of refinement of mind or literary taste, a man of science, or a philosopher. Yet is it so? Were not the Apostles in great necessities? had not St. Paul to work for his livelihood? did they eat and drink at their will? did they know one day where they should get their meal or lay their head the next? Surely not; yet they were as expressly told as others, "Seek ye first the kingdom of God and His righteousness" (Mt 6:33). And then it is promised with an express reference to those anxieties about food and clothing, "And all these things shall be added unto you." This passage in our Saviour's Sermon on the Mount shows us most undeniably, that poverty must not be allowed to make us,—is no excuse for our being,—what poor people so often are, anxious, fretful, close, deceitful, dull-minded, suspicious, envious, or ungrateful. No; much as we ought to feel for the poor, yet, if our Saviour's words be true, there is nothing to hinder the poorest man from living the life of an Angel, living in all the unearthly contemplative blessedness of a saint in glory, except so far as sin interferes with it. I mean, it is *sin*, and not poverty which is the hindrance.

Such is the case with the poor; now again take the case of those who have a competency. They too are swallowed up in the cares or interests of life as much as the poor are. While want keeps the one from God by unsettling his mind, a competency keeps the other by the seductions of ease and plenty. The poor man says, "I cannot go to Church or to the Sacrament of the Lord's Supper, till I am more at ease in my mind; I am troubled, and my thoughts are not my own." The rich man does not make any excuses,—he comes; but his "heart goeth after his covetousness." It is not enlarged by being rid of care; but is as little loosened from what is seen, as little expatiates in the free and radiant light of Gospel day, as if that day had not been poured upon it. No; such an one may be far other than a mere man of the world,—he may be a religious man, in the common sense of the word; he may be exemplary in his conduct, as far as the social duties of life go; he may be really and truly, and not in pretence, kind, benevolent, sincere, and in a manner serious: but so it is, his mind has never been unchained to soar aloft, he does not look out with longing into the infinite spaces in which, as a Christian, he has free range. Our Lord praises those who *"hunger and thirst* after righteousness." *This* is what men in general are without. They are more or less "full, and have need of nothing," in religious matters; they do not feel how great a thing it is to be a Christian, and how far they fall short of it. They are contented with themselves on the whole; they are quite conscious indeed that they do act up to their standard, but it is their standard that is low. A sort of ordinary obedience suffices them as well as the poor. A person in straitened circumstances will say, "I have enough to do to take care of my wife and children"; another says, "I have lost my husband and friends, and have enough to do to take care of myself"; bystanders say, "What a mockery to call on a starving population, to watch, fast, and pray, and aim at perfection." Well, let me turn, I say, to the rich men, and speak to them; what say the rich? *They* put aside all such hungering and thirsting after righteousness as visionary, high-flown, and what they call romantic. They have a certain definite and clear view of their duties; they think that the summit of perfection is to be decent and respectable in their calling, to enjoy moderately the pleasures of life, to eat and drink, and marry and give in marriage, and buy and sell, and plant and build, and to take care that religion does not *engross* them. Alas! and is it so? Is the superhuman life enjoined on us in the Gospel but a dream? Is there no meaning in our own case, of the texts about the strait gate and the narrow way, and Mary's good part, and the rule of perfection, and the saying which "all cannot receive save they to whom it is given?" Holy men, certainly, do not throw themselves out of their stations. They are not gloomy, or morose, or overbearing, or restless; but still they are pursuing in their daily walk, and by their secret thoughts and actions, a conduct *above* the world. Whether rich or poor, high-born or low-born, married or single, they have never wedded themselves to the world; they have never surrendered themselves to be its captives; never looked out for station, fashion, comfort, credit, as the end of life. They have kept up the feeling which young people often have, who at first ridicule the artificial forms and usages of society, and find it difficult to conform themselves to its pomp and pretence. Of course it is not wise to ridicule and run counter to any thing that is in its nature indifferent; and as they have grown older they have learned this; but the feeling remains of want of sympathy with what surrounds them; whereas these are the very things which men of the world are most proud of, their appointments, and their dress, and their bearing, and their gentility, and their acquaintance with great men, and their connexions, and their power of managing, and their personal importance.

God grant to us a simple, reverent, affectionate, temper, that we may truly be the Church's children, and fit subjects of her instructions! This gained, the rest through His grace will follow. This is the temper of those "little ones," whose Angels "do always behold the face" of our heavenly Father; of those for whom Apostles endured all things, to whom the Ordinances of grace minister, and whom Christ "nourisheth and cherisheth" even as His own flesh.

SERMON XIV

The Greatness and Littleness of Human Life

"The days of the years of my pilgrimage are an hundred and thirty years: few and evil have the days of the years of my life been; and have not attained unto the days of the years of the life of my fathers, in the days of their pilgrimage."—Gn 47:9

Why did the aged Patriarch call his days few, who had lived twice as long as men now live, when he spoke? Why did he call them evil, seeing he had on the whole lived in riches and honour, and, what is more, in God's favour? Yet he described his time as short, his days as evil, and his life as but a pilgrimage. Or if we allow that his afflictions were such as to make him reasonably think cheaply of his life, in spite of the blessings which attended it, yet that he should call it short, considering he had so much more time for the highest purposes of his being than we have, is at first sight surprising. He alludes indeed to the longer life which had been granted to his fathers, and perhaps felt a decrepitude greater than theirs had been; yet this difference between him and them could hardly be the real ground of his complaint in the text, or more than a confirmation or occasion of it. It was not because Abraham had lived one hundred and seventy-five years, and Isaac one hundred and eighty, and he himself, whose life was not yet finished, but one hundred and thirty, that he made this mournful speech. For it matters not, when time is gone, what length it has been; and this doubtless was the real cause why the Patriarch spoke as he did, not because his life was shorter than his fathers', but because it was well nigh over. When life is past, it is all one whether it has lasted two hundred years or fifty. And it is this characteristic, stamped on human life in the day of its birth, viz., that it is mortal, which makes it under all circumstances and in every form equally feeble and despicable. All the points in which men differ, health and strength, high or low estate, happiness or misery, vanish before this common lot, mortality. Pass a few years, and the longest-lived will be gone; nor will what is past profit him then, except in its consequences.

PAROCHIAL AND PLAIN SERMONS

And this sense of the nothingness of life, impressed on us by the very fact that it comes to an end, is much deepened, when we contrast it with the capabilities of us who live it. Had Jacob lived Methuselah's age, he would have called it short. This is what we all feel, though at first sight it seems a contradiction, that even though the days as they go be slow, and be laden with many events, or with sorrows or dreariness, lengthening them out and making them tedious, yet the year passes quick though the hours tarry, and time bygone is as a dream, though we thought it would never go while it was going. And the reason seems to be this; that, when we contemplate human life in itself, in however small a portion of it, we see implied in it the presence of a soul, the energy of a spiritual existence, of an accountable being; consciousness tells us this concerning it every moment. But when we look back on it in memory, we view it but externally, as a mere lapse of time, as a mere earthly history. And the longest duration of this external world is as dust and weighs nothing, against one moment's life of the world within. Thus we are ever expecting great things from life, from our internal consciousness every moment of our having souls; and we are ever being disappointed, on considering what we have gained from time past, or can hope from time to come. And life is ever promising and never fulfilling; and hence, however long it be, our days are few and evil. This is the particular view of the subject on which I shall now dwell.

Our earthly life then gives promise of what it does not accomplish. It promises immortality, yet it is mortal; it contains life in death and eternity in time; and it attracts us by beginnings which faith alone brings to an end. I mean, when we take into account the powers with which our souls are gifted as Christians, the very consciousness of these fills us with a certainty that they must last beyond this life; that is in the case of good and holy men, whose present state I say, is to them who know them well, an earnest of immortality. The greatness of their gifts, contrasted with their scanty time for exercising them, forces the mind forward to the thought of another life, as almost the necessary counterpart and consequence of this life, and certainly implied in this life, provided there be a righteous Governor of the world who does not make man for nought.

This is a thought which will come upon us not always, but under circumstances. And many perhaps of those who at first hearing may think they never felt it, may recognize what I mean, while I describe it.

I mean, when one sees some excellent person, whose graces we know, whose kindliness, affectionateness, tenderness, and generosity,—when we see him dying (let him have lived ever so long; I am not supposing a premature death; let him live out his days), the thought is forced upon us with a sort of surprise; "Surely, he is not to die yet; he has not yet had any opportunity of exercising duly those excellent gifts with which God has endowed him." Let him have lived seventy or eighty years, yet it seems as if he had done nothing at all, and his life were scarcely begun. He has lived all his days perhaps in a private sphere; he has been engaged on a number of petty matters which died with the day, and yielded no apparent fruit. He has had just enough of trial under various circumstances, to evidence, but not adequately to employ, what was in him. He has, we perhaps perceive, a noble benevolence of mind, a warmth of heart, and a beneficent temper, which, had it the means, would scatter blessings on every side; yet he has never been rich,—he dies poor. We have been accustomed to say to ourselves, "What would such a one be were he wealthy?" not as fancying he ever *will* have riches, but from feeling how he would become them; yet, when he actually does die as he lived, without them, we feel somehow disappointed,—there has been a failure,—his mind, we think, has never reached its scope,— he has had a treasure within him which has never been used. His days have been but few and evil, and have become old unseasonably, compared with his capabilities; and we are driven by a sense of these, to look on to a future state as a time when they will be brought out and come into effect. I am not attempting by such reflections to prove that there is a future state; let us take that for granted. I mean, over and above our positive belief in this great truth, we are actually driven to a belief, we attain a sort of sensible conviction of that life to come, a certainty striking home to our hearts and piercing them, by this imperfection in what is present. The very greatness of our powers makes this life look pitiful; the very pitifulness of this life forces on our thoughts to another; and the prospect of another gives a dignity and value to this life which promises it; and thus this life is at once great and little, and we rightly contemn it while we exalt its importance.

And, if this life is short, even when longest, from the great disproportion between it and the powers of regenerate man, still more is this the case, of course, where it is cut short, and death comes prematurely. Men there are, who, in a single moment of their lives, have shown a superhuman height and majesty of mind which it would take ages for them to employ on its proper objects, and, as it were, to exhaust; and who by such passing flashes, like rays of the sun, and the darting of lightning, give token of their immortality, give token to us that they are but Angels in disguise, the elect of God sealed for eternal life, and destined to judge the world and to reign with Christ for ever. Yet they are suddenly taken away, and we have hardly recognized them when we lose them. Can we believe that they are not removed for higher things elsewhere? This is sometimes said with reference to our intellectual powers; but it is still more true of our moral nature. There is something in moral truth and goodness, in faith, in firmness, in heavenly-mindedness, in meekness, in courage, in loving-kindness, to which this world's circumstances are quite unequal, for which the longest life is insufficient, which makes the highest opportunities of this world disappointing, which must burst the prison of this world to have its appropriate range. So that when a good man dies, one is led to say, "He has not half showed himself, he has had nothing to exercise him; his days are gone like a shadow, and he is withered like grass."

I say the word "disappointing" is the only word to express our feelings on the death of God's saints. Unless our faith be very active, so as to pierce beyond the grave, and realize the future, we feel depressed at what seems like a failure of great things. And from this very feeling surely, by a sort of contradiction, we may fairly take hope; for if this life be so disappointing, so unfinished, surely it is not the whole. This feeling of disappointment will often come upon us in an especial way on happening to hear of or to witness the deathbeds of holy men. The hour of death seems to be a season, of which, in the hands of providence, much might be *made*, if I may use the term; much might be done for the glory of God, the good of man, and the manifestation of the person dying. And beforehand friends will perhaps look forward, and expect that great things are then to take place, which they shall never forget. Yet, "how dieth the wise man? as the fool" (Eccl 2:16). Such is the preacher's experience, and our own bears witness to it. King Josiah, the zealous servant of the Living God, died the death of wicked Ahab, the worshipper of Baal. True Christians die as other men. One dies by a sudden accident, another in battle, another without friends to see how he dies, a fourth is insensible or not himself. Thus the opportunity seems thrown away, and we are forcibly reminded that "the manifestation of the sons of God" (Rom 8:19) is hereafter; that "the earnest expectation of the creature" is but waiting for it; that this life is unequal to the burden of so great an office as the due exhibition of those secret ones who shall one day "shine forth as the sun in the kingdom of their Father" (Mt 13:43).

But further (if it be allowable to speculate), one can even conceive the same kind of feeling, and a most transporting one, to come over the soul of the faithful Christian, when just separated from the body, and conscious that his trial is once for all over. Though his life has been a long and painful discipline, yet when it is over, we may suppose him to feel at the moment the same sort of surprise at its being ended, as generally follows any exertion in this life, when the object is gained and the anticipation over. When we have wound up our minds for any point of time, any great event, an interview with strangers, or the sight of some wonder, or the occasion of some unusual trial, when it comes, and is gone, we have a strange reverse of feeling from our changed circumstances. Such, but without any mixture of pain, without any lassitude, dulness, or disappointment, may be the happy contemplation of the disembodied spirit; as if it said to itself, "So all is now over; this is what I have so long waited for; for which I have nerved myself; against which I have prepared, fasted, prayed, and wrought righteousness. Death is come and gone,—it is over. Ah! is it possible? What an easy trial, what a cheap price for eternal glory! A few sharp sicknesses, or some acute pain awhile, or some few and evil years, or some struggles of mind, dreary desolateness for a season, fightings and fears, afflicting bereavements, or the scorn and ill-usage of the world,—how they fretted me, how much I thought of them, yet how little really they are! How contemptible a thing is human life,—contemptible in itself, yet in its effects invaluable! for it has been to me like a small seed of easy purchase, germinating and ripening into bliss everlasting."

Such being the unprofitableness of this life, viewed in itself, it is plain how we should regard it while we go through it. We should remember that it is scarcely more than an accident of our being—that it is no part of ourselves, who are immortal; that we are immortal spirits, independent of time and space, and that this life is but a sort of outward stage, on which we act for a time, and which is only sufficient and only intended to answer the purpose of trying whether we will serve God or no. We should consider ourselves to be in this world in no fuller sense than players in any game are in the game; and life to be a sort of dream, as detached and as different from our real eternal existence, as a dream differs from waking; a serious dream, indeed, as affording a means of judging us, yet in itself a kind of shadow without substance, a scene set before us, in which we seem to be, and in which it is our duty to act just as if all we saw had a truth and reality, because all that meets us influences us and our destiny. The regenerate soul is taken into communion with Saints and Angels, and its "life is hid with Christ in God" (Col 3:3); it has a place in God's court, and is not of this world,—looking into this world as a spectator might look at some show or pageant, except when called from time to time to take a part. And while it obeys the instinct of the senses, it does so for God's sake, and it submits itself to things of time so far as to be brought to perfection by them, that, when the veil is withdrawn and it sees itself to be, where it ever has been, in God's kingdom, it may be found worthy to enjoy it. It is this view of life, which removes from us all surprise and disappointment that it is so incomplete: as well might we expect any chance event which happens in the course of it to be complete, any casual conversation with a stranger, or the toil or amusement of an hour.

Let us then thus account of our present state: It is precious as revealing to us, amid shadows and figures, the existence and attributes of Almighty God and His elect people: It is precious, because it enables us to hold intercourse with immortal souls who are on their trial as we are. It is momentous, as being the scene and means of our trial; but beyond this it has no claims upon us. "Vanity of vanities, says the Preacher, all is vanity." We may be poor or rich, young or old, honoured or slighted, and it ought to affect us no more, neither to elate us nor depress us, than if we were actors in a play, who know that the characters they represent are not their own, and that though they may appear to be superior one to another, to be kings or to be peasants, they are in reality all on a level. The one desire which should move us should be, first of all, that of seeing Him face to face, who is now hid from us; and next of enjoying eternal and direct communion, in and through Him, with our friends around us, whom at present we know only through the medium of sense, by precarious and partial channels, which give us little insight into their hearts.

These are suitable feelings towards this attractive but deceitful world. What have we to do with its gifts and honours, who, having been already baptized into the world to come, are no longer citizens of this? Why should we be anxious for a long life, or wealth, or credit, or comfort, who know that the next world will be every thing which our hearts can wish, and that not in appearance only, but truly and everlastingly? Why should we rest in this world, when it is the token and promise of another? Why should we be content with its surface, instead of appropriating what is stored beneath it? To those who live by faith, every thing they see speaks of that future world; the very glories of nature, the sun, moon, and stars, and the richness and the beauty of the earth, are as types and figures witnessing and teaching the invisible things of God. All that we see is destined one day to burst forth into a heavenly bloom, and to be transfigured into immortal glory. Heaven at present is out of sight, but in due time, as snow melts and discovers what it lay upon, so will this visible creation fade away before those greater splendours which are behind it, and on which at present it depends. In that day shadows will retire, and the substance show itself. The sun will grow pale and be lost in the sky, but it will be before the radiance of Him whom it does but image, the Sun of Righteousness, with healing on His wings, who will come forth in visible form, as a bridegroom out of his chamber, while His perishable type decays. The stars which surround it will be replaced by Saints and Angels circling His throne. Above and below, the clouds of the air, the trees of the field, the waters of the great deep will be found impregnated with the forms of everlasting spirits, the servants of God which do His pleasure. And our own mortal bodies will then be found in like manner to contain within them an inner man, which will then receive its due proportions, as the soul's harmonious organ, instead of that gross mass of flesh and blood which sight and touch are sensible of. For this glorious manifestation the whole creation is at present in travail, earnestly desiring that it may be accomplished in its season.

These are thoughts to make us eagerly and devoutly say, "Come, Lord Jesus, to end the time of waiting, of darkness, of turbulence, of disputing, of sorrow, of care." These are thoughts to lead us to rejoice in every day and hour that passes, as bringing us nearer the time of His appearing, and the termination of sin and misery. They are thoughts which ought thus to affect us; and so they would, were it not for the load of guilt which weighs upon us, for sins committed against light and grace. Oh, that it were otherwise with us! Oh, that we were fitted duly to receive this lesson which the world gives us, and had so improved the gifts of life, that while we felt it to be perishing, we might rejoice in it as precious! Oh, that we were not conscious of deep stains upon our souls, the accumulations of past years, and of infirmities continually besetting us! Were it not for all this,—were it not for our unprepared state, as in one sense it may truly be called, how gladly should we hail each new month and year as a token that our Saviour is so much nearer to us than He ever has been yet! May He grant His grace abundantly to us, to make us meet for His presence, that we may not be ashamed before Him at His coming! May He vouchsafe to us the full grace of His ordinances: May He feed us with His choicest gifts: May He expel the poison from our souls: May He wash us clean in His precious blood, and give us the fulness of faith, love, and hope, as foretastes of the heavenly portion which He destines for us!

SERMON XV

Moral Effects of Communion with God

"One thing have I desired of the Lord, which I will require; even that I may dwell in the house of the Lord all the days of my life, to behold the fair beauty of the Lord, and to visit His Temple."—Ps 27:4

What the Psalmist desired, we Christians enjoy to the full,—the liberty of holding communion with God in His Temple all through our life. Under the Law, the presence of God was but in one place; and therefore could be approached and enjoyed only at set times. For far the greater part of their lives, the chosen people were in one sense "cast out of the sight of His eyes" (Ps 31:24); and the periodical return to it which they were allowed, was a privilege highly coveted and earnestly expected. Much more precious was the privilege of continually dwelling in His sight, which is spoken of in the text. "One thing," says the Psalmist, "have I desired of the Lord . . . that I may dwell in the house of the Lord all the days of my life, to behold the fair beauty of the Lord, and to visit His Temple." He desired to have continually that communion with God in prayer, praise, and meditation, to which His presence admits the soul; and this, I say, is the portion of Christians. Faith opens upon us Christians the Temple of God wherever we are; for that Temple is a spiritual one, and so is everywhere present. "We have access," says the Apostle,—that is, we have admission or introduction, "by faith into this grace wherein we stand, and rejoice in hope of the glory of God." And hence he says elsewhere, "Rejoice in the Lord alway, and again I say, Rejoice." "Rejoice evermore, pray without ceasing; in every thing give thanks." And St. James, "Is any afflicted? let him pray: is any merry? let him sing Psalms" (Rom 5:2; Phil 4:4; 1 Thes 5:16–18; Jas 5:13). Prayer, praise, thanksgiving, contemplation, are the peculiar privilege and duty of a Christian, and that for their own sakes, from the exceeding comfort and satisfaction they afford him, and without reference to any definite results to which prayer tends, without reference to the answers which are promised to it, from a general sense of the blessedness of being under the shadow of God's throne.

I propose, then, in what follows, to make some remarks on communion with God, or prayer in a large sense of the word; not as regards its external consequences, but as it may be considered to affect our own minds and hearts.

What, then, is prayer? It is (if it may be said reverently) *conversing* with God. We converse with our fellow-men, and then we use familiar language, because they *are* our fellows. We converse with God, and then we use the lowliest, awfullest, calmest, concisest language we can, because He *is* God. Prayer, then, is *divine* converse, differing from human as God differs from man. Thus St. Paul says, "Our conversation is in heaven" (Phil 3:20)—not indeed thereby meaning converse of words only, but intercourse and manner of living generally; yet still in an especial way converse of words or prayer, because language is the special means of all intercourse. Our intercourse with our fellow-men goes on, not by sight, but by sound, not by eyes, but by ears. Hearing is the social sense, and language is the social bond. In like manner, as the Christian's conversation is in heaven, as it is his duty, with Enoch and other Saints, *to walk with God*, so his voice is in heaven, his heart "inditing of a good matter," of prayers and praises. Prayers and praises are the mode of his intercourse with the next world, as the converse of business of recreation is the mode in which this world is carried on in all its separate courses. He who does not pray, does not claim his citizenship with heaven, but lives, though an heir of the kingdom, as if he were a child of earth.

Now, it is not surprising if that duty or privilege, which is the characteristic token of our heavenly inheritance, should also have an especial influence upon our fitness for claiming it. He who does not use a gift, loses it; the man who does not use his voice or limbs, loses power over them, and becomes disqualified for the state of life to which he is called. In like manner, he who neglects to pray, not only suspends the enjoyment, but is in a way to lose the possession, of his divine citizenship. We are members of another world; we have been severed from the companionship of devils, and brought into that invisible kingdom of Christ which faith alone discerns,—that mysterious Presence of God which encompasses us, which is in us, and around us, which is in our heart, which enfolds us as though with a robe of light, hiding our scarred and discoloured souls from the sight of Divine Purity, and making them shining as the Angels; and which flows in upon us too by means of all forms of beauty and grace which this visible world contains, in a starry host or (if I may so say) a milky way of divine companions, the inhabitants of Mount Zion, where we dwell. Faith, I say, alone apprehends all this; but yet there *is* something which is not left to faith,—our own tastes, likings, motives, and habits. Of these we are conscious in our degree, and we can make ourselves more and more conscious; and as consciousness tells us what they are, reason tells us whether they are such as become, as correspond with, that heavenly world into which we have been translated.

I say then, it is plain to common sense that the man who has not accustomed himself to the language of heaven will be no fit inhabitant of it when, in the Last Day, it is perceptibly revealed. The case is like that of a language or style of speaking of this world; we know well a foreigner from a native. Again, we know those who have been used to kings' courts or educated society from others. By their voice, accent, and language, and not only so, by their gestures and gait, by their usages, by their mode of conducting themselves and their principles of conduct, we know well what a vast difference there is between those who have lived in good society and those who have not. What indeed is called "*good* society" is often very worthless society. I am not speaking of it to praise it; I only mean, that, as the manners which men call refined or courtly are gained only by intercourse with courts and polished circles, and as the influence of the words there used (that is, of the ideas which those words, striking again and again on the ear, convey to the mind), extends in a most subtle way over all that men do, over the turn of their sentences, and the tone of their questions and replies, and their general bearing, and the spontaneous flow of their thoughts, and their mode of viewing things, and the general maxims or heads to which they refer them, and the motives which determine them, and their likings and dislikings, hopes and fears, and their relative estimate of persons, and the intensity of their perceptions towards particular objects; so a habit of prayer, the practice of turning to God and the unseen world, in every season, in every place, in every emergency (let alone its supernatural effect of prevailing with God),—prayer, I say, has what may be called a *natural* effect, in spiritualizing and elevating the soul. A man is no longer what he was before; gradually, imperceptibly to himself, he has imbibed a new set of ideas, and become imbued with fresh principles. He is as one coming from kings' courts, with a grace, a delicacy, a dignity, a propriety, a justness of thought and taste, a clearness and firmness of principle, all his own. Such is the power of God's secret grace acting through those ordinances which He has enjoined us; such the evident fitness of those ordinances to produce the results which they set before us. As speech is the organ of human society, and the means of human civilization, so is prayer the instrument of divine fellowship and divine training.

I will give, for the sake of illustration, some instances in detail of one particular fault of mind, which among others a habit of prayer is calculated to cure.

For instance; many a man seems to have no grasp at all of doctrinal truth. He cannot get himself to think it of importance what a man believes, and what not. He tries to do so; for a time he does; he does for a time think that a certain faith is necessary for salvation, that certain doctrines are to be put forth and maintained in charity to the souls of men. Yet though he thinks so one day, he changes the next; he holds the truth, and then lets it go again. He is filled with doubts; suddenly the question crosses him, "Is it possible that such and such a doctrine *is* necessary?" and he relapses into an uncomfortable sceptical state, out of which there is no outlet. Reasonings do not convince him; he *cannot* be convinced; he has no grasp of truth. Why? Because the next world is not a reality to him; it only exists in his mind in the form of certain conclusions from certain reasonings. It is but an inference; and never can be more, never can be present to his mind, until he acts, instead of arguing. Let him but act as if the next world were before him; let him but give himself to such devotional exercises as we ought to observe in the presence of an Almighty, All-holy, and All-merciful God, and it will be a rare case indeed if his difficulties do not vanish.

Or again: A man may have a natural disposition towards caprice and change; he may be apt to take up first one fancy, then another, from novelty or other reason; he may take sudden likings or dislikings, or be tempted to form a scheme of religion for himself, of what he thinks best or most beautiful out of all the systems which divide the world.

Again: He is troubled perhaps with a variety of unbecoming thoughts, which he would fain keep out of his mind if he could. He finds himself unsettled and uneasy, dissatisfied with his condition, easily excited, sorry at sin one moment, forgetting it the next, feeble-minded, unable to rule himself, tempted to dote upon trifles, apt to be caught and influenced by vanities, and to abandon himself to languor or indolence.

Once more: He has not a clear perception of the path of truth and duty. This is an especial fault among us now-a-days: Men are actuated perhaps by the best feelings and the most amiable motives, and are not fairly chargeable with insincerity; and yet there is a want of straightforwardness in their conduct. They allow themselves to be guided by expediency, and defend themselves, and perhaps so plausibly, that though you are not convinced, you are silenced. They attend to what others think, more than to what God says; they look at Scripture more as a gift to man than as a gift from God; they consider themselves at liberty to modify its plain precepts by a certain discretionary rule; they listen to the voice of great men, and allow themselves to be swayed by them; they make comparisons and strike the balance between the impracticability of the whole that God commands, and the practicability of effecting a part, and think they may consent to give up something, if they can secure the rest. They shift about in opinion, going first a little this way, then a little that, according to the loudness and positiveness with which others speak; they are at the mercy of the last speaker, and they think they observe a safe, judicious, and middle course, by always keeping a certain distance behind those who go furthest. Or they are rash in their religious projects and undertakings, and forget that they may be violating the lines and fences of God's law, while they move about freely at their pleasure. Now, I will not judge another; I will not say that in this or that given case the fault of mind in question (for any how it is a fault), does certainly arise from some certain cause which I choose to guess at: but at least there *are* cases where this wavering of mind *does* arise from scantiness of prayer; and if so, it is worth a man's considering, who is thus unsteady, timid, and dimsighted, whether this scantiness be not perchance the true reason of such infirmities in his own case, and whether a "continuing instant in prayer,"—by which I mean, not merely prayer morning and evening, but some thing suitable to his disease, something extraordinary, as medicine is extraordinary, a "redeeming of time" from society and recreation in order to pray more,—whether such a change in his habits would not remove them?

For what is the very promise of the New Covenant but stability? What is it, but a clear insight into the truth, such as will enable us to know how to walk, how to profess, how to meet the circumstances of life, how to withstand gainsayers? Are we built upon a rock or upon the sand? Are we after all tossed about on the sea of opinion, when Christ has stretched out His hand to us, to help and encourage us? "Thou wilt keep him in perfect peace whose mind is stayed on Thee, because he trusteth in Thee" (Is 26:3). Such is the word of promise. Can we possibly have apprehensions about what man will do to us or say of us, can we flatter the great ones of earth, or timidly yield to the many, or be dazzled by talent, or drawn aside by interest, who are in the habit of divine conversations? "Ye have an unction from the Holy One," says St. John, "and ye know all things. I have not written unto you because ye know not the truth, but because ye know it, and that no lie is of the truth. . . . The anointing which ye have received of Him abideth in you, and ye need not that any man teach you. . . . Whosoever is born of God, doth not commit sin, for his seed remaineth in him; and he cannot sin, because he is born of God" (1 Jn 2:20, 21, 27; 3:9). This is that birth, by which the baptized soul not only enters, but actually embraces and realizes the kingdom of God. This is the true and effectual regeneration, when the seed of life takes root in man and thrives. Such men have accustomed themselves to speak to God, and God has ever spoken to them; and they feel "the powers of the world to come" as truly as they feel the presence of this world, because they have been accustomed to speak and act as if it were real. All of us must rely on something; all must look up to, admire, court, make themselves one with something. Most men cast in their lot with the visible world; but true Christians with Saints and Angels.

Such men are little understood by the world because they are not of the world; and hence it sometimes happens that even the better sort of men are often disconcerted and vexed by them. It cannot be otherwise; they move forward on principles so different from what are commonly assumed as true. They take for granted, as first principles, what the world wishes to have proved in detail. They have become familiar with the sights of the next world, till they talk of them as if all men admitted them. The immortality of truth, its oneness, the impossibility of falsehood coalescing with it, what truth is, what it should lead one to do in particular cases, how it lies in the details of life,—all these points are mere matters of debate in the world, and men go through long processes of argument, and pride themselves on their subtleness in defending or attacking, in making probable or improbable, ideas which are assumed without a word by those who have lived in heaven, as the very ground to start from. In consequence, such men are called bad disputants, inconsecutive reasoners, strange, eccentric, or perverse thinkers, merely because they do not take for granted, nor go to prove, what others do,—because they do not go about to define and determine the sights (as it were), the mountains and rivers and plains, and sun, moon, and stars, of the next world. And hence in turn they are commonly unable to enter into the ways of thought or feelings of other men, having been engrossed with God's thoughts and God's ways. Hence, perhaps, they seem abrupt in what they say and do; nay, even make others feel constrained and uneasy in their presence. Perhaps they appear reserved too, because they take so much for granted which might be drawn out, and because they cannot bring themselves to tell all their thoughts from their sacredness, and because they are drawn off from free conversation to the thought of heaven, on which their minds rest. Nay, perchance, they appear severe, because their motives are not understood, nor their sensitive jealousy for the honour of God and their charitable concern for the good of their fellow-Christians duly appreciated. In short, to the world they seem like *foreigners*. We know how foreigners strike us; they are often to *our* notions strange and unpleasing in their manners; why is this? merely *because* they are of a different country. Each country has its own manners,—one may not be better than other; but we naturally like our own ways, and we do not understand other. We do not see their meaning. We misconstrue them; we think they mean something unpleasant, something rude, or over-free, or haughty, or unrefined, when they do not. And in like manner, the world at large, not only is not Christian, but cannot discern or understand the Christian. Thus our Blessed Lord Himself was not recognized or honoured by His relatives, and (as is plain to every reader of Scripture) He often seems to speak abruptly and severely. So too St. Paul was considered by the Corinthians as contemptible in speech. And hence St. John, speaking of "what manner of love the Father hath bestowed upon us that we should be called the sons of God," adds, "therefore the world *knoweth* us not, because it knew Him not" (1 Jn 3:1). Such is the effect of divine meditations: admitting us into the next world, and withdrawing us from this; making us children of God, but withal "strangers unto our brethren, even aliens unto our mother's children" (Ps 69:8). Yea, though the true servants of God increase in meekness and love day by day, and to those who know them will seem what they really are; and though their good works are evident to all men, and cannot be denied, yet such is the eternal Law which goes between the Church and the world—we cannot be friends of both; and they who take their portion with the Church, will seem, except in some remarkable cases, unamiable to the world, for the "world knoweth them not," and does not like them though it can hardly tell why; yet (as St. John proceeds) they have this blessing, that "when He shall appear, they shall be like Him, for they shall see Him as He is" (1 Jn 3:2).

And if, as it would seem, we must choose between the two, surely the world's friendship may be better parted with than our fellowship with our Lord and Saviour. What indeed have we to do with courting men, whose faces are turned towards God? We know how men feel and act when they come to die; they discharge their worldly affairs from their minds, and try to realize the unseen state. Then this world is nothing to them. It may praise, it may blame; but they feel it not. They are leaving their goods, their deeds, their sayings, their writings, their names, behind them; and they care not for it, for they wait for Christ. To one thing alone they are alive, His coming; they watch against it, if so be they may then be found without shame. Such is the conduct of dying men; and what all but the very hardened do at the last, if their senses fail not and their powers hold, that does the true Christian all life long. He is ever dying while he lives; he is on his bier, and the prayers for the sick are saying over him. He has no work but that of making his peace with God, and preparing for the judgment. He has no aim but that of being found worthy to escape the things that shall come to pass and to stand before the Son of man. And therefore day by day he unlearns the love of this world, and the desire of its praise; he can bear to belong to the nameless family of God, and to seem to the world strange in it and out of place, for so he is.

And when Christ comes at last, blessed indeed will be his lot. He has joined himself from the first to the conquering side; he has risked the present against the future, preferring the chance of eternity to the certainty of time; and then his reward will be but beginning, when that of the children of this world is come to an end. In the words of the wise man, "Then shall the righteous man stand in great boldness before the face of such as have afflicted him, and made no account of his labours. When they see it they shall be troubled with terrible fear, and shall be amazed at the strangeness of His salvation, so far beyond all that they looked for. And they, repenting and groaning for anguish of spirit, shall say within themselves, This is he whom we had sometimes in derision and a proverb of reproach; we fools counted his life madness, and his end to be without honour. How is he numbered among the children of God, and his lot is among the saints!" (Wis 5:1–5).

SERMON XVI

Christ Hidden from the World

"The light shineth in darkness; and the darkness comprehended it not."—Jn 1:5

Of all the thoughts which rise in the mind when contemplating the sojourn of our Lord Jesus Christ upon earth,* none perhaps is more affecting and subduing than the obscurity which attended it. I do not mean His obscure condition, in the sense of its being humble; but the obscurity in which He was shrouded, and the secrecy which He observed. This characteristic of His first Advent is referred to very frequently in Scripture, as in the text, "The light shineth in darkness, and the darkness comprehended it not"; and is in contrast with what is foretold about His second Advent. Then "every eye shall see Him"; which implies that all shall recognize Him; whereas, when He came for the first time, though many saw Him, few indeed discerned Him. It had been prophesied, "When we shall see Him there is no beauty that we should desire Him"; and at the very end of His ministry, He said to one of His twelve chosen friends, "Have I been so long time with you, and yet hast thou not known Me, Philip?" (Is 53:2; Jn 14:9).

I propose to set before you one or two thoughts which arise from this very solemn circumstance, and which may, through God's blessing, be profitable.

1. And first, let us review some of the circumstances which marked His sojourn when on earth.

His condescension in coming down from heaven, in leaving His Father's glory and taking flesh, is so far beyond power of words or thought, that one might consider at first sight that it mattered little whether He came as a prince or a beggar. And yet after all, it *is* much more wonderful that He came in low estate, for this reason; because it might have been thought beforehand, that, though He condescended to come on earth, yet He would not submit to be overlooked and despised:

---

* Preached on Christmas Day.

Now the rich are not despised by the world, and the poor are. If He had come as a great prince or noble, the world without knowing a whit more that He was God, yet would at least have looked up to Him and honoured Him, as being a prince; but when He came in a low estate, He took upon Him one additional humiliation, *contempt*,—being contemned, scorned, rudely passed by, roughly profaned by His creatures.

What were the actual circumstances of His coming? His Mother is a poor woman; she comes to Bethlehem to be taxed, travelling, when her choice would have been to remain at home. She finds there is no room in the inn; she is obliged to betake herself to a stable; she brings forth her firstborn Son, and lays Him in a manger. That little babe, so born, so placed, is none other than the Creator of heaven and earth, the Eternal Son of God.

Well; he was born of a poor woman, laid in a manger, brought up to a lowly trade, that of a carpenter; and when He began to preach the Gospel He had not a place to lay His head: lastly, He was put to death, to an infamous and odious death, the death which criminals then suffered.

For the three last years of His life, He preached the Gospel, I say, as we read in Scripture; but He did not begin to do so till He was thirty years old. For the first thirty years of His life, He seems to have lived, just as a poor man would live now. Day after day, season after season, winter and summer, one year and then another, passed on, as might happen to any of us. He passed from being a babe in arms to being a child, and then He became a boy, and so He grew up "like a tender plant," increasing in wisdom and stature; and then He seems to have followed the trade of Joseph, his reputed father; going on in an ordinary way without any great occurrence, till He was thirty years old. How very wonderful is all this! that He should live here, doing nothing great, so long; living here, as if for the sake of living; not preaching, or collecting disciples, or apparently in any way furthering the cause which brought Him down from heaven. Doubtless there were deep and wise reasons in God's counsels for His going on so long in obscurity; I only mean, that *we* do not know them.

And it is remarkable that those who were about Him, seem to have treated Him as one of their equals. His brethren, that is, His near relations, His cousins, did not believe in Him. And it is very observable, too, that when He began to preach and a multitude collected, we are told, "When His friends heard of it they went out to lay hold on Him; for they said, He is beside Himself" (Mk 3:21). They treated Him as we might be disposed, and rightly, to treat any ordinary person now, who began to preach in the streets. I say "rightly," because such persons generally preach a *new* Gospel, and therefore must be wrong. Also, they preach without being sent, and against authority; all which is wrong too. Accordingly we are often tempted to say that such people are "beside themselves," or made, and not unjustly. It is often charitable to say so, for it is better to be mad than to be disobedient. Well, what we should say of such persons, this is what our Lord's friends said of Him. They had lived so long with Him, and yet did not know Him; did not understand what He was. They saw nothing to mark a difference between Him and them. He was dressed as others, He ate and drank as others, He came in and went out, and spoke, and walked, and slept, as others. He was in all respects a man, except that He did not sin, and this great difference the many would not detect, because none of us understands those who are much better than himself: so that Christ, the sinless Son of God, might be living close to us, and we not discover it.

2. I say that Christ, the sinless Son of God, might be living now in the world as our next door neighbour, and perhaps we not find it out. And this is a thought that should be dwelt on. I do not mean to say that there are not a number of persons, who we could be sure were not Christ; of course, no persons who lead bad and irreligious lives. But there are a number of persons who are in no sense irreligious or open to serious blame, who are very much like each other at first sight, yet in God's eyes are very different. I mean the great mass of what are called respectable men, who vary very much: Some are merely decent and outwardly correct persons, and have no great sense of religion, do not deny themselves, have no ardent love of God, but love the world; and, whereas their interest lies in being regular and orderly, or they have no strong passions, or have early got into the way of being regular, and their habits are formed accordingly, they are what they are, decent and correct, but very little more. But there are others who look just the same to the world, who in their hearts are very different; they make no great show, they go on in the same quiet ordinary way as the others, but really they are training to be saints in Heaven. They do all they can to change themselves, to become like God, to obey God, to discipline themselves, to renounce the world; but they do it in secret, both because God tells them so to do, and because they do not like it to be known. Moreover, there are a number of others between these two with more or less of worldliness and more or less of faith. Yet they all look about the same, to common eyes, because true religion is a hidden life in the heart; and though it cannot exist without deeds, yet these are for the most part secret deeds,

secret charities, secret prayers, secret self-denials, secret struggles, secret victories.

Of course in proportion as persons are brought out into public life, they will be seen and scrutinized, and (in a certain sense) known more; but I am talking of the ordinary condition of people in private life, such as our Saviour was for thirty years; and these look very like each other. And there are so many of them, that unless we get very near them, we cannot see any distinction between one and another; we have no means to do so, and it is no business of ours. And yet, though we have no right to judge others, but must leave this to God, it is very certain that a really holy man, a true saint, though he looks like other men, still has a sort of secret power in him to attract others to him who are like-minded, and to influence all who have any thing in them like him. And thus it often becomes a test, whether we are like-minded with the Saints of God, whether they have influence over us. And though we have seldom means of knowing at the time who are God's own Saints, yet after all is over we have; and then on looking back on what is past, perhaps after they are dead and gone, if we knew them, we may ask ourselves what power they had over us, whether they attracted us, influenced us, humbled us, whether they made our hearts burn within us. Alas! too often we shall find that we were close to them for a long time, had means of knowing them, and knew them not; and that is a heavy condemnation on us, indeed. Now this was singularly exemplified in our Saviour's history, by how much He was so very holy. The holier a man is, the less he is understood by men of the world. All who have any spark of living faith will understand him in a measure, and the holier he is, they will, for the most part, be attracted the more; but those who serve the world will be blind to him, or scorn and dislike him, the holier he is. This, I say, happened to our Lord. He was All-holy, but "the light shined in darkness, and the darkness comprehended it not." His near relations did not believe in Him. And if this was really so, and for the reason I have said, it surely becomes a question whether we should have understood Him better than they: whether though He had been our next door neighbour, or one of our family, we should have understood Him better than they: whether though He had been our next door neighbour, or one of our family, we should have distinguished Him from any one else, who was correct and quiet in his deportment; or rather, whether we should not, though we respected Him, (alas, what a word! what language towards the Most High God!) yet even if we went as far as this, whether we should not have thought Him strange, eccentric, extravagant, and fanciful. Much less should we have detected any sparks of that glory which He had with the Father before the world was, and which was merely hidden not quenched by His earthly tabernacle. This, truly, is a very awful thought; because if He were near us for any long time, and we did not see any thing wonderful in Him, we might take it as a clear proof that we were not His, for "His sheep know His voice, and follow Him"; we might take it as a clear proof that we should not know Him, or admire His greatness, or adore His glory, or love His excellency, if we were admitted to His presence in heaven.

3. And here we are brought to another most serious thought, which I will touch upon. We are very apt to wish we had been born in the days of Christ, and in this way we excuse our misconduct, when conscience reproaches us. We say, that had we had the advantage of being with Christ, we should have had stronger motives, stronger restraints against sin. I answer, that so far from our sinful habits being reformed by the presence of Christ, the chance is, that those same habits would have hindered us from recognizing Him. We should not have known He was present; and if He had even told us who He was, we should not have believed Him. Nay, had we seen His miracles (incredible as it may seem), even they would not have made any lasting impression on us. Without going into this subject, consider only the possibility of Christ being close to us, even though He did no miracle, and our not knowing it; yet I believe this literally would have been the case with most men. But enough on this subject. What I am coming to is this: I wish you to observe what a fearful light this casts upon our prospects in the next world. We think heaven must be a place of happiness to us, if we do but get there; but the great probability is, if we can judge by what goes on here below, that a bad man, if brought to heaven, would not know he was in heaven;—I do not go to the further question, whether, on the contrary, the very fact of his being in heaven with all his unholiness upon him, would not be a literal torment to him, and light up the fires of hell within him. This indeed would be a most dreadful way of finding out where he was. But let us suppose the lighter case: Let us suppose he could remain in heaven unblasted, yet it would seem that at least he would not know that he was there. He would see nothing wonderful there. Could men come nearer to God than when they seized Him, struck Him, spit on Him, hurried Him along, stripped Him, stretched out His limbs upon the cross, nailed Him to it, raised it up, stood gazing on Him, jeered Him, gave Him vinegar, looked close whether He was dead, and then pierced Him with a spear? Oh, dreadful thought, that the nearest ap-

proaches man has made to God upon earth have been in blasphemy! Whether of the two came closer to Him, St. Thomas, who was allowed to reach forth his hand and reverently touch His wounds, and St. John, who rested on His bosom, or the brutal soldiers who profaned Him limb by limb, and tortured Him nerve by nerve? His Blessed Mother, indeed, came closer still to Him; and we, if we be true believers, still closer, who have Him really, though spiritually, within us; but this is another, an inward sort of approach. Of those who approached Him externally, they came nearest, who knew nothing about it. So it is with sinners: They would walk close to the throne of God; they would stupidly gaze at it; they would touch it; they would meddle with the holiest things; they would go on intruding and prying, not meaning any thing wrong by it, but with a sort of brute curiosity, till the avenging lightings destroyed them;—all because they have no *senses* to guide them in the matter. Our bodily senses tell us of the approach of good or evil on earth. By sound, by scent, by feeling we know what is happening to us. We know when we are exposing ourselves to the weather, when we are exerting ourselves too much. We have warnings, and feel we must not neglect them. Now, sinners have no spiritual senses; they can presage nothing; they do not know what is going to happen the next moment to them. So they go fearlessly further and further among precipices, till on a sudden they fall, or are smitten and perish. Miserable beings! and this is what sin does for immortal souls; that they should be like the cattle which are slaughtered at the shambles, yet touch and smell the very weapons which are to destroy them!

4. But you may say, how does this concern us? Christ is not here; *we* cannot thus or in any less way insult His Majesty. Are we so sure of this? Certainly we cannot commit such open blasphemy; but it is another matter whether we cannot commit as great. For often sins are greater which are less startling; insults more bitter, which are not so loud; and evils deeper, which are more subtle. Do we not recollect a very awful passage? "Whosoever speaketh a word against the Son of man, it shall be forgiven him; but whosoever speaketh against the Holy Ghost, it shall not be forgiven him" (Mt 12:32). Now, I am not deciding whether or no this denunciation can be fulfilled in the case of Christians now, though when we recollect that we *are* at present under the ministration of that very Spirit of whom our Saviour speaks, this is a very serious question; but I quote it to show that there may be sins greater even than insult and injury offered to Christ's Person, though we should think that impossi-

ble, and though they could not be so flagrant or open. With this thought let it be considered:—

First, that Christ is still on earth. He said expressly that He would come again. The Holy Ghost's coming is so really His coming, that we might as well say that He was not here in the days of His flesh, when He was visibly in this world, as deny that He is here now, when He is here by His Divine Spirit. This indeed is a mystery, how God the Son and God the Holy Ghost, two Persons, can be one, how He can be in the Spirit and the Spirit in Him; but so it is.

Next, if He is still on earth, yet is not visible (which cannot be denied), it is plain that He keeps Himself still in the condition which He chose in the days of His flesh. I mean, He is a hidden Saviour, and may be approached (unless we are careful) without due reverence and fear. I say, wherever He is (for that is a further question), still He is here, and again He is secret; and whatever be the tokens of His Presence, still they must be of a nature to admit of persons doubting where it is; and if they will argue, and be sharpwitted and subtle, they may perplex themselves and others, as the Jews did even in the days of His flesh, till He seems to them nowhere present on earth now. And when they come to think Him far away, of course they *feel* it to be impossible so to insult Him as the Jews did of old; and if nevertheless He *is* here, they *are* perchance approaching and insulting Him, though they so feel. And this was just the case of the Jews, for they too were ignorant what they were doing. It is probable, then, that we can now commit at least as great blasphemy towards Him as the Jews did first, because we are under the dispensation of that Holy Spirit, against whom even more heinous sins *can* be committed; next, because His Presence now as little witnesses of itself, or is impressive to the many, as His bodily presence formerly.

We see a further reason for this apprehension, when we consider what the tokens of His Presence now are; for they will be found to be of a nature easily to lead men into irreverence, unless they be humble and watchful. For instance, the Church is called "His Body": what His material Body was when He was visible on earth, such is the Church now. It is the instrument of His Divine power; it is that which we must approach, to gain good from Him; it is that which by insulting we awaken His anger. Now, what is the Church but, as it were, a body of humiliation, almost provoking insult and profaneness, when men do not live by faith? an earthen vessel, far more so even than His body of flesh, for that was at least pure from all sin, and the Church is defiled in all her members. We know that her ministers at best are but imperfect and erring, and of like passions with their brethren; yet of them He has said, speaking not to the Apostles merely but to all the seventy disciples (to whom Christian ministers are in office surely equal), "He that heareth you, heareth Me, and He that despiseth you despiseth Me, and he that despiseth Me, despiseth Him that sent Me."

Again: He has made the poor, weak, and afflicted, tokens and instruments of His Presence; and here again, as is plain, the same temptation meets us to neglect or profane it. What He was, such are His chosen followers in this world; and as His obscure and defenceless state led men to insult and ill-treat Him, so the like peculiarities, in the tokens of His Presence, lead men to insult Him now. That such are His tokens is plain from many passages of Scripture: for instance, He says of children, "Whoso shall receive one such little child in My Name, receiveth Me." Again: He said to Saul, who was persecuting His followers, "Why persecutest thou Me?" And He forewarns us, that at the Last Day He will say to the righteous, "I was an hungered, and ye gave Me meat; I was thirsty, and ye gave Me drink; I was a stranger, and ye took Me in; naked, and ye clothed Me; I was sick and ye visited Me; I was in prison, and ye came unto Me." And He adds, "Inasmuch as ye have done it unto the least of these My brethren, ye have done it unto Me" (Mt 18:5; Acts 9: 4; Mt 25:35–40). He observes the same connexion between Himself and His followers in His words to the wicked. What makes this passage the more awful and apposite, is this, which has been before now remarked,* that neither righteous nor wicked *knew* what they had done; even the righteous are represented as unaware that they had approached Christ. They say, "Lord, *when* saw we Thee an hungered, and fed Thee, or thirsty, and gave Thee drink?" In every age, then, Christ is both in the world, and yet not publicly so more than in the days of His flesh.

And a similar remark applies to His Ordinances, which are at once most simple, yet most intimately connected with Him. St. Paul, in his First Epistle to the Corinthians, shows both how easy and how fearful it is to profane the Lord's Supper, while he states how great the excess of the Corinthians had been, yet also that it was a want of "*discerning* the Lord's Body. When He was born into the world, the world knew it not. He was laid in a rude manger, among the cattle, but 'all the Angels of God worshipped Him.' " Now too He is present upon a table, homely

---

* See Pascal's *Thoughts*.

perhaps in make, and dishonoured in its circumstances; and faith adores, but the world passes by.

Let us then pray Him ever to enlighten the eyes of our understanding, that we may belong to the Heavenly Host, not to this world. As the carnal-minded would not perceive Him even in Heaven, so the spiritual heart may approach Him, possess Him, see Him, even upon earth.

SERMON XVII

Christ Manifested in Remembrance

"He shall glorify Me."—Jn 16:14

When our Lord was leaving His Apostles, and they were sorrowful, He consoled them by the promise of another Guide and Teacher, on whom they might rely instead of Him, and who should be more to them even than He had been. He promised them the Third Person in the Ever-blessed Trinity, the Holy Ghost, the Spirit of Himself and of His Father, who should come invisibly, and with the greater power and comfort, inasmuch as He was invisible; so that His presence would be more real and efficacious by how much it was more secret and inscrutable. At the same time this new and most gracious Comforter, while bringing a higher blessedness, would not in any degree obscure or hide what had gone before. Though He did more for the Apostles than Christ had done, He would not throw into the shade and supersede Him whom He succeeded. How could that be? who could come greater or holier than the Son of God? who could obscure the Lord of glory? how could the Holy Ghost, who was one with the Son, and the Spirit proceeding from the Son, do otherwise than manifest the Son, while manifesting Himself? how could He fail to illuminate the mercies and perfections of Him, whose death upon the cross opened a way for Himself, the Holy Ghost, to be gracious to man also? Accordingly, though it was expedient that the Son should go away, in order that the Comforter might come, we did not lose the sight of the Son in the presence of the Comforter. On the contrary, Christ expressly announced to the Apostles concerning Him, in the words of the text, "He shall glorify Me."

Now these words lead us first to consider in what special way the Holy Ghost gives glory to the Son of God; and next to inquire whether there is not in this appointment some trace of a general law of Divine providence, which is observed, as in Scripture, so in the world's affairs.

The special way in which God the Holy Ghost gave glory to God the Son, seems to have been His revealing Him as the Only-begotten

Son of the Father, who had appeared as the Son of man. Our Saviour said most plainly, that He was the Son of God; but it is one thing to declare the whole truth, another to receive it. Our Saviour said all that need be said, but His Apostles understood Him not. Nay, when they made confession, and that in faith, and by the secret grace of God, and therefore acceptably to Christ, still they understood not fully what they said. St. Peter acknowledged Him as the Christ, the Son of God. So did the centurion who was present at His crucifixion. Did that centurion, when he said, "Truly, this was the Son of God," understand his own words? Surely not. Nor did St. Peter, though he spoke, not through flesh and blood, but by the revelation of the Father. Had he understood, could he so soon after, when our Lord spoke of His passion which lay before Him, have presumed to "take Him, and begin to rebuke Him?" Certainly he did not understand that our Lord, as being the Son of God, was not the creature of God, but the Eternal Word, the Only-begotten Son of the Father, one with Him in substance, distinct in Person.

And when we look into our Saviour's conduct in the days of His flesh, we find that He purposely concealed that knowledge, which yet He gave; as if intending it should be enjoyed, but not at once; as if His words were to stand, but to wait awhile for their interpretation; as if reserving them for His coming, who at once was to bring Christ and His words into the light. Thus when the young ruler came to Him, and said, "Good Master," He showed Himself more desirous of correcting him than of revealing Himself, desirous rather to make him weigh his words, than Himself to accept them. At another time, when He had so far disclosed Himself that the Jews accused Him of blasphemy, in that He, being a man, made Himself God, far from repeating and insisting on the sacred Truth which they rejected, He invalidated the terms in which He had conveyed it, by intimating that even the Prophets of the Old Testament were called gods as well as He. And when He stood before Pilate, He refused to bear witness to Himself, or say what He was, or whence He came.

Thus He was among them "as he that serveth." Apparently, it was not till after His resurrection, and especially after His ascension, when the Holy Ghost descended, that the Apostles understood who had been with them. When all was over they knew it, not at the time.

Now here we see, I think, the trace of a general principle, which comes before us again and again both in Scripture and in the world, that God's presence is not discerned at the time when it is upon us, but afterwards, when we look back upon what is gone and over.

Our Saviour's history itself will supply instances in evidence of the existence of this remarkable law.

St. Philip, for instance, when he asked to see the Almighty Father, little understood the privilege he had already so long enjoyed; accordingly, our Lord answered, "Have I been so long time with you, and yet hast thou not known Me, Philip?"

Again, on another occasion, He said to St. Peter, "What I do thou knowest not now, but thou shalt know hereafter" (Jn 13:7). Again, "These things understood not His disciples at the first; but when Jesus was glorified, then remembered they that these things were written of Him, and that they had done these things unto Him" (Jn 12:16).

And in like manner while He talked with the two disciples going to Emmaus, their eyes were holden that they did not know Him. When they recognized Him, at once He vanished out of their sight. *Then* "they said one to another, Did not our heart burn within us, while He talked with us by the way?" (Lk 24:32).

Such too are the following, taken from the Old Testament. Jacob, when he fled from his brother, "lighted upon a certain place, and tarried there all night, because the sun was set." In his sleep he saw the vision of Angels, and the Lord above them. Accordingly when he awaked out of his sleep, he said, "Surely the Lord is in this place, and I knew it not. And he was afraid, and said, How dreadful is this place! This is none other but the house of God, and this is the gate of heaven" (Gn 28:11–17).

Again, after wrestling all night with the Angel, not knowing who it was, and asking after His name, then at length "Jacob called the name of the place Peniel; for I have seen God face to face, and my life is preserved" (Gn 32:30).

So again, after the Angel had departed from Gideon, who had treated Him like a man, then, and not till then, he discovered who had been with him, and he said, "Alas, O Lord God; for because I have seen an Angel of the Lord face to face" (Jgs 6:22).

And so in like manner, after the Angel had departed from Manoah and his wife, then, and not till then, they discovered Him. Then "they fell on their faces to the ground. . . . And Manoah said unto his wife, We shall surely die, because we have seen God" (Jgs 13:20, 22).

Such is God's rule in Scripture, to dispense His blessings, silently and secretly; so that we do not discern them at the time, except by faith, afterwards only. Of which, as I have said, we have two special instances in the very outline of the Gospel history; the mission of our Saviour, who was not understood till afterwards to be the Son of God Most High, and the mission of the Holy Ghost, which was still more laden with spiritual benefits, and is still more secret. Flesh and blood could not discern the Son of God, even when He wrought visible miracles; the natural man still less discerns the things of the Spirit of God; yet in the next world all shall be condemned, for not believing here what it was never given them to see. Thus the Presence of God is like His glory as it appeared to Moses; He said, "Thou canst not see my face . . . and live"; but He passed by, and Moses saw that glory, as it retired, which he might not see in front, or in passing; he saw it, and he acknowledged it, and "made haste and bowed his head toward the earth, and worshipped" (Ex 33:20; 34:8).

Now consider how parallel this is to what takes place in the providences of daily life. Events happen to us pleasant or painful; we do not know at the time the meaning of them, we do not see God's hand in them. If indeed we have faith, we confess what we do not see, and take all that happens as His; but whether we will accept it in faith or not, certainly there is no other way of accepting it. We see nothing. We see not why things come, or whither they tend. Jacob cried out on one occasion, "All these things are against me" (Gn 42:36); certainly so they seemed to be. One son made away with by the rest, another in prison in a foreign land, a third demanded;—"Me have ye bereaved of my children; Joseph is not, and Simeon is not, and ye will take Benjamin away: all these things are against me." Yet all these things were working for good. Or pursue the fortunes of the favourite and holy youth who was the first taken from him; sold by his brethren to strangers, carried into Egypt, tempted by a very perilous temptation, overcoming it but not rewarded, thrown into prison, the iron entering into his soul, waiting there till the Lord should be gracious, and "look down from heaven"; but waiting— why? and how long? It is said again and again in the sacred narrative, "The Lord was with Joseph"; but do you think he saw at the time any tokens of God? any tokens, except so far as by faith he realized them, in faith he saw them? His faith was its own reward; which to the eye of reason was no reward at all, for faith forsooth did but judge of things by that standard which it had originally set up, and pronounce that Joseph was happy because he ought to be so. Thus though the Lord was with him, apparently all things were against him. Yet afterwards he saw, what was so mysterious at the time;—"God did send me before you," he said to his brethren, "to preserve life. . . . It was not you that sent me hither, but God; and He hath made me a father to Pharaoh, and lord of all his house, and a ruler throughout all the land of Egypt."

Wonderful providence indeed, which is so silent, yet so efficacious, so constant, so unerring! This is what baffles the power of Satan. He cannot discern the Hand of God in what goes on; and though he would fain meet it and encounter it, in his mad and blasphemous rebellion against heaven, he cannot find it. Crafty and penetrating as he is, yet his thousand eyes and his many instruments avail him nothing against the majestic serene silence, the holy imperturbable calm which reigns through the providences of God. Crafty and experienced as he is, he appears like a child or a fool, like one made sport of, whose daily bread is but failure and mockery, before the deep and secret wisdom of the Divine Counsels. He makes a guess here, or does a bold act there, but all in the dark. He knew not of Gabriel's coming, and the miraculous conception of the Virgin,* or what was meant by that Holy Thing which was to be born, being called the Son of God. He tried to kill Him, and he made martyrs of the innocent children; he tempted the Lord of all with hunger and with ambitious prospects; he sifted the Apostles, and got none but one who already bore his own name, and had been already given over as a devil. He rose against his God in his full strength, in the hour and power of darkness, and then he seemed to conquer; but with his utmost effort, and as his greatest achievement, he did no more than "whatsoever Thy hand and Thy counsel determined before to be done" (Acts 4:28). He brought into the world the very salvation which he feared and hated. He accomplished the Atonement of that world, whose misery he was plotting. Wonderfully silent, yet resistless course of God's providence! "Verily, Thou art a God that hidest Thyself, O God of Israel, the Saviour"; and if even devils, sagacious as they are, spirits by nature and experienced in evil, cannot detect His hand, while He works, how can we hope to see it except by that way which the devils cannot take, by a loving faith? how can we see it except afterwards as a reward to our faith, beholding the cloud of glory in the distance, which when present was too rare and impalpable for mortal sense?

And so, again, in a number of other occurrences, not striking, not grievous, not pleasant, but ordinary, we are able afterwards to discern that He has been with us, and, like Moses, to worship Him. Let a person who trusts he is on the whole serving God acceptably, look back upon

---

* See Ignat. ad Eph. 19.

his past life, and he will find how critical were moments and acts, which at the time seemed the most indifferent: as for instance, the school he was sent to as a child, the occasion of his falling in with those persons who have most benefited him, the accidents which determined his calling or prospects whatever they were. God's hand is ever over His own, and He leads them forward by a way they know not of. The utmost they can do is to believe, what they cannot see now, what they shall see hereafter; and as believing, to act together with God towards it.

And hence perchance it is, that years that are past bear in retrospect so much of fragrance with them, though at the time perhaps we saw little in them to take pleasure in; or rather we did not, could not realize that we *were* receiving pleasure, though we received it. We received pleasure, because we were in the presence of God, but we knew it not; we knew not what we received; we did not bring home to ourselves or reflect upon the pleasure we were receiving; but afterwards, when enjoyment is past, reflection comes in. We feel at the time; we recognize and reason afterwards. Such, I say, is the sweetness and softness with which days long passed away fall upon the memory, and strike us. The most ordinary years, when we seemed to be living for nothing, these shine forth to us in their very regularity and orderly course. What was sameness at the time, is now stability; what was dulness, is now a soothing calm; what seemed unprofitable, has now its treasure in itself; what was but monotony, is now harmony; all is pleasing and comfortable, and we regard it all with affection. Nay, even sorrowful times (which at first sight is wonderful) are thus softened and illuminated afterwards: yet why should they not be so, since then, more than at other times, our Lord is present, when He seems leaving His own to desolateness and orphanhood? The planting of Christ's Cross in the heart is sharp and trying; but the stately tree rears itself aloft, and has fair branches and rich fruit, and is good to look upon. And if all this be true, even of sad or of ordinary times, much more does it hold good of seasons of religious obedience and comfort.

Such are the feelings with which men often look back on their childhood, when any accident brings it vividly before them. Some relic or token of that early time, some spot, or some book, or a word, or a scent, or a sound, brings them back in memory to the first years of their discipleship, and they then see, what they could not know at the time, that God's Presence went up with them and gave them rest. Nay, even now perhaps they are unable to discern fully what it was which made that time so bright and glorious. They are full of tender, affectionate thoughts towards those first years, but they do not know why. They think it is those very years which they yearn after, whereas it is the presence of God which, as they now see, was then over them, which attracts them. They think that they regret the past, when they are but longing after the future. It is not that they would be children again, but that they would be Angels and would see God; they would be immortal beings, crowned with amaranth, robed in white, and with palms in their hands, before His throne.

What happens in the fortunes of individuals, happens also to the Church. Its pleasant times are pleasant in memory. We cannot know who are great and who are little, what times are serious and what are their effects, till afterwards. Then we make much of the abode, and the goings out and the comings in of those who in their day lived familiarly with us, and seemed like other men. Then we gather up the recollection of what they did here, and what they said there. Then their persecutors, however powerful, are not known or spoken of, except by way of setting off *their* achievements and triumphs in the Gospel. "Kings of the earth, and the great men, and rich men, and the chief captains, and the mighty men," who in their day so magnified themselves, so ravaged and deformed the Church, that it could not be seen except by faith, then are found in nowise to have infringed the continuity of its outlines, which shine out clear and glorious, and even more delicate and tender for the very attempt to obliterate them. It needs very little study of history to prove how really this is the case; how little schism and divisions and disorders and troubles and fears and persecutions and scatterings and threatenings interfere with the glory of Christ Mystical, as looked upon afterwards, though at the time they almost hid it. Great Saints, great events, great privileges, like the everlasting mountains, grow as we recede from them.

And it is a sort of instinct, felt by the multitude, that they really are in possession of that which they neither see nor in faith accept, which (as some have remarked) makes them so unwilling just at the last moment to give up those privileges which they have so long possessed without valuing or using. Sometimes at the last moment, when mercies are about to be withdrawn, when it is too late, or all but too late, a feeling comes over them that something precious is going from them. They seem to hear the sound of arms, and the voices in the Temple saying, "Let us depart hence"; and they attempt to retain what they cannot see;—penitents, when the day of grace is over.

Once more: Every one of us surely must have experienced this general feeling most strongly, at one time or other, as regards the Sacraments and Ordinances of the Church. At the time, we cannot realize, we can but believe that Christ is with us; but after an interval a sweetness breathes from them, as from His garments, "of myrrh, aloes, and cassia." Such is the memory of many a Holy Communion in Church, of Holy Communions solemnized at a sick-bed, of Baptisms assisted in, of Confirmation, of Marriage, of Ordination; nay, Services which at the time we could not enjoy, from sickness, from agitation, from restlessness,—Services which at the time, in spite of our belief in their blessedness, yet troubled our wayward hearts,—Services which we were tempted to think long, feared beforehand, nay, and wished over when they were performing (alas! that we should be so blind and dead to our highest good), yet afterwards are full of God. We come, like Jacob, in the dark, and lie down with a stone for our pillow; but when we rise again, and call to mind what has passed, we recollect we have seen a vision of Angels, and the Lord manifested through them, and we are led to cry out, "How dreadful is this place! This is *none other* than the house of God, and this is the gate of heaven."

To conclude. Let us profit by what every day and hour teaches us, as it flies. What is dark while it is meeting us, reflects the Sun of Righteousness when it is past. Let us profit by this in future, so far as this, to have *faith in what* we cannot see. The world seems to go on as usual. There is nothing of heaven in the face of society; in the news of the day there is nothing of heaven; in the faces of the many, or of the great, or of the rich, or of the busy, there is nothing of heaven; in the words of the eloquent, or the deeds of the powerful, or the counsels of the wise, or the resolves of the lordly, or the pomps of the wealthy, there is nothing of heaven. And yet the Ever-blessed Spirit of God is here; the Presence of the Eternal Son, ten times more glorious, more powerful than when He trod the earth in our flesh, is with us. Let us ever bear in mind this divine truth,—the more secret God's hand is, the more powerful—the more silent, the more awful. We are under the awful ministration of the Spirit, against whom whoso speaks, hazards more than can be reckoned up; whom whoso grieves, loses more of blessing and glory than can be fathomed. The Lord was with Joseph, and the Lord was with David, and the Lord, in the days of His flesh, was with His Apostles; but now, He is with us in the Spirit. And inasmuch as the Divine Spirit is more than flesh and blood; inasmuch as the risen and glorified Saviour is more powerful than when He was in the form of a servant; inasmuch as the Eternal Word, spiritualizing His own manhood, has more of virtue for us, and grace, and blessing, and life, than when concealed in it, and subject to temptation and pain; inasmuch as faith is more blessed than sight; by so much more are we now more highly privileged, have more title to be called kings and priests unto God, even than the disciples who saw and touched Him. He who glorified Christ, imparts Him thus glorified to us. If He could work miracles in the days of His flesh, how much more can He work miracles now? and if His visible miracles were full of power, how much more His miracles invisible? Let us beg of Him grace wherewith to enter into the depth of our privileges,—to enjoy what we possess,—to believe in, to use, to improve, to glory in our present gifts as "members of Christ, children of God, and inheritors of the kingdom of heaven."

SERMON XXI

Faith and Love

"Though I have all Faith, so that I could remove mountains, and have no Charity, I am nothing."—1 Cor 13:2

I suppose that all thoughtful readers of the chapter from which these words are taken, have before now been struck with surprise at the varied characteristics which are there ascribed to the excellent grace called love, or charity. What *is* charity? St. Paul answers, by giving a great number of properties of it, all distinct and special. It is patient, it is kind, it has no envy, no self-importance, no ostentation, no indecorum, no selfishness, no irritability, no malevolence. Which of all these is it? for if it is all at once, surely it is a name for all virtues at once.

And what makes this conclusion still more plausible, is, that St. Paul elsewhere actually calls charity "the fulfilling of the Law": and our Saviour, in like manner, makes our whole duty consist in loving God and loving our neighbour. And St. James calls it "the royal law": and St. John says, "We know that we have passed from death unto life, because we love the brethren" (Rom 13:10; Mt 22:40; Jas 2:8; 1 Jn 3:14). Thus the chapter from which the text is taken seems but an exemplification in detail of what is declared in general terms by the inspired writers.

It is well too, by way of contrast, to consider the description of faith given elsewhere by the same Apostle, who, in the chapter before us, describes charity. In his Epistle to the Hebrews he devotes a much longer chapter to it: but his method in treating it is altogether different. He starts with a definition of it, and then he illustrates his clear and precise account of it in a series of instances. The chapter is made up of a repetition again and again, in Noah, in Abraham, in Moses, in David, and in the Prophets, of one and the same precisely marked excellence, called faith, which is such as no one can mistake. Again mention is made of it in the text; and then, though in a different Epistle, and in the midst of a train of thought altogether different, its description, as far as it goes, accurately agrees with what is said in the Hebrews; "... faith, so that I could remove mountains"; which moreover is the very account of it given by our Lord, and expresses surely the same habit of mind as that by which Noah, Abraham, Moses, and David, preached righteousness, obtained promises, renounced the world, waxed valiant in fight. How then is it that faith is of so definite a character, and love so large and comprehensive?

Now the reason seems to be pretty much what at first sight is the difficulty. The difficulty is whether, if love be such as St. Paul describes, it is not all virtues at once; and I answer, that in one sense it *is* all virtues at once, and therefore St. Paul cannot describe it more definitely, more restrictedly than he does. In other words, it is the root of all holy dispositions, and grows and blossoms into them: they are its parts; and when it is described, they of necessity are mentioned. Love is the material (so to speak) out of which all graces are made, the quality of mind which is the fruit of regeneration, and in which the Spirit dwells; according to St. John's words, "Every one that loveth is born of God"; "he that dwelleth in love, dwelleth in God, and God in him" (1 Jn 4:7,16). Such is love, and, as being such, it will last for ever. "Charity," or love, "never faileth." Faith and hope are graces of an imperfect state, and they cease with that state; but love is greater, because it is perfection. Faith and hope are graces, as far as we belong to this world,—which is for a time; but love is a grace, because we are creatures of God whether here or elsewhere, and partakers in a redemption which is to last for ever. Faith will not be when there is sight, nor hope when there is enjoyment; but love will (as we believe) increase more and more to all eternity. Faith and hope are means by which we express our love: We believe God's word, because we love it; we hope after heaven, because we love it. We should not have any hope or concern about it, unless we loved it; we should not trust or confide in the God of heaven, unless we loved Him. Faith, then, and hope are but instruments or expressions of love; but as to love itself, we do not love because we believe, for the devils believe, yet do not love; nor do we love because we hope, for hypocrites hope, who do not love. But we love for no cause beyond itself: We love, because it is our nature to love; and it is our nature, because God the Holy Ghost has made it our nature. Love is the immediate fruit and the evidence of regeneration.

It is expressing the same thing in other words, to say, as we may, that faith and hope are not in themselves necessarily graces, but only as grafted on and found in love. Balaam had faith and hope, but not love. "May I die the death of the righteous!" is an act of hope. "The word that the Lord putteth into my mouth, that will I speak," is an act of faith; but his conduct showed that neither his faith nor his hope was loving. The servant in the parable, who fell down at his Lord's feet, and begged to be excused his debt, had both faith and hope. He believed his lord able, and he hoped him willing, to forgive him. He went out, and saw a fellow-servant who owed him a small sum, and he behaved at once unmercifully to him, and unthankfully by his lord. He had neither love of God, because he was high-minded, nor love of his brother, because he was hard-hearted. There are then two kinds of faith in God, a good faith and a worthless faith; and two kinds of hope in God, good and worthless: but there are not two kinds of love of God. Love must always be heavenly; it is always the sign of the regenerate. Faith and hope are not in themselves signs, but only that faith "which worketh by love," and that hope which "loves the thing which God commandeth, and desires that which God doth promise." In the text it is said, "Though I had all faith, yet without love I am nothing": It is nowhere said, "Though I have all love, without faith I am nothing."

Love, then, is the seed of holiness, and grows into all excellences, not indeed destroying their peculiarities, but making them what they are. A weed has stalk, leaves, and flowers; so has a sweet-smelling plant; because the latter is sweet-smelling, it does not cease to have stalk, leaves, and flowers; but they are all pleasant, because they come of it. In like manner, the soul which is quickened with the spirit of love has faith and hope, and a number of faculties and habits, some of which it might have without love, and some not; but anyhow, in that soul one and all exist *in* love, though distinct from it; as stalk, leaves, and flowers are as distinct and entire in one plant as in another, yet vary in their quality, according to the plant's nature.

But here it may be asked, whether Scripture does not make faith, not love, the root, and all graces its fruits. I think not; on the contrary, it pointedly intimates that something besides faith is the root, not only in the text, but in our Lord's parable of the Sower; in which we read of persons who, "when they hear, receive the word with joy," yet having no "root" (Lk 8:13), fall away. Now, receiving the word with joy, surely implies faith; faith, then, is certainly distinct from the *root*, for these persons receive with joy, yet have "*no* root." However, it is allowable to call faith the root, because, in a certain sense at least, works *do* proceed from it. And hence Scripture speaks of "faith *working* by love," which would imply in the form of expression that faith was prior to love. And again: In the chapter in which the text occurs, we read of "faith, hope, and charity," an order of words which seems to imply that faith precedes love, or charity. And again, St. Paul says elsewhere, "The *end* of the commandment is *charity*, out of a pure heart, and of a good conscience, and *of faith unfeigned*" (1 Tm 1:5), where faith is spoken of as if it were the origin of love.

This must be granted then; and accordingly a question arises, how to adjust these opposite modes of speaking; in *what* sense faith is the beginning of love, and in what sense love is the origin of faith; whether love springs from faith, or faith from love, which comes first, and which last. I observe, then, as follows:—

Faith is the first element of *religion*, and love, of *holiness;* and as holiness and religion are distinct, yet united, so are love and faith. Holiness can exist without religion; religion cannot exist without holiness. Baptized infants, before they come to years of understanding, are holy; they are not religious. Holiness is love of the Divine Law. When God regenerates an infant, He imparts to it the gift of His Holy Spirit; and what is the Spirit thus imparted but the Law written on its heart? Such was the promise, "I will put My laws into their mind, and write them in their hearts." And hence it is said, "This is the love of God, that we keep His *commandments*" (Heb 8:10; 1 Jn 5:3). God comes to us as a Law, before He comes as a Lawgiver; that is, He sets up His throne within us, and enables us to obey Him, before we have learned to reflect on our own sensations, and to know the voice of God. Such, as if in a type, was Samuel's case; he knew not who it was who called him, till Eli the priest told him. Eli stands for religion, Samuel for holiness; Eli for faith, Samuel for love.

Love then is the motion within us of the new spirit, the holy and renewed heart which God the Holy Ghost gives us; and, as being such, we see how it may exist in infants, who obey the inward law without knowing it, by a sort of natural service, as plants and trees fulfil the functions of their own nature; a service which is most acceptable to God, as being moral and spiritual, though not intellectual. And this, for what we know, may be the state of those little ones who are baptized and taken away before they have learned either to reason or to sin. They may be as the stones of the Everlasting Pavement, crying out continually in praise to God; dimly visible, as if absorbed in the glory which encompasses God's throne; or as the wonderful wheels described by the Prophet, which were living, yet in a way instrumental; for in heaven, where there is no gross matter, the very framework of the Temple is composed of spirits.

Love, then, is the life of those who know not an external world, but who worship God as manifested within them. Such a life however can last but a little while on earth. The eyes see and the reason embraces a lower world, sun, moon, stars, and earth, and men, and all that man does or makes; and this external world does not speak of God upon the face of it. It shows as if it were itself God, and an object of worship, or at least it becomes the creature of a usurper, who has made himself "the god of this world." We are at once forced to reflect, reason, decide, and act; for we are between two, the inward voice speaking one thing within us, and the world speaking another without us; the world tempting, and the Spirit whispering warnings. Hence faith becomes necessary; in other words, God has most mercifully succoured us in this contest, by speaking not only in our hearts, but through the sensible world; and this Voice we call Revelation. God has overruled this world of sense, and put a word in its mouth, and bid it prophesy of Him. And thus there are two voices even in the external world; the voice of the tempter calling us to fall down and worship him, and he will give us all; and the voice of God, speaking in aid of the voice in our hearts: and as love is that which hears the voice within us, so faith is that which hears the voice without us; and as love worships God within the shrine, faith discerns Him in the world; and as love is the life of God in the solitary soul, faith is the guardian of love in our intercourse with men; and, while faith ministers to love, love is that which imparts to faith its praise and excellence.

And thus it is that faith is to love as religion to holiness; for religion is the Divine Law as coming to us from without, as holiness is the acquiescence in the same Law as written within. Love then is meditative, tranquil, pure, gentle, abounding in all offices of goodness and truth; and faith is strenuous and energetic, formed for this world, combating it, training the mind towards love, fortifying it in obedience, and overcoming sense and reason by representations more urgent than their own.

Moreover it is plain, that, while love is the root out of which faith grows, faith by receiving the wonderful tidings of the Gospel, and presenting before the soul its sacred Objects, the mysteries of the faith, the Holy Trinity, and the Incarnate Saviour, expands our love, and raises it to a perfection which otherwise it could never reach.

And thus our duty lies in faith working by love; love is the sacrifice we offer to God, and faith is the sacrificer. Yet they are not distinct from each other except in our way of viewing them. Priest and sacrifice are one; the loving faith and the believing love.

And thus I answer the question concerning the connexion of love and faith. Love is the condition of faith; and faith in turn is the cherisher and maturer of love; it brings love out into works, and therefore is called the root of *works* of love; the substance of the works is love, the outline and direction of them is faith.

This being so, surely we need not be surprised at St. Paul's language, as in the text and verses following. Love is the true ruling principle of the regenerate soul, and faith ministers to it. Love is the end, faith the means; and if the means be difficult, much more is the end. St. Paul says that faith which could remove mountains will not avail without love; and in truth, faith is only half way (as it were) to heaven. By faith we give up this world, but by love we reach into the next world; and it often happens from one cause or another, men are able to get as far as the one, without going on to the other. Too true is it, that the mass of men live neither with faith nor love; they live to themselves, they love themselves selfishly, and do not desire any thing beyond the visible framework of things. This world is their all in all. But I speak of religious persons; and these, I think, will confess that distaste for the world is quite a distinct thing from the spirit of love. As years go on, the disappointments, troubles, and cares of life, wean a religious mind from attachment to this world. A man sees it is but vanity. He neither receives, nor looks for enjoyment from it. He does not look to the future with hope; he has no prospects; he cares not for the world's smile or frown; for what it can do, what it can withhold. Nay, even his friends are nothing to him; he knows they cannot help him really in his greatest needs, and he has no dependence that they will be continued to him. And thus in the course of time, with a very scanty measure of true divine love, he is enabled, whatever his sphere is, to act above the world, in his degree; to do his plain straightforward duty, because reason tells him he should do it, and because he has no great temptation seducing him from it. Observe, *why* he keeps God's commandments; from *reason*, because he knows he ought, and because he has no strong motives keeping him from doing so. Alas! not from *love* towards those commandments. He has only just so much of the spirit of love as suffices to hinder his resignation from being despondency, and his faith from being dead. Or again, he has had experience of the misery of a laden conscience, the misery of the pollution involved in the numberless little sins of every day, the odiousness of his pride, vanity, fretfulness, wilfulness, arrogance, irritability, profaneness, hardness of heart, and all the other evils which beset him; and he desires earnestly to be cleansed;—yet rather from dislike of sin than direct love of God and Christ.

This then is that middle state in which some of us may be standing in our progress from earth to heaven, and which the text warns us against. It tells us that faith at most only makes a hero, but that love makes a saint; that faith can but put us above the world, but that love brings us under God's throne; that faith can but make us sober, but love makes us happy. It warns us that it is possible for a man to have the clearest, calmest, exactest view of the realities of heaven; that he may most firmly realize and act upon the truths of the Gospel; that he may understand that all about him is but a veil, not a substance; that he may have that full confidence in God's Word as to be able to do miracles; that he may have such simple absolute faith as to give up his property, give up all his goods to feed the poor; that he may so scorn the world, that he may with so royal a heart trample on it, as even to give his body to be burned by a glorious martyrdom; and yet—I do not say, be without love; God forbid! I do not suppose the Apostle means there ever *was* actually such a case, but that it is abstractedly possible; that no one of the proper acts of faith, in itself, and necessarily, implies love; that it is distinct from love. He says this,—that, though a person *be* all that has been said, yet unless he be also something besides, unless he have love, it profiteth him nothing. Oh, fearful lesson, to all those who are tempted to pride themselves in their labours, or sufferings, or sacrifices, or works! We are Christ's, not by faith merely, nor by works merely, but by love; not by hating the world, nor by hating sin, nor by venturing for the world to come, nor by calmness, nor by magnanimity,—though we must do and be all this; and if we *have* love in perfection we *shall*,—but it is love makes faith, not faith love. We are saved, not by any of these things, but by that heavenly flame within us, which, while it consumes what is seen, aspires to what is unseen. Love is the gentle, tranquil, satisfied acquiescence and adherence of the soul in the contemplation of God; not only a preference of God before all things, but a delight in Him because He is God, and because His commandments are good; not any violent emotion or transport, but as St. Paul describes it, long-suffering, kind, modest, unassuming, innocent, simple, orderly, disinterested, meek, pure-hearted, sweet-tempered, patient, enduring. Faith without charity is dry, harsh, and sapless; it has nothing sweet, engaging, winning, soothing; but it was charity which brought Christ down. Charity is but another name for the Comforter. It is eternal charity which is the bond of all things in heaven and earth; it is charity wherein the Father and the Son are one in the unity of the Spirit; by which the Angels in heaven are one, by which all Saints are one with God, by which the Church is one upon earth.

SERMON XXII

Watching

"Take ye heed, watch and pray; for ye know not when the time is."—Mk 13:33

Our Saviour gave this warning when He was leaving this world,—leaving it, that is, as far as His visible presence is concerned. He looked forward to the many hundred years which were to pass before He came again. He knew His own purpose and His Father's purpose gradually to leave the world to itself, gradually to withdraw from it the tokens of His gracious presence. He contemplated, as contemplating all things, the neglect of Him which would spread even among his professed followers; the daring disobedience, and the loud words, which would be ventured against Him and His Father by many whom He had regenerated: and the coldness, cowardice, and tolerance of error which would be displayed by others, who did not go so far as to speak or to act against Him. He foresaw the state of the world and the Church, as we see it this day, when His prolonged absence has made it practically thought, that He never will come back in visible presence: and in the text, He mercifully whispers into our ears, not to trust in what we see, not to share in that general unbelief, not to be carried away by the world, but to "take heed, watch,* pray," and look out for His coming.

Surely this gracious warning should be ever in our thoughts, being so precise, so solemn, so earnest. He foretold His first coming, yet He took His Church by surprise when He came; much more will He come suddenly the second time, and overtake men, now that He has not measured out the interval before it, as then He did, but left our watchfulness to the keeping of faith and love.

Let us then consider this most serious question, which concerns every one of us so nearly;—What it is to *watch* for Christ? He says, "*Watch* ye therefore, for ye know not when the Master of the house cometh; at even, or at midnight, or at the cock-crowing, or in the morn-

---

* ἀγρυπνεῖτε.

ing; lest coming suddenly He find you sleeping. And what I say unto you, I say unto all, *Watch*" (Lk 12:39). And again, "If the goodman of the house had known what hour the thief would come, he would have *watched*, and not have suffered his house to be broken through" (Mk 13: 35–37, γρηγορεῖτε). A like warning is given elsewhere both by our Lord and by His Apostles. For instance; we have the parable of the Ten Virgins, five of whom were wise and five foolish; on whom the bridegroom, after tarrying came suddenly, and five were found without oil. On which our Lord says, "*Watch* therefore, for ye know neither the day nor the hour wherein the Son of man cometh" (Mt 25:13). Again He says, "Take heed to yourselves, lest at any time your hearts be overcharged with surfeiting and drunkenness, and cares of this life, and so that day come upon you unawares; for as a snare shall it come on all them that dwell on the face of the whole earth. *Watch* ye therefore, and pray always, that ye may be accounted worthy to escape all these things that shall come to pass, and to stand before the Son of man" (Lk 21:36). In like manner He upbraided Peter thus: "Simon, sleepest thou? couldest not thou *watch* one hour?" (Mk 14:37).

In like manner St. Paul in his Epistle to the Romans. "Now it is high time to awake out of sleep. . . . The night is far spent, the day is at hand" (Rom 13:11,12). Again, "*Watch* ye, stand fast in the faith, quit you like men, be strong" (1 Cor 16:13). "Be strong in the Lord, and in the power of His might; put on the whole armour of God, that ye may be able to stand against the wiles of the devil; . . . that ye may be able to withstand in the evil day, and having done all to stand" (Eph 6:10–13). "Let us not sleep as do others, but let us *watch* and be sober" (1 Thes 5: 6). In like manner St. Peter, "The end of all things is at hand; be ye therefore sober, and *watch* unto prayer." "Be sober, be *vigilant*, because your adversary the devil, as a roaring lion, walketh about seeking whom he may devour" (1 Pt 6:7 νήψατε). And St. John, "Behold I come as a thief; blessed is he that *watcheth* and keepeth his garments" (Rv 16:15).

Now I consider this word *watching*, first used by our Lord, then by the favoured disciple, then by the two great Apostles, Peter and Paul, is a remarkable word, remarkable because the idea is not so obvious as might appear at first sight, and next because they all inculcate it. We are not simply to believe, but to watch; not simply to love, but to watch; not simply to obey, but to watch; to watch for what? for that great event, Christ's coming. Whether then we consider what is the obvious meaning of the word, or the Object towards which it directs us, we seem to see a special duty enjoined on us, such as does not naturally come into our minds. Most of us have a general idea what is meant by believing, fearing, loving, and obeying; but perhaps we do not contemplate or apprehend what is meant by watching.

And I conceive it is one of the main points, which, in a practical way, will be found to separate the true and perfect servants of God from the multitude called Christians; from those who are, I do not say false and reprobate, but who are such that we cannot speak much about them, nor can form any notion what will become of them. And in saying this, do not understand me as saying, which I do not, that we can tell for certain who are the perfect, and who the double-minded or incomplete Christians; or that those who discourse and insist upon these subjects are necessarily on the right side of the line. I am but speaking of two *characters*, the true and consistent character, and the inconsistent; and these I say will be found in no slight degree discriminated and distinguished by this one mark,—true Christians, whoever they are, watch, and inconsistent Christians do not. Now what is watching?

I conceive it may be explained as follows:—Do you know the feeling in matters of this life, of expecting a friend, expecting him to come, and he delays? Do you know what it is to be in unpleasant company, and to wish for the time to pass away, and the hour strike when you may be at liberty? Do you know what it is to be in anxiety lest something should happen which may happen or may not, or to be in suspense about some important event, which makes your heart beat when you are reminded of it, and of which you think the first thing in the morning? Do you know what it is to have a friend in a distant country, to expect news of him, and to wonder from day to day what he is now doing, and whether he is well? Do you know what it is to live upon a person who is present with you, that your eyes follow his, that you read his soul, that you see all its changes in his countenance, that you anticipate his wishes, that you smile in his smile, and are sad in his sadness, and are downcast when he is vexed, and rejoice in his successes? To watch for Christ is a feeling such as all these; as far as feelings of this world are fit to shadow out those of another.

He watches for Christ who has a sensitive, eager, apprehensive mind; who is awake, alive, quick-sighted, zealous in seeking and honouring Him; who looks out for Him in all that happens, and who would not be surprised, who would not be over-agitated or overwhelmed, if he found that He was coming at once.

And he watches *with* Christ, who, while he looks on to the future, looks back on the past, and does not so contemplate what his Saviour has purchased for him, as to forget what He has suffered for him. He watches with Christ, who ever commemorates and renews in his own person Christ's Cross and Agony, and gladly takes up that mantle of affliction which Christ wore here, and left behind Him when he ascended. And hence in the Epistles, often as the inspired writers show their desire for His second coming, as often do they show their memory of His first, and never lose sight of His Crucifixion in His Resurrection. Thus if St. Paul reminds the Romans that they "wait for the redemption of the body" at the Last Day, he also says, "If so be that we *suffer with Him*, that we may be also glorified together." If he speaks to the Corinthians of "waiting for the coming of our Lord Jesus Christ," he also speaks of "always bearing about in the body the *dying* of the Lord Jesus, *that* the life also of Jesus might be made manifest in our body." If to the Philippians of "the power of His resurrection," he adds at once *"and the fellowship of His sufferings,* being made conformable unto His death." If he consoles the Colossians with the hope "when Christ shall appear," of their "appearing with Him in glory, he has already declared that he *"fills up that which remains of the afflictions of Christ* in his flesh for His body's sake, which is the Church" (Rm 8:17–28; 1 Cor 1:7; 2 Cor 4:10; Pl 3:10; Cl 3:4; 1:24). Thus the thought of what Christ is, must not obliterate from the mind the thought of what He was; and faith is always sorrowing with Him while it rejoices. And the same union of opposite thoughts is impressed on us in Holy Communion, in which we see Christ's death and resurrection together, at one and the same time; we commemorate the one, we rejoice in the other; we make an offering, and we gain a blessing.

This then is to watch; to be detached from what is present, and to live in what is unseen; to live in the thought of Christ as He came once, and as He will come again; to desire His second coming, from our affectionate and grateful remembrance of His first. And this it is, in which we shall find that men in general are wanting. They are indeed without faith and love also; but at least they profess to have these graces, nor is it easy to convince them that they have not. For they consider they have faith, if they do but own that the Bible came from God, or that they trust wholly in Christ for salvation; and they consider they have love if they obey some of the most obvious of God's commandments. Love and faith they think they have; but surely they do not even fancy that they watch. What is meant by watching, and how it is a duty, they have no definite idea; and thus it accidentally happens that watching is a suitable test of a Christian, in that it is that particular property of faith and love, which, essential as it is, men of this world do not even profess; that particular property, which is the life or energy of faith and love, the way in which faith and love, if genuine, show themselves.

It is easy to exemplify what I mean, from the experience which we all have of life. Many men indeed are open revilers of religion, or at least openly disobey its laws; but let us consider those who are of a more sober and conscientious cast of mind. They have a number of good qualities, and are in a certain sense and up to a certain point religious; but they do not watch. Their notion of religion is briefly this: loving God indeed, but loving this world too; not only doing their *duty*, but finding their chief and highest *good*, in that state of life to which it has pleased God to call them, resting in it, taking it as their portion. They serve God, and they seek Him; but they look on the present world as if it were the eternal, not a mere temporary, scene of their duties and privileges, and never contemplate the prospect of being separated from it. It is not that they forget God, or do not live by principle, or forget that the goods of this world are His gift; but they love them for their own sake more than for the sake of the Giver, and reckon on their remaining, as if they had that permanence which their duties and religious privileges have. They do not understand that they are called to be strangers and pilgrims upon the earth, and that their worldly lot and worldly goods are a sort of accident of their existence, and that they really have no property, though human law guarantees property to them. Accordingly, they set their heart upon their goods, be they great or little, not without a sense of religion the while, but still idolatrously. *This* is their fault,—an identifying God with this world, and therefore an idolatry towards this world; and so they are rid of the trouble of looking out for their God, for they think they have found Him in the goods of this world. While, then, they are really praiseworthy in many parts of their conduct, benevolent, charitable, kind, neighbourly, and useful in their generation, nay, constant perhaps in the ordinary religious duties which custom has established, and while they display much right and amiable feeling, and much correctness in opinion, and are even in the way to improve in character and conduct as time goes on, correct much that is amiss, gain greater command over themselves, mature in judgment, and are much looked up to in consequence; yet still it is plain that they love this world, would be loth to leave it, and wish to have more of its good things. They like wealth, and distinction, and credit, and influence. They may improve in conduct, but not in aims; they advance, but they do not mount; they are moving on a low level, and were they to move on for centuries, would never rise above the atmosphere of this world. "I will stand upon my watch, and set me upon the tower, and will watch to see what He will say unto me, and what I shall answer when I am reproved" (Hb 2:1). This is the temper of mind which they have not; and when we reflect how rarely it *is* found among professing Christians, we shall see why our Lord is so urgent in enforcing it;—as if He said, "I am not warning you, My followers, against open apostasy; that will not be; but I foresee that very few will keep awake and watch while I am away. Blessed are the servants who do so; few will open to me *immediately,* when I knock. They will have something to do first; they will have to get ready. They will have to recover from the surprise and confusion which overtake them on the first news of My coming, and will need time to collect themselves, and summon about them their better thoughts and affections. They feel themselves very well off as they are; and wish to serve God as they are. They are satisfied to remain on earth; they do not wish to move; they do not wish to change."

Without denying, then, to these persons the praise of many religious habits and practices, I would say that they want the tender and sensitive heart which hangs on the thought of Christ, and lives in His love. The breath of the world has a peculiar power in what may be called rusting the soul. The mirror within them, instead of reflecting back the Son of God their Saviour, has become dim and discoloured; and hence, though (to use a common expression) they have a good deal of good *in* them, it is only *in* them, it is not through them, around them, and upon them. An evil crust is *on* them: They think with the world; they are full of the world's notions and modes of speaking; they appeal to the world, and have a sort of reverence for what the world will say. There is a want of naturalness, simplicity, and childlike teachableness in them. It is difficult to touch them, or (what may be called) get at them, and to persuade them to a straightforward course in religion. They start off when you least expect it: They have reservations, make distinctions, take exceptions, indulge in refinements, in questions where there are really but two sides, a right and a wrong. Their religious feelings do not flow forth easily, at times when they ought to flow; either they are diffident, and can say nothing, or else they are affected and strained in their mode of conversing. And as a rust preys upon metal and eats into it, so does this worldly spirit penetrate more and more deeply into the soul which once admits it. And this is one great end, as it would appear, of afflictions, viz., to rub away and clear off these outward defilements, and to keep the soul in a measure of its baptismal purity and brightness.

Now, it cannot surely be doubted that multitudes in the Church are such as I have been describing, and that they would not, could not, at once welcome our Lord on His coming. We cannot, indeed, apply what has been said to this or that individual; but on the whole, viewing the multitude, one cannot be mistaken. There may be exceptions; but after all conceivable deductions, a large body must remain thus double-minded, thus attempting to unite things incompatible. This we might be sure of, though Christ had said nothing on the subject; but it is a most affecting and solemn thought, that He has actually called our attention to this very danger, the danger of a worldly religiousness, for so it may be called, though it *is* religiousness; this mixture of religion and unbelief, which serves God indeed, but loves the fashions, the distinctions, the pleasures, the comforts of this life,—which feels a satisfaction in being prosperous in circumstances, likes pomps and vanities, is particular about food, raiment, house, furniture, and domestic matters, courts great people, and aims at having a position in society. He warns His disciples of the danger of having their minds drawn off from the thought of Him, by whatever cause; He warns them against *all* excitements, *all* allurements of this world; He solemnly warns them that the world will not be prepared for His coming, and tenderly intreats of them not to take their portion with the world. He warns them by the instance of the rich man whose soul was required, of the servant who ate and drank, and of the foolish virgins. When He comes, they will one and all want time; their head will be confused, their eyes will swim, their tongue falter, their limbs totter, as men who are suddenly awakened. They will not all at once collect their senses and faculties. Oh, fearful thought! the bridal train is sweeping by,—Angels are there,—the just made perfect are there,—little children, and holy teachers, and white-robed saints, and martyrs washed in blood; the marriage of the Lamb is come, and His wife hath made herself ready. She has already attired herself: While we have been sleeping, she has been robing; she has been adding jewel to jewel, and grace to grace; she has been gathering in her chosen ones, one by one, and has been excercising them in holiness, and purifying them for her Lord; and now her marriage hour is come. The holy Jerusalem is descending, and a loud voice proclaims, "Behold, the bridegroom cometh; go ye out to meet Him!" but we, alas! are but dazzled with the blaze of light, and neither welcome the sound, nor obey it,—and all for what? what shall we have gained then? what will this world have then done for us? wretched, deceiving world! which will then be burned up, unable not only to profit us, but to save itself. Miserable hour, indeed, will that be, when the full consciousness breaks on us of what we will not believe now, viz., that we *are* at present serving the world. We trifle with our conscience now; we deceive our better judgment; we repel the hints of those who tell us that we are joining ourselves to this perishing world. We *will* taste a little of its pleasures, and follow its ways, and think it no harm, so that we do not altogether neglect religion. I mean, we allow ourselves to covet what we have not, to boast in what we have, to look down on those who have less; or we allow ourselves to profess what we do not try to practise, to argue for the sake of victory, and to debate when we should be obeying; and we pride ourselves on our reasoning powers, and think ourselves enlightened, and despise those who had less to say for themselves, and set forth and defend our own theories; or we are over-anxious, fretful, and care-worn about worldly matters, spiteful, envious, jealous, discontented, and evil-natured: In one or other way we take our portion with this world, and we will not believe that we do. We obstinately refuse to believe it; we know we are not altogether irreligious, and we persuade ourselves that we are religious. We learn to think it is possible to be too religious; we have taught ourselves that there is nothing high or deep in religion, no great exercise of our affections, no great food for our thoughts, no great work for our exertions. We go on in a self-satisfied or a self-conceited way, not looking out of ourselves, not standing like soldiers on the watch in the dark night; but we kindle our own fire, and delight ourselves in the sparks of it. This is our state, or something like this, and the Day will declare it; the Day is at hand, and the Day will search our hearts, and bring it home even to ourselves, that we have been cheating ourselves with words, and have not served Christ, as the Redeemer of the soul claims, but with a meagre, partial, worldly service, and without really contemplating Him who is above and apart from this world.

Year passes after year silently; Christ's coming is ever nearer than it was. Oh, that, as He comes nearer earth, we may approach nearer heaven! O my brethren, pray Him to give you the heart to seek Him in sincerity. Pray Him to make you in earnest. You have one work only, to bear your cross after Him. Resolve in His strength to do so. Resolve to be no longer beguiled by "shadows of religion," by words, or by disputings, or by notions, or by high professions, or by excuses, or by the world's promises or threats. Pray Him to give you what Scripture calls "an honest and good heart," or "a perfect heart," and, without waiting, begin at once to obey Him with the best heart you have. Any obedience is better than none,—any profession which is disjoined from obedience, is a mere pretence and deceit. Any religion which does not bring you nearer to God is of the world. You have to seek His face; obedience is the only way of seeking Him. All your duties are obediences. If you are to believe the truths He has revealed, to regulate yourselves by His precepts, to be frequent in His ordinances, to adhere to His Church and people, why is it, except because *He* has bid you? and to do what He bids is to obey Him, and to obey Him is to approach Him. Every act of obedience is an approach,—an approach to Him who is not far off, though He seems so, but close behind this visible screen of things which hides Him from us. He is behind this material framework; earth and sky are but a veil going between Him and us; the day will come when He will rend that veil, and show Himself to us. And then, according as we have waited for Him, will He recompense us. If we have forgotten Him, He will not know us; but "blessed are those servants whom the Lord, when He cometh, shall find watching. . . . He shall gird Himself, and make them sit down to meat, and will come forth and serve them. And if He shall come in the second watch, or come in the third watch, and find them so, blessed are those servants" (Lk 12:37,38). May this be the portion of every one of us! It is hard to attain it; but it is woeful to fail. Life is short; death is certain; and the world to come is everlasting.

Volume V

SERMON I

Worship, a Preparation for Christ's Coming

(ADVENT)

"Thine eyes shall see the King in His beauty: they shall behold the land that is very far off."—Is 33:17

Year after year, as it passes, brings us the same warnings again and again, and none perhaps more impressive than those with which it comes to us at this season. The very frost and cold, rain and gloom, which now befall us, forebode the last dreary days of the world, and in religious hearts raise the thought of them. The year is worn out; spring, summer, autumn, each in turn, have brought their gifts and done their utmost; but they are over, and the end is come. All is past and gone, all has failed, all has sated; we are tired of the past; we would not have the seasons longer; and the austere weather which succeeds, though ungrateful to the body, is in tone with our feelings, and acceptable. Such is the frame of mind which befits the end of the year; and such the frame of mind which comes alike on good and bad at the end of life. The days have come in which they have no pleasure; yet they would hardly be young again, could they be so by wishing it. Life is well enough in its way; but it does not satisfy. Thus the soul is cast forward upon the future, and in proportion as its conscience is clear and its perception keen and true, does it rejoice solemnly that "the night is far spent, the day is at hand," that there are "new heavens and a new earth" to come, though the former are failing; nay, rather that, because they are failing, it will "soon see the King in His beauty," and "behold the land which is very far off." These are feelings for holy men in winter and in age, waiting, in some dejection perhaps, but with comfort on the whole, and calmly though earnestly, for the Advent of Christ.

And such, too, are the feelings with which we now come before Him in prayer day by day. The season is chill and dark, and the breath of the morning is damp, and worshipers are few, but all this befits those who are by profession penitents and mourners, watchers and pilgrims. More dear to them that loneliness, more cheerful that severity, and more bright that gloom, than all those aids and appliances of luxury by which men nowadays attempt to make prayer less disagreeable to them. True faith does not covet comforts. It only complains when it is forbidden to kneel, when it reclines upon cushions, is protected by curtains, and encompassed by warmth. Its only hardship is to be hindered, or to be ridiculed, when it would place itself as a sinner before its Judge. They who realize that awful Day when they shall see Him face to face, whose eyes are as a flame of fire, will as little bargain to pray pleasantly now, as they will think of doing so then.

One year goes and then another, but the same warnings recur. The frost or the rain comes again; the earth is stripped of its brightness; there is nothing to rejoice in. And then, amid this unprofitableness of earth and sky, the well-known words return; the Prophet Isaiah is read; the same Epistle and Gospel, bidding us "awake out of sleep," and welcome Him "that cometh in the Name of the Lord"; the same Collects, beseeching Him to prepare us for judgment. Oh, blessed they who obey these warning voices, and look out for Him whom they have not seen, because they "love His appearing!"

We cannot have fitter reflections at this Season than those which I have entered upon. What may be the destiny of other orders of beings we know not;—but this we know to be our own fearful lot, that before us lies a time when we must have the sight of our Maker and Lord face to face. We know not what is reserved for other beings; there may be some, which, knowing nothing of their Maker, are never to be brought before Him. For what we can tell, this may be the case with the brute creation. It may be the law of their nature that they should live and die, or live on an indefinite period, upon the very outskirts of His government, sustained by Him, but never permitted to know or approach Him. But this is not our case. We are destined to come before Him; nay, and to come before Him in judgment; and that on our first meeting; and that suddenly. We are not merely to be rewarded or punished, we are to be judged. Recompense is to come upon our actions, not by a mere general provision or course of nature, as it does at present, but from the Lawgiver Himself in person. We have to stand before His righteous Presence, and that one by one. One by one we shall have to endure His holy and searching eye. At present we are in a world of shadows. What we see is not substantial. Suddenly it will be rent in twain and vanish away, and our Maker will appear. And then, I say, that first appearance will be nothing less than a personal intercourse between the Creator and every creature. He will look on us, while we look on Him.

I need hardly quote any of the numerous passages of Scripture which tell us this, by way of proof; but it may impress the truth of it upon our hearts to do so. We are told then expressly, that good and bad shall see God. On the one hand holy Job says, "Though after my skin worms destroy this body, yet in my flesh shall I see God: whom I shall see for myself, and mine eyes shall behold, and not another." On the other hand unrighteous Balaam says, "I shall see Him, but not now; I shall behold Him, but not nigh; there shall come a Star out of Jacob, and a Sceptre shall rise out of Israel." Christ says to His disciples, "Look up, and lift up your heads, for your redemption draweth nigh"; and to His enemies, "Hereafter ye shall see the Son of man sitting on the right hand of power, and coming in the clouds of heaven." And it is said generally of all men, on the one hand, "Behold He cometh with clouds; and every eye shall see Him, and they also which pierced Him; and all kindreds of the earth shall wail because of Him." And on the other, "When He shall appear, we shall be like Him; for we shall see Him as He is." Again, "Now we see through a glass, darkly; but then face to face"; and again, "They shall see His face; and His Name shall be in their foreheads" (Jb 19:26, 27; Nm 24:17; Lk 21:28; Mt 26:64; Rv 1:7; 1 Jn 3:2; 1 Cor 13: 12; Rv 22:4).

And, as they see Him, so will He see them, for His coming will be to judge them. "We must all appear before the judgment-seat of Christ," says St. Paul. Again, "We shall all stand before the judgment-seat of Christ. For it is written, As I live, saith the Lord, every knee shall bow to Me, and every tongue shall confess to God. So then every one of us shall give account of himself to God." And again, "When the Son of man shall come in His glory, and all the holy Angels with Him, then shall He sit upon the throne of His glory. And before Him shall be gathered all nations; and He shall separate them one from another, as a shepherd divideth his sheep from the goats" (2 Cor 5:10; Rom 14:10–12; Mt 25:31, 32).

Such is our first meeting with our God; and, I say, it will be as sudden as it is intimate. "Yourselves know perfectly," says St. Paul, "that the day of the Lord so cometh as a thief in the night. For when they shall say, Peace and safety, then sudden destruction cometh upon them." This is said of the wicked,—elsewhere He is said to surprise good as well as bad. "While the Bridegroom tarried," the wise and foolish virgins "all slumbered and slept. And at midnight there was a cry made, Behold, the Bridegroom cometh; go ye out to meet Him" (1 Thes 5:2, 3; Mt 25:5, 6).

Now, when this state of the case, the prospect which lies before us, is brought home to our thoughts, surely it is one which will lead us anxiously to ask, Is this all that we are told, all that is allowed to us, or done for us? Do we know only this, that all is dark now, and all will be light then; that now God is hidden, and one day will be revealed? that we are in a world of sense, and are to be in a world of spirits? For surely it is our plain wisdom, our bounden duty, to prepare for this great change;—and if so, are any directions, hints, or rules given us *how* we are to prepare? "Prepare to meet thy God," "Go ye out to meet Him," is the dictate of natural reason, as well as of inspiration. But *how* is this to be?

Now observe, that it is scarcely a sufficient answer to this question to say that we must strive to obey Him, and so to approve ourselves to Him. This indeed might be enough, were reward and punishment to follow in the mere way of nature, as they do in this world. But, when we come steadily to consider the matter, appearing before God, and dwelling in His presence, is a very different thing from being merely subjected to a system of moral laws, and would seem to require another preparation, a special preparation of thought and affection, such as will enable us to endure His countenance, and to hold communion with Him as we ought. Nay, and, it may be, a preparation of the soul itself for His presence, just as the bodily eye must be exercised in order to bear the full light of day, or the bodily frame in order to bear exposure to the air.

But, whether or not this be safe reasoning, Scripture precludes the necessity of it, by telling us that the Gospel Covenant is intended, among its other purposes, to prepare us for this future glorious and wonderful destiny, the sight of God,—a destiny which, if not most glorious, will be most terrible. And in the worship and service of Almighty God, which Christ and His Apostles have left to us, we are vouchsafed means, both moral and mystical, of approaching God, and gradually learning to bear the sight of Him.

This indeed is the most momentous reason for religious worship, as far as we have grounds for considering it a true one. Men sometimes ask, Why need they *profess* religion? Why need they go to church? Why need they observe certain rites and ceremonies? Why need they watch, pray, fast, and meditate? Why is it not enough to be just, honest, sober, benevolent, and otherwise virtuous? Is not this the true and real worship of God? Is not activity in mind and conduct the most acceptable way of approaching Him? How can they please Him by submitting to certain religious forms, and taking part in certain religious acts? Or if they must do so, why may they not choose their own? Why must they come to church for them? Why must they be partakers in what the Church calls Sacraments? I answer, they must do so, first of all and especially, because God tells them so to do. But besides this, I observe that we see this plain reason why, that they are one day to change their state of being. They are not to be here for ever. Direct intercourse with God on their part now, prayer and the like, may be necessary to their meeting Him suitably hereafter: and direct intercourse on His part with them, or what we call sacramental communion, may be necessary in some incomprehensible way, even for preparing their very nature to bear the sight of Him.

Let us then take this view of religious service; it is "going out to meet the Bridegroom," who, if not seen "in His beauty," will appear in consuming fire. Besides its other momentous reasons, it is a preparation for an awful event, which shall one day be. What it would be to meet Christ at once without preparation, we may learn from what happened even to the Apostles when His glory was suddenly manifested to them. St. Peter said, "Depart from me, for I am a sinful man, O Lord." And St. John, "when he saw Him, fell at His feet as dead" (Lk 5:8; Rv 1:17).

This being the case, it is certainly most merciful in God to vouchsafe to us the means of preparation, and such means as He has actually appointed. When Moses came down from the Mount, and the people were dazzled at his countenance, he put a veil over it. That veil is so far removed in the Gospel, that we are in a state of preparation for its being altogether removed. We are with Moses in the Mount so far, that we have a sight of God; we are with the people beneath it so far, that Christ does not visibly show Himself. He has put a veil on, and He sits among us silently and secretly. When we approach Him, we know it only by faith; and when He manifests Himself to us, it is without our being able to realize to ourselves that manifestation.

Such then is the spirit in which we should come to all His ordinances, considering them as anticipations and first-fruits of that sight of

Him which one day must be. When we kneel down in prayer in private, let us think to ourselves, Thus shall I one day kneel down before His very footstool, in this flesh and this blood of mine; and He will be seated over against me, in flesh and blood also, though divine. I come, with the thought of that awful hour before me, I come to confess my sin to Him now, that He may pardon it then, and I say, "O Lord, Holy God, Holy and Strong, Holy and Immortal, in the hour of death and in the day of judgment, deliver us, O Lord!"

Again, when we come to church, then let us say:—The day will be when I shall see Christ surrounded by His Holy Angels. I shall be brought into that blessed company, in which all will be pure, all bright. I come then to learn to endure the sight of the Holy One and His Servants; to nerve myself for a vision which is fearful before it is ecstatic, and which they only enjoy whom it does not consume. When men in this world have to undergo any great thing, they prepare themselves beforehand, by thinking often of it, and they call this making up their mind. Any unusual trial they thus make familiar to them. Courage is a necessary step in gaining certain goods, and courage is gained by steady thought. Children are scared, and close their eyes, at the vision of some mighty warrior or glorious king. And when Daniel saw the Angel, like St. John, "his comeliness was turned in him into corruption, and he retained no strength" (Dn 10:8). I come then to church, because I am an heir of heaven. It is my desire and hope one day to take possession of my inheritance: and I come to make myself ready for it, and I would not see heaven yet, for I could not bear to see it. I am allowed to be in it without seeing it, that I may learn to see it. And by psalm and sacred song, by confession and by praise, I learn my part.

And what is true of the ordinary services of religion, public and private, holds in a still higher or rather in a special way, as regards the sacramental Ordinances of the Church. In these is manifested in greater or less degree, according to the measure of each, that Incarnate Saviour, who is one day to be our Judge, and who is enabling us to bear His Presence then, by imparting it to us in measure now. A thick black veil is spread between this world and the next. We mortal men range up and down it, to and fro, and see nothing. There is no access through it into the next world. In the Gospel this veil is not removed; it remains, but every now and then marvellous disclosures are made to us of what is behind it. At times we seem to catch a glimpse of a Form which we shall hereafter see face to face. We approach, and in spite of the darkness, our hands, or our head, or our brow, or our lips become, as it were, sensible of the contact of something more than earthly. We know not where we are, but we have been bathing in water, and a voice tells us that it is blood. Or we have a mark signed upon our foreheads, and it spake of Calvary. Or we recollect a hand laid upon our heads, and surely it had the print of nails in it, and resembled His who with a touch gave sight to the blind and raised the dead. Or we have been eating and drinking; and it was not a dream surely, that One fed us from His wounded side, and renewed our nature by the heavenly meat He gave. Thus in many ways He, who is Judge to us, prepares us to be judged,—He, who is to glorify us, prepares us to be glorified, that He may not take us unawares; but that when the voice of the Archangel sounds, and we are called to meet the Bridegroom, we may be ready.

Now consider what light these reflections throw upon some remarkable texts in the Epistle to the Hebrews. If we have in the Gospel this supernatural approach to God and to the next world, no wonder that St. Paul calls it an "enlightening," "a tasting of the heavenly gift," a being "made partaker of the Holy Ghost," a "tasting of the good word of God, and the powers of the world to come." No wonder, too, that utter apostasy after receiving it should be so utterly hopeless; and that in consequence, any profanation of it, any sinning against it, should be so perilous in proportion to its degree. If He, who is to be our Judge, condescend here to manifest Himself to us, surely if that privilege does not fit us for His future glory, it does but prepare us for His wrath.

And what I have said concerning Ordinances, applies still more fully to Holy Seasons, which include in them the celebration of many Ordinances. They are times when we may humbly expect a larger grace, because they invite us especially to the means of grace. This in particular is a time for purification of every kind. When Almighty God was to descend upon Mount Sinai, Moses was told to "sanctify the people," and bid them "wash their clothes," and to "set bounds to them round about": Much more is this a season for "cleansing ourselves from all defilement of the flesh and spirit, perfecting holiness in the fear of God" (Ex 19:10-12; 2 Cor 7:1); a season for chastened hearts and religious eyes; for severe thoughts, and austere resolves, and charitable deeds; a season for remembering what we are and what we shall be. Let us go out to meet Him with contrite and expectant hearts; and though He delays His coming, let us watch for Him in the cold and dreariness which must one day have an end. Attend His summons we must, at any rate, when He strips us of the body; let us anticipate, by a voluntary act, what will one day come on us of necessity. Let us wait for Him solemnly, fearfully, hopefully, patiently, obediently; let us be resigned to His will, while active in good works. Let us pray Him ever, to "remember us when He cometh in His kingdom"; to remember all our friends; to remember our enemies; and to visit us according to His mercy here, that He may reward us according to His righteousness hereafter.

SERMON X

Righteousness Not of Us, but in Us

(EPIPHANY)

"Of Him are ye in Christ Jesus, who of God is made unto us wisdom, and righteousness, and sanctification, and redemption; that, according as it is written, he that glorieth, let him glory in the Lord."—1 Cor 1:30, 31

St. Paul is engaged, in the chapter from which these words are taken, in humbling the self-conceit of the Corinthians. They had had gifts given them; they did not forget they had them; they used, they abused them; they forgot, not that they were theirs, but that they were given them. They seem to have thought that those gifts were theirs by a sort of right, because they were persons of more cultivation of mind than others, of more knowledge, more refinement. Corinth was a wealthy place; it was a place where all nations met, and where men saw much of the world; and it was a place of science and philosophy. It had indeed some good thing in it which Athens had not. The wise men of Athens heard the Apostle and despised him, but of Corinth it was said to him by Christ Himself, "I have much people in this city" (Acts 18:10). Yet, though there were elect of God at Corinth, yet in a place of so much luxury and worldly wisdom, difficulties so great stood in the way of a simple, humble faith, as to seduce, if it were possible, even the elect,— as to bring it to pass that those who were saved were saved "as by fire." In spite of the clear views which the Apostle had doubtless given them on their conversion of their utter nothingness in themselves; in spite too of their confessing it (for we can hardly suppose that they said in so many words that their gifts were their own), yet they did not feel that they came from God. They seemed, as it were, to claim them, or at least to view their possession of them as a thing of course; they acted as if they were their own, not with humbleness and gratitude towards their Giver, not with a sense of responsibility, not with fear and trembling, but as if they were lords over them, as if they had sovereign power to do what they would with them, as if they might use them from themselves and for themselves.

Our bodily powers and limbs also come from God, but they are in such sense part of our original formation, or (if I may say so) of our essence, that though we ought ever to lift up our hearts in gratitude to God while we use them, yet we use them as *our* instruments, organs and ministers. They spring from us, and (as I may say) hold of us, and we use them for our own purposes. Well, this seems to have been the way in which the Corinthians used their supernatural gifts, viz., as if they were parts of themselves,—as natural faculties, instead of influences *in* them, but not *of* them, *from* the Giver of all good,—not with awe, not with reverence, not with worship. They considered themselves, not members of the kingdom of Saints, and dependent on an unseen Lord, but were members of an earthly community, still rich men, still scribes, still philosophers, still disputants, who had the *addition* of certain gifts, who had aggrandized their existing position by the reception of Christianity. They became proud, when they should have been thankful. They had forgotten that to be members of the Church they must become as little children; that they must give up all, that they might win Christ; that they must become poor in spirit to gain the true riches; that they must put off philosophy, if they would speak wisdom among the perfect. And, therefore, St. Paul reminds them that "not many wise men after the flesh, not many mighty, not many noble are called"; and that all true power, all true wisdom flows from Christ, who is "the power of God, and the wisdom of God"; and that all who are Christians indeed, renounce their own power and their own wisdom, and come to Him that He may be the Source and Principle of their power, and of their wisdom; that they may depend on Him, and hold of Him, not of themselves; that they may exist in Him, or have Him in them; that they may be (as it were) His members; that they may glory simply in Him, not in themselves. For, whereas the wisdom of the world is but foolishness in God's sight, and the power of the world but weakness, God had set forth His Only-begotten Son to be the First-born of creation, and the standard and original of true life; to be a wisdom of God and a power of God, and a "righteousness, sanctification, and redemption" of God, to all those who are found in Him. "Of Him," says he, "are ye in Christ Jesus, who is made unto us a wisdom from God, namely, righteousness, and sanctification, and redemption; that according as it is written, He that glorieth, let him glory in the Lord."

In every age of the Church, not in the primitive age only, Christians have been tempted to pride themselves on their gifts, or at least to forget that they were gifts, and to take them for granted. Ever have they been tempted to forget their own responsibilities, their having received what they are bound to improve, and the duty of fear and trembling, while improving it. On the other hand, how they ought to behave under a sense of their own privileges, St. Paul points out when he says to the Philippians, "Work out your own salvation with fear and trembling, *for* it is God which worketh in you both to will and to do of His good pleasure" (Phil 2:13). God is in you for righteousness, for sanctification, for redemption, through the Spirit of His Son, and you must use His influences, His operations, not as your own (God forbid!), not as you would use your own mind or your own limbs, irreverently, but as His presence in you. All your knowledge is from Him; all good thoughts are from Him; all power to pray is from Him; your Baptism is from Him; the consecrated elements are from Him; your growth in holiness is from Him. You are not your own, you have been bought with a price, and a mysterious power is working in you. Oh, that we felt all this as well as were convinced of it!

This then is one of the first elements of Christian knowledge and a Christian spirit, to refer all that is good in us, all that we have of spiritual life and righteousness, to Christ our Saviour; to believe that He works in us, or, to put the same thing more pointedly, to believe that saving truth, life, light, and holiness are not *of* us, though they must be *in* us. I shall now enlarge on each of these two points.

1. Whatever we have, is not of us, but of God. This surely it will not take many words to prove. Our unassisted nature is represented in Scripture as the source of much that is evil, but not of anything that is good. We read much in Scripture of *evil* coming out of the natural heart, but nothing of good coming out of it. When did not the multitude of men turn away from Him who is their life? When was it that the holy were not the few, and the unholy the many? and what does this show but that the law of man's nature tends towards evil, not towards good? As is the tree, so is its fruit; if the fruit be evil, therefore the tree must be evil. When was the face of human society, which is the fruit of human nature, other than evil? When was the power of the world an upholder of God's truth? When was its wisdom an interpreter of it? or its rank an image of it? Shall we look at the early age of the world? What fruit do we find there? "The earth was corrupt before God, and the earth was filled with violence." "God saw that the wickedness of man was great upon the earth, and that every imagination of the thoughts of his heart was only

evil continually. And it repented the Lord that He had made man on the earth, and it grieved Him at His heart." Shall we find good in man's nature after the flood more easily than before? "And the Lord said, Behold, the people is one, and they have all one language; and this they begin to do, and now nothing will be restrained from them which they have imagined to do. . . . So the Lord scattered them abroad from thence upon the face of all the earth." Shall we pass on to the days of David? "The Lord looked down from heaven upon the children of men, to see if there were any that did understand and seek God. They are all gone aside, they are all together become filthy; there is none that doeth good, no not one." Thus three times did God look down from heaven, and three times was man the same, God's enemy, a rebel against his Maker. Let us see if Solomon will lighten this fearful testimony. He says, "The heart of the sons of men is full of evil, and madness is in their heart while they live, and after that they go to the dead." Shall we ask of the prophet Isaiah? He answers, "We are all as an unclean thing, and all our righteousness are as filthy rags; and we all do fade as a leaf; and our iniquities as the wind have taken us away." Or Jeremiah? "The heart is deceitful above all things, and desperately wicked." Or what did our Lord Himself, when He came in the flesh, witness of the fruits of the heart? He said, "Out of the heart proceed evil thoughts, murders, adulteries, fornications, thefts, false witnesses, blasphemies." And will His coming have improved the world? How will it be, when He comes again? "When the Son of Man cometh, shall He find faith on the earth?" (Gn 6:11, 5, 6, 11:6–8; Ps 14:2, 3; Eccl 9:3; Is 64:6; Jer 17:9; Mt 15:19; Lk 18:8) What then human nature *tends* to, is very plain, and according to the end, so I say must be the beginning. If the end is evil, so is the beginning; if the termination is astray, the first direction is wrong. "Out of the abundance of the heart the mouth speaketh," and the hand worketh; and such as is the work and the word, such is the heart. Nothing then can be more certain, if we go by Scripture, not to speak of experience, than that the present nature of man is evil, and not good; that evil things come from it, and not good things. If good things come from it, they are the exception, and therefore not of it, but in it merely; first given to it, and then coming from it; not of it by nature, but in it by grace. Our Lord says expressly, "That which is born of the flesh, is flesh; and that which is born of the Spirit, is spirit. Marvel not that I say unto thee, Ye must be born again" (Jn 3:7). And again, "Without Me ye can do nothing" (Jn 15:5); and St. Paul, "I can do all things through Christ, that strengtheneth me." And again, in the Epistle before us, "Who maketh thee to differ from another? and what hast thou that thou didst not receive? now if thou didst receive it, why dost thou glory, as if thou hadst not received it?" (1 Cor 4:7).

This is that great truth which is at the foundation of all true doctrine as to the way of salvation. All teaching about duty and obedience, about attaining heaven, and about the office of Christ towards us, is hollow and unsubstantial, which is not built *here*, in the doctrine of our original corruption and helplessness; and, in consequence, of original guilt and sin. Christ Himself indeed is the foundation, but a broken, self-abased, self-renouncing heart is (as it were) the ground and soil in which the foundation must be laid; and it is but building on the sand to profess to believe in Christ, yet not to acknowledge that without Him we can do nothing. It is what is called the Pelagian heresy, of which many of us perhaps have heard the name. I am not, indeed, formally stating what that heresy consists in, but I mean, that, speaking popularly, I may call it the belief, that "holy desires, good counsels, and just works," can come of *us*, can be *from* us, as well as *in* us: whereas they are from God only; from whom, and not from ourselves, is that righteousness, sanctification, and redemption, which is in us,—from whom is the washing away of our inward guilt, and the implanting in us of a new nature. But when men take it for granted that they are natural objects of God's favour,—when they view their privileges and powers as natural things,—when they look upon their Baptism as an ordinary work, bringing about its results as a matter of course,—when they come to Church without feeling that they are highly favoured in being allowed to come,—when they do not understand the necessity of prayer for God's grace,—when they refer everything to system, and subject the provisions of God's free bounty to the laws of cause and effect,—when they think that education will do everything, and that education is in their own power,—when, in short, they think little of the Church of God, which is the great channel of God's mercies, and look upon the Gospel as a sort of literature or philosophy, contained in certain documents, which they may use as they use the instruction of other books; then, not to mention other instances of the same error, are they practically Pelagians, for they make themselves their own centre, instead of depending on Almighty God and His ordinances.

2. And, secondly, while truth and righteousness are not of us, it is quite as certain that they are also in us if we be Christ's; not merely nominally given to us and imputed to us, but really implanted in us by the operation of the Blessed Spirit. Our Lord and Saviour Jesus Christ,

when He came on earth in our flesh, made a perfect atonement, "sacrifice, oblation, and satisfaction for the sins of the whole world." He was born of a woman, He wrought miracles, He fasted and was tempted in the desert, He suffered and was crucified, He was dead and buried; He rose again from the dead, He ascended on high, and "liveth ever" with the Father,—all for our sakes. And as His incarnation and death were in order to our salvation, so also He really accomplished the end which that humiliation had in view. All was done that needed to be done, except what could not be done at a time, when they were not yet in existence on whom it was to be done. All was done for us except the actual grant of mercy made to us one by one. He saved us by anticipation, but we were not yet saved in fact, for as yet we were not. But everything short of this was then finished. Satan was vanquished; sin was atoned for; the penalty was paid; God was propitiated; righteousness, sanctification, redemption, life, all were provided for the sons of Adam, and all that remained to do was to dispense, to impart, these divine gifts to them one by one. This was not done, because it could not be done all at once; it could not be done forthwith to individuals, and salvation was designed in God's counsels to be an individual gift. He did not once for all restore the whole race, and change the condition of the world in His sight immediately on Christ's death. The sun on Easter-day did not rise, nor did He rise from the grave, on a new world, but on the old world, the sinful rebellious outcast world as before. Men were just what they had been, both in themselves and in His sight. They were guilty and corrupt before His crucifixion, and so they were after it; so they remain to this day, except so far as He by His free bounty and at His absolute will, vouchsafes to impart the gift of His passion to this man or that. He provided, not gave salvation, when He suffered; and there must be a giving or applying in the case of all those who are to be saved. The gift of life is in us, as truly as it is not of us; it is not only *from* Him but it is *unto* us. This must carefully be borne in mind, for as there are those who consider that life, righteousness, and salvation are of us, so there are others who hold that they are not in us; and as there are many who more or less forget that justification is of God, so there are quite as many who more or less forget that justification must be in man if it is to profit him. And it is hard to say which of the two errors is the greater.

But there is another ground for saying that Christ did not finish His gracious economy by His death, viz., because the Holy Spirit came in order to finish it. When He ascended, He did not leave us to ourselves, so far the work was not done. He sent His Spirit. Were all finished as regards individuals, why should the Holy Ghost have condescended to come? But the Spirit came to finish in us, what Christ had finished in Himself, but left unfinished as regards us. To Him it is committed to apply to us severally all that Christ had done for us. As then His mission proves on the one hand that salvation is not from ourselves, so does it on the other that it must be wrought in us. For if all gifts of grace are with the Spirit, and the presence of the Spirit is within us, it follows that these gifts are to be manifested and wrought in us. If Christ is our sole hope, and Christ is given to us by the Spirit, and the Spirit be an inward presence, our sole hope is in an inward change. As a light placed in a room pours out its rays on all sides, so the presence of the Holy Ghost imbues us with life, strength, holiness, love, acceptableness, righteousness. God looks on us in mercy, because He sees in us "the mind of the Spirit," for whoso has this mind has holiness and righteousness within him. Henceforth all his thoughts, words, and works as done in the Spirit, are acceptable, pleasing, just before God; and whatever remaining infirmity there be in him, that the presence of the Spirit hides. That divine influence, which has the fulness of Christ's grace to purify us, has also the power of Christ's blood to justify.

Let us never lose sight of this great and simple view, which the whole of Scripture sets before us. What was actually done by Christ in the flesh eighteen hundred years ago, is in type and resemblance really wrought in us one by one even to the end of time. He was born of the Spirit, and we too are born of the Spirit. He was justified by the Spirit, and so are we. He was pronounced the well-beloved Son, when the Holy Ghost descended on Him; and we too cry Abba, Father, through the Spirit sent into our hearts. He was led into the wilderness by the Spirit; He did great works by the Spirit; He offered Himself to death by the Eternal Spirit; He was raised from the dead by the Spirit; He was declared to be the Son of God by the Spirit of holiness on His resurrection: We too are led by the same Spirit into and through this world's temptations; we, too, do our works of obedience by the Spirit; we die from sin, we rise again unto righteousness through the Spirit; and we are declared to be God's sons,—declared, pronounced, dealt with as righteous,—through our resurrection unto holiness in the Spirit. Or, to express the same great truth in other words; Christ Himself vouchsafes to repeat in each of us in figure and mystery all that He did and suffered in the flesh. He is formed in us, born in us, suffers in us, rises again in us, lives in us; and this not by a succession of events, but all at once: for He comes to us as a Spirit, all dying, all rising again, all living. We are ever receiving our birth, our justification, our renewal, ever dying to sin, ever rising to righteousness. His whole economy in all its parts is ever in us all at once; and this divine presence constitutes the title of each of us to heaven; this is what He will acknowledge and accept at the Last Day. He will acknowledge Himself,—His image in us,—as though we reflected Him, and He, on looking round about, discerned at once who were His; those, namely, who gave back to Him His image. He impresses us with the seal of the Spirit, in order to avouch that we are His. As the king's image appropriates the coin to him, so the likeness of Christ in us separates us from the world and assigns us over to the kingdom of heaven.

Scripture is full of texts to show that salvation is such an inward gift. For instance: What is it that rescues us from being reprobates? "Know ye not," says St. Paul, "that Jesus Christ is in you, except ye be reprobates?" What is our hope? "Christ in us, the hope of glory." What is it that hallows and justifies? "The Name of the Lord Jesus, and the Spirit of our God." What makes our offerings acceptable? "Being sanctified by the Holy Ghost." What is our life? "The Spirit is life because of righteousness." How are we enabled to fulfil the law? "The righteousness of the law is fulfilled in us who walk not after the flesh, but after the Spirit." Who is it makes us righteous? "The fruit of the *Spirit* is in all goodness, and righteousness, and truth" (2 Cor 13:5; Col 1:27; 1 Cor 6:11; Rom 15:16, 8:10; Eph 5:9).

To conclude—I have said that there are two opposite errors: one, the holding that salvation is not of God; the other, that it is not in ourselves. Now it is remarkable that the maintainers of both the one and the other error, whatever their differences in other respects, agree in this,—in depriving a Christian life of its mysteriousness. He who believes that he can please God of himself, or that obedience can be performed by his own powers, of course has nothing more of awe, reverence, and wonder in his personal religion, than when he moves his limbs and uses his reason, though he might well feel awe then also. And in like manner he also who considers that Christ's passion once undergone on the cross absolutely secured his own personal salvation, may see mystery indeed in that cross (as he ought), but he will see no mystery, and feel little solemnity, in prayer, in Ordinances, or in his attempts at obedience. He will be free, familiar, and presuming, in God's Presence. Neither will "work out their salvation with fear and trembling"; for neither will realize, though they use the words, that God is in them "to will and to do." Both the one and the other will be content with a low standard of duty:

the one, because he does not believe that God requires much; the other, because he thinks that Christ in His own Person has done all. Neither will honour and make much of God's Law: the one, because he brings down the Law to his own power of obeying it; the other, because he thinks that Christ has taken away the Law by obeying it in his stead. They only feel awe and true seriousness who think that the Law remains; that it claims to be fulfilled by them; and that it can be fulfilled in them through the power of God's grace. Not that any man alive arises up to that perfect fulfilment, but that such fulfilment is not impossible; that it is begun in all true Christians; that they all are tending to it; are growing into it; and are pleasing to God because they are becoming, and in proportion as they are becoming like Him who, when He came on earth in our flesh, fulfilled the Law perfectly.

SERMON XV

Sins of Infirmity

"The flesh lusteth against the Spirit, and the Spirit against the flesh; and these are contrary the one to the other, so that ye cannot do the things that ye would."—Gal 5:17

It is not uncommonly said of the Church Catholic, and we may humbly and thankfully receive it, that though there is error, variance, and sin in an extreme degree in its separate members, yet what they do all in common, what they do in combination, what they do gathered together in one, or what they universally receive or allow, is divine and holy; that the sins of individuals are overruled, and their wanderings guided and brought round, so that they end in truth, in spite, or even in one sense, by means of error. Not as if error had any power of arriving at truth, or were a necessary previous condition of it, but that it pleases Almighty God to work out His great purposes in and through human infirmity and sin. Thus Balaam had a word put in his mouth in the midst of his enchantments, and Caiaphas prophesied in the act of persuading our Lord's death.

What is true of the Church as a body, is true also of each member of it who fulfills his calling: The continual results, as I may call them, of his faith, are righteous and holy, but the process through which they are obtained is one of imperfection; so that could we see his soul as Angels see it, he would, when seen at a distance, appear youthful in countenance, and bright in apparel; but approach him, and his face has lines of care upon it, and his dress is tattered. His righteousness then seems, I do not mean superficial, this would be to give a very wrong idea of it, but though reaching deep within him, yet not whole and entire in the depth of it; but, as it were, wrought out of sin, the result of a continual struggle,—not spontaneous nature, but habitual self-command.

True faith is not shown here below in peace, but rather in conflict; and it is no proof that a man is not in a state of grace that he continually sins, provided such sins do not remain on him as what I may call ultimate results, but are ever passing on into something beyond and unlike themselves, into truth and righteousness. As we gain happiness through suffering, so do we arrive at holiness through infirmity, because man's very condition is a fallen one, and in passing out of the country of sin, he necessarily passes through it. And hence it is that holy men are kept from regarding themselves with satisfaction, or resting in any thing short of our Lord's death, as their ground of confidence; for, though that death has already in a measure wrought life in them, and effected the purpose for which it took place, yet to themselves they seem but sinners, their renewal being hidden from them by the circumstances attending it. The utmost they can say of themselves is, that they are not in the commission of any such sins as would plainly exclude them from grace; but how little of firm hope can be placed on such negative evidence is plain from St. Paul's own words on the subject, who, speaking of the censures passed upon him by the Corinthians, says, "I know nothing by myself," that is, I am conscious of nothing, "yet am I not hereby justified; but He that judgeth me is the Lord." As men in a battle cannot see how it is going, so Christians have no certain signs of God's presence in their hearts, and can but look up towards their Lord and Saviour, and timidly hope. Hence they will readily adopt the well-known words, not as expressing a matter of doctrine, but as their own experience about themselves. "The little fruit which we have in holiness, it is, God knoweth, corrupt and unsound; we put no confidence at all in it; . . . our continual suit to Him is, and must be, to bear with our infirmities and pardon our offences."*

Let us then now enumerate some of the infirmities which I speak of; infirmities which, while they certainly beset those who are outcasts from God's grace, and that with grievous additions and fatal aggravations, yet are also possible in a state of acceptance, and do not in themselves imply the absence of true and lively faith. The review will serve to humble all of us, and perhaps may encourage those who are depressed by a sense of their high calling, by reminding them that they are not reprobate, though they be not all they should be.

1. Now of the sins which stain us, though without such a consent of the will as to forfeit grace, I must mention first original sin. How it is that we are born under a curse which we did not bring upon us, we do not know; it is a mystery; but when we become Christians, that curse is removed. We are no longer under God's wrath; our guilt is forgiven us, but still the infection of it remains. I mean, we still have an evil principle

---

* Hooker on Justification, §9.

within us, dishonouring our best services. How far, by God's grace, we are able in time to chastise, restrain, and destroy this infection, is another question; but still it is not removed at once by Baptism, and if not, surely it is a most grievous humiliation to those who are striving to "walk worthy of the Lord unto all pleasing" (Col 1:10). It is involuntary, and therefore does not cast us out of grace; yet in itself it is very miserable and very humbling: and every one will discover it in himself, if he watches himself narrowly. I mean, what is called the old Adam, pride, profaneness, deceit, unbelief, selfishness, greediness, the inheritance of the Tree of the knowledge of good and evil; sins which the words of the serpent sowed in the hearts of our first parents, which sprang up and bore fruit, some thirty-fold, some sixty, some an hundred, and which have been by carnal descent transmitted to us.

2. Another class of involuntary sins, which often are not such as to throw us out of grace, any more than the infection of nature, but are still more humbling and distressing, consists of those which arise from our former habits of sin, though now long abandoned. We cannot rid ourselves of sin when we would; though we repent, though God forgives us, yet it remains in its power over our souls, in our habits, and in our memories. It has given a colour to our throughts, words, and works; and though, with many efforts, we would wash it out from us, yet this is not possible except gradually. Men have been slothful, or self-conceited, or self-willed, or impure, or worldly-minded in their youth, and afterwards they turn to God, and would fain be other than they have been, but their former self clings to them, as a poisoned garment, and eats into them. They cannot do the things that they would, and from time to time they seem almost reduced back again to that heathen state, which the Apostle describes, when he cries out, "Oh, wretched man that I am! who shall deliver me from the body of this death?" (Rom 7:24).

3. Another class of involuntary sins are such as arise from want of self-command; that is, from the mind being possessed of more light than strength, the conscience being informed, but the governing principle weak. The soul of man is intended to be a well-ordered polity, in which there are many powers and faculties and each has its due place; and for these to exceed their limits is sin; yet they cannot be kept within those limits except by being governed, and we are unequal to this task of governing ourselves except after long habit. While we are learning to govern ourselves, we are constantly exposed to the risk, or rather to the occurrence, of numberless failures. We have failures by the way, though we triumph in the end; and thus, as I just

now implied, the process of learning to obey God is, in one sense, a process of sinning, from the nature of the case. We have much to be forgiven; nay, we have the more to be forgiven the more we attempt. The higher our aims, the greater our risks. They who venture much with their talents, gain much, and in the end they hear the words, "Well done, good and faithful servant"; but they have so many losses in trading by the way, that to themselves they seem to do nothing but fail. They cannot believe that they are making any progress; and though they do, yet surely they have much to be forgiven in all their services. They are like David, men of blood; they fight the good fight of faith, but they are polluted with the contest.

I am not speaking of cases of extraordinary devotion, but of what every one must know in his own case, how difficult it is to command himself, and do that he wishes to do;—how weak the governing principle of his mind is, and how poorly and imperfectly he comes up to his own notions of right and truth; how difficult it is to command his feelings, grief, anger, impatience, joy, fear; how difficult to govern his tongue, to say just what he would; how difficult to rouse himself to do what he would, at this time or that; how difficult to rise in the morning; how difficult to go about his duties and not be idle; how difficult to eat and drink just what he should, how difficult to fix his mind on his prayers; how difficult to regulate his thoughts through the day; how difficult to keep out of his mind what should be kept out of it.

We are feeble-minded, excitable, effeminate, wayward, irritable, changeable, miserable. We have no lord over us, because we are but partially subject to the dominion of the true King of Saints. Let us try to do right as much as we will, let us pray as earnestly, yet we do not, in a time of trial, come up even to our own notions of perfection, or rather we fall quite short of them, and do perhaps just the reverse of what we had hoped to do. While there is no external temptation present, our passions sleep, and we think all is well. Then we think, and reflect, and resolve what we will do; and we anticipate no difficulty in doing it. But when the temptation is come, where are we then? We are like Daniel in the lions' den; and our passions are the lions; except that we have not Daniel's grace to prevail with God for the shutting of the lions' mouths lest they devour us. Then our reason is but like the miserable keeper of wild beasts, who in ordinary seasons is equal to them, but not when they are excited. Alas! Whatever the affection of mind may be, how miserable it is! It may be a dull, heavy sloth, or cowardice, which throws its huge limbs around us, binds us close, oppresses our breath, and makes us despise ourselves, while we are impotent to resist it; or it may be anger, or other baser passion, which, for the moment, escapes from our control after its prey, to our horror and our disgrace; but anyhow, what a miserable den of brute creatures does the soul then become, and we at the moment (I say) literally unable to help it! I am not, of course, speaking of *deeds* of evil, the fruits of wilfulness,—malice, or revenge, or uncleanness, or intemperance, or violence, or robbery, or fraud;—alas the sinful heart often goes on to commit sins which hide from it at once the light of God's countenance; but I am supposing what was Eve's case, when she looked at the Tree and saw that the fruit was good, but before she plucked it, when lust had conceived and was bringing forth sin, but ere sin was finished and had brought forth death. I am supposing that we do not exceed so far as to estrange God from us, that He mercifully chains the lions at our cry, before they do more than frighten us by their moanings or their roar,—before they fall on us to destroy us: yet, at best, what misery, what pollution, what sacrilege, what a chaos is there then in that consecrated spot, which is the temple of the Holy Ghost! How is it that the lamp of God does not go out in it at once, when the whole soul seems tending to hell, and hope is almost gone? Wonderful mercy indeed it is, which bears so much! Incomprehensible patience in the Holy One, so to dwell, in such a wilderness, with the wild beasts! Exceeding and divine virtue in the grace given us, that it is not stifled! Yet such is the promise, not to those who sin contentedly after they have received grace; there is no hope while they so sin; but where sin is not part of a course, though it is still sin, whether sin of our birth, or of habits formed long ago, or of want of self-command which we are trying to gain, God mercifully allows and pardons it, and "the blood of Jesus Christ cleanseth us from" it all.

4. Further, I might dwell upon sins which we fall into from being taken unawares,—when the temptation is sudden,—as St. Peter, when he first denied Christ; though whether it became of a different character, when he denied twice and thrice, is a further question.

5. And again, those sins which rise from the devil's temptations, inflaming the wounds and scars of past sins healed, or nearly so; exciting the memory, and hurrying us away; and thus making use of our former selves against our present selves contrary to our will.

6. And again, I might speak of those which rise from a deficiency of practical experience, or from ignorance how to perform duties which we set about. Men attempt to be munificent, and their acts are prodigal; they wish to be firm and zealous, and their acts are cruel; they wish to be

benevolent, and they are indulgent and weak; they do harm when they mean to do good; they engage in undertakings, or they promote designs, or they put forth opinions, or they set a pattern, of which evil comes; they countenance evil; they mistake falsehood for truth; they are zealous for false doctrines; they oppose the cause of God. One can hardly say all this is without sin, and yet in them it may be involuntary sin and pardonable on the prayer of faith.

7. Or I might speak of those unworthy motives, low views, mistakes in principle, false maxims, which abound on all sides of us, and which we catch (as it were) from each other;—that spirit of the world which we breathe, and which defiles all we do, yet which can hardly be said to be a wilful pollution; but rather it is such sin as is consistent with the presence of the grace of God in us, which that grace will blot out and put away.

8. And, lastly, much might be said on the subject of what the Litany calls "negligences and ignorances," on forgetfulnesses, heedlessnesses, want of seriousness, frivolities, and a variety of weaknesses, which we may be conscious of in ourselves, or see in others.

Such are some of the classes of sins which may be found, if it so happen, where the will is right, and faith lively; and which in such cases are not inconsistent with the state of grace, or may be called infirmities. Of course it must be ever recollected, that infirmities are not always to be regarded *as* infirmities; they attach also to those who live in the commission of wilful sins, and who have no warrant whatever for considering themselves in a saving state. Men do not cease to be under the influence of original sin, or sins of past years, they do not gain self-command, or unlearn negligences and ignorances, by adding to these offences others of a more grievous character. Those who are out of grace, have infirmities and much more. And there will always be a tendency in such persons to explain away their wilful sins into infirmities. This is ever to be borne in mind. I am not attempting to draw the line between infirmities and transgressions; I only say, that to whomsoever besides such infirmities do attach, they may happen to attach to those who are free from transgressions, and who need not despond, or be miserable on account of failings which in them are not destructive of faith or incompatible with grace. Who these are He only knows for certain, who "tries the reins and the heart," who "knoweth the mind of the Spirit," and "discerns between the righteous and the wicked." He is able, amid the maze of contending motives and principles within us, to trace out the perfect work of righteousness steadily going on there, and the rudiments of a new world rising from out the chaos. He can discriminate between what is habitual and what is accidental; what is on the growth and what is in decay; what is a result and what is indeterminate; what is of us and what is in us. He estimates the difference between a will that is honestly devoted to Him, and one that is insincere. And where there is a willing mind, He accepts it "according to that a man hath, and not according to that he hath not" (2 Cor 8:12). In those whose wills are holy, He is present for sanctification and acceptance; and, like the sun's beams in some cave of the earth, His grace sheds light on every side, and consumes all mists and vapours as they rise.

We indeed have not knowledge such as His; were we ever so high in God's favour, a certainty of our justification would not belong to us. Yet, even to know only thus much, that infirmities are no necessary mark of reprobation, that God's elect have infirmities, and that our own sins may possibly be no more than infirmities, this surely, by itself, is a consolation. And to reflect that at least God continues us visibly in His Church; that He does not withdraw from us the ordinances of grace; that He gives us means of instruction, patterns of holiness, religious guidance, good books; that He allows us to frequent His house, and to present ourselves before Him in prayer and Holy Communion; that He gives us opportunities of private prayer; that He has given us a care for our souls; an anxiety to secure our salvation; a desire to be more strict and conscientious, more simple in faith, more full of love than we are; all this will tend to soothe and encourage us, when the sense of our infirmities makes us afraid. And if further, God seems to be making us His instruments for any purpose of His, for teaching, warning, guiding, or comforting others, resisting error, spreading the knowledge of the truth, or edifying His Church, this too will create in us the belief, not that God is certainly pleased with us, for knowledge of mysteries may be separated from love, but that He has not utterly forsaken us in spite of our sins, that He still remembers us, and knows us by name, and desires our salvation. And further, if, for all our infirmities, we can point to some occasions on which we have sacrificed anything for God's service, or to any habit of sin or evil tendency of nature which we have more or less overcome, or to any habitual self-denial which we practice, or to any work which we have accomplished to God's honour and glory; this perchance may fill us with the humble hope that God is working in us, and therefore is at peace with us. And, lastly, if we have, through God's mercy, an inward sense of our own sincerity and integrity, if we feel that we can appeal to God with St. Peter, that we love Him only, and desire to please Him in all things,—in proportion as we feel this, or at such times as we feel it, we have an assurance shed abroad on our hearts, that we are at present in His favour, and are in training for the inheritance of His eternal kingdom.

SERMON XVI

Sincerity and Hypocrisy

"If there be first a willing mind, it is accepted according to that a man hath, and not according to that he hath not."—2 Cor 8:12

Men may be divided into two great classes, those who profess religious obedience, and those who do not; and of those who do profess to be religious, there are again those who perform as well as profess, and those who do not. And thus on the whole there are three classes of men in the world, open sinners, consistent Christians, and between the two, (as speaking with the one, and more or less acting with the other), professing Christians, or, as they are sometimes called, nominal Christians. Now the distinction between open sinners and consistent Christians is so clear, that there is no mistaking it; for they agree in nothing; they neither profess the same things nor practise the same. But the difference between professing Christians and true Christians is not so clear, for this reason, that true Christians, however consistent they are, yet do sin, as being not yet perfect; and so far as they sin, are inconsistent, and this is all that professing Christians are. What then, it may be asked, is the real difference between true and professing Christians, since both the one and the other profess more than they practise? Again, if you put the question to one of the latter class, however inconsistent his life may be, yet he will be sure to say that he wishes he was better; that he is sorry for his sins; that the flesh is weak; that he cannot overcome it; that God alone can overcome it; that he trusts God will, and that he prays to Him to enable him to do it. There is no form of words conceivable which a mere professing Christian cannot use,—nay, more, there appears to be no sentiment which he cannot feel,—as well as the true Christian, and at first sight apparently with the same justice. He *seems* just in the very position of the true Christian, only perhaps behind him; not *so* consistent, not advanced so much; still, on the same line. Both confess to a struggle within them; both sin, both are sorry; what then is the difference between them?

There are many differences; but, before going on to mention that one to which I shall confine my attention, I would have you observe that I am speaking of differences in God's sight. Of course, we men may after all be unable altogether, and often are unable, to see differences between those who, nevertheless, are on different sides of the line of life. Nor may we judge anything absolutely before the time, whereas God "searcheth the hearts." He alone, "who searcheth the hearts," "knoweth what is the mind of the Spirit." We do not even know ourselves absolutely. "Yea, I judge not mine own self," says St. Paul, "but He that judgeth me is the Lord." God alone can unerringly discern between sincerity and insincerity, between the hypocrite and the man of perfect heart. I do not, of course, mean that we can form no judgment at all upon ourselves, or that it is not useful to do so; but here I will chiefly insist upon the point of *doctrine,* viz., how does the true Christian differ in God's sight from the insincere and double-minded?—leaving any practical application which it admits, to be incidentally brought out in the course of my remarks.

Now the real difference between the true and the professing Christian seems to be given us in the text,—"If there be a willing mind, it is accepted." St. Paul is speaking of almsgiving; but what he says seems to apply generally. He is laying down a principle, which applies of course in many distinct cases, though he uses it with reference to one in particular. An honest, unaffected *desire* of doing right is the test of God's true servants. On the other hand, a double mind, a pursuing other ends besides the truth, and in consequence an inconsistency in conduct, and a half-consciousness (to say the least) of inconsistency, and a feeling of the necessity of defending oneself to oneself, and to God, and to the world; in a word, hypocrisy; these are the signs of the merely professed Christian. Now I am going to give some instances of this distinction, in Scripture and in fact.

For instance. The two great Christian graces are faith and love. Now, how are these characterised in Scripture?—By their being honest or single-minded. Thus St. Paul, in one place, speaks of "the end of the commandment being love"; what love?—"love *out of a pure heart*," he proceeds, "and of a *good conscience*"; and still further, "and of faith,"—what kind of faith?—"faith *unfeigned*"; or, as it may be more literally translated, "unhypocritical faith"; for so the word means in Greek. Again, elsewhere he speaks of his "calling to remembrance the *unfeigned* faith" which dwelt in Timothy, and in his mother and grandmother before him; that is, literally, "unhypocritical faith." Again, he speaks of the

Apostles approving themselves as the Ministers of God, "by kindness, by the Holy Ghost, by love *unfeigned*," or, more literally, "unhypocritical love." Again, as to love towards man. "Let love be *without dissimulation*," or, more literally, as in the other cases, "let love be unhypocritical." In like manner, St. Peter speaks of Christians "having purified their souls in obeying the truth through the Spirit unto unhypocritical love of the brethren." And in like manner, St. James speaks of "the wisdom that is from above, being first *pure*. . ." and, presently, "without partiality, and *without hypocrisy*" (2 Cor 6:6; Rom 12:9; 1 Pt 1:22; Jas 3:17). Surely it is very remarkable that three Apostles, writing on different subjects and occasions, should each of them thus speak about whether faith or love as without hypocrisy.

A true Christian, then, may almost be defined as one who has a ruling sense of God's presence within him. As none but justified persons have that privilege, so none but the justified have that practical perception of it. A true Christian, or one who is in a state of acceptance with God, is he, who, in such sense, has faith in Him, as to live in the thought that He is present with him,—present not externally, not in nature merely, or in providence, but in his innermost heart, or in his *conscience*. A man is justified whose conscience is illuminated by God, so that he habitually realizes that all his thoughts, all the first springs of his moral life, all his motives and his wishes, are open to Almighty God. Not as if he was not aware that there is very much in him impure and corrupt, but he wishes that all that is in him should be bare to God. He believes that it is so, and he even joys to think that it is so, in spite of his fear and shame at its being so. He alone admits Christ into the shrine of his heart; whereas others wish in some way or other, to be by themselves, to have a home, a chamber, a tribunal, a throne, a self where God is not,—a home within them which is not a temple, a chamber which is not a confessional, a tribunal without a judge, a throne without a king;—that self may be king and judge; and that the Creator may rather be dealt with and approached as though a second party, instead of His being that true and better self, of which self itself should be but an instrument and minister.

Scripture tells us that God the Word, who died for us and rose again, and now lives for us, and saves us, is "quick and powerful, and sharper than any two-edged sword, piercing even to the dividing asunder of soul and spirit, and of the joints and marrow, and a discerner of the thoughts and intents of the heart. Neither is there any creature that is not manifest in His sight; but all things are naked and opened unto the eyes of Him with whom we have to do" (Heb 4:12, 13). Now the true

PAROCHIAL AND PLAIN SERMONS

Christian realizes this; and what is the consequence?—Why, that he enthrones the Son of God in his conscience, refers to Him as a sovereign authority, and uses no reasoning with Him. He does not reason, but he says, "Thou, God, seest me." He feels that God is too near him to allow of argument, self-defence, excuse, or objection. He appeals in matters of duty, not to his own reason, but to God Himself, whom with the eyes of faith he sees, and whom he makes the Judge; not to any fancied fitness, or any preconceived notion, or any abstract principle, or any tangible experience.

The Book of Psalms continually instances this temper of profound, simple, open-hearted confidence in God. "O Lord, Thou hast searched me out and known me. Thou knowest my downsitting and mine uprising. Thou understandest my thoughts long before.... There is not a word in my tongue but Thou knowest it altogether." "My soul hangeth upon Thee. Thy right hand hath upholden me." "When I wake up, I am present with Thee." "Into Thy hands I commend my spirit, for Thou hast redeemed me, O Lord, Thou God of Truth." "Commit thy way unto the Lord, and put thy trust in Him, and He shall bring it to pass. He shall make thy righteousness as clear as the light, and thy just dealing as the noonday." "Against Thee only have I sinned, and done this evil in Thy sight." "Hear the right, O Lord, consider my complaint, and hearken unto my prayer that goeth not out of feigned lips. Let my sentence come forth from Thy presence, and let Thine eyes look upon the thing that is equal. Thou hast proved and visited mine heart in the night season. Thou hast tried me, and shalt find no wickedness in me; for I am utterly purposed that my mouth shall not offend." Once more, "Thou shalt guide me with Thy counsel, and after that receive me with glory. Whom have I in heaven but Thee? and there is none upon earth that I desire in comparison of Thee. My flesh and my heart faileth, but God is the strength of mine heart and my portion for ever" (Ps 139:1, 2, 4; 63:8; 31:5; 37:5, 6; 51:4; 17:1–3; 73:24–26).

Or, again, consider the following passage in St. John's First Epistle. "If our heart condemn us, God is greater than our heart and knoweth all things. Beloved, if our heart condemn us not, then have we confidence towards God." And in connexion with this, the following from the same Epistle: "God is Light, and in Him is no darkness at all. If we say that we have fellowship with Him, and walk in darkness, we lie, and do not the truth.... If we confess our sins, He is faithful and just to forgive us our sins, and to cleanse us from all unrighteousness." Again, "The darkness is past, and the true light now shineth." Again, "Hereby we know that He abideth in us, by the Spirit which He hath given us." And again, "He that believeth on the Son of God, hath the witness in himself." And, in the same connexion, consider St. Paul's statement, that "the Spirit itself beareth witness with our spirit, that we are the children of God" (1 Jn 3:20, 21, 1:5–9, 2:8, 3:24, 5:10; Rom 8:16).

And, now, on the other hand, let us contrast such a temper of mind, which loves to walk in the light, with that of the merely professing Christian, or, in Scripture language, of the *hypocrite*. Such are they who have two ends which they pursue, religion *and* the world; and hence St. James calls them "double-minded." Hence, too, our Lord, speaking of the Pharisees who were hypocrites, says, "Ye cannot serve God *and* mammon" (Lk 16:13). A double-minded man, then, as having two ends in view, dare not come to God, lest he should be discovered; for "all things that are reproved are made manifest by the light" (Eph 5:13). Thus, whereas the Prodigal Son "rose and came to his father," on the contrary, Adam hid himself among the trees of the garden. It was not simple dread of God, but dread joined to an unwillingness to be restored to God. He had a secret in his heart which he kept from God. He felt towards God,—as it would seem, or at least his descendants so feel,—as one man often feels towards another in the intercourse of life. You sometimes say of a man, "he is friendly, or courteous, or respectful, or considerate, or communicative; but, after all, there is something, perhaps without his knowing it, in the background. He professes to be agreed with me; he almost displays his agreement; he says he pursues the same objects as I; but still I do not know him, I do not make progress with him, I have no confidence in him, I do not know him better than the first time I saw him." Such is the way in which the double-minded approach the Most High,—they have a something private, a hidden self at bottom. They look on themselves, as it were, as independent parties, treating with Almighty God as one of their fellows. Hence, so far from seeking God, they hardly like to be sought by Him. They would rather keep their position and stand where they are,—on earth, and so make terms with God in heaven; whereas, "he that doeth truth, cometh to the light, that his deeds may be made manifest that they are wrought in God" (Jn 3:21).

This being the case, there being in the estimation of the double-minded man two parties, God and self, it follows (as I have said), that reasoning and argument is the mode in which he approaches his Saviour and Judge; and that for two reasons,—first, because he will not *give* himself up to God, but stands upon his rights and appeals to his notions of fitness: and next, because he has some secret misgiving after all that he is dishonest, or some consciousness that he may appear so to others; and therefore, he goes about to fortify his position, to explain his conduct, or to excuse himself.

Some such argument or excuse had the unprofitable servant, when called before his Lord. The other servants said, "Lord, Thy pound hath gained ten," or "five pounds." They said no more; nothing more was necessary; the case spoke for itself. But the unprofitable servant did not dare leave his conduct to tell its own tale at God's judgment-seat; he said not merely, "Lord, I have kept Thy pound laid up in a napkin": He appealed, as it were, to the reasonableness of his conduct against his Maker: he felt he must make out a case, and he went on to attempt it. He trusted not his interests to the Eternal and All-perfect Reason of God, before whom he stood, but entrenched himself in his own.

Again:—When our Lord said to the scribe, who had answered Him that eternal life was to be gained by loving God and his neighbour, "Thou hast answered right," this ought to have been enough. But his object was not to please God, but to exalt himself. And, therefore, he went on to make an objection. "But he, willing to *justify himself*, said unto Jesus, And who is my neighbour?" whereas they only are justified in God's judgment, who give up the notion of justifying themselves by word or deed, who start with the confession that they are unjust, and who come to God, not upon their own merits, but for His mercy.

Again: We have the same arguing and insincere spirit exposed in the conduct of the Pharisees, when they asked Christ for the authority on which He acted. They said, "By what authority doest thou these things?" This might be the question of sincere inquirers or mere objectors, of faith or of hypocrisy. Observe how our Lord detects it. He asked them about St. John's baptism; meaning to say, that if they acknowledged St. John, they must acknowledge Himself, of whom St. John spake. They, unwilling to submit to Christ as a teacher and Lord, preferred to deny John to going on to acknowledge Him. Yet, on the other hand, they dare not openly deny the Baptist, because of the people; so, between hatred of our Lord and dread of the people, they would give no answer at all. "They *reasoned* among themselves," we are told. In consequence, our Lord left them to their reasonings; He refused to tell them what, had they reasoned sincerely, they might learn for themselves.

What is seen in the Gospels, had taken place from the beginning. Our first parents were as ready with excuses, as their posterity when Christ came. First, Adam says, "I hid myself, for I was afraid"; though fear and shame were not the sole or chief reasons why he fled, but an incipient hatred, if it may be said, of his Maker. Again, he says, "The woman, whom Thou gavest me . . . she gave me of the tree." And the woman says, "The serpent beguiled me." They did not honestly surrender themselves to their offended God, but had something to say in their behalf. Again, Cain says, when asked where his brother was, whom he had murdered, "Am I my brother's keeper?"

Balaam, again, is a most conspicuous instance of a double mind, or of hypocrisy. He has a plausible reason for whatever he does; he can so skillfully defend himself, that to this day he looks like a good man, and his conduct and fortunes are a perplexity to many minds. But it is one thing to have good excuses, another to have good motives. He had not the love of the truth, the love of God, in his heart; he was covetous of worldly goods; and, therefore, all his excuses only avail to mark him as double-minded.

Again:—Saul is another very remarkable instance of a man acting for his own ends, and yet having plausible *reasons* for what he did. He offered sacrifice on one occasion, not having a commission; this was a sin; yet what was his excuse?—a very fair one. Samuel had promised to come to offer the sacrifice, and did not. Saul waited some days, the people grew discouraged, his army fell off, and the enemy was at hand,—so, as he says, he "*forced* himself" (1 Sm 13:12).

Such is the conduct of insincere men in difficulty. Perhaps their difficulty may be a real one; but in this they differ from the sincere:—the latter seek God *in* their difficulty, feeling that He only who imposes it can remove it; but insincere men do not like to go to God; and to them the difficulty is only so much gain, for it gives them an apparent reason, a sort of excuse, for not going by God's rule, but for deciding in their own way. Thus Saul took his own course; thus Jeroboam, when in a difficulty, put up calves of gold and instituted a new worship without Divine command. Whereas, when Hezekiah was in trouble, he took the letter of Sennacherib, "and went up into the house of the Lord, and spread it before the Lord" (Is 37:14). And when St. Peter was sinking in the water, he cried out to Christ, "Lord, save me" (Mt 14:30). And in like manner holy David, after he had sinned in numbering the people, and was told to choose between three punishments offered him, showed the same honest and simple-hearted devotion in choosing that of the three which might be the most exactly called falling into the Lord's hands. If he must suffer, let the Lord chastise him.—"I am in a great strait," he says; "let us fall now into the hands of the Lord; for His mercies are great; and let me not fall into the hand of man" (2 Sm 24:14).

Great, then, is the difference between sincere and insincere Christians, however like their words may be to each other; and it is needless to say, that what I have shown in a few examples, might be instanced again and again from every part of Scripture, particularly from the history of the Jews, as contained in the Prophets. All men, even after the gift of God's grace, sin: God's true servants profess and sin,—sin, and are sorry; and hypocrites profess and sin,—sin and are sorry. Thus the two parties look like each other. But the word of God discriminates one from the other by this test,—that Christ dwells in the conscience of one, not of the other; that the one opens his heart to God, the other does not; the one views Almighty God only as an accidental guest, the other as Lord and owner of all that he is; the one admits Him as if for a night, or some stated season, the other gives himself over to God, and considers himself God's servant and instrument now and for ever. Not more different is the intimacy of friends from mere acquaintance; not more different is it to know a person in society, to be courteous and obliging to him, to interchange civilities, from opening one's heart to another, admitting him into it, seeing into his, loving him, and living in him;— than the external worship of the hypocrite, from the inward devotion of true faith; approaching God with the lips, from believing on Him with the heart; so opening to the Spirit that He opens to us, from so living to self as to exclude the light of heaven.

Now, as to applying what I have been showing from Scripture to ourselves, this shall here be left, my brethren, to the consciences of each of us, and a few words will suffice to do this. Do you, then, habitually thus unlock your hearts and subject your thoughts to Almighty God? Are you living in this conviction of His Presence, and have you this special witness that that Presence is really set up within you unto your salvation, viz., that you live in the sense of it? Do you believe, and act on the belief, that His light penetrates and shines through your heart, as the sun's beams through a room? You know how things look when the sun's beams are on it,—the very air then appears full of impurities, which, before it came out, were not seen. So is it with our souls. We are full of stains and corruptions, we see them not, they are like the air before the sun shines; but though we see them not, God sees them: He pervades us as the sunbeam. Our souls, in His view, are full of things which offend, things which must be repented of, forgiven, and put away. He, in the words of the Psalmist, "has set our misdeeds before Him, our secret sins in the light of His countenance" (Ps 90:8). This is most true, though it be not at all welcome doctrine to many. We cannot hide ourselves from Him; and our wisdom, as our duty, lies in embracing this truth, acquiescing in it, and acting upon it. Let us then beg Him to teach us the Mystery of His Presence in us, that, by acknowledging it, we may thereby possess it fruitfully. Let us confess it in faith, that we may possess it unto justification. Let us so own it, as to set Him before us in everything. "I have set God always before me," says the Psalmist, "for He is on my right hand, therefore I shall not fall" (Ps 16:8). Let us, in all circumstances, thus regard Him. Whether we have sinned, let us not dare keep from Him, but with the Prodigal Son, rise and go to Him. Or, if we are conscious of nothing, still let us not boast in ourselves or justify ourselves, but feel that "He who judgeth us is the Lord." In all circumstances, of joy or sorrow, hope or fear, let us aim at having Him in our inmost heart; let us have no secret apart from Him. Let us acknowledge Him as enthroned within us at the very springs of thought and affection. Let us submit ourselves to His guidance and sovereign direction; let us come to Him that He may forgive us, cleanse us, change us, guide us, and save us.

This is the true life of saints. This is to have the Spirit witnessing with our spirits that we are sons of God. Such a faith alone will sustain the terrors of the Last Day; such a faith alone will be proof against those fierce flames which are to surround the Judge, when He comes with His holy Angels to separate between "those who serve God, and those who serve Him not?" (Mal 3:18).

SERMON XXII

The Thought of God, the Stay of the Soul

(QUINQUAGESIMA)

"Ye have not received the spirit of bondage again to fear, but ye have received the Spirit of adoption, whereby we cry, Abba, Father."—Rom 8:15

When Adam fell, his soul lost its true strength; he forfeited the inward light of God's presence, and became the wayward, fretful, excitable, and miserable being which his history has shown him to be ever since; with alternate strength and feebleness, nobleness and meanness, energy in the beginning and failure in the end. Such was the state of his soul in itself, not to speak of the Divine wrath upon it, which followed, or was involved in the Divine withdrawal. It lost its spiritual life and health, which was necessary to complete its nature, and to enable it to fulfil the ends for which it was created,—which was necessary both for its moral integrity and its happiness; and as if faint, hungry, or sick, it could no longer stand upright, but sank on the ground. Such is the state in which every one of us lies as born into the world; and Christ has come to reverse this state, and restore us the great gift which Adam lost in the beginning. Adam fell from his Creator's favour to be a bond-servant; and Christ has come to set us free again, to impart to us the Spirit of adoption, whereby we become God's children, and again approach Him as our Father.

I say, by birth we are in a state of defect and want; we have not all that is necessary for the perfection of our nature. As the body is not complete in itself, but requires the soul to give it a meaning, so again the soul till God is present with it and manifested in it, has faculties and affections without a ruling principle, object, or purpose. Such it is by birth, and this Scripture signifies to us by many figures; sometimes calling human nature blind, sometimes hungry, sometimes unclothed, and calling the gift of the Spirit light, health, food, warmth, and raiment; all by way of teaching us what our first state is, and what our gratitude should be to Him who has brought us into a new state. For instance, "Because thou sayest, I am rich, and increased in goods, and have need of nothing; and knowest not that thou art wretched, and miserable, and poor, and blind, and naked: I counsel thee to buy of Me gold tried in the fire, that thou mayest be rich; and white raiment, that thou mayest be clothed, . . . and anoint thine eyes with eye-salve, that thou mayest see." Again, "God, who commanded the light to shine out of darkness, hath shined in our hearts, to give the light of the knowledge of the glory of God, in the face of Jesus Christ." Again, "Awake, thou that sleepest, and arise from the dead, and Christ shall give thee light." Again, "Whosoever drinketh of the water that I shall give him, shall never thirst; but the water that I shall give him shall be in him a well of water springing up into everlasting life." And in the Book of Psalms, "They shall be satisfied with the plenteousness of Thy house; and Thou shalt give them drink of Thy pleasures as out of the river. For with Thee is the well of life, and in Thy Light shall we see light." And in another Psalm, "My soul shall be satisfied, even as it were with marrow and fatness, when my mouth praiseth Thee with joyful lips." And so again, in the Prophet Jeremiah, "I will satiate the souls of the priests with fatness; and My people shall be satisfied with My goodness. . . . I have satiated the weary soul, and I have replenished every sorrowful soul" (Rv 3:17, 18; 2 Cor 4:6; Eph 5:14; Jn 4:14; Ps 36:8, 9, 63:5; Jer 31:14, 25).

Now the doctrine which these passages contain is often truly expressed thus: that the soul of man is made for the contemplation of its Maker; and that nothing short of that high contemplation is its happiness; that, whatever it may possess besides, it is unsatisfied till it is vouchsafed God's Presence, and lives in the light of it. There are many aspects in which the same solemn truth may be viewed; there are many ways in which it may be signified. I will now dwell upon it as I have been stating it.

I say, then, that the happiness of the soul consists in the exercise of the affections; not in sensual pleasures, not in activity, not in excitement, not in self-esteem, not in the consciousness of power, not in knowledge; in none of these things lies our happiness, but in our affections being elicited, employed, supplied. As hunger and thirst, as taste, sound, and smell, are the channels through which this bodily frame receives pleasure, so the affections are the instruments by which the soul has pleasure.

When they are exercised duly, it is happy; when they are undeveloped, restrained, or thwarted, it is not happy. This is our real and true bliss, not to know, or to affect, or to pursue; but to love, to hope, to joy, to admire, to revere, to adore. Our real and true bliss lies in the possession of those objects on which our hearts may rest and be satisfied.

Now, if this be so, here is at once a reason for saying that the thought of God, and nothing short of it, is the happiness of man; for though there is much besides to serve as subject of knowledge, or motive for action, or means of excitement, yet the affections require a something more vast and more enduring than anything created. What is novel and sudden excites, but does not influence; what is pleasurable or useful raises no awe; self moves no reverence, and mere knowledge kindles no love. He alone is sufficient for the heart who made it. I do not say, of course, that nothing short of the Almighty Creator can awaken and answer to our love, reverence, and trust; man can do this for man. Man doubtless is an object to rouse his brother's love, and repays it in his measure. Nay, it is a great duty, one of the two chief duties of religion, thus to be minded towards our neighbor. But I am not speaking here of what we can do, or ought to do, but what it is our happiness to do: and surely it may be said that though the love of the brethren, the love of all men, be one half of our obedience, yet exercised by itself, were that possible, which it is not, it would be no part of our reward. And for this reason, if for no other, that our hearts require something more permanent and uniform than man can be. We gain much for a time from fellowship with each other. It is a relief to us, as fresh air to the fainting, or meat and drink to the hungry, or a flood of tears to the heavy in mind. It is a soothing comfort to have those whom we may make our confidants; a comfort to have those to whom we may confess our faults; a comfort to have those to whom we may look for sympathy. Love of home and family in these and other ways is sufficient to make this life tolerable to the multitude of men, which otherwise it would not be; but still, after all, our affections exceed such exercise of them, and demand what is more stable. Do not all men die? are they not taken from us? are they not as uncertain as the grass of the field? We do not give our hearts to things irrational, because these have no permanence in them. We do not place our affections in sun, moon, and stars, or this rich and fair earth, because all things material come to nought, and vanish like day and night. Man, too, though he has an intelligence within him, yet in his best estate he is altogether vanity. If our happiness consists in our affections being employed and recompensed, "man that is born of a woman" cannot be our happiness; for how can he stay another, who "continueth not in one stay" himself?

But there is another reason why God alone is the happiness of our souls, to which I wish rather to direct attention:—the contemplation of Him, and nothing but it, is able fully to open and relieve the mind, to unlock, occupy, and fix our affections. We may indeed love things created with great intenseness, but such affection, when disjoined from the love of the Creator, is like a stream running in a narrow channel, impetuous, vehement, turbid. The heart runs out, as it were, only at one door; it is not an expanding of the whole man. Created natures cannot open us, or elicit the ten thousand mental senses which belong to us, and through which we really live. None but the presence of our Maker can enter us; for to none besides can the whole heart in all its thoughts and feelings be unlocked and subjected. "Behold," He says, "I stand at the door and knock; if any man hear My voice and open the door, I will come in to him, and will sup with him, and he with Me." "My Father will love him, and We will come unto him, and make Our abode with him." "God hath sent forth the Spirit of His Son into your hearts." "God is greater than our heart, and knoweth all things" (Rv 3:20; Jn 14: 23; Gal 4:6; 1 Jn 3:20). It is this feeling of simple and absolute confidence and communion, which soothes and satisfies those to whom it is vouchsafed. We know that even our nearest friends enter into us but partially, and hold intercourse with us only at times; whereas the consciousness of a perfect and enduring Presence, and it alone, keeps the heart open. Withdraw the Object on which it rests, and it will relapse again into its state of confinement and constraint; and in proportion as it is limited, either to certain seasons or to certain affections, the heart is straitened and distressed. If it be not over bold to say it, He who is infinite can alone be its measure; He alone can answer to the mysterious assemblage of feelings and thoughts which it has within it. "There is no creature that is not manifest in His sight, but all things are naked and opened unto the eyes of Him with whom we have to do" (Heb 4:13).

This is what is meant by the peace of a good conscience; it is the habitual consciousness that our hearts are open to God, with a desire that they should be open. It is a confidence in God, from a feeling that there is nothing in us which we need be ashamed or afraid of. You will say that no man on earth is in such a state; for we are all sinners, and that daily. It is so; certainly we are quite unfitted to endure God's all-searching Eye, to come into direct contact (if I may so speak) with His glorious Presence, without any medium of intercourse between Him and us. But, first, there may be degrees of this confidence in different men, though the perfection of it be in none. And again, God in His great mercy, as we all well know, has revealed to us that there is a Mediator between the sinful soul and Himself. And as His merits most wonderfully intervene between our sins and God's judgment, so the thought of those merits, when present with the Christian, enables him, in spite of his sins, to lift up his heart to God; and believing, as he does, that he is (to use Scripture language) in Christ, or, in other words, that he addresses Almighty God, not simply face to face, but in and through Christ, he can bear to submit and open his heart to God, and to wish it open. For while he is very conscious both of original and actual sin, yet still a feeling of his own sincerity and earnestness is possible; and in proportion as he gains as much as this, he will be able to walk unreservedly with Christ his God and Saviour, and desire His continual presence with him, though he be a sinner, and will wish to be allowed to make Him the one Object of his heart. Perhaps, under somewhat of this feeling, Hagar said, "Thou, God, seest me." It is under this feeling that holy David may be supposed to say, "Examine me, O Lord, and prove me; try out my reins and my heart." "Try me, O God, and seek the ground of my heart; prove me, and examine my thoughts. Look well, if there be any way of wickedness in me; and lead me in the way everlasting" (Ps 26:2, 139:23, 24). And especially is it instanced in St. Paul, who seems to delight in the continual laying open of his heart to God, and submitting it to His scrutiny, and waiting for His Presence upon it; or, in other words, in the joy of a good conscience. For instance, "I have lived in all good conscience before God until this day." "Herein do I exercise myself, to have always a conscience void of offence toward God, and toward men." "I say the truth in Christ, I lie not; my conscience also bearing me witness in the Holy Ghost." "Our rejoicing is this, the testimony of our conscience, that in simplicity and godly sincerity, not with fleshly wisdom, but by the grace of God, we have had our conversation in the world, and more abundantly to you-ward" (Acts 23:1, 24:16; Rom 9:1; 2 Cor 1:12). It is, I say, the characteristic of St. Paul, as manifested to us in his Epistles, to live in the sight of Him who "searcheth the reins and the heart," to love to place himself before Him, and, while contemplating God, to dwell on the thought of God's contemplating him.

And, it may be, this is something of the Apostle's meaning, when he speaks of the witness of the Spirit. Perhaps he is speaking of that satisfaction and rest which the soul experiences in proportion as it is able to surrender itself wholly to God, and to have no desire, no aim, but to please Him. When we are awake, we are conscious we are awake, in a sense in which we cannot fancy we are, when we are asleep. When we have discovered the solution of some difficult problem in science, we have a conviction about it which is distinct from that which accompanies fancied discoveries or guesses. When we realize a truth we have a feeling which they have not, who take words for things. And so, in like manner, if we are allowed to find that real and most sacred Object on which our heart may fix itself, a fulness of peace will follow, which nothing but it can give. In proportion as we have given up the love of the world, and are dead to the creature, and, on the other hand, are born of the Spirit unto love of our Maker and Lord, this love carries with it its own evidence whence it comes. Hence the Apostle says, "The Spirit itself beareth witness with our spirit, that we are the children of God." Again, he speaks of Him "who hath sealed us, and given the earnest of the Spirit in our hearts" (Rom 8:16; 2 Cor 1:22).

I have been saying that our happiness consists in the contemplation of God;—(such a contemplation is alone capable of accompanying the mind always and everywhere, for God alone can be always and everywhere present);—and that what is commonly said about the happiness of a good conscience, confirms this; for what is it to have a good conscience, when we examine the force of our words, but to be ever reminded of God by our own hearts, to have our hearts in such a state as to be led thereby to look up to Him, and to desire His eye to be upon us through the day? It is in the case of holy men the feeling attendant on the contemplation of Almighty God.

But, again, this sense of God's presence is not only the ground of the peace of a good conscience, but of the peace of repentance also. At first sight it might seem strange how repentance can have in it anything of comfort and peace. The Gospel, indeed, promises to turn all sorrow into joy. It makes us take pleasure in desolateness, weakness, and contempt. "We glory in tribulations also," says the Apostle, "because the love of God is shed abroad in our hearts by the Holy Ghost which is given unto us." It destroys anxiety: "Take no thought for the morrow, for the morrow shall take thought for the things of itself." It bids us take comfort under bereavement: "I would not have you ignorant, brethren, concerning them which are asleep, that ye sorrow not, even as others which have no hope" (Rom 5:3, 5; Mt 6:34; 1 Thes 4:18). But if there be one sorrow, which might seem to be unmixed misery, if there be one misery left under the Gospel, the awakened sense of having abused the

Gospel might have been considered that one. And, again, if there be a time when the Presence of the Most High would at first sight seem to be intolerable, it would be then, when first the consciousness vividly bursts upon us that we have ungratefully rebelled against Him. Yet so it is that true repentance cannot be without the thought of God; it has the thought of God, for it seeks Him; and it seeks Him, because it is quickened with love; and even sorrow must have a sweetness, if love be in it. For what is to repent but to surrender ourselves to God for pardon or punishment; as loving His Presence for its own sake, and accounting chastisement from Him better than rest and peace from the world? While the Prodigal Son remained among the swine, he had sorrow enough, but no repentance; remorse only; but repentance led him to rise and go to his Father, and to confess his sins. Thus he relieved his heart of its misery, which before was like some hard and fretful tumour weighing upon it. Or, again, consider St. Paul's account of the repentance of the Corinthians; there is sorrow in abundance, nay, anguish, but no gloom, no dryness of spirit, no sternness. The penitents afflict themselves, but it is from the fulness of their hearts, from love, gratitude, devotion, horror of the past, desire to escape from their present selves into some state holier and more heavenly. St. Paul speaks of their "earnest desire, their mourning, their fervent mind towards him." He rejoices, "not that they were made sorry, but that they sorrowed to repentance." "For ye were made sorry," he proceeds, "after a godly manner, that ye might receive damage by us in nothing." And he describes this "sorrowing after a godly sort," to consist in "carefulness, which it wrought in them," "clearing of themselves," — "indignation," — "fear," — "vehement desire," — "zeal," — "revenge" (2 Cor 7:7, 9, 11), — feelings, all of them, which open the heart, yet, without relaxing it, in that they terminate in acts or works.

On the other hand, remorse, or what the Apostle calls "the sorrow of the world," worketh death. Instead of coming to the Fount of Life, to the God of all consolation, remorseful men feed on their own thoughts, without any confidant of their sorrow. They disburden themselves to no one: to God they will not, to the world they cannot confess. The world will not attend to their confession; it is a good associate, but it cannot be an intimate. It cannot approach us or stand by us in trouble; it is no Paraclete; it leaves all our feelings buried within us, either tumultuous, or, at best, dead: It leaves us gloomy or obdurate. Such is our state, while we live to the world, whether we be in sorrow or in joy. We are pent up within ourselves, and are therefore miserable. Perhaps we may not be able to analyse our misery, or even to realize it, as persons oftentimes who are in bodily sicknesses. We do not know, perhaps, what or where our pain is; we are so used to it that we do not call it pain. Still so it is; we need a relief to our hearts, that they may be dark and sullen no longer, or that they may not go on feeding upon themselves; we need to escape from ourselves to something beyond; and much as we may wish it otherwise, and may try to make idols to ourselves, nothing short of God's Presence is our true refuge; everything else is either a mockery, or but an expedient useful for its season or in its measure.

    How miserable then is he, who does not practically know this great truth! Year after year he will be a more unhappy man, or, at least, he will emerge into a maturity of misery at once, when he passes out of this world of shadows into that kingdom where all is real. He is at present attempting to satisfy his soul with that which is not bread; or he thinks the soul can thrive without nourishment. He fancies he can live without an object. He fancies that he is sufficient for himself; or he supposes that knowledge is sufficient for his happiness; or that exertion, or that the good opinion of others, or (what is called) fame, or that the comforts and luxuries of wealth, are sufficient for him. What a truly wretched state is that coldness and dryness of soul, in which so many live and die, high and low, learned and unlearned. Many a great man, many a peasant, many a busy man, lives and dies with closed heart, with affections undeveloped, unexercised. You see the poor man, passing day after day, Sunday after Sunday, year after year, without a thought in his mind, to appearance almost like a stone. You see the educated man, full of thought, full of intelligence, full of action, but still with a stone heart, as cold and dead as regards his affections, as if he were the poor ignorant countryman. You see others, with warm affections, perhaps, for their families, with benevolent feelings towards their fellow-men, yet stopping there; centring their hearts on what is sure to fail them, as being perishable. Life passes, riches fly away, popularity is fickle, the senses decay, the world changes, friends die. One alone is constant; One alone is true to us; One alone can be true; One alone can be all things to us; One alone can supply our needs; One alone can train us up to our full perfection; One alone can give a meaning to our complex and intricate nature; One alone can give us tune and harmony; One alone can form and possess us. Are we allowed to put ourselves under His guidance? this surely is the only question. Has He really made us His children, and taken possession of us by His Holy Spirit? Are we still in His kingdom of grace, in spite of our sins? The question is not whether we should go, but whether He will receive. And we trust, that, in spite of our sins, He will receive us still, every one of us, if we seek His face in love unfeigned, and holy fear. Let us then do our part, as He has done His, and much more. Let us say with the Psalmist, "Whom have I in heaven but Thee? and there is none upon earth I desire in comparison of Thee. My flesh and my heart faileth; but God is the strength of my heart, and my portion for ever" (Ps 73:25, 26).

Volume VI

SERMON IV

Christ's Privations a Meditation for Christians

(FIFTH SUNDAY IN LENT)

"Ye know the grace of our Lord Jesus Christ, that, though He was rich, yet for your sakes He became poor, that ye through His poverty might be rich."—2 Cor 8:9

As time goes on, and Easter draws nearer, we are called upon not only to mourn over our sins, but especially over the various sufferings which Christ our Lord and Saviour underwent on account of them. Why is it, my brethren, that we have so little feeling on the matter as we commonly have? Why is it that we are used to let the season come and go just like any other season, not thinking more of Christ than at other times, or, at least, not feeling more? Am I not right in saying that this is the case? and if so, have I not cause for asking why it is the case? We are not moved when we hear of the bitter passion of Jesus Christ, the Son of God, for us. We neither bewail our sins which caused it, nor have any sympathy with it. We do not suffer *with* Him. If we come to church, we hear, and then we go away again; not distressed at all; or if distressed, only for the moment. And many do not come to church at all; and to them, of course, this holy and solemn time is like other times. They eat, and drink, and sleep, and rise up, and go about their business and their pleasure, just as usual. They do not carry the thought of Him who died for them, along with them,—with them wherever they are,—with them "whether they eat, or drink, or whatever they do." They in no sense "live," to use St. Paul's words, "by the faith of the Son of God, who loved them and gave Himself for them."

This, alas! cannot be denied. Yet, if it be so, that the Son of God came down from heaven, put aside His glory, and submitted to be despised, cruelly treated, and put to death by His own creatures,—by those whom He had made, and whom He had preserved up to that day, and was then upholding in life and being,—is it reasonable that so great an event should not move us? Does it not stand to reason that we must be in a very irreligious state of mind, unless we have some little gratitude, some little sympathy, some little love, some little awe, some little self-reproach, some little self-abasement, some little repentance, some little desire of amendment, in consequence of what He has done and suffered for us? Or, rather, may not so great a Benefactor demand of us some overflowing gratitude, keen sympathy, fervent love, profound awe, bitter self-reproach, earnest repentance, eager desire and longing after a new heart? Who can deny all this? Why then, O my brethren, is it not so? why are things with us as they are? Alas! I sorrowfully foretell that time will go on, and Passion-tide, Good Friday, and Easter-Day will pass by, and the weeks after it, and many of you will be just what you were—not at all nearer heaven, not at all nearer Christ in your hearts and lives, not impressed lastingly or savingly with the thought of His mercies and your own sins and demerits.

But why is this? why do you so little understand the Gospel of your salvation? why are your eyes so dim, and your ears so hard of hearing? why have you so little faith? so little of heaven in your hearts? For this one reason, my brethren, if I must express my meaning in one word, because you so little *meditate*. You do not meditate, and therefore you are not impressed.

What is meditating on Christ? it is simply this, thinking habitually and constantly of Him and of His deeds and sufferings. It is to have Him before our minds as One whom we may contemplate, worship, and address when we rise up, when we lie down, when we eat and drink, when we are at home and abroad, when we are working, or walking, or at rest, when we are alone, and again when we are in company; this is meditating. And by this, and nothing short of this, will our hearts come to feel as they ought. We have stony hearts, hearts as hard as the highways; the history of Christ makes no impression on them. And yet, if we would be saved, we must have tender, sensitive, living hearts; our hearts must be broken, must be broken up like ground, and dug, and watered, and tended, and cultivated, till they become as gardens, gardens of Eden, acceptable to our God, gardens in which the Lord God may walk and dwell; filled, not with briars and thorns, but with all sweet-smelling and useful plants, with heavenly trees and flowers. The dry and barren waste must burst forth into springs of living water. This change must take place in our hearts if we would be saved; in a word, we must have what we have not by nature, faith and love; and how is this to be effected, under God's grace, but by godly and practical meditation through the day?

St. Peter describes what I mean, when he says, speaking of Christ, "Whom having not seen ye love: in whom, though now ye see Him not, yet believing, ye rejoice with joy unspeakable and full of glory" (1 Pt 1:8).

Christ is gone away; He is not seen; we never saw Him, we only read and hear of Him. It is an old saying, "Out of sight, out of mind." Be sure, so it *will* be, so it *must* be with us, as regards our blessed Saviour, unless we make continual efforts all through the day to think of Him, His love, His precepts, His gifts, and His promises. We must recall to mind what we read in the Gospels and in holy books about Him; we must bring before us what we have heard in church; we must pray God to enable us to do so, to bless the doing so, and to make us do so in a simple-minded, sincere, and reverential spirit. In a word, we must meditate, for all this is meditation; and this even the most unlearned person can do, and will do, if he has a will to do it.

Now of such meditation, or thinking over Christ's deeds and sufferings, I will say two things; the first of which would be too plain to mention, except that, did I not mention it, I might seem to forget it, whereas I grant it. It is this: that such meditation is not at all pleasant at first. I know it; people will find it at first very irksome, and their minds will gladly slip away to other subjects. True: but consider, if Christ thought your salvation worth the great sacrifice of voluntary sufferings for you, should not you think (what is your own concern) your own salvation worth the slight sacrifice of learning to meditate upon those sufferings? Can a less thing be asked of you, than, when He has done the work, that you should only have to believe in it and accept it?

And my second remark is this: that it is only by slow degrees that meditation is able to soften our hard hearts, and that the history of Christ's trials and sorrows really moves us. It is not once thinking of Christ or twice thinking of Christ that will do it. It is by going on quietly and steadily, with the thought of Him in our mind's eye, that by little and little we shall gain something of warmth, light, life, and love. We shall not perceive ourselves changing. It will be like the unfolding of the leaves in spring. You do not see them grow; you cannot, by watching, detect it. But every day, as it passes, has done something for them; and you are able, perhaps, every morning to say that they are more advanced than yesterday. So is it with our souls; not indeed every morning, but at certain periods, we are able to see that we are more alive and religious than we were, though during the interval we were not conscious that we were advancing.

Now, then, as if by way of specimen, I will say a few words upon the voluntary self-abasement of Christ, to suggest to you thoughts, which you ought, indeed, to bear about you at all times, but especially at this most holy season of the year; thoughts which will in their poor measure (please God) prepare you for seeing Christ in heaven, and, in the meanwhile, will prepare you for seeing Him in His Easter Festival. Easter-Day comes but once a year; it is short, like other days. Oh, that we may make much of it, that we may make the most of it, that we may enjoy it! Oh, that it may not pass over like other days, and leave us no fragrance after it to remind us of it!

Come then, my brethren, at this time, before the solemn days are present, and let us review some of the privations of the Son of God made man, which should be your meditation through these holy weeks.

And, chiefly, He seems to speak to the poor. He came in *poverty*. St. Paul says, in the text, "Ye know the grace of our Lord Jesus Christ, that though He was rich, yet for your sakes He became poor, that ye through His poverty might be rich." Let not the poor suppose that their hardships are their own only, and that no one else ever felt them. The Most High God, God the Son, who had reigned with the Father from everlasting, supremely blessed, He, even He, became a poor man, and suffered the hardships of the poor. What are their hardships? I suppose such as these:—that they have bad lodging, bad clothing, not enough to eat, or of a poor kind, that they have few pleasures or amusements, that they are despised, that they are dependent upon others for their living, and that they have no prospects for the future. Now how was it with Christ, the Son of the Living God? Where was He born? In a stable. I suppose not many men suffer an indignity so great; born, not in quiet and comfort, but amid the brute cattle; and what was His first cradle, if I may so call it? a manger. Such were the beginnings of His earthly life; nor did His condition mend as life went on. He says on one occasion, "Foxes have holes, and birds of the air have nests, but the Son of Man hath not where to lay His head" (Lk 9:58). He had no home. He was, when He began to preach, what would now be called with contempt a vagrant. There are persons who are obliged to sleep where they can; such, in good measure, seems to have been our blessed Lord. We hear of Martha who was hospitable to Him, and of others; but, though little is told us, He seems, from what *is* told, to have lived a rougher life than any village peasant. He was forty days in the wilderness: where do you think He slept then? in caves of the rock. And who were His companions then? worse companions even than those He was born among. He was born in a cave; He passed forty nights in a cave; but on His birth, at least, they were tame beasts whom He was among, the ox and the ass. But during His forty days' temptation He "was with the wild beasts." Those caverns in the wilderness are filled with fierce and poisonous creatures. There Christ slept; and doubtless, but for His Father's unseen arm and His own sanctity, they would have fallen upon Him.

Again, cold is another hardship which sensibly afflicts us. This, too, Christ endured. He remained whole nights in prayer upon the mountains. He rose before day and went into solitary places to pray. He was on the sea at night.

Heat is a suffering which does not afflict us much in our country, but is very formidable in the eastern parts, where our Saviour lived. Men keep at home when the sun is high, lest it should harm them; yet we read of His sitting down on Jacob's well at mid-day, being wearied with His journey.

Observe this also, to which I have already referred. He was constantly journeying during His ministry, and journeying on foot. Once He rode into Jerusalem, to fulfil a prophecy.

Again, He endured hunger and thirst. He was athirst at the well, and asked the Samaritan woman to give Him water to drink. He was hungry in the wilderness, when He fasted forty days. At another time, when actively engaged in His works of mercy, He and His disciples had no time to eat bread (Mk 6:31). And, indeed, wandering about as He did, He seldom could have been certain of a meal. And what was the kind of food He lived on? He was much in the neighbourhood of an inland sea or lake, called the sea of Gennesaret, or Tiberias, and He and His Apostles lived on bread and fish; as spare a diet as poor men have now, or sparer. We hear, on one well-known occasion, of five barley loaves and two small fishes. After His resurrection He provided for His Apostles—"a fire, and fish laid thereon, and bread" (Jn 21:9), as it would seem, their usual fare.

Yet it deserves notice that, in spite of this penury, He and His were in the custom of giving something to the poor notwithstanding. They did not allow themselves to make the most even of the little they had. When the traitor Judas rose up and went out to betray Him, and Jesus spoke to him, some of the Apostles thought that He was giving directions about alms to the poor; this shows His practice.

And He was, as need scarcely be added, quite dependent on others. Sometimes rich men entertained Him. Sometimes, as I have said, pious persons ministered to Him of their substance (Lk 8:3). He lived, in His own blessed words, like the ravens, whom God feeds, or like the grass of the field, which God clothes.

Need I add that He had few pleasures, few recreations? It is hardly in place to speak on such a topic in the case of One who came from God, and who had other thoughts and ways than we have. Yet there are innocent enjoyments which God gives us here to counterbalance the troubles of life; our Lord was exposed to the trouble, and might have taken also its compensation. But He refrained. It has been observed, that He is never spoken of as mirthful; we often read of His sighing, groaning, and weeping. He was "a man of sorrows and acquainted with grief."

Now let us proceed to other greater sufferings, which He took on Himself when He became poor. Contempt, hatred, and persecution from the world was one of these. Even in His infancy Mary had to flee with Him into Egypt to hinder Herod from killing Him. When He returned, it was not safe to dwell in Judea, and He was brought up at Nazareth, a place of evil name, where the holy Virgin had been when Gabriel the Angel came to her. I need not say how He was set at nought and persecuted by the Pharisees and priests when He began to preach, and had again and again to flee for His life, which they were bent on taking.

Another great suffering from which our Lord did not withdraw Himself, was what in our case we call bereavement, the loss of relations or friends by death. This, indeed, it was not easy for Him to sustain, who had but one earthly near relation, and so few friends; but even this affliction He tasted for our sakes. Lazarus was His friend, and He lost him. He knew, indeed, that He could restore him, and He did. Yet still He bitterly lamented him, for whatever reason, so that the Jews said, "Behold how He loved him." But a greater and truer bereavement, as far as we dare speak of it, was His original act of humiliation itself, in leaving His heavenly glory and coming down on earth. This, of course, is a great mystery to us from beginning to end; still, He certainly vouchsafes to speak, through His Apostle, of His "emptying Himself" of His glory; so that we may fairly and reverently consider it as an unspeakable and wondrous bereavement, which He underwent, in being for the time, as it were, disinherited, and made in the likeness of sinful flesh.

But all these were but the beginning of sorrows with Him; to see their fulness we must look on to His passion. In the anguish which He then endured, we see all His other sorrows concentrated and exceeded; though I shall say little of it now, when His "time is not yet come."

But I will observe thus much; first, what is very wonderful and awful, the overwhelming fear He had of His sufferings before they came. This shows how great they were; but it would seem besides this, as if He had decreed to go through all trials for us, and, among them, the trial of fear. He says, "Now is My soul troubled, and what shall I say? Father, save Me from this hour; but for this cause came I unto this hour." And when the hour came, this terror formed the beginning of His sufferings, and caused His agony and bloody sweat. He prayed, "O My Father, if it be possible, let this cup pass from Me; nevertheless, not My will, but Thine, be done." St. Luke adds, "And being in an agony, He prayed more earnestly, and His sweat was as it were great drops of blood falling down to the ground" (Jn 12:27; Mt 26:39; Lk 22:44).

Next, He was betrayed to death by one of His own friends. What a bitter stroke was this! He was lonely enough without this: but in this last trial, one of the twelve Apostles, His own familiar friend, betrayed Him; and the others forsook Him and fled; though St. Peter and St. John afterwards recovered heart a little, and followed Him. Yet soon St. Peter himself incurred a worse sin, by denying Him thrice. How affectionately He felt towards them, and how He drew towards them with a natural movement of heart upon the approach of His trial, though they disappointed Him, is plain from the words He used towards them at His Last Supper; "He said unto them, With desire I have desired to eat this passover with you before I suffer" (Lk 22:15).

Soon after this His sufferings began; and both in soul and in body was this Holy and Blessed Saviour, the Son of God, and Lord of life, given over to the malice of the great enemy of God and man. Job was given over to Satan in the Old Testament, but within prescribed limits; first, the Evil One was not allowed to touch his person, and afterwards, though his person, yet not his life. But Satan had power to triumph, or what he thought was triumphing, over the life of Christ, who confesses to His persecutors, "This is your hour, and the power of darkness" (Lk 22:53). His head was crowned and torn with thorns, and bruised with staves; His face was defiled with spitting; His shoulders were weighed down with the heavy cross; His back was rent and gashed with scourges; His hands and feet gored through with nails; His side, by way of contumely, wounded with the spear; His mouth parched with intolerable thirst; and His soul so bedarkened, that He cried out, "My God, My God, why hast Thou forsaken Me?" (Mt 27:46). And thus He hung upon the cross for six hours, His whole body one wound, exposed almost naked to the eyes of men, "despising the shame" (Heb 12:2), and railed at, taunted, and cursed by all who saw Him. Surely to Him alone, in their fulness, apply the Prophet's words; "Is it nothing to you, all ye that pass by? behold, and see if there be any sorrow like unto My sorrow which is done unto Me, wherewith the Lord hath afflicted Me in the day of His fierce anger" (Lam 1:12).

How little are our sorrows to these! how little is our pain, our hardships, our persecutions, compared with those which Christ voluntarily undertook for us! If He, the sinless, underwent these, what wonder is it that we sinners should endure, if it so be, the hundredth part of them? How base and miserable are we, for understanding them so little, for being so little impressed by them! Alas! if we felt them as we ought, of course they would be to us, at seasons such as that now coming, far worse than what the death of a friend is, or his painful illness. We should not be able at such times to take pleasure in this world; we should lose our enjoyment of things of earth; we should lose our appetite, and be sick at heart, and only as a matter of duty eat, and drink, and go about our work. The Holy Season on which we shall soon enter would be a week of mourning, as when a dead body is in a house. We cannot, indeed, thus feel, merely because we wish and ought so to feel. We cannot force ourselves into so feeling. I do not exhort this man or that so to feel, since it is not in his power. We cannot work ourselves up into such feelings; or, if we can, it is better we should not, because it *is* a working up, which is bad. Deep feeling is but the natural or necessary attendant on a holy heart. But though we cannot at our will thus feel, and at once, we can go the way thus to feel. We can grow in grace till we thus feel. And, meanwhile, we can observe such an outward abstinence from the innocent pleasures and comforts of life, as may prepare us for thus feeling; such an abstinence as we should spontaneously observe if we did thus feel. We may meditate upon Christ's sufferings; and by this meditation we *shall* gradually, as time goes on, be brought to these deep feelings. We may pray God to do for us what we cannot do for ourselves, to *make* us feel; to give us the spirit of gratitude, love, reverence, self-abasement, godly fear, repentance, holiness, and lively faith.

Volume VII

SERMON I

The Lapse of Time

"Whatsoever thy hand findeth to do, do it with thy might; for there is no work, nor device, nor knowledge, nor wisdom, in the grave, whither thou goest."—Eccl 9:10

Solomon's advice that we should do whatever our hand findeth to do with our might, naturally directs our thoughts to that great work in which all others are included, which will outlive all other works, and for which alone we really are placed here below—the salvation of our souls. And the consideration of this great work, which must be done with all our might, and completed before the grave, whither we go, presents itself to our minds with especial force at the commencement of a new year. We are now entering on a fresh stage of our life's journey; we know well by how it will end, and we see where we shall stop in the evening, though we do not see the road. And we know in what our business lies while we travel, and that it is important for us to do it with our "might; for there is no work, nor device, nor knowledge, nor wisdom, in the grave." This is so plain, that nothing need be said in order to convince us that it is true. We know it well; the very complaint which numbers commonly make when told of it, is that they know it already, that it is nothing new, that they have no need to be told, and that it is tiresome to hear the same thing said over and over again, and impertinent in the person who repeats it. Yes; thus it is that sinners silence their conscience, by quarreling with those who appeal to it; they defend themselves, if it may be called a defense, by pleading that they already know what they should do and do not; that they know perfectly well that they are living at a distance from God, and are in peril of eternal ruin; that they know they are making themselves children of Satan, and denying the Lord that bought them, and want no one to tell them so. Thus they witness against themselves.

However, though we already know well enough that we have much to do before we die, yet (if we will but attend) it may be of use to hear the fact dwelt upon; because by thinking over it steadily and seriously, we may possibly, through God's grace, gain some deep conviction of it; whereas while we keep to general terms, and confess that this life is important and is short, in the mere summary way in which men commonly confess it, we have, properly speaking, no knowledge of that great truth at all.

Consider, then, what it is to die; "there is no work, device, knowledge, or wisdom, in the grave." Death puts an end absolutely and irrevocably to all our plans and works, and it is inevitable. The Psalmist speaks to "high and low, rich and poor, one with another." "No man can deliver his brother, nor make agreement unto God for him." Even "wise men die, as well as the ignorant and foolish, and leave their riches for other (Ps 49:2–10)." Difficult as we may find it to bring it home to ourselves, to realize it, yet as surely as we are here assembled together, so surely will every one of us, sooner or later, one by one, be stretched on the bed of death. We naturally shrink from the thought of death, and of its attendant circumstances; but all that is hateful and fearful about it will be fulfilled in our case, one by one. But all this is nothing compared with the consequences implied in it. Death stops us; it stops our race. Men are engaged about their work, or about their pleasure; they are in the city, or the field; any how they are stopped; their deeds are suddenly gathered in—a reckoning is made—all is sealed up till the great day. What a change is this! In the words used familiarly in speaking of the dead, they are no more. They were full of schemes and projects; whether in a greater or humbler rank, they had their hopes and fears, their prospects, their pursuits, their rivalries; all these are now come to an end. One builds a house, and its roof is not finished; another buys merchandise, and it it not yet sold. And all their virtues and pleasing qualities which endeared them to their friends are, as far as this world is concerned, vanished. Where are they who were so active, so sanguine, so generous? the amiable, the modest, and the kind? We were told that they were dead; they suddenly disappeared; that is all we know about it. They were silently taken from us; they are not met in the seat of the elders, nor in the assemblies of the people; in the mixed concourse of men, nor in the domestic retirement which they prized. As Scripture describes it, "the wind has passed over them, and they are gone, and their place shall know them no more." And they have burst the many ties which held them; they were parents, brothers, sisters, children, and friends; but the bond of kindred is broken, and the silver cord of love is loosed. They have been followed by the vehement grief of tears, and the long sorrow of aching hearts; but they make no return, they answer not; they do not even satisfy our wish to know that they sorrow for us as we for them. We talk about them thenceforth as if they were persons we do not know; we talk about them as third persons; whereas they used to be always with us, and every other thought which was within us was shared by them. Or perhaps, if our grief is too deep, we do not mention their names at all. And their possessions, too, all fall to others. The world goes on without them; it forgets them. Yes, so it is; the world contrives to forget that men have souls, it looks upon them all as mere parts of some great visible system. This continues to move on; to this the world ascribes a sort of life and personality. When one or other of its members die, it considers them only as falling out of the system, and as come to nought. For a minute, perhaps, it thinks of them in sorrow, then leaves them—leaves them for ever. It keeps its eye on things seen and temporal. Truly whenever a man dies, rich or poor, an immortal soul passes to judgment; but somehow we read of the deaths of persons we have seen or heard of, and this reflection never comes across us. Thus does the world really cast off men's souls, and recognizing only their bodies, it makes it appear as if "that which befalleth them, as the one dieth so dieth the other; yea, they have all one breath, so that a man hath no pre-eminence over a beast, for all is vanity." (Eccl 3:19).

But let us follow the course of a soul thus casting off the world, and cast off by it. It goes forth as a stranger on a journey. Man seems to die and to be no more, when he is but quitting us, and is really beginning to live. Then he sees sights which before it did not even enter into his mind to conceive, and the world is even less to him than he to the world. Just now he was lying on the bed of sickness, but in that moment of death what an awful change has come over him! What a crisis for him! There is stillness in the room that lately held him; nothing is doing there, for he is gone, he now belongs to others; he now belongs entirely to the Lord who bought him; to Him he returns; but whether to be lodged safely in His place of hope, or to be imprisoned against the great Day, that is another matter, that depends on the deeds done in the body, whether good or evil. And now what are his thoughts? How infinitely important now appears the value of time, now when it is nothing to him! Nothing; for though he spend centuries waiting for Christ, he cannot now alter his state from bad to good, or from good to bad. What he dieth that he must be for ever; as the tree falleth so must it lie. This is the comfort of the true servant of God, and the misery of the transgressor. His lot is cast once and for all, and he can but wait in hope or in dread. Men on their death-beds have declared, that no one could form a right idea of the value of time till he came to die; but if this has truth in it, how much more truly can it be said after death! What an estimate shall we form of time while we are waiting for judgment! Yes, it is we—all this, I repeat, belongs to us most intimately. It is not to be looked at as a picture, as a man might read a light book in a leisure hour. *We* must die, the youngest, the healthiest, the most thoughtless; *we* must be thus unnaturally torn in two, soul from body; and only united again to be made more thoroughly happy or to be miserable for ever.

Such is death considered in its inevitable necessity, and its unspeakable importance—nor can we ensure to ourselves any certain interval before its coming. The time may be long; but it may also be short. It is plain, a man may die any day; all we can say is, that it is unlikely that he will die. But of this, at least, we are certain, that, come it sooner or later, death is continually on the move towards us. We are ever nearer and nearer to it. Every morning we rise we are nearer that grave in which there is no work, nor device, than we were. We are now nearer the grave, than when we entered this Church. Thus life is ever crumbling away under us. What should we say to a man, who was placed on some precipitous ground, which was ever crumbling under his feet, and affording less and less secure footing, yet was careless about it? Or what should we say to one who suffered some precious liquor to run from its receptacle into the thoroughfare of men, without a thought to stop it? who carelessly looked on and saw the waste of it, becoming greater and greater every minute? But what treasure can equal time? It is the seed of eternity: Yet we suffer ourselves to go on, year after year, hardly using it at all in God's service, or thinking it enough to give Him at most a tithe or a seventh of it, while we strenuously and heartily sow to the flesh, that from the flesh we may reap corruption. We try how little we can safely give to religion, instead of having the grace to give abundantly. "Rivers of water run down mine eyes, because men keep not Thy law"; so says the holy Psalmist. Doubtless an inspired prophet saw far more clearly than we can see, the madness of men in squandering that treasure upon sin, which is meant to buy their chief good;—but if so, what must this madness appear in God's sight! What an inveterate malignant evil is it in the hearts of the sons of men, that thus leads them to sit down to eat, and drink, and rise up to play, when time is hurrying on and judgment coming? We have been told what He thinks of man's unbelief, though we cannot enter into the depths of His thoughts. He showed it to us in act and deed, as far as we could receive it, when He even sent His Only-begotten Son into the world as at this time, to redeem us from the world,—which, most surely, was not lightly done; and we also learn His thoughts about it from the words of that most merciful Son,—which most surely were not lightly spoken, "The wicked," He says, "shall go into everlasting punishment."

Oh, that there were such a heart in us that we would fear God and keep His commandments always! But it is of no use to speak; men know their duty—they will not do it. They say they do not need or wish to be told it, that it is an intrusion, and a rudeness, to tell them of death and judgment. So must it be,—and we, who have to speak to them, must submit to this. Speak we must, as an act of duty to God, whether they will hear, or not, and then must leave our words as a witness. Other means for rousing them we have none. We speak from Christ our gracious Lord, their Redeemer, who has already pardoned them freely, yet they will not follow Him with a true heart; and what can be done more?

Another year is now opening upon us; it speaks to the thoughtful, and is heard by those, who have expectant ears, and watch for Christ's coming. The former year is gone, it is dead, there it lies in the grave of past time, not to decay however, and be forgotten, but kept in the view of God's omniscience, with all its sins and errors irrevocably written, till, at length, it will be raised again to testify about us at the last day; and who among us can bear the thought of his own doings, in the course of it?—all that he has said and done, all that has been conceived within his mind, or been acted on, and all that he has not said and done, which it was a duty to say or do. What a dreary prospect seems to be before us, when we reflect that we have the solemn word of truth pledged to us, in the last and most awful revelation, which God has made to us about the future, that in that day, the books will be opened, "and another book opened, which is the book of life, and the dead judged out of those things which were written in the books according to their works" (Rv 20:12). What would a man give, any one of us, who has any real insight into his polluted and miserable state, what would he give to tear away some of the leaves there preserved! For how heinous are the sins therein written! Think of the multitude of sins done by us since we first knew the difference between right and wrong. We have forgotten them, but there we might read them clearly recorded. Well may holy David exclaim, "Remember not the sins of my youth nor my transgressions, according to Thy mercy remember Thou me." Conceive, too, the multitude of sins which have so grown into us as to become part of us, and in which we now live, not knowing, or but partially knowing, that they are sins; habits of pride, self-reliance, self-conceit, sullenness, impurity, sloth, selfishness, worldliness. The history of all these, their beginnings, and their growth, is recorded in those dreadful books; and when we look forward to the future, how many sins shall we have committed by this time next year,—though we try ever so much to know our duty, and overcome ourselves! Nay, or rather shall we have the opportunity of obeying or disobeying God for a year longer? Who knows whether by that time our account may not be closed for ever?

"Remember me, O Lord, when Thou comest into Thy kingdom" (Lk 23:42). Such was the prayer of the penitent thief on the cross, such must be our prayer. Who can do us any good, but He, who shall also be our Judge? When shocking thoughts about ourselves come across us and afflict us, "Remember me," this is all we have to say. We have "no work, nor device, nor knowledge, nor wisdom" of our own, to better ourselves withal. We can say nothing to God in defence of ourselves,—we can but acknowledge that we are grievous sinners, and addressing Him as suppliants, merely beg Him to bear us in mind in mercy, for His Son's sake to do us some favour, not according to our deserts, but for the love of Christ. The more we try to serve Him here, the better; but after all, so far do we fall short of what we should be, that if we had but what we are in ourselves to rely upon, wretched are we,—and we are forced out of ourselves by the very necessity of our condition. To whom should we go? Who can do us any good, but He who was born into this world for our regeneration, was bruised for our iniquities, and rose again for our justification? Even though we have served Him from our youth up, though after His pattern we have grown, as far as mere man can grow, in wisdom as we grew in stature, though we ever have had tender hearts, and a mortified will, and a conscientious temper, and an obedient spirit; yet, at the very best, how much have we left undone, how much done, which ought to be otherwise! What He can do for our nature, in the way of sanctifying it, we know indeed in a measure; we know, in the case of His Saints; and we certainly do not know the limit of His carrying forward in those objects of His special favour the work of purification, and renewal through His Spirit. But for ourselves, we know full well that much as we may have attempted, we have done very little, that our very best service is nothing worth,—and the more we attempt, the more clearly we shall see how little we have hitherto attempted.

Those whom Christ saves are they who at once attempt to save themselves, yet despair of saving themselves; who aim to do all, and confess they do nought; who are all love, and all fear; who are the most holy, and yet confess themselves the most sinful; who ever seek to please Him, yet feel they never can; who are full of good works, yet of works of penance. All this seems a contradiction to the natural man, but it is not so to those whom Christ enlightens. They understand in proportion to their illumination, that it is possible to work out their salvation, yet to have it wrought out for them, to fear and tremble at the thought of judgment, yet to rejoice always in the Lord, and hope and pray for His coming.

SERMON VII

The Duty of Self-Denial

"Surely I have behaved and quieted myself, as a child that is weaned of his mother: my soul is even as a weaned child."—Ps 131:2

Self-denial of some kind or other is involved, as is evident, in the very notion of renewal and holy obedience. To change our hearts is to learn to love things which we do not naturally love—to unlearn the love of this world; but this involves, of course, a thwarting of our natural wishes and tastes. To be righteous and obedient implies self-command; but to possess power we must have gained it; nor can we gain it without a vigorous struggle, a persevering warfare against ourselves. The very notion of being religious implies self-denial, because by nature we do not love religion.

Self-denial, then, is a subject never out of place in Christian teaching; still more appropriate is it at a time like this, when we have entered upon the forty days of Lent, the season of the year set apart for fasting and humiliation.

This indeed is not all that is meant by self-denial; but before proceeding with the subject, I would ask whether the generality of mankind go as far as this: It is plain that they do not. They do not go so far as to realize to themselves that religious obedience involves a thwarting of those wishes and inclinations which are natural to them. They do not like to be convinced, much less will they act upon the notion, that religion is difficult. You may hear men of the world say plainly, and as if in the way of argument, "that God will not punish us for indulging the passions with which we are born; that it is no praise to be unnatural; and no crime to be a man." This, however, may seem an extreme case; yet are there not a great many decent and respectable men, as far as outward character goes, who at least fix their thoughts on worldly comfort, as the greatest of goods, and who labour to place themselves in easy circumstances, under the notion that, when they can retire from the business of their temporal calling, then they may (in a quiet, unexceptionable way of course) consult their own tastes and likings, take their pleasure, and indulge themselves in self-importance and self-satisfaction, in the enjoyment of wealth, power, distinction, popularity, and credit? I am not at this moment asking whether such indulgences are in themselves allowable or not, but whether the life which centres in them does not imply the absence of any very deep views of sanctification as a process, a change, a painful toil, of working out our own salvation with fear and trembling, of preparing to meet our God, and waiting for the judgment? You may go into mixed society; you will hear men conversing on their friend's prospects, openings in trade, or realized wealth, on his advantageous situation, the pleasant connexions he has formed, the land he has purchased, the house he has built; then they amuse themselves with conjecturing what this or that man's property may be, where he lost, where he gained, his shrewdness, or his rashness, or his good fortune in this or that speculation. Observe, I do not say that such conversation is wrong; I do not say that we must always have on our lips the very thoughts which are deepest in our hearts, or that it is safe to judge of individuals by such speeches; but when this sort of conversation is the customary standard conversation of the world, and when a line of conduct answering to it is the prevalent conduct of the world (and this is the case), is it not a grave question for each of us, as living in the world, to ask himself what abiding notion we have of the necessity of self-denial, and how far we are clear of the danger of resembling that evil generation which "ate and drank, which married wives, and were given in marriage, which bought and sold, planted, and builded, till it rained fire and brimstone from heaven, and destroyed them all" (Lk 17:27–29)?

   It is strange, indeed, how far this same forgetfulness and transgression of the duty of self-denial at present spreads. Take another class of persons, very different from those just mentioned, men who profess much love for religion—I mean such as maintain, that if a man has faith he will have works without his trouble, so that he need be at no pains about performing them. Such persons at best seem to say, that religious obedience is to follow as a matter of course, an easy work, or rather a necessary consequence, from having some strong urgent motive, or from some bright vision of the Truth acting on the mind; and thus they dismiss from their religion the notion of self-denial, or the effort and warfare of faith against our corrupt natural will, whether they actually own that they dismiss it or not. I say that they do this at best; for it often happens, as I just now intimated, that they actually avow their belief that faith is all-sufficient, and do not let their minds dwell at all on the necessity of works of righteousness. All this being considered, surely I am not wrong in saying that the notion of self-denial as a distinct religious duty, and, much more (as it may well be called), the essence of religious obedience, is not admitted into the minds of the generality of men.

But let it be observed, I have hitherto spoken of self-denial not as a distinct duty actually commanded in Scripture, but merely as it is involved in the very notion of sanctification, as necessarily attendant on that change of nature which God the Holy Spirit vouchsafes to work within us. But now let us consider it in the light of the Scripture precepts concerning it, and we shall come to a still more serious view of it, serious (I mean) to those who are living to the world; it is this,—that it is our duty, not only to deny ourselves in what is sinful, but even, in a certain measure, in lawful things, to keep a restraint over ourselves even in innocent pleasures and enjoyments.

Now the first proof I shall give of this will at the same time explain what I mean.

Fasting is clearly a Christian duty, as our Saviour implies in His Sermon on the Mount. Now what is fasting but a refraining from what is lawful; not merely from what is sinful, but what is innocent?—from that bread which we might lawfully take and eat with thanksgiving, but which at certain times we do not take, in order to deny ourselves. Such is Christian self-denial,—not merely a mortification of what is sinful, but an abstinence even from God's blessings.

Again: Consider the following declaration of our Saviour: He first tells us, "Strait is the gate, and narrow is the way which leadeth unto life, and few there be that find it." And again: "Strive to enter in, for many, I say unto you, will seek (only seek) to enter in, and shall not be able." Then He explains to us what this peculiar difficulty of a Christian's life consists in: "If any man come to Me, and hate not his father, and mother, and wife, and children, and brethren, and sisters, yea, and his own life also, he cannot be My disciple" (Mt 7:14; Lk 13:24, 14:26). Now whatever is precisely meant by this (which I will not here stop to inquire), so far is evident, that our Lord enjoins a certain refraining, not merely from sin, but from innocent comforts and enjoyments of this life, or a self-denial in things lawful.

Again, He says, "If any man will come after Me, let him deny himself, and take up his cross daily, and follow Me" (Lk 9:23). Here He shows us from His own example what Christian self-denial is. It is taking on us a cross after His pattern, not a mere refraining from sin, for He had no sin, but a giving up what we might lawfully use. This was the peculiar character in which Christ came on earth. It was this spontaneous and exuberant self-denial which brought Him down. He who was one with God, took upon Him our nature, and suffered death—and why? to save us whom He needed not save. Thus He denied Himself, and took up His cross. This is the very aspect, in which God, as revealed in Scripture, is distinguished from that exhibition of His glory, which nature gives us: power, wisdom, love, mercy, long-suffering—these attributes, though far more fully and clearly displayed in Scripture than in nature, still are in their degree seen on the face of the visible creation; but self-denial, if it may be said, this incomprehensible attribute of Divine providence, is disclosed to us only in Scripture. "God so loved the world that He gave His Son" (Jn 3:16). Here is self-denial. And the Son of God so loved us, that "though He was rich yet for our sakes He became poor" (2 Cor 8:9). Here is our Saviour's self-denial. "He pleased not Himself."

And what Christ did when He came on earth, that have all His Saints done both before and since His coming. Even the Saints of the Old Testament so conducted themselves, to whom a temporal promise was made, and who, if any, might have surrendered themselves to the enjoyment of it. They had a temporal promise, they had a present reward; yet, with a noble faith, and a largeness of soul (how they put us to shame who have so much higher privileges!) the Jewish believers grudged themselves the milk and honey of Canaan, as seeking a better country, that is a heavenly. Elijah, how unlike is he to one who had a temporal promise! Or take again the instance of Daniel, which is still more striking,—"They that wear soft clothing are in kings' houses." Daniel was first in power in the palace of the greatest monarchs of his time. Yet what do we read of him? First of his living upon pulse and water, afterwards of his fasting in sackcloth and ashes, at another time of his mourning three full weeks, eating no pleasant bread, neither flesh nor wine coming in his mouth, nor anointing himself at all, till those three weeks were fulfilled. Can any thing more clearly show the duty of self-denial, even in lawful things, in the case of Christians, when even God's servants, before Christ came and commanded it, in proportion as they had evangelical gifts, observed it?

Or again, consider the words of the text spoken by David, who, if any, had riches and power poured upon him by the hand of God. He says, he has "behaved and quieted" himself lest he should be proud, and made himself "as a weaned child." What an impressive word is "weaned!" David had put away the unreserved love and the use of this world. We naturally love the world, and innocently; it is before us, and meets our eyes and hands first; its pleasures are dear to us, and many of them not in themselves sinful, only in their excess, and some of them not sinful at all;—those, for instance, which we derive from our home, our friends, and our prospects, are the first and natural food of our mind. But as children are weaned from their first nourishment, so must our souls put away childish things, and be turned from the pleasures of earth to those of heaven; we must learn to compose and quiet ourselves as a weaned child, to put up with the loss of what is dear to us, nay, voluntarily to give it up for Christ's sake.

Much more after Christ came does St. Paul give us this same lesson in the ninth chapter of his first Epistle to the Corinthians: "Every one that striveth for the mastery is temperate in all things," i.e., has power over himself, and keeps himself in subjection, as he presently says. Again, in the seventh chapter, "The time is short; it remaineth that both they that have wives be as though they had none, and they that weep as though they wept not, and they that rejoice as though they rejoiced not, and they that buy as though they possessed not, and they that use this world as not abusing it." Here the same doctrine of moderation or temperance in lawful indulgences is strongly enforced; to weep, to rejoice, to buy, to possess, to marry, to use this world, are not unlawful, yet we must not use God's earthly gifts to the full, but in all things we must be self-denying.

Such is Christian self-denial, and it is incumbent upon us for many reasons. The Christian denies himself in things lawful because he is aware of his own weakness and liability to sin; he dares not walk on the edge of a precipice; instead of going to the extreme of what is allowable, he keeps at a distance from evil, that he may be safe. He abstains lest he should not be temperate; he fasts lest he should eat and drink with the drunken. As is evident, many things are in themselves right and unexceptionable which are inexpedient in the case of a weak and sinful creature: His case is like that of a sick person; many kinds of food, good for a man in health, are hurtful when he is ill—wine is poison to a man in a fierce fever. And just so, many acts, thoughts, and feelings, which would have been allowable in Adam before his fall, are prejudicial or dangerous in man fallen. For instance, anger is not sinful in itself. St. Paul implies this, when he says, "Be ye angry and sin not" (Eph 4:26). And our Saviour on one occasion is said to have been angry, and He was sinless. Almighty God, too, is angry with the wicked. Anger, then, is not in itself a sinful feeling; but in man, constituted as he is, it is so highly dangerous to indulge it, that self-denial here is a duty from mere prudence. It is almost impossible for a man to be angry only so far as he ought to be; he will exceed the right limit; his anger will degenerate into pride, sullenness, malice, cruelty, revenge, and hatred. It will inflame his diseased soul, and poison it. Therefore, he must abstain from it, as if it were *in itself* a sin (though it is not), for it is practically such to him.

Again, the love of praise is in itself an innocent passion, and might be indulged, were the world's opinion right and our hearts sound; but, as things are, human applause, if listened to, will soon make us forget how weak and sinful we are; so we must deny ourselves, and accept the praise even of good men, and those we love, cautiously and with reserve.

So, again, love of power is commonly attendant on a great mind; but he is the greatest of a sinful race who refrains himself, and turns from the temptation of it; for it is at once unbecoming and dangerous in a son of Adam. "Whosoever will be great among you, let him be your minister," says our Lord; "and whosoever will be chief among you, let him be your servant" (Mt 20:26, 27). His reward will be hereafter; to reign with Christ, to sit down with Him on His throne, to judge angels,—yet without pride.

Again, even in affection towards our relations and friends, we must be watchful over ourselves, lest it seduce us from the path of duty. Many a father, from a kind wish to provide well for his family, neglects his own soul. Here, then, is a fault; not that we can love our relations too well, but that that strong and most praiseworthy affection for them may, accidentally, ensnare and corrupt our weak nature.

These considerations will show us the meaning of our Saviour's words already cited, about the duty of hating our friends. To hate is to feel that perfect distaste for an object, that you wish it put away and got rid of; it is to turn away from it, and to blot out the thought of it from your mind. Now this is just the feeling we must cherish towards all earthly blessings, so far as Christ does not cast His light upon them. He (blessed be His name) has sanctioned and enjoined love and care for our relations and friends. Such love is a great duty; but should at any time His guidance lead us by a strange way, and the light of His providence pass on, and cast these objects of our earthly affection into the shade, then they must be at once in the shade to *us*,—they must, for the time, disappear from our hearts. "He that loveth father or mother more than Me, is not worthy of Me." So He says; and at such times, though still loving them, we shall seem to hate them; for we shall put aside the thought of them, and act as if they did not exist. And in this sense an ancient and harsh proverb is true: We must always so love our friends as feeling that one day or other we may perchance be called upon to hate them,—that is, forget them in the pursuit of higher duties.

Here, again, then, is an instance of self-denial in lawful things; and if a person says it is painful thus to feel, and that it checks the spontaneous and continual flow of love towards our friends to have this memento sounding in our ears, we must boldly acknowledge that it *is* painful. It is a sad thought, not that we can ever be called upon actually to put away the love of them, but to have to act as if we did not love them,—as Abraham when called on to slay his son. And this thought of the uncertainty of the future, doubtless, does tinge all our brightest affections (as far as this world is concerned) with a grave and melancholy hue. We need not shrink from this confession, remembering that this life is not our rest or happiness;—"*that* remaineth" to come. This sober chastised feeling is the very temper of David, when he speaks of having composed and quieted his soul, and weaned it from the babe's nourishment which this world supplies.

I hope I have made it clear, by these instances, what is meant by Christian self-denial. If we have good health, and are in easy circumstances, let us beware of high-mindedness, self-sufficiency, self-conceit, arrogance; of delicacy of living, indulgences, luxuries, comforts. Nothing is so likely to corrupt our hearts, and to seduce us from God, as to surround ourselves with comforts,—to have things our own way,—to be the centre of a sort of world, whether of things animate or inanimate, which minister to us. For then, in turn, we shall depend on them; they will become necessary to us; their very service and adulation will lead us to trust ourselves to them, and to idolize them. What examples are there in Scripture of soft luxurious men! Was it Abraham before the Law, who wandered through his days, without a home? or Moses, who gave the Law, and died in the wilderness? or David under the Law, who "had no proud looks," and was "as a weaned child?" or the Prophets, in the latter days of the Law, who wandered in sheep-skins and goat-skins? or the Baptist, when the Gospel was superseding it, who was clad in raiment of camel's hair, and ate the food of the wilderness? or the Apostles, who were "the offscouring of all things"? or our blessed Saviour, who "had not a place to lay His head"? Who are the soft luxurious men in Scripture? There was the rich man, who "fared sumptuously every day," and then "lifted up his eyes in hell, being in torments." There was that other, whose "ground brought forth plentifully," and who said, "Soul, thou hast much goods laid up for many years"; and his soul was required of him that night. There was Demas, who forsook St. Paul, "having loved this present world." And, alas! there was that highly favoured, that divinely inspired king, rich and wise Solomon, whom it availed nothing to have measured the earth, and numbered its inhabitants, when in his old age he "loved many strange women," and worshipped their gods.

Far be it from us, soldiers of Christ, thus to perplex ourselves with this world, who are making our way towards the world to come. "No man that warreth, entangleth himself with the affairs of this life, that he may please Him who hath chosen him to be a soldier. If a man also strive for masteries, yet is he not crowned, except he strive lawfully." This is St. Paul's rule, as has already been referred to: accordingly, in another place, he bears witness of himself that he "died daily." Day by day he got more and more dead to this world; he had fewer ties to earth, a larger treasure in heaven. Nor let us think that it is over-difficult to imitate him, though we be not Apostles, nor are called to any extraordinary work, nor are enriched with any miraculous gifts: He would have all men like himself, and all may be like him, according to their place and measure of grace. If we would be followers of the great Apostle, first let us with him fix our eyes upon Christ our Saviour; consider the splendour and glory of His holiness, and try to love it. Let us strive and pray that the love of holiness may be created within our hearts; and then acts will follow, such as befit us and our circumstances, in due time, without our distressing ourselves to find what they should be. You need not attempt to draw any precise line between what is sinful and what is only allowable: Look up to Christ, and deny yourselves every thing, whatever its character, which you think He would have you relinquish. You need not calculate and measure, if you love much: You need not perplex yourselves with points of curiosity, if you have a heart to venture after Him. True, difficulties will sometimes arise, but they will be seldom. He bids you take up your cross; therefore accept the daily opportunities which occur of yielding to others, when you need not yield, and of doing unpleasant services, which you might avoid. He bids those who would be highest, live as the lowest: Therefore, turn from ambitious thoughts, and (as far as you religiously may) make resolves against taking on you authority and rule. He bids you sell and give alms; therefore, hate to spend money on yourself. Shut your ears to praise, when it grows loud: Set your face like a flint, when the world ridicules, and smile at its threats. Learn to master your heart, when it would burst forth into vehemence, or prolong a barren sorrow, or dissolve into unseasonable tenderness. Curb your tongue, and turn away your eye, lest you fall into temptation. Avoid the dangerous air which relaxes you, and brace yourself upon the heights.

Be up at prayer "a great while before day," and seek the true, your only Bridegroom, "by night on your bed." So shall self-denial become natural to you, and a change come over you, gently and imperceptibly; and, like Jacob, you will lie down in the waste, and will soon see Angels, and a way opened for you into heaven.

Volume VIII

SERMON XIII

Truth Hidden When Not Sought After

"They shall turn away their ears from the truth, and shall be turned unto fables."—2 Tm 4:4

From these words of the blessed Apostle, written shortly before he suffered martyrdom, we learn, that there is such a thing as religious truth, and therefore there is such a thing as religious error. We learn that religious truth is *one*—and therefore that all views of religion *but* one are wrong. And we learn, moreover, that so it was to be (for his words are a prophecy) that professed Christians, forgetting this, should turn away their ears from the one Truth, and should be turned, not to one, but to many fables. All this is fulfilled before our eyes; our religious creeds and professions at this day are many; but Truth is one: Therefore they cannot all be right, or rather almost all of them must be wrong. That is, the multitude of men are wrong, so far as they differ; and as they differ, not about trivial points, but about great matters, it follows that the multitude of men, whether by their own fault or not, are wrong even in the greater matters of religion.

This is a most solemn thought, and a perplexing one. However, there is another which, though it ought not to be perplexing, is perplexing still, and perhaps has greater need to be considered and explained; I mean that men of learning and ability are so often wrong in religious matters also. It is a stumbling-block to many, when they find that those who seem the legitimate guides furnished by God's providence, who are in some sense the natural prophets and expounders of the Truth, that these too are on many sides, and therefore many of them on the side of error also. There are persons who can despise the opinions of the *many*, and feel that *they* are not right, but that Truth, if it be to be found, lies with the *few*; and since men of ability *are* among the few, they think that

Truth lies with men of ability, and when after all they are told that able men are ranged on contrary sides in religious questions, they either hastily deny the fact, or they are startled, and stagger in their faith.

But on the contrary, let us honestly confess what is certain, that not the ignorant, or weak-minded, or dull, or enthusiastic, or extravagant only turn their ears from the Truth and are turned unto fables, but also men of powerful minds, keen perceptions, extended views, ample and various knowledge. Let us, I say, confess it; yet let us not believe in the Truth the less on account of it.

I say that in the number of the adversaries of the Truth, there are many men of highly endowed and highly cultivated minds. Why should we deny this? It is unfair to do so; and not only unfair, but very unnecessary. What is called ability and talent does not make a man a Christian; nay, often, as may be shown without difficulty, it is the occasion of his rejecting Christianity, or this or that part of it. Not only in the higher ranks of society do we see this; even in the humble and secluded village, it will commonly be found, that those who have greater gifts of mind than others around them, who have more natural quickness, shrewdness, and wit, are the very persons who are the most likely to turn out ill—who are least under the influence of religious principles—and neither obey nor even revere the Gospel of salvation which Christ has brought us.

Now if we consult St. Paul's Epistles to the Corinthians, we shall find the same state of things existing even in the first age of Christianity. Even the Apostle speaks of those who were blind, or to whom his Gospel was hid; and he elsewhere describes them, not as the uneducated and dull of understanding, but as the wise of this world, the scribe and the disputer. Even then, before the Apostle's prophecy in the text was fulfilled, there were many who erred from the truth even in the midst of light, and in spite of superior intellectual endowments and acquirements.

Does not our Saviour Himself say the same thing, when He thanks His Father, Lord of heaven and earth, that He hath hid these things from the wise and prudent, and revealed them unto babes?

Now it should not surprise us when men of acute and powerful understandings more or less reject the Gospel, for this reason, that the Christian revelation addresses itself to our hearts, to our love of truth and goodness, our fear of sinning, and our desire to gain God's favour; and quickness, sagacity, depth of thought, strength of mind, power of comprehension, perception of the beautiful, power of language, and the like, though they are excellent gifts, are clearly quite of a different kind from these spiritual excellences—a man may have the one without having the other. *This*, then, is the plain reason why able, or again why learned men are so often defective Christians, because there is no necessary connexion between faith and ability; because faith is one thing and ability is another; because ability of mind is a *gift*, and faith is a *grace*. Who would ever argue that a man could, like Samson, conquer lions or throw down the gates of a city, because he was able, or accomplished, or experienced in the business of life? Who would ever argue that a man could see because he could hear, or run with the swift because he had "the tongue of the learned" (Is 1:4)? These gifts are different in kind. In like manner, powers of mind and religious principles and feelings are distinct gifts; and as all the highest spiritual excellence, humility, firmness, patience, would never enable a man to read an unknown tongue, or to enter into the depths of science, so all the most brilliant mental endowments, wit, or imagination, or penetration, or depth, will never of themselves make us wise in religion. And as we should fairly and justly deride the savage who wished to decide questions of science or literature by the sword, so may we justly look with amazement on the error of those who think that they can master the high mysteries of spiritual Truth, and find their way to God, by what is commonly called reason, i.e., by the random and blind efforts of mere mental acuteness, and mere experience of the world.

That Truth, which St. Paul preached, addresses itself to our spiritual nature: It will be rightly understood, valued, accepted, by none but lovers of truth, virtue, purity, humility, and peace. Wisdom will be justified of her children. Those, indeed, who are thus endowed may and will go on to use their powers of mind, whatever they are, in the service of religion; none but they can use them aright. Those who reject revealed truth wilfully, are such as do not love moral and religious truth. It is bad men, proud men, men of hard hearts, and unhumbled tempers, and immoral lives, these are they who reject the Gospel. These are they of whom St. Paul speaks in another Epistle—"If our Gospel be hid, it is hid to them that are lost, in whom the god of this world hath blinded the minds of them which believe not." With this agree the instances of turning the ears from the Truth which the New Testament affords us. Who were they who were the enemies of Christ and His Apostles? The infidel Sadducees, the immoral, hard-hearted, yet hypocritical Pharisees, Herod, who married his brother Philip's wife (Mt 14:3), and Felix, who trembled when St. Paul reasoned of righteousness, temperance, and judgment to come (Acts 24:25). On the other hand, men of holy and consistent lives, as Cornelius the Centurion, and those who were frequenters of religious ordinances, as Simeon and Anna, these became Christians. So it is now. If men turn unto fables of their own will, they do it on account of their pride, or their love of indolence and self-indulgence.

This should be kept in mind when Christians are alarmed, as they sometimes are, on hearing instances of infidelity or heresy among those who read, reflect, and inquire; whereas, however we may mourn over such instances, we have no reason to be surprised at them. It is quite enough for Christians to be able to show, as they well can, that belief in revealed religion is not inconsistent with the highest gifts and acquirements of mind, that men even of the strongest and highest intellect have been Christians; but they have as little reason to be perplexed at finding *other* men of ability not true believers, as at finding that certain *rich* men are not true believers, or certain *poor* men, or some in every rank and circumstance of life. A belief in Christianity has hardly more connexion with what is called talent, than it has with riches, station, power, or bodily strength.

Now let me explain what I have said by a further remark. Is it not plain that earnestness is necessary for gaining religious Truth? On the other hand, is it not a natural effect of ability to save us trouble, and even to tempt us to dispense with it, and to lead us to be indolent? Do not we see this even in the case of children—the more clever are the more idle, because they rely on their own quickness and power of apprehension? Is indolence the way to gain knowledge from God? Yet this surely is continually forgotten in the world. It is forgotten in a measure even by the best of Christians, for no man on earth seeks to know God's will, and to do His duty with an earnestness suitable to the importance of the object. But not to speak thus rigorously, let us consider for an instant how eagerly men in general pursue objects of this world; now with what portion of this eagerness do they exert themselves to know the Truth of God's word? Undeniable, then, as is the doctrine that God does not reveal Himself to those who do not seek Him, it is certain that its Truth is not really felt by us, or we should seek Him more earnestly than we do.

Nothing is more common than to think that we shall gain religious knowledge as a thing of course, without express trouble on our part. Though there is no art or business of this world which is learned without time and exertion, yet it is commonly conceived that the knowledge of God and our duty will come as if by accident or by a natural process.

Men go by their feelings and likings; they take up what is popular, or what comes first to hand. They think it much if they now and then have serious thoughts, if they now and then open the Bible; and their minds recur with satisfaction to such seasons, as if they had done some very great thing, never remembering that to seek and gain religious Truth is a long and systematic work. And others think that education will do every thing for them, and that if they learn to read, and use religious words, they understand religion itself. And others again go so far as to maintain that exertion is *not* necessary for discovering the Truth. They say that religious Truth is simple and easily acquired; that Scripture, being intended for all, is at once open to all, and that if it had difficulties, that very circumstance would be an objection to it. And others, again, maintain that there *are* difficulties in religion, and that this shows that it is an indifferent matter whether they seek or not as to those matters which are difficult.

In these and other ways do men deceive themselves into a carelessness about religious Truth. And is not all this varied negligence sufficient to account for the varieties of religious opinion which we see all around us? Do not these two facts just illustrate each other; the discordance of our religious opinions needing some explanation; and our actual indolence and negligence in seeking the Truth accounting for it? How many sects, all professing Christianity, but opposed to each other, dishonour this country! Doubtless if men sought the Truth with one tenth part of the zeal with which they seek to acquire wealth or secular knowledge, their differences would diminish year by year. Doubtless if they gave a half or a quarter of the time to prayer for Divine guidance which they give to amusement or recreation, or which they give to dispute and contention, they would ever be approximating to each other. We differ in opinion; therefore we cannot all be right; many must be wrong; many must be turned from the Truth; and why is this, but on account of that undeniable fact which we see before us, that we do not pray and seek for the Truth?

But this melancholy diversity is sometimes explained, as I just now hinted, in another way. Some men will tell us that this difference of opinion in religious matters which exists, is a proof, not that the Truth is withheld from us on account of our negligence in seeking it, but that religious Truth is not worth seeking at all, or that it is not given us. The present confused and perplexed state of things, which is really a proof of God's anger at our negligence, these men say is a proof that religious Truth cannot be obtained; that there is no such thing as religious Truth;

that there is no right or wrong in religion; that, provided we *think* ourselves right, one set of opinions is as good as another; that we shall all come right in the end if we do but mean well, or rather if we do not mean ill. That is, we create confusion by our negligence and disobedience, and then excuse our negligence by the existence of that confusion. It is no uncommon thing, I say, for men to say, "that in religious matters God has willed that men should differ," and to support their opinion by no better argument than the fact that they *do* differ; and they go on to conclude that *therefore* we need not perplex ourselves about matters of *faith*, about which, after all, we cannot be certain. Others, again, in a similar spirit, argue that forms and ordinances are of no account; that they are little matters; that it is uncertain what is right and what is wrong in them, and that to insist on them as important to religion is the mark of a narrow mind. And others, again, it is to be feared, go so far as to think that indulgence of the passions, or self-will, or selfishness, or avarice, is not wrong, because it is the way of the world and cannot be prevented.

To all such arguments against religious Truth, it is sufficient to reply, that no one who does not seek the Truth with all his heart and strength, can tell what is of importance and what is not; that to attempt carelessly to decide on points of faith or morals is a matter of serious presumption; that no one knows *whither* he will be carried *if* he seeks the Truth perseveringly, and therefore, that since he cannot see at first starting the course into which his inquiries will be divinely directed, he *cannot* possibly say beforehand whether they may not lead him on to certainty as to things which at present he thinks trifling or extravagant or irrational. "What I do," said our Lord to St. Peter, "thou knowest not now, but thou shalt know hereafter." "*Seek*, and ye shall find"; this is the Divine rule, "If thou *criest* after knowledge, and *liftest up* thy voice for understanding; if thou seekest her as silver, and searchest for her as *for hid* treasures; *then* shalt thou understand the fear of the Lord, and find the knowledge of God" (Prv 2:3–5).

This is a subject which cannot too strongly be insisted on. Act up to your light, though in the midst of difficulties, and you will be carried on, you do not know how far. Abraham obeyed the call and journeyed, not knowing whither he went; so we, if we follow the voice of God, shall be brought on step by step into a new world, of which before we had no idea. This is His gracious way with us: He gives, not all at once, but by measure and season, wisely. To him that hath, more shall be given. But we must begin at the beginning. Each truth has its own order; we cannot join the way of life at any point of the course we please; we cannot learn advanced truths before we have learned primary ones. "Call upon Me," says the Divine Word, "and I will answer thee, and show thee great and mighty things which thou knowest not" (Jer 33:3). Religious men are always learning; but when men refuse to profit by light already granted, their light is turned to darkness. Observe our Lord's conduct with the Pharisees. They asked Him on what authority He acted. He gave them no direct answer, but referred them to the mission of John the Baptist—"The baptism of John, whence was it? from heaven or from men?" (Mt 21:25). They refused to say. Then He said, "Neither tell I you by what authority I do these things." That is, they would not profit by the knowledge they already had from St. John the Baptist, who spoke of Christ—therefore no more was given them.

All of us may learn a lesson here, for all of us are in danger of hastily finding fault with others, and condemning their opinions or practices; not considering, that unless we have faithfully obeyed our conscience and improved our talents, we are no fit judges of them at all. Christ and His Saints are alike destitute of form or comeliness in the eyes of the world, and it is only as we labour to change our nature, through God's help, and to serve Him truly, that we begin to discern the beauty of holiness. Then, at length, we find reason to suspect our own judgments of what is truly good, and perceive our own blindness; for by degrees we find that those whose opinions and conduct we hitherto despised or wondered at as extravagant or unaccountable or weak, really know more than ourselves, and are above us—and so, ever as we rise in knowledge and grow in spiritual illumination, they (to our amazement) rise also, while we look at them. The better we are, the more we understand their excellence; till at length we are taught something of their Divine Master's perfections also, which before were hid from us, and see why it is that, though the Gospel is set on a hill in the midst of the world, like a city which cannot be hid, yet to multitudes it is notwithstanding hid, since He taketh the wise in their own craftiness, and the pure in heart alone can see God.

How are the sheep of Christ's flock scattered abroad in the waste world! He came to gather them together in one; but they wander again and faint by the way, as having lost their Shepherd. What religious opinion can be named which some men or other have not at some time held? All are equally confident in the truth of their own doctrines, though the many must be mistaken. In this confusion let us, my brethren, look to ourselves, each to himself. There must be a right and a wrong, and no matter whether others agree with us or not, it is to us a solemn practical concern not to turn away our ears from the truth. Let not the diversity of opinion in the world dismay you, or deter you from seeking all your life long true wisdom. It is not a search for this day or that, but as you should ever grow in grace, so should you ever grow also in the knowledge of our Lord and Saviour Jesus Christ. Care not for the perplexing question which many will put to you, "How can you be sure that you are right more than others?" Others are nothing to you, if they are not holy and devout in their conversation—and we all know what is meant by being holy; we know whom we should call holy; to be holy is to be like an Apostle. Seek truth in the way of *obedience;* try to act up to your conscience, and let your opinions be the result, not of mere chance reasoning or fancy, but of an improved heart. This way, I say, carries with it an evidence to ourselves of its being the right way, if any way be right; and that there is a right and a wrong way conscience also tells us. God surely will listen to none but those who strive to obey Him. Those who thus proceed, watching, praying, taking all means given them of gaining the truth, studying the Scriptures, and doing their duty; in short, those who seek religious truth by principle and habit, as the main business of their lives, humbly not arrogantly, peaceably not contentiously, shall not be "turned unto fables." "The secret of the Lord is with them that fear Him"; but in proportion as we are conscious to ourselves that we are indolent, and transgress our own sense of right and wrong, in the same proportion we have cause to fear, not only that we are not in a safe state, but, further than this, that we do not know what is a safe state, and what an unsafe—what is light and what is darkness, what is truth and what is error; which way leads to heaven and which to hell. "The way of the wicked is in darkness; they know not at what they stumble" (Prv 4:19).

    I know we shall find it very hard to rouse ourselves, to break the force of habit, to resolve to serve God, and persevere in doing so. And assuredly we must expect, even at best, and with all our efforts, perhaps backslidings, and certainly much continual imperfection all through our lives, in all we do. But this should create in us a horror of disobedience, not a despair at overcoming ourselves. We are not under the law of nature, but under grace; we are not bid do a thing above our strength, because, though our hearts are naturally weak, we are not left to ourselves. According to the command, so is the gift. God's grace is sufficient for us. Why, then, should we fear? Rather, why should we not make any sacrifice, and give up all that is naturally pleasing to us, rather than that light and truth should have come into the world, yet we not find them? Let us be willing to endure toil and trouble; and should times of comparative quiet be given to us, should for a while temptation be withdrawn, or the Spirit of comfort poured upon us, let us not inconsiderately rest in these accidental blessings. While we thank God for them, let us remember that in its turn the time of labour and fear, and danger and anxiety, will come upon us; and that we must act our part well in it. We live here to struggle and to endure: The time of eternal rest will come hereafter.

"Blessed are the undefiled in the way, who walk in the law of the Lord. Blessed are they that keep His testimonies, and that seek Him with the whole heart" (Ps 119:1, 2). "The path of the just is as the shining light, that shineth more and more unto the perfect day" (Prv 4:18).

Sermons Bearing on Subjects of the Day

SERMON VII

Faith and the World

"Though hand join in hand, the wicked shall not be unpunished: but the seed of the righteous shall be delivered."
—Prv 11:21

When we hear speak of the wicked, we are apt to think that men of abandoned lives and unprincipled conduct, cruel, crafty, or profligate men, can alone be meant. This obtains almost universally; we think that evil, in any sufficient sense of the word, is something external to us, and at a distance. Thus in the case of children, when they hear of bad men and wicked men, they have no conception that evil can really be near them. They fancy, with a fearful curiosity, something which they have not seen, something foreign and monstrous, as if brought over the seas, or the production of another sphere; though, in truth, evil, and in its worst and most concentrated shape, is born with them, lives within them, is not subdued except by a supernatural gift from God, and is still in them, even when God's grace has brought it under. And so, when we grow up, whether we are thrown upon the world or not, we commonly do not understand that what Scripture says of sin, of its odiousness and its peril, applies to us. The world itself, even though we see it, appears not to be the world; that is, not the world which Scripture speaks of. We do not discern, we do not detect, the savour of its sinfulness; its ways are pleasant to us; and what Scripture says of wickedness, and of misery as attending on it, does not, as we think, apply to the world we see.

And hence it is, that when we read, as in the text, of the short triumph and the overthrow of wickedness, when we read that "though hand join in hand, the wicked shall not be unpunished," we have a picture brought before us of some overbearing tyranny, or some perfidious conspiracy, or some bold and avowed banding against religion, some event of a generation or a century, and nothing short of it. And such specimens of evil doubtless are especially intended by the sacred writer; still, after all, much more is included in his meaning, much which is ordinary, much which we see before our eyes.

SERMONS BEARING ON SUBJECTS OF THE DAY

Can it indeed be otherwise? Is not the world in itself evil? Is it an accident, is it an occasion, is it but an excess, or a crisis, or a complication of circumstances, which constitutes its sinfulness? or, rather, is it not one of our three great spiritual enemies, at all times, and under all circumstances and all changes, ungodly, unbelieving, seducing, and antichristian? Surely we must grant it to be so. Why else in Baptism do we vow to wage war against it? Why else does Scripture speak of it in the terms which we know so well, if we will but attend to them? St. James says, that "the friendship of the world is enmity with God" (Jas 4:4), so that "whosoever will be a friend of the world is the enemy of God." And St. Paul speaks of "walking according to the course of this world, according to the prince of the power of the air, the spirit that now worketh in the children of disobedience" (Eph 2:2); and exhorts us not to be "conformed to this world," but to be "transformed by the renewing of our mind" (Rom 12:2); and he says that Christ "gave Himself for our sins, that He might deliver us from this present evil world" (Gal 1:4). In like manner St. John says, "Love not the world, neither the things that are in the world. If any man love the world, the love of the Father is not in him" (1 Jn 2:15). Let us be quite sure, then, that confederacy of evil which Scripture calls the world, that conspiracy against Almighty God of which Satan is the secret instigator, is something wider, and more subtle, and more ordinary, than mere cruelty, or craft, or profligacy; it is that very world in which we are; it is not a certain body or party of men, but it is human society itself. This it is which is our greatest enemy; and this it is of which the text in its fulness speaks, when it says that "though hand join in hand, the wicked shall not be unpunished." It is powerful at present, but in the end it shall be overthrown; and then these its separate members "shall not be unpunished," but "the seed of the righteous shall be delivered."

Now I shall attempt an explanation of what may be supposed to be meant in the text by "hand joining in hand," and of the sense in which it is fulfilled in the course of human affairs in every age. The one peculiar and characteristic sin of the world is this, that whereas God would have us live for the life to come, the world would make us live for this life. This, I say, is the world's sin; it lives for this life, not for the next. It takes, as the main scope of human exertion, an end which God forbids; and consequently all that it does becomes evil, because directed to a wrong end.

This is a thing which seems easy to say, but which should be steadily considered. In this respect the temptations of the world differ from temptations of the flesh. The flesh is not rational, nor appeals to reason; but the world reasons. The works of the flesh are such as St. Paul describes them,—variance, hatred, murders, adulteries, uncleanness, and drunkenness. Pride, cruelty, wrath, revenge, obstinacy, sensuality, are works of the flesh. They are the spontaneous fruit of the unrenewed mind, as thorns and thistles are the natural growth of the earth. But the case is different as regards the world. The world has many sins, but its peculiar offence is that of daring to reason contrary to God's Word and will. It puts wrong aims before itself, and acts towards them. It goes wrong as if on principle, and prefers its own way of viewing things to God's way. When Eve saw that the forbidden fruit was good for food, she was tempted through the flesh; and when the serpent said, "Ye shall not surely die," he used the temptation proper to the world—false reason.

Now you will see this by taking a survey of the world, and seeing how and why it disobeys God. God, in Scripture, says one thing; the world says another. God says that we should live for the life to come; the world says that we should live for this life. How is it able to say so? what are the arguments it uses? Let us consider.

Men seem made for this world; this is what prevails on them to neglect the next world: They think they have reason for concluding, they think they see, that this world is the world for which they are to labour, and to which they are to devote their faculties. And therefore they persist in denying that they must live for the next world. It is not that they profess to run counter to God's Word, but they deny that He has said that they must live directly for the next world. As the Israelites did not avowedly cast off the God of Abraham when they worshipped the golden calf, but professed to worship Him under that symbol, so men generally, when they pursue this world as their supreme good, and as their god, deny that they *are* disowning their Lord and Maker, but maintain that He wishes them to worship Him by means of and in this world.

Now these are the sort of considerations which seduce them to think that this world is all in all:—

1. For instance, there are a number of faculties and talents which seem only to exist in this world, and to be impossible in another. Consider the varieties of mental gifts which are in active exercise on all sides of us, and you will see what I mean; such as talent for business, or talent for the useful arts, mechanical talent. Or, again, consider the talents which go to make up a great warrior. They seem as if evidently made for this world, and this world only. If such ability is not to be used, it may

be asked, why is it given? If a person lives only for the next world, what is the use of it? Our aim then, they say, must be an aim of this life, our end of action must be in this world, because our talents point that way. Talents are not necessary for religion, talents are not necessary for preparing for the life to come; yet they are given, therefore they are given for this life. Thus men argue: I do not say that they bring out their full meaning in words; but this is the argument latent in their minds. They say or think that if religion disowns the wisdom of this world; if it disowns, as its real and true ground, power, and rank, and might, and knowledge, and ability,—which it does; then, all these things may disown religion, do not belong to religion, need not aim at religion. It parts with them, they part with it. Religion, therefore (they say), is not for this world. It is a private thing for each man's own conscience, but not for society, not for acting upon on a large scale. And this, both because man has faculties which religion does not deign to make its instruments; and also because these faculties do not exist beyond this life, and therefore, if they are to be employed, must be employed here.

2. Another consideration of the same kind, which is adapted to influence men of this world in the same direction, if they give their minds to consider the matter, is the existence of national character. This seems to them to be a providential mark of what this world is intended to be. The character of *one individual* may be accidental, and may arise from his own caprice or wilfulness; but when a whole multitude are one and the same, this cannot arise from themselves, it must arise from their very nature, it must be a token of the will of God. That character, they say, whatever it is, must be pleasing to God. Now one nation is manly, and another is brave but cruel, and a third sagacious, and a fourth energetic and busy. These then, it is argued, are the qualities of mind for which this life is intended. Where was there ever a religious nation? or, at least, how is it possible, in the nature of things, that nations, differing as they do, and so complete in their differences, should have been intended for one form or creed? Religion, then, is for the next world, not for this. No (thus men seem to proceed), energy and activity, enterprise, adventure, rivalry, and invention,—war, politics, and trade,—these are what men are made for here; not for faith, fear, humiliation, prayer, self-discipline, penance, tenderness of conscience, sanctity. It is very well if individuals feel themselves called this way; but it is a private matter for themselves, not to be urged on others. Or again, if we look at the religion of different men, one develops one set of ideas, another another; one

adopts a strict creed, another is free and bold. All religions then are matters of opinion, because they are matters of disposition and habit.

3. I have spoken of nations, because the argument then can be made to look specious; but men generally apply it to the case of individuals. They go into the world, and they find individuals of this or that character, and not religious; and hence they argue that religion is but a theory, because it is not on the face of society. This is what they call seeing life and knowing the world, and it leads them to despise strict principle and religious conduct as narrow-minded. They say that religion is very well for a domestic circle, but will not do for the world; for they take men as facts, as they might take the materials of the physical world, stones or vegetables; as if they were what they were, and could not be otherwise; and as one cannot change the elements, but must take them for what they are, and use them, so they think we ought to deal with human beings. And as a person would be called a theorist, who cherished certain ideas about the natural world, to which the facts of that world did not answer, so they think a man a mere dreamer, who says that men ought not to be what they confessedly are; who comes to them with a doctrine which is above them, refuses to deal with them as he finds them, and tries to raise them, and change them, and to make them what they are not. As they would think a man a madman who waited for rivers to have done flowing, or mountains to make way before him, so they think it obstinate, impracticable, perverse, and almost insane, to run counter to the natural man, to thwart his wishes, to condemn his opinions, and to insist on his submitting to a rule foreign to him. Great philosophers have said, that in the case of the material creation we overcome nature by yielding to it, and because this is true of matter, the world would have it in the same sense true of mind.

4. Another consideration which the world urges in its warfare against religion, as I have already implied, is, that religion is unnatural. It is objected (what indeed cannot be denied, and is almost a truism) that religion does not bring the elementary and existing nature of man to its highest perfection, but thwarts and impairs it, and provides for a second and new nature. It is said, and truly, that religion treats the body hardly, and is severe with the soul. How different is the world, which conceives that the first object of life is to treat our inferior nature indulgently, that all methods of living are right which do this, and all wrong which do not! Hence men lay it down, that wealth is the measure of all good, and the end of life; for a state of wealth may be described as a state of ease and

comfort to body and mind. They say that every act of civil government is wrong, which does not tend to what they thus consider to be man's happiness; that utility and expedience, or, in other words, whatever tends to produce wealth, is the only rule on which laws should be framed; that what tends to higher objects is not useful or expedient; that higher objects are a mere dream; that the only thing substantial is this life, and the only wisdom, to cherish and enjoy it. And they are so obstinate in this their evil view of things, that they will not let other people take their own view and rest in it; but are bent on making all men (what they call) happy in their way. In their plans of social and domestic economy, their projects of education, their mode of treating the poor, the one object which they think sufficient for happiness is, that men should have the necessaries of life according to their condition. On the other hand, they think that religion in all its duties clashes with this life, and is therefore unnatural. Almsgiving they think the virtue of a barbarous or half-civilized or badly managed community. Fasting and watching are puerile and contemptible, for such practices interfere with nature, which prompts us to eat and sleep. Prayer again is a mere indolence. It is better, they say, to put the shoulder to the wheel, than to spend time in wishing it to move. Again, making a stand for particular doctrines is thought unnecessary and unmeaning, as if there were any excellence or merit in believing this rather than that, or believing any thing at all.

These are some of the arguments on which the world relies, in defending the interests of this life against those of the next. It says, that the constitution of our body and the powers of our mind tend towards an end short of the next life; and therefore that religion, or the thought of the next world, is unnatural. I answer by admitting that religion is in this sense unnatural; but I maintain that Christ came to bring in a higher nature into this world of men, and that this could not be done except by interfering with the nature which originally belongs to it. Where the spiritual system runs counter to the natural, the natural must give way. God has graciously willed to bring us to heaven; to practice a heavenly life on earth, certainly, is a thing above earth. It is like trying to execute some high and refined harmony on an insignificant instrument. In attempting it, that instrument would be taxed beyond its powers, and would be sacrificed to great ideas beyond itself. And so, in a certain sense, this life, and our present nature, is sacrificed for heaven and the new creature; that while our outward man perishes, our inward man may be renewed day by day.

If, indeed, men will urge that religion is against nature, as an objection to religion, certainly we must become infidels at once; for can any thing be so marvellously and awfully beyond nature, both the nature of man and the nature of God, as that the Eternal Son of God should take flesh and be born of a virgin, and suffer and die on the cross, and rise again? Let us cease, then, to fear this taunt, that religion makes us lead an unnatural or rather supernatural life, seeing it has no force, except it withal persuade us to disown our Saviour, who for us took on Him another nature not His own, and was in the economy of grace what by His Divine generation from the Father He could not be.

5. But to proceed: The strongest argument which the world uses in its favour, is the actual success of its experiment in cultivating the natural faculties of body and mind; for success seems a fresh mark of God's will, over and above the tendencies of nature. This is what influences men most especially to neglect the words of Scripture. Any thing that is used for an end unsuited to it is likely to fail; but human nature, when used for this world, does not fail, but does its work well, and therefore it seems as if it ought so to be used. For instance, we argue that a certain animal is the work of God; why? because its parts fit in together and sustain one another. We bring it as a proof of design, a proof that it is made by God, and does not come of chance, that its teeth and its claws are fitted to its nature and habits, and to each other. Now human society, or this world our enemy, seems in like manner to bear about it marks of design, and therefore to come from God. Enter the mixed multitude of men, and see how they go on. Men may or may not have the fear of God before their eyes, yet they seem to go on equally well either way. Each has his own occupation, his own place; he may be an irreligious and immoral man, a scoffer, or covetous, or heartless, or he may be serious and correct in his conduct, yet none of these things interfere much one way or the other with the development of our social state, the formation of communities, the provisions for mutual protection, the interchange of good offices, and the general intercourse of man with man. Punctuality, honesty, business-like despatch, perseverance, sobriety, friendliness, trust in each other, steady co-operation, these are the sort of virtues which seem sufficient for carrying on the great empires of the world; what a man's character is besides, seems nothing to the purpose. Each nation testifies to each, north to south, and east to west, as to what is enough, and what is required, and Christianity is not included in the list of requisites. East and west, north and south, are of different religions,— here there is no agreement; the form of religion may be this or may be that, and the world goes on the same; but the value of such qualities as I

have named is acknowledged every where. If these did not constitute the true excellence of our nature, it is argued, they would not be enough to live by. No vital part can be wanting in the world, because, in fact, it has life.

I am obliged to state this in an abstract way, and cannot proceed to instances, because I should become familiar. But let any one betake himself to the world, and go through but one day in it; let him consider the course of occurrences through which he passes, only by taking a journey and passing day or night among strangers, or at an inn; and he will recognize what I mean. He will understand what this argument is, which the very face of society presents; viz., that religion is not needed for this world, and therefore is of no great importance.

Now, let it be observed, what I have already implied, men of the world do not deny the existence and power of God. No; they only hold this—(I do not mean in words, but implicitly)—they hold, I say, not that there is not an Almighty Ruler, whose subjects they are, but they deny in their hearts all that is meant by religion, or religious service; they deny their duty towards God; they deny His personal existence, and their subjection to Him. Yes; and if they are obliged at any time to own the existence of religious duty, then they say, to get rid of the subject, in an insincere way, lightly, heartlessly, sometimes scoffingly, that the best kind of religion is "to do their duty in this world," that this is the true worship of God; in other words, that the pursuit of money, of credit, of power, that the gratification of self, and the worship of self, is doing their duty. This unbelief you see in a variety of shapes. For instance, many persons openly defend the aim at rising in the world, and speak in applause of an honourable ambition; as if the prizes of this world were from heaven, and the steps of this world's ladder were the ascent of Angels which Jacob saw. Others, again, consider that their duty lies simply in this,—in making money for their families. The soldier thinks that fighting for his king is his sufficient religion; and the statesman, even when he is most blameless, that serving his country is religion. God's service, as such, as distinct from the service of this world, is in no sense recognized. Faith, hope, love, devotion, are mere names; some visible idol is taken as the substitute for God.

And will God Almighty thus be defrauded of what is due to Him? Will He allow the seductions of this world's sophistry, against which He has Himself warned us, to excuse us in His sight at the last day? Will it be sufficient to acquit us at His judgment-seat for neglecting His Word, that we have trusted the world? for scoffing at faith, that we have lived by sight? Will it compensate for neglecting the God and Father of our Lord Jesus Christ, that we have been Pantheists? is not this our very calling as Christians, to live by faith? If we do not, it is mere trifling to call ourselves Christians at all. The world promises that, if we trust it, we cannot go wrong. Why? because it is so many—there are so many men in it; they must be right. This is what it seems boldly to say,—"God cannot punish so many." So it is, we know, in human law. The magistrate never can punish a very great number of the community at once; he is obliged to let the multitude of culprits escape him, and he makes examples;—and this is what we cannot help fancying God will do. We do not allow ourselves to take in the idea that He can, and that He has said He will, punish a thousand as easily as one. What the poor and ignorant man, who lives irreligiously, professes, is what all really profess. He, when taxed with neglect of religion, says that "he is as good as his neighbours," he speaks out; he speaks abruptly, but he does but say what multitudes feel who do not say it. They think that this world is too great an evil for God to punish; or rather that therefore it is not an evil, because it is a great one. They cannot compass the idea that God should allow so great an evil to exist, as the world would be, if it is evil; and therefore, since He does allow it, it is not an evil. In vain does Scripture assure them that it is an evil, though God allows it. In vain does the whole Psalter, from beginning to the end, proclaim and protest that the world is against the truth, and that the saints must suffer. In vain do Apostles tell us, that the world lieth in wickedness; in vain does Christ Himself declare, that broad is the way that leadeth to destruction, and many there be that go in thereat. In vain do Prophets tell us, that in the end the Saints shall possess the kingdom,—implying they do not possess it now. In vain is the vast judgment of the Deluge; in vain the instant death of the first-born in Egypt, and of the hosts of Sennacherib. No, we will not believe; the words of the Tempter ring in our ears,—"Ye shall not surely die!" and we stake our eternal interests on sight and reason, rather than on the revealed Word of God.

O how miserable in that day, when the dead bones rise from their graves, and the millions who once lived are summoned before their Omnipotent Judge, whose breath is a fiery stream, and whose voice is like the sound of many waters! How vain to call upon the rocks to fall on us; or to attempt to hide ourselves among the trees of the garden, and to make our brother's sin cover our own; when we are in His presence, who is every where at once, and is as fully and entirely our God and Judge, as if there were no other creature but each of us in the whole world! Why will we not learn here, what then to a certainty we shall discover, that number is not strength? Never was a greater fallacy than to suppose that the many must necessarily be stronger than the few; on the contrary, power is ever concentrated and one, in order to be power. God is one. The heathen raged, the people imagined a vain thing; the kings of the earth and the rulers joined hands and took counsel together; and Christ was one. Such is the Divine rule. "There is one Body and one Spirit," and "one hope," and "one Lord, one faith, one baptism, one God and Father of all." No; the number of the wicked will be but an increase of their misery; they will but crowd their prison.

Let us then leave the world, manifold and various as it is; let us leave it to follow its own devices, and let us turn to the living and true God, who has revealed Himself to us in Jesus Christ. Let us be sure that He is more true than the whole world, though with one voice all its inhabitants were to speak against Him. And if we doubt where the truth lies, let us pray to Him to reveal it to us; let us pray Him to give us humility, that we may seek aright; honesty, that we may have no concealed aims; love, that we may desire the truth; and faith, that we may accept it. So that when the end comes, and the multitudes who have joined hands in evil are punished, we may be of those who, in the words of the text, are "delivered." Let us put off all excuses, all unfairness and insincerity, all trifling with our consciences, all self-deception, all delay of repentance. Let us be filled with one wish,—to please God; and if we have this, I say it confidently, we shall no longer be deceived by this world, however loud it speaks, and however plausibly it argues, as if God were with it, for we shall "have an unction from the Holy One," and shall "know all things."

SERMON XIX

The Apostolical Christian

"Know ye not, that they which run in a race run all, but one receiveth the prize? so run, that ye may obtain."—1 Cor 9:24

There was one who came running to Christ, and kneeled to Him, yet he did not obtain; for that haste of his and hurry was no type of the inward earnestness with which the true soul goes sedately forward unto salvation. He was one of the many who, in some sort, run the race, yet do not receive the prize, because they run in self-will, or lightness of mind. "If a man strive for masteries, yet is he not crowned, except he strive lawfully." "I have not sent" them, says the Lord by His Prophet, "yet they ran" (2 Tm 2:5; Jer 23:21). Many there are, who are not open sinners, who do not deny Christ, who honour Him with their lips—may, in some sort with their lives—who, like the young man, are religious in a certain sense, and yet obtain not the crown. For they are not of those who, with the blessed Apostle who speaks in the text, observe the rules of the contest. They have no claim upon the prize, because they run on their own ground, or at their own time; or, in other respects, after their own pleasure. They make a religion for themselves, and they have a private idea what a Christian ought to be; and they never get beyond, even if they attain, the regulation of their lives and conduct upon this self-devised standard of truth. They can never be said to have "finished their course," for, in truth, they have never entered on it. Or they begin it, and turn aside in some other direction, mistaking the path. "Ye did run well," says St. Paul to the Galatians; "who did hinder you that ye should not obey the truth?" (Gal 5:7).

Let us then, with this thought before us, leave for a while our own private judgment of what is pleasing to God and not pleasing, and turn to consider the picture which Scripture gives us of the true Christian life, and then attempt to measure our own life by it. He alone who gives us eternal happiness, has the power of determining the conditions for attaining it. Let us not take it for granted that we shall know them by our own common sense. Let us betake ourselves to Scripture to learn them.

SERMONS BEARING ON SUBJECTS OF THE DAY

Now it is very certain, that the New Testament abounds in notices, suggestions, and descriptions of the temper and mode of living of the disciples of Christ; that is, as they were characterized at the time when it was written. The idea of a Christian, as set forth in Scripture, is something very definite. We may conceive we have some general notion from Scripture what a Jew was, but we know much more what a Christian was. As a Jew had a very peculiar character, as an Englishman has a character all his own, so the Christian, as described in the inspired writings, is like himself, and unlike any one else. He is not like Pharisee, not like Sadducee, not like Herodian, not like Greek, not like Roman, not like Samaritan; but he is like a follower of Christ, and none but him. Now, whether Christians at this day need be like what Christians were in the primitive times, is a further question. I want, in the first place, to consider *what* the primitive Christians were like, as represented in Scripture. As an historical question, as a matter of fact, thus only I would consider the subject; afterwards will be time enough for us to apply it to our own case, and to settle how far it is necessary for men of this day to conform their lives to the pattern given them once for all by inspiration.

Now so far is certain, that this one peculiar Christian character and life, and none but it, is attributed in Scripture to our Lord, to St. John Baptist, to the Apostles, and to Christians generally. Very different is our Lord from St. John Baptist; very different St. John from the Apostles; very different the Apostles from private Christians. John came in the garb of an ascetic, dressed in a garment of camel's hair, and eating locusts and wild honey. Our Lord came eating and drinking; He lived in the world as St. John in the desert. The Apostles were the teachers of grace, as St. John of repentance; and Christians in general were hearers, not preachers; numbers of them besides were women, and thereby still more unlike Christ and St. John and the Apostles: and yet on the whole one only character distinguishes all of them in Scripture; Christ Himself, and the Baptist, and St. Peter, and St. John, and St. Paul, and the Christian multitude, men and women. And now to draw out what that character is; though, in doing so, I shall say nothing, my brethren, but what you know well already, and shall be doing little more than quoting texts of Scripture. And yet you have heard these texts so often, that perhaps they fall dead upon your ear, and they leave you as they found you, impressing no definite image of their meaning upon your minds.

1. Now the first great and obvious characteristic of a Bible Christian, if I may use that much abused term, is to be without worldly ties or objects, to be living in this world, but not for this world. St. Paul says,

"our conversation is in heaven" (Phil 3:20), or in other words, heaven is our city. We know what it is to be a citizen of this world; it is to have interests, rights, privileges, duties, connexions, in some particular town or state; to depend upon it, and to be bound to defend it; to be part of it. Now all this the Christian is in respect to heaven. Heaven is his city, earth is not. Or, at least, so it was as regards the Christians of Scripture. "Here," as the same Apostle says in another place, "we have no continuing city, but we seek one to come" (Heb 13:14). And therefore he adds to the former of these texts, "from whence also we look for the Saviour, the Lord Jesus Christ." This is the very definition of a Christian,—one who looks for Christ; not who looks for gain, or distinction, or power, or pleasure, or comfort, but who looks "for the Saviour, the Lord Jesus Christ." This, according to Scripture, is the essential mark, this is the foundation of a Christian, from which every thing else follows; whether he is rich or poor, high or low, is a further matter, which may be considered apart; but he surely is a primitive Christian, and he only, who has no aim of this world, who has no wish to be other in this world than he is; whose thoughts and aims have relation to the unseen, the future world; who has lost his taste for this world, sweet and bitter being the same to him; who fulfils the same Apostle's exhortation in another Epistle, "Set your affection on things above, not on things on the earth, for ye are dead, and your life is hid with Christ in God. When Christ, who is our life, shall appear, then shall ye also appear with Him in glory" (Col 3:2–4).

Hence it follows, that watching is a special mark of the Scripture Christian, as our Lord so emphatically sets before us: "Watch therefore, for ye know not what hour your Lord doth come.... Be ye also ready, for in such an hour as ye think not the Son of man cometh" (Mt 24:42, 44). "At midnight there was a cry made, Behold, the bridegroom cometh, go ye out to meet Him.... Watch therefore, for ye know neither the day nor the hour wherein the Son of man cometh" (Mt 25:6, 13). "Watch ye therefore, for ye know not when the Master of the house cometh, at even, or at midnight, or at the cock-crowing, or in the morning; lest coming suddenly he find you sleeping; and what I say unto you, I say unto all, Watch" (Mk 13:35–37). And St. Peter, who once suffered for lack of watching, repeats the lesson: "The end of all things is at hand: be ye therefore sober, and watch unto prayer" (1 Pt 4:7).

And accordingly, prayer, as St. Peter enjoins in the last text, is another characteristic of Christians as described in Scripture. They knew not what hour their Lord would come, and therefore they watched and prayed in every hour, lest they should enter into temptation. "They were continually in the temple praising and blessing God" (Lk 24:53). "These all continued with one accord in prayer and supplication with the women" (Acts 1:14). "They, continuing daily with one accord in the temple, and breaking bread from house to house, did eat their meat with gladness and singleness of heart" (Acts 2:46). "They were all with one accord in one place" (Acts 2:1), at "the third hour of the day." Again, "Peter and John went up together into the temple at the hour of prayer, being the ninth hour" (Acts 3:1). "Cornelius, . . . a devout man, . . . which gave much alms to the people, and prayed to God alway," saw "in a vision evidently about the ninth hour of the day an angel of God" (Acts 10:1–3); and he says himself, "I was fasting until this hour, and at the ninth hour I prayed in my house." "Peter went up upon the house-top to pray about the sixth hour." "At midnight Paul and Silas prayed, and sang praises unto God" (Acts 16:25). "And they all brought us on our way, with wives and children, till we were out of the city; and we kneeled down on the shore, and prayed" (Acts 21:5). This habit of prayer then, recurrent prayer, morning, noon, and night, is one discriminating point in Scripture Christianity, as arising from the text with which I began, "our conversation is in heaven."

In a word, there was no barrier, no cloud, no earthly object, interposed between the soul of the primitive Christian and its Saviour and Redeemer. Christ was in his heart, and therefore all that came from his heart, his thoughts, words, and actions, savoured of Christ. The Lord was his light, and therefore he shone with the illumination. For, "The light of the body is the eye: if therefore thine eye be single, thy whole body shall be full of light. But if thine eye be evil, thy whole body shall be full of darkness" (Mt 6:22, 23). And, "Out of the abundance of the heart the mouth speaketh. A good man out of the good treasure of the heart bringeth forth good things: and an evil man out of the evil treasure, bringeth forth evil things" (Mt 12:34, 35). Or, as Christ says elsewhere, "Cleanse first that which is within the cup and platter, that the outside of them may be clean also" (Mt 23:26). Observe this well, my brethren; religion, you see, begins with the heart, but it does not end with the heart. It begins with the conversion of the heart from earth to heaven, the stripping off and casting away all worldly aims; but it does not end there; it did not end there in the Christians whom Scripture describes, whom our Lord's precepts formed: It drew up all the faculties of the soul, all the members of the body, to Him who was in their heart. Let us then now go on to see in what that inward Christianity issued; what

SERMONS BEARING ON SUBJECTS OF THE DAY

Christians then, in that early time, looked like outwardly, who were citizens of heaven within.

2. Christians, then, were a simple, innocent, grave, humble, patient, meek, and loving body, without earthly advantages or worldly influence, as every page of the New Testament shows us. A description of them is given in the beginning of the Acts: "The multitude of them that believed were of one heart and of one soul; neither said any of them that ought of the things which he possessed was his own, but they had all things common.... Neither was there any among them that lacked: for as many as were possessors of lands or houses sold them, and brought the prices of the things that were sold, and laid them down at the Apostles' feet: and distribution was made unto every man according as he had need" (Acts 4:32-35).

Such, of course, was the natural consequence of a deep conviction of the nothingness of this world, and the all-importance of the other. Those who understood that they were "fellow-citizens with the saints, and of the household of God," could not but show it in their actions. In circumstances like theirs they would have been using idle words, had they said that their conversation was in heaven, yet had gone on eating, and drinking, and conversing like children of men. But here our Lord's words may well take the place of ours. Consider, then, how solemnly He had warned them.

"As the days of Noe were, so shall also the coming of the Son of man be. For as in the days that were before the flood, they were eating and drinking, marrying and giving in marriage, until the day that Noe entered into the ark, and knew not until the flood came, and took them all away; so shall also the coming of the Son of man be" (Mt 24:37-39). "They did eat, they drank, they married wives, they were given in marriage, until the day that Noe entered into the ark, and the flood came, and destroyed them all. Likewise also as it was in the days of Lot; they did eat, they drank, they bought, they sold, they planted, they builded; but the same day that Lot went out of Sodom, it rained fire and brimstone from heaven, and destroyed them all" (Lk 17:27-29). Again, "They all with one consent began to make excuse. The first said unto him, I have bought a piece of ground, and I must needs go and see it: I pray thee have me excused. And another said, I have bought five yoke of oxen, and I go to prove them: I pray thee have me excused. And another said, I have married a wife, and therefore I cannot come" (Lk 14:18-20). Again, "There was a certain rich man, which was clothed in purple and fine linen, and fared sumptuously every day" (Lk 16:19). Again, "Take heed and beware of covetousness.... The ground of a certain rich man brought forth plentifully; ... and he said ... I will say to my soul, Soul, thou hast much goods laid up for many years; take thine ease, eat, drink, and be merry. But God said unto him, Thou fool, this night thy soul shall be required of thee." Again, "Sell that ye have, and give alms: provide yourselves bags which wax not old, a treasure in the heavens that faileth not, where no thief approacheth, neither moth corrupteth; for where your treasure is, there will your heart be also. Let your loins be girded about, and your lights burning" (Lk 12:15–20, 33–35). Again, "How hardly shall they that have riches enter into the kingdom of God" (Mk 10:23). Again, "Take no thought, saying, What shall we eat? or, What shall we drink? or, Wherewithal shall we be clothed?" (Mt 6:31). And hence St. Paul, after the pattern of his Lord and Saviour, is careful to remind us that "the time is short" (1 Cor 7:29);—we are labourers in the eleventh hour of the day. "The time is short; it remaineth that both they that have wives be as though they had none; and they that weep, as though they wept not; and they that rejoice, as though they rejoiced not; and they that buy, as though they possessed not; and they that use this world, as not abusing it, for the fashion of this world passeth away." And again, "No man that warreth entangleth himself with the affairs of this life; that he may please him who hath chosen him to be a soldier" (2 Tm 2:4).

This separation from the world which marked the Christian character as drawn by Christ and His Apostles, is displayed in a variety of details scattered up and down the sacred volume. "Love not the world, neither the things that are in the world" (1 Jn 2:15), says St. John. "Be not conformed to this world, but be ye transformed by the renewing of your mind" (Rom 12:2), says St. Paul. Again, of himself, "By the Cross of Christ ... the world is crucified unto me, and I unto the world" (Gal 6:14). The first Christians were separated from their earthly kindred and friends. "Henceforth," says he, "know we no man after the flesh; yea, though we have known Christ after the flesh, yet now henceforth know we Him no more. Therefore, if any man be in Christ, he is a new creature: old things are passed away, behold all things are become new" (2 Cor 5:16, 17). Or, in our Lord's words, "He that loveth father or mother more than Me, is not worthy of Me; and he that loveth son or daughter more than Me, is not worthy of Me" (Mt 10:37). They parted with property: "Every one that hath forsaken houses, ... or lands, for My Name's sake, shall receive an hundredfold, and shall inherit everlasting life" (Mt 19:29). They put off from them things personal: "Provide neither gold, nor silver, nor brass, in your purses, nor scrip for your journey, neither two coats, neither shoes, nor yet staves: for the workman is worthy of his meat" (Mt 10:9, 10). They sacrificed to Christ their dearest wishes and objects, things nearer and closer to them than the very garments they had on them: "If thy hand or thy foot offend thee," says our Lord, in figurative language, "cut them off, and cast them from thee; it is better for thee to enter into life halt or maimed, rather than having two hands or two feet to be cast into everlasting fire. And if thine eye offend thee, pluck it out, and cast it from thee: it is better for thee to enter into life with one eye, rather than having two eyes to be cast into hell fire" (Mt 18:8, 9). They forfeited the common sympathy of humanity, and were cruelly used, or rather, hunted down, as some separate race of beings less than man: "Ye shall be hated of all men for My Name's sake. . . . The disciple is not above his Master, nor the servant above his Lord. . . . If they have called the Master of the house Beelzebub, how much more shall they call them of his household!" (Mt 10:22, 24, 25).

This, to speak briefly on a great subject, is the picture of a Christian as drawn in the New Testament. Christians are those who profess to have the love of the truth in their hearts; and when Christ asks them whether they so love Him as to be able to drink of His cup, and partake of His Baptism, they answer, "We are able," and their profession issues in a wonderful fulfilment. They love God and they give up the world.

3. And here we are brought to a third and last characteristic of the Christianity of the New Testament, which necessarily follows from the other two. If the first disciples so unreservedly gave up the world, and if, secondly, they were so strictly and promptly taken at their word, what do you think would follow, if they were true men and not hypocrites? this—they would rejoice to be so taken. This, then, is the third chief grace of primitive Christianity—joy in all its forms; not only a pure heart, not only a clean hand, but, thirdly, a cheerful countenance. I say joy in all its forms, for in true joyfulness many graces are included; joyful people are loving; joyful people are forgiving; joyful people are munificent. Joy, if it be Christian joy, the refined joy of the mortified and persecuted, makes men peaceful, serene, thankful, gentle, affectionate, sweet-tempered, pleasant, hopeful; it is graceful, tender, touching, winning. All this were the Christians of the New Testament, for they had obtained what they desired. They had desired to sacrifice the kingdom of the world and all its pomps for the love of Christ, whom they had seen, whom they loved, in whom they believed, in whom they delighted; and when their wish was granted, they could but "rejoice in that day,

and leap for joy, for, behold, their reward was great in heaven" (Lk 6: 23): Blessed were they, thrice blessed, because they in their lifetime had evil things (Lk 16:25), and their consolation was to come hereafter.

Such, I say, was the joy of the first disciples of Christ, to whom it was granted to suffer shame and to undergo toil for His Name's sake; and such holy, gentle graces were the fruit of this joy, as every part of the Gospels and Epistles shows us. "We glory in tribulations," says St. Paul, "knowing that tribulation worketh patience, and patience experience, and experience hope, and hope maketh not ashamed, because the love of God is shed abroad in our hearts by the Holy Ghost which is given unto us" (Rom 5:3–5). Again, "Even unto this present hour we both hunger and thirst, and are naked, and are buffeted, and have no certain dwelling-place, and labour working with our own hands: being reviled, we bless; being persecuted, we suffer it; being defamed, we intreat; we are made as the filth of the earth, and are the off-scouring of all things unto this day" (1 Cor 4:11–13). How is the very same character set before us in the Beatitudes, so holy, so tender, so serene, so amiable! "Blessed are the poor in spirit, for theirs is the kingdom of heaven; blessed are they that mourn, for they shall be comforted; blessed are the meek, they which do hunger and thirst after righteousness, the merciful, the pure in heart, the peace-makers, they which are persecuted for righteousness' sake" (Mt 5:3–10). And again, "Let your communication be yea, yea, nay, nay; for whatsoever is more than these cometh of evil" (Mt 5:37). "I say unto you, That ye resist not evil; but whosoever shall smite thee on thy right cheek, turn to him the other also": "love your enemies, bless them that curse you, do good to them that hate you, and pray for them which despitefully use you and persecute you; that ye may be the children of your Father which is in heaven." Again, "Judge not, that ye be not judged; . . . and why beholdest thou the mote that is in thy brother's eye, but considerest not the beam that is in thine own eye?" (Mt 7:1, 3). And again, "In your patience possess ye your souls" (Lk 21: 19). Again, "If I then, your Lord and Master, have washed your feet, ye also ought to wash one another's feet" (Jn 13:14). Again, "By this shall all men know that ye are My disciples, if ye have love one to another." And again, "Peace I leave with you, My peace I give unto you, not as the world giveth, give I unto you. Let not your heart be troubled, neither let it be afraid" (Jn 14:27). Or again, consider the special prayer which the Lord Himself taught us, as a pattern of all prayer, and see how it corresponds to that one idea of a Christian which I have been drawing out. It consists of seven petitions; three have reference to Almighty God, four to the petitioners; and could any form of words be put together which so well could be called the Prayer of the Pilgrim? We often hear it said, that the true way of serving God is to serve man, as if religion consisted merely in acting well our part in life, not in direct faith, obedience, and worship: How different is the spirit of this prayer! Evil round about him, enemies and persecutors in his path, temptation in prospect, help for the day, sin to be expiated, God's will in his heart, God's Name on his lips, God's kingdom in his hopes: This is the view it gives us of a Christian. What simplicity! what grandeur! and what definiteness! how one and the same, how consistent with all that we read of him elsewhere in Scripture!

Alas! my brethren, so it is, when you have subjects like this dwelt upon, too many of you are impatient of them, and wish to hurry past them, and are eager to be reminded by the preacher in the same breath with his presenting them—nay, you remind yourselves—that you of this day can have no immediate interest in them,—that times are changed. Times *are* changed, I grant; but without going on to the question of the obligation now of such a profession of the Gospel as I have been describing, do persuade yourselves, I entreat you, to contemplate the picture. Do not shut your eyes, do not revolt from it, do not fret under it, but look at it. Bear to look at the Christianity of the Bible; bear to contemplate the idea of a Christian, traced by inspiration, without gloss, or comment, or tradition of man. Bear to hear read to you a number of texts; texts which might be multiplied sevenfold; texts which can be confronted by no others; which are no partial selections, but a specimen of the whole of the New Testament. Before you go forward to the question, "How do they affect us, must we obey them, or why need we not?" prevail on yourselves to realize the idea of a Scriptural Christian, and the fact that the first Christians really answered to it. Granting you have to apply and modify the pattern given you, before you can use it yourselves, which I am not denying, yet after all, your pattern it is; you have no other pattern of a Christian any where. No other view of Christianity is given you in Scripture. If Scripture is used, you must begin with accepting that pattern; how can you apply what you will not study? Study what a Bible Christian is; be silent over it; pray for grace to comprehend it, to accept it.

And next ask yourselves this question, and be honest in your answer. This model of a Christian, though not commanding your literal imitation, still is it not the very model which has been fulfilled in others in every age since the New Testament was written? You will ask me in whom? I am loth to say; I have reason to ask you to be honest and candid; for so it is, as if from consciousness of the fact, and dislike to have it urged upon us, we and our forefathers have been accustomed to scorn and ridicule these faithful, obedient persons, and, in our Saviour's very words, to "cast out their *name* as evil, for the Son of man's sake." But, if the truth must be spoken, what are the humble monk, and the holy nun, and other regulars, as they are called, but Christians after the very pattern given us in Scripture? What have they done but this—perpetuate in the world the Christianity of the Bible? Did our Saviour come on earth suddenly, as He will one day visit it, in whom would He see the features of the Christians whom He and His Apostles left behind them, but in them? Who but these give up home and friends, wealth and ease, good name and liberty of will, for the kingdom of heaven? Where shall we find the image of St. Paul, or St. Peter, or St. John, or of Mary the mother of Mark, or of Philip's daughters, but in those who, whether they remain in seclusion, or are sent over the earth, have calm faces, and sweet plaintive voices, and spare frames, and gentle manners, and hearts weaned from the world, and wills subdued; and for their meekness meet with insult, and for their purity with slander, and for their gravity with suspicion, and for their courage with cruelty; yet meet with Christ every where—Christ, their all-sufficient, everlasting portion, to make up to them, both here and hereafter, all they suffer, all they dare, for His Name's sake?

And, lastly, apply this pattern to yourselves; for there only will you have power to apply it rightly. You know very well, most of us know it too well, that such precepts and examples do not directly apply to every one of us. We are not severally bound to give up the world by so literal a surrender. The case of Ananias and Sapphira is enough to show us this. Their sin lay in professing to do what they need not have done; in making pretence of a voluntary renunciation which they did not execute. They kept back part of the price of the land which they made a show of giving up: and St. Peter urged it against them. "Whiles it remained, was it not thine own? and after it was sold, was it not in thine own power?" A most awful warning to every one, not to affect greater sanctity or self-denial than he attempts; but a proof withal, that those great surrenders which Scripture speaks of, are not incumbent on all Christians. They could not be voluntary if they were duties; they could not be meritorious if they were not voluntary. But though they are not duties to all, they may be duties to you; and though they are voluntary, you may have a call to them. It may be your duty to follow after merit. And whether it is you cannot learn, till first you have fairly surrendered your mind to the contemplation of that Christianity which Scripture delineates. After all, it may prove to be your duty to remain as others, and you may serve Him best and most acceptably in a secular life. But you cannot tell till you inquire; enough do we hear of private judgment in matters of doctrine; alas! that we will not exercise it where it is to a certain extent allowable and religious; in points, not public and ecclesiastical and eternal and independent of ourselves, but personal,—in the choice of life, in matters of duty!

Discourses Addressed to Mixed Congregations

Discourse XVI

Mental Sufferings of Our Lord in His Passion

Every passage in the history of our Lord and Saviour is of unfathomable depth, and affords inexhaustible matter of contemplation. All that concerns Him is infinite, and what we first discern is but the surface of that which begins and ends in eternity. It would be presumptuous for any one short of saints and doctors to attempt to comment on His words and deeds, except in the way of meditation; but meditation and mental prayer are so much a duty in all who wish to cherish true faith and love towards Him, that is may be allowed us, my brethren, under the guidance of holy men who have gone before us, to dwell and enlarge upon what otherwise would more fitly be adored than scrutinised. An certain times of the year, this especially,* call upon us to consider, as closely and minutely as we can, even the more sacred portions of the Gospel history. I would rather be thought feeble or officious in my treatment of them, than wanting to the Season; and so I now proceed because the religious usage of the Church requires it, and though any individual preacher may well shrink from it, to direct your thoughts to a subject, especially suitable now, and about which many of us perhaps think very little, the sufferings which our lord endured in His innocent and sinless soul.

You know, my brethren, that our Lord and Saviour, though He was God, was also perfect man; and hence He had not only a body, but a soul likewise, such as ours, though pure from all stain of evil. He did not take a body without a soul, God forbid! for that would not have been to become man. How would He have sanctified our nature by taking a nature which was not ours? Man without a soul is on a level with the beasts of the field; but our Lord came to save a race capable of praising and obeying Him, possessed of immortality, though that immortality had lost its promised blessedness. Man was created in the image of God, and that image is in his soul; when then his Maker, by an unspeakable condescen-

---

* Passion-tide.

sion, came in his nature, He took on Himself a soul in order to take on Him a body; He took on Him a soul as the means of His union with a body; He took on Him in the first place the soul, then the body of man, both at once, but in this order, the soul and the body; He Himself created the soul which He took on Himself, while He took His body from the flesh of the Blessed Virgin, His Mother. Thus He became perfect man with body and soul; and as He took on Him a body of flesh and nerves, which admitted of wounds and death, and was capable of suffering, so did He take a soul, too, which was susceptible of that suffering, and moreover was susceptible of the pain and sorrow which are proper to a human soul; and, as His atoning passion was undergone in the body, so it was undergone in the soul also.

As the solemn days proceed, we shall be especially called on, my brethren, to consider His sufferings in the body, His seizure, His forced journeyings to and fro, His blows and wounds, His scourging, the crown of thorns, the nails, the cross. They are all summed up in the crucifix itself, as it meets our eyes; they are represented all at once on His sacred flesh, as it hangs up before us—and meditation is made easy by the spectacle. It is otherwise with the sufferings of His soul; they cannot be painted for us, nor can they even be duly investigated: they are beyond both sense and thought; and yet they anticipated His bodily sufferings. The agony, a pain of the soul, not of the body, was the first act of His tremendous sacrifice; "My soul is sorrowful even unto death," He said; nay; if He suffered in the body, it really was in the soul, for the body did but convey the infliction on to that which was the true recipient and seat of the suffering.

This it is very much to the purpose to insist upon; I say, it was not the body that suffered, but the soul in the body; it was the soul and not the body which was the seat of the suffering of the Eternal Word. Consider, then, there is no real pain, though there may be apparent suffering, when there is no kind of inward sensibility or spirit to be the seat of it. A tree, for instance, has life, organs, growth, and decay; it may be wounded and injured; it droops, and is killed; but it does not suffer, because it has no mind or sensible principle within it. But wherever this gift of an immaterial principle is found, there pain is possible, and greater pain according to the quality of the gift. Had we no spirit of any kind, we should feel as little as a tree feels; had we no soul, we should not feel pain more acutely than a brute feels it; but, being men, we feel pain in a way in which none but those who have souls can feel it.

Living beings, I say, feel more or less according to the spirit which is in them; brutes feel far less than man, because they cannot reflect on what they feel; they have no advertence or direct consciousness of their sufferings. This it is that makes pain so trying, viz., that we cannot help thinking of it, while we suffer it. It is before us, it possesses the mind, it keeps our thoughts fixed upon it. Whatever draws the mind off the thought of it lessens it; hence friends try to amuse us when we are in pain, for amusement is a diversion. If the pain is slight, they sometimes succeed with us; and then we are, so to say, without pain, even while we suffer. And hence it continually happens that in violent exercise or labour, men meet with blows or cuts, so considerable and so durable in their effect, as to bear witness to the suffering which must have attended their infliction, of which nevertheless they recollect nothing. And in quarrels and in battles wounds are received which, from the excitement of the moment, are brought home to the consciousness of the combatant, not by the pain at the time of receiving them, but by the loss of blood that follows.

I will show you presently, my brethren, how I mean to apply what I have said to the consideration of our Lord's sufferings; first I will make another remark. Consider, then, that hardly any one stroke of pain is intolerable; it is intolerable when it continues. You cry out perhaps that you cannot bear more; patients feel as if they could stop the surgeon's hand, simply because he continues to pain them. Their feeling is that they have borne *as much* as they can bear; as if the continuance and not the intenseness was what made it too much for them. What does this mean, but that the memory of the foregoing moments of pain acts upon and (as it were) edges the pain that succeeds? If the third or fourth or twentieth moment of pain could be taken by itself, if the succession of the moments that preceded it could be forgotten, it would be no more than the first moment, as bearable as the first (taking away the shock which accompanies the first); but what makes it unbearable is, that it *is* the twentieth; that the first, the second, the third, on to the nineteenth moment of pain, are all concentrated in the twentieth; so that every additional moment of pain has all the force, the ever-increasing force, of all that has preceded it. Hence, I repeat, it is that brute animals would seem to feel so little pain, because, that is, they have not the power of reflection or of consciousness. They do not know they exist; they do not contemplate themselves; they do not look backwards or forwards; every moment as it succeeds is their all; they wander over the face of the earth, and see this thing and that, and feel pleasure and pain, but still they take everything as it comes, and then let it go again, as men do in dreams.

They have memory, but not the memory of an intellectual being; they put together nothing, they make nothing properly one and individual to themselves out of the particular sensations which they receive; nothing is to them a reality, or has a substance, beyond those sensations; they are but sensible of a number of successive impressions. And hence, as their other feelings, so their feeling of pain is but faint and dull, in spite of their outward manifestations of it. It is the intellectual comprehension of pain, as a whole diffused through successive moments, which gives it its special power and keenness, and it is the soul only, which a brute has not, which is capable of that comprehension.

Now apply this to the sufferings of our Lord;—do you recollect their offering Him wine mingled with myrrh, when He was on the point of being crucified? He would not drink of it; why? because such a portion would have stupefied His mind, and He was bent on bearing the pain in all its bitterness. You see from this, my brethren, the character of His sufferings; He would have fain escaped them, had that been His Father's will; "If it be possible," He said, "let this chalice pass from Me"; but since it was not possible, He says calmly and decidedly to the Apostle, who would have rescued Him from suffering, "The chalice which My Father hath given Me, shall I not drink it?" If He was to suffer, He gave Himself to suffering; He did not come to suffer as little as He could; He did not turn away His face from the suffering; He confronted it, or, as I may say, He breasted it, that every particular portion of it might make its due impression on Him. And as men are superior to brute animals, and are affected by pain more than they, by reason of the mind within them, which gives a substance to pain, such as it cannot have in the instance of brutes; so, in like manner, our Lord felt pain of the body, with an advertence and a consciousness, and therefore with a keenness and intensity, and with a unity of perception, which none of us can possibly fathom or compass, because His soul was so absolutely in His power, so simply free from the influence of distractions, so fully directed *upon* the pain, so utterly surrendered, so simply subjected to the suffering. And thus He may truly be said to have suffered the whole of His passion in every moment of it.

Recollect that our Blessed Lord was in this respect different from us, that, though He was perfect man, yet there was a power in Him greater than His soul, which ruled His soul, for He was God. The soul of other men is subjected to its own wishes, feelings, impulses, passions, perturbations; His soul was subjected simply to His Eternal and Divine Personality. Nothing happened to His soul by chance, or on a sudden;

He never was taken by surprise; nothing affected Him without His willing beforehand that it should affect Him. Never did He sorrow, or fear, or desire, or rejoice in spirit, but He first willed to be sorrowful, or afraid, or desirous, or joyful. When we suffer, it is because outward agents and the uncontrollable emotions of our minds bring suffering upon us. We are brought under the discipline of pain involuntarily, we suffer from it more or less acutely according to accidental circumstances, we find our patience more or less tried by it according to our state of mind, and we do our best to provide alleviations or remedies of it. We cannot anticipate beforehand how much of it will come upon us, or how far we shall be able to sustain it; nor can we say afterwards why we have felt just what we have felt, or why we did not bear the suffering better. It was otherwise with our Lord. His Divine Person was not subject, could not be exposed, to the influence of His own human affections and feelings, except so far as He chose. I repeat, when He chose to fear, He feared; when He chose to be angry, He was angry; when He chose to grieve, He was grieved. He was not open to emotion, but He opened upon Himself voluntarily the impulse by which He was moved. Consequently, when He determined to suffer the pain of His vicarious passion, whatever He did, He did, as the Wise Man says, *instanter*, "earnestly," with His might; He did not do it by halves; He did not turn away His mind from the suffering as we do—(how should He, who came to suffer, who could not have suffered but of His own act?) no, He did not say and unsay, do and undo; He said and He did; He said, "Lo, I come to do Thy will, O God; sacrifice and offering Thou wouldest not, but a body hast Thou fitted to Me." He took a body in order that He might suffer; He became man, that He might suffer as man; and when His hour was come, that hour of Satan and of darkness, the hour when sin was to pour its full malignity upon Him, it followed that He offered Himself wholly, a holocaust, a whole burnt-offering;—as the whole of His body, stretched out upon the cross, so the whole of His soul, His whole advertence, His whole consciousness, a mind awake, a sense acute, a living co-operation, a present, absolute intention, not a virtual permission, not a heartless submission, this did He present to His tormentors. His passion was an action; He lived most energetically, while He lay languishing, fainting, and dying. Nor did He die, except by an act of the will; for He bowed His head, in command as well as in resignation, and said, "Father, into Thy hands I commend My Spirit"; He gave the word, He surrendered His soul, He did not lose it.

Thus you see, my brethren, had our Lord only suffered in the body, and in it not so much as other men, still as regards the pain, He would have really suffered indefinitely more, because pain is to be measured by the power of realising it. God was the sufferer; God suffered in His human nature; the sufferings belonged to God, and were drunk up, were drained out to the bottom of the chalice, because God drank them; not tasted or sipped, not flavoured, disguised by human medicaments, as man disposes of the cup of anguish. And what I have been saying will further serve to answer an objection, which I shall proceed to notice, and which perhaps exists latently in the minds of many, and leads them to overlook the part which our Lord's soul had in His gracious satisfaction for sin.

Our Lord said, when His agony was commencing, "My soul is sorrowful unto death"; now you may ask, my brethren, whether He had not certain consolations peculiar to Himself, impossible in any other, which diminished or impeded the distress of His soul, and caused Him to feel, not more, but less than an ordinary man. For instance, He had a sense of innocence which no other sufferer could have; even His persecutors, even the false Apostle who betrayed Him, the judge who sentenced Him, and the soldiers who conducted the execution, testified His innocence. "I have condemned the innocent blood," said Judas; "I am clear from the blood of this just Person," said Pilate; "Truly this was a just Man," cried the centurion. And if even they, sinners, bore witness to His sinlessness, how much more did His own soul! And we know well that even in our own case, sinners as we are, on the consciousness of innocence or of guilt mainly turns our power of enduring opposition and calumny; how much more, you will say, in the case of our Lord, did the sense of inward sanctity compensate for the suffering and annihilate the shame! Again, you may say that He knew that His sufferings would be short, and that their issue would be joyful, whereas uncertainty of the future is the keenest element of human distress; but He could not have anxiety, for He was not in suspense; nor despondency or despair, for He never was deserted. And in confirmation you may refer to St. Paul, who expressly tells us that, "for the joy set before Him," our Lord "despised the shame." And certainly there is a marvellous calm and self-possession in all He does: Consider His warning to the Apostles, "Watch and pray, lest ye enter into temptation; the spirit indeed is willing, but the flesh is weak"; or His words to Judas, "Friend, wherefore art thou come?" and "Judas, betrayest thou the Son of Man with a kiss?" or to Peter, "All that take the sword shall perish with the sword"; or to the man who struck Him, "If I have spoken evil, bear witness of the evil; but if well, why smitest thou Me?" or to His Mother, "Woman, behold thy Son."

DISCOURSES TO MIXED CONGREGATIONS

All this is true and much to be insisted on; but it quite agrees with, or rather illustrates, what I have been observing. My brethren, you have only said (to use a human phrase) that He was always Himself. His mind was its own centre, and was never in the slightest degree thrown off its heavenly and most perfect balance. What He suffered, He suffered because He put Himself under suffering, and that deliberately and calmly. As He said to the leper, "I will, be thou clean"; and to the paralytic, "Thy sins be forgiven thee"; and to the centurion, "I will come and heal him"; and of Lazarus, "I go to wake him out of sleep"; so He said, "Now I will begin to suffer," and He did begin. His composure is but the proof how entirely He governed His own mind. He drew back, at the proper moment, the bolts and fastenings, and opened the gates, and the floods fell right upon His soul in all their fulness. That is what St. Mark tells us of Him; and he is said to have written his Gospels from the very mouth of St. Peter, who was one of three witnesses present at the time. "They came," he says, "to the place which is called Gethsemani; and He saith to His disciples, Sit you here while I pray. And He taketh with Him Peter and James and John, and He *began to be* frightened and to be very heavy." You see how deliberately He acts; He comes to a certain spot; and then, giving the word of command, and withdrawing the support of the Godhead from His soul, distress, terror, and dejection at once rush in upon it. Thus He walks forth into a mental agony with as definite an action as if it were some bodily torture, the fire or the wheel.

This being the case, you will see at once, my brethren, that it is nothing to the purpose to say that He would be supported under His trial by the consciousness of innocence and the anticipation of triumph; for His trial consisted in the withdrawal, as of other causes of consolation, so of that very consciousness and anticipation. The same act of the will which admitted the influence upon His soul of any distress at all, admitted all distresses at once. It was not the contest between antagonist impulses and views, coming from without, but the operation of an inward resolution. As men of self-command can turn from one thought to another at their will, so much more did He deliberately deny Himself the comfort, and satiate Himself with the woe. In that moment His soul thought not of the future, He thought only of the present burden which was upon Him, and which He had come upon earth to sustain.

And now, my brethren, what was it He had to bear, when He thus opened upon His soul the torrent of this predestinated pain? Alas! He had to bear what is well known to us, what is familiar to us, but what to Him was woe unutterable. He had to bear that which is so easy a thing to us, so natural, so welcome, that we cannot conceive of it as of a great endurance, but which to Him had the scent and the poison of death—He had, my dear brethren, to bear the weight of sin; He had to bear your sins; He had to bear the sins of the whole world. Sin is an easy thing to us; we think little of it; we do not understand how the Creator can think much of it; we cannot bring our imagination to believe that it deserves retribution, and, when even in this world punishments follow upon it, we explain them away or turn our minds from them. But consider what sin is in itself; it is rebellion against God; it is a traitor's act who aims at the overthrow and death of His sovereign; it is that, if I may use a strong expression, which, could the Divine Governor of the world cease to be, would be sufficient to bring it about. Sin is the mortal enemy of the All-holy, so that He and it cannot be together; and as the All-holy drives it from His presence into the outer darkness, so, if God could be less than God, it is sin that would have power to make Him less. And here observe, my brethren, that when once Almighty Love, by taking flesh, entered this created system, and submitted Himself to its laws, then forthwith this antagonist of good and truth, taking advantage of the opportunity, flew at that flesh which He had taken, and fixed on it, and was its death. The envy of the Pharisees, the treachery of Judas, and the madness of the people, were but the instrument or the expression of the enmity which sin felt towards Eternal Purity as soon as, in infinite mercy towards men, He put Himself within its reach. Sin could not touch His Divine Majesty; but it could assail Him in that way in which He allowed Himself to be assailed, that is, through the medium of His humanity. And in the issue, in the death of God incarnate, you are but taught, my brethren, what sin is in itself, and what it was which then was falling, in its hour and in its strength, upon His human nature, when He allowed that nature to be so filled with horror and dismay at the very anticipation.

There, then, in that most awful hour, knelt the Saviour of the world, putting off the defences of His divinity, dismissing His reluctant Angels, who in myriads were ready at His call, and opening His arms, baring His breast, sinless as He was, to the assault of His foe,—of a foe whose breath was a pestilence, and whose embrace was an agony. There He knelt, motionless and still, while the vile and horrible fiend clad His spirit in a robe steeped in all that is hateful and heinous in human crime, which clung close round His heart, and filled His conscience, and found its way into every sense and pore of His mind, and spread over Him a moral leprosy, till He almost felt Himself to be that which He never could be, and which His foe would fain have made Him. Oh, the horror, when He looked, and did not know Himself, and felt as a foul and loathsome sinner, from His vivid perception of that mass of corruption which poured over His head and ran down even to the skirts of His garments! Oh, the distraction, when He found His eyes, and hands, and feet, and lips, and heart, as if the members of the Evil One, and not of God! Are these the hands of the Immaculate Lamb of God, once innocent, but now red with ten thousand barbarous deeds of blood? are these His lips, not uttering prayer, and praise, and holy blessings, but as if defiled with oaths, and blasphemies, and doctrines of devils? or His eyes, profaned as they are by all the evil visions and idolatrous fascinations for which men have abandoned their adorable Creator? And His ears, they ring with sounds of revelry and of strife; and His heart is frozen with avarice, and cruelty, and unbelief; and His very memory is laden with every sin which has been committed since the fall, in all regions of the earth, with the pride of the old giants, and the lusts of the five cities, and the obduracy of Egypt, and the ambition of Babel, and the unthankfulness and scorn of Israel. Oh, who does not know the misery of a haunting thought which comes again and again, in spite of rejection, to annoy, if it cannot seduce? or of some odious and sickening imagination, in no sense one's own, but forced upon the mind from without? or of evil knowledge, gained with or without a man's fault, but which he would give a great price to be rid of at once and for ever? And adversaries such as these gather around Thee, Blessed Lord, in millions now; they come in troops more numerous than the locust or the palmer-worm, or the plagues of hail, and flies, and frogs, which were sent against Pharaoh. Of the living and of the dead and of the as yet unborn, of the lost and of the saved, of Thy people and of strangers, of sinners and of saints, all sins are there. Thy dearest are there, Thy Saints and Thy chosen are upon Thee; Thy three Apostles, Peter, James, and John; but not as comforters, but as accusers, like the friends of Job, "sprinkling dust towards heaven," and heaping curses on Thy head. All are there but one; one only is not there, one only; for she who had no part in sin, she only could console Thee, and therefore she is not nigh. She will be near Thee on the cross, she is separated from Thee in the garden. She has been Thy companion and Thy confidant through Thy life, she interchanged with Thee the pure thoughts and holy meditations of thirty years; but her virgin ear may not take in, nor may her immaculate heart conceive, what now is in vision before Thee. None was equal to the weight but God; sometimes before Thy saints Thou hast brought the image of a single sin, as it appears in the light of Thy countenance, or of venial sins, not mortal; and they have told us that the sight did all but kill them, nay, would have killed them, had it not been instantly withdrawn. The Mother of God, for all her sanctity, nay by reason of it, could not have borne even one brood of that innumerable progeny of Satan which now compasses Thee about. It is the long history of a world, and God alone can bear the load of it. Hopes blighted, vows broken, lights quenched, warnings scorned, opportunities lost; the innocent betrayed, the young hardened, the penitent relapsing, the just overcome, the aged failing; the sophistry of misbelief, the wilfulness of passion, the obduracy of pride, the tyranny of habit, the canker of remorse, the wasting fever of care, the anguish of shame, the pining of disappointment, the sickness of despair; such cruel, such pitiable spectacles, such heartrending, revolting, detestable, maddening scenes; nay, the haggard faces, the convulsed lips, the flushed cheek, the dark brow of the willing slaves of evil, they are all before Him now; they are upon Him and in Him. They are with Him instead of that ineffable peace which has inhabited His soul since the moment of His conception. They are upon Him, they are all but His own; He cries to His Father as if He were the criminal, not the victim; His agony takes the form of guilt and compunction. He is doing penance, He is making confession, He is exercising contrition, with a reality and a virtue infinitely greater than that of all saints and penitents together; for He is the One Victim for us all, the sole Satisfaction, the real Penitent, all but the real sinner.

He rises languidly from the earth, and turns around to meet the traitor and his band, now quickly nearing the deep shade. He turns, and lo! there is blood upon His garment and in His footprints. Whence come these first-fruits of the passion of the Lamb? no soldier's scourge has touched His shoulders, nor the hangman's nails His hands and feet. My brethren, He has bled before His time; He has shed blood; yes, and it is His agonising soul which has broken up His framework of flesh and poured it forth. His passion has begun from within. That tormented Heart, the seat of tenderness and love, began at length to labour and to beat with vehemence beyond its nature; "the foundations of the great deep were broken up"; the red streams rushed forth so copious and fierce as to overflow the veins, and bursting through the pores, they stood in a thick dew over His whole skin; then forming into drops, they rolled down full and heavy, and drenched the ground.

"My soul is sorrowful even unto death," He said. It has been said of that dreadful pestilence which now is upon us, that it begins with death; by which is meant that it has no stage or crisis, that hope is over when it comes, and that what looks like its course is but the death agony and the process of dissolution; and thus our Atoning Sacrifice, in a much higher sense, began with this passion of woe, and only did not die, because at His Omnipotent will His Heart did not break, nor Soul separate from Body, till He had suffered on the cross.

No; He has not yet exhausted that full chalice, from which at first His natural infirmity shrank. The seizure and the arraignment, and the buffeting, and the prison, and the trial, and the mocking, and the passing to and fro, and the scourging, and the crown of thorns, and the slow march to Calvary, and the crucifixion, these are all to come. A night and a day, hour after hour, is slowly to run out before the end comes, and the satisfaction is completed.

And then, when the appointed moment arrived, and He gave the word, as His passion had begun with His soul, with the soul did it end. He did not die of bodily exhaustion, or of bodily pain; at His will His tormented Heart broke, and He commended His Spirit to the Father.

"O Heart of Jesus, all Love, I offer Thee these humble prayers for myself, and for all those who unite themselves with me in Spirit to adore Thee. O holiest Heart of Jesus most lovely, I intend to renew and to offer to Thee these acts of adoration and these prayers, for myself a wretched sinner, and for all those who are associated with me in Thy adoration, through all moments while I breathe, even to the end of my life. I recommend to Thee, O my Jesus, Holy Church, Thy dear spouse and our true Mother, all just souls and all poor sinners, the afflicted, the dying, and all mankind. Let not Thy Blood be shed for them in vain. Finally, deign to apply it in relief of the souls in Purgatory, of those in particular who have practised in the course of their life this holy devotion of adoring Thee."

Sermons Preached on Various Occasions

SERMON II

The Religion of the Pharisee, the Religion of Mankind

(PREACHED IN THE UNIVERSITY CHURCH, DUBLIN)

Evang. sec. Luc., c. xviii. v. 13.

Deus, propitius esto mihi peccatori. O God, be merciful to me, a sinner.

These words set before us what may be called the characteristic mark of the Christian Religion, as contrasted with the various forms of worship and schools of belief, which in early or in later times have spread over the earth. They are a confession of sin and a prayer for mercy. Not indeed that the notion of transgression and of forgiveness was introduced by Christianity, and is unknown beyond its pale; on the contrary, most observable it is, the symbols of guilt and pollution, and rites of deprecation and expiation, are more or less common to them all; but what is peculiar to our divine faith, as to Judaism before it, is this, that confession of sin enters into the idea of its highest saintliness, and that its pattern worshipers and the very heroes of its history are only, and can only be, and cherish in their hearts the everlasting memory that they are, and carry with them into heaven the rapturous avowal of their being, redeemed, restored transgressors. Such an avowal is not simply wrung from the lips of the neophyte, or of the lapsed; it is not the cry of the common run of men alone, who are buffeting with the surge of temptation in the wide world; it is the hymn of Saints, it is the triumphant ode sounding from the heavenly harps of the Blessed before the Throne, who sing to their Divine Redeemer, "Thou wast slain, and hast redeemed us to God in Thy blood, out of every tribe, and tongue, and people, and nation."

SERMONS PREACHED ON VARIOUS OCCASIONS

And what is to the Saints above a theme of never-ending thankfulness, is, while they are yet on earth, the matter of their perpetual humiliation. Whatever be their advance in the spiritual life, they never rise from their knees, they never cease to beat their breasts, as if sin could possibly be strange to them while they were in the flesh. Even our Lord Himself, the very Son of God in human nature, and infinitely separate from sin,—even His Immaculate Mother, encompassed by His grace from the first beginnings of her existence, and without any part of the original stain,—even they, as descended from Adam, were subjected at least to death, the direct, emphatic punishment of sin. And much more, even the most favoured of that glorious company, whom He has washed clean in His Blood; they never forget what they were by birth; they confess, one and all, that they are children of Adam, and of the same nature as their brethren, and compassed with infirmities while in the flesh, whatever may be the grace given them and their own improvement of it. Others may look up to them, but they ever look up to God; others may speak of their merits, but they only speak of their defects. The young and unspotted, the aged and most mature, he who has sinned least, he who has repented most, the fresh innocent brow, and the hoary head, they unite in this one litany, "O God, be merciful to me, a sinner." So it was with St. Aloysius; so, on the other hand, was it with St. Ignatius; so was it with St. Rose, the youngest of the saints, who, as a child, submitted her tender frame to the most amazing penances; so was it with St. Philip Neri, one of the most aged, who, when some one praised him, cried out, "Begone! I am a devil, and not a saint"; and when going to communicate, would protest before his Lord, that he "was good for nothing, but to do evil." Such utter self-prostration, I say, is the very badge and token of the servant of Christ;—and this indeed is conveyed in His own words, when He says, "I am not come to call the just, but sinners"; and it is solemnly recognized and inculcated by Him, in the words which follow the text, "Every one that exalteth himself, shall be humbled, and he that humbleth himself, shall be exalted."

This, you see, my brethren, is very different from that merely general acknowledgment of human guilt, and of the need of expiation, contained in those old and popular religions, which have before now occupied, or still occupy, the world. In them, guilt is an attribute of individuals, or of particular places, or of particular acts of nations, of bodies politic or their rulers, for whom, in consequence, purification is necessary. Or it is the purification of the worshiper, not so much personal as ritual, before he makes his offering, and an act of introduction to his religious service. All such practices indeed are remnants of true religion, and tokens and witnesses of it, useful both in themselves and in their import; but they do not rise to the explicitness and the fulness of the Christian doctrine. "There is not any man just." "All have sinned, and do need the glory of God." "Not by the works of justice, which we have done, but according to His mercy." The disciples of other worships and other philosophies thought and think, that the many indeed are bad, but the few are good. As their thoughts passed on from the ignorant and erring multitude to the select specimens of mankind, they left the notion of guilt behind, and they pictured for themselves an idea of truth and wisdom, perfect, indefectible, and self-sufficient. It was a sort of virtue without imperfection, which took pleasure in contemplating itself, which needed nothing, and which was, from its own internal excellence, sure of a reward. Their descriptions, their stories of good and religious men, are often beautiful, and admit of an instructive interpretation; but in themselves they have this great blot, that they make no mention of sin, and that they speak as if shame and humiliation were no properties of the virtuous. I will remind you, my brethren, of a very beautiful story, which you have read in a writer of antiquity; and the more beautiful it is, the more it is fitted for my present purpose, for the defect in it will come out the more strongly by the very contrast, viz., the defect that, though in some sense it teaches piety, humility it does not teach. I say, when the Psalmist would describe the happy man, he says, "Blessed are they whose iniquities are forgiven, and whose sins are covered; blessed is the man to whom the Lord hath not imputed sin." Such is the blessedness of the Gospel; but what is the blessedness of the religions of the world? A celebrated Greek sage once paid a visit to a prosperous king of Lydia, who, after showing him all his greatness and his glory, asked him whom he considered to have the happiest lot, of all men whom he had known. On this, the philosopher, passing by the monarch himself, named a countryman of his own, as fulfilling his typical idea of human perfection. The most blessed of men, he said, was Tellus of Athens, for he lived in a flourishing city, and was prospered in his children, and in their families; and then at length when war ensued with a border state, he took his place in the battle, repelled the enemy, and died gloriously, being buried at the public expense where he fell, and receiving public honours. When the king asked who came next to him in Solon's judgment, the sage went on to name two brothers, conquerors at the games, who, when the oxen were not forthcoming, drew their mother, who was priestess, to the temple, to the great admiration of the assembled multitude; and who, on her praying for them the best of possible rewards, after sacrificing and feasting, lay down to sleep in the temple, and never rose again. No one can deny the beauty of these pictures; but it is for that reason I select them; they are the pictures of men who were not supposed to have any grave account to settle with heaven, who had easy duties, as they thought, and who fulfilled them.

Now perhaps you will ask me, my brethren, whether this heathen idea of religion be not really higher than that which I have called pre-eminently Christian; for surely to obey in simple tranquility and unsolicitous confidence, is the noblest conceivable state of the creature, and the most acceptable worship he can pay to the Creator. Doubtless it is the noblest and most acceptable worship; such has ever been the worship of the Angels; such is the worship now of the spirits of the just made perfect; such will be the worship of the whole company of the glorified after the general resurrection. But we are engaged in considering the actual state of man, as found in this world; and I say, considering what he is, any standard of duty, which does not convict him of real and multiplied sins, and of incapacity to please God of his own strength, is untrue; and any rule of life, which leaves him contented with himself, without fear, without anxiety, without humiliation, is deceptive; it is the blind leading the blind; yet such, in one shape or other, is the religion of the whole earth, beyond the pale of the Church.

The natural conscience of man, if cultivated from within, if enlightened by those external aids which in varying degrees are given him in every place and time, would teach him much of his duty to God and man, and would lead him on, by the guidance both of providence and grace, into the fulness of religious knowledge; but, generally speaking, he is contented that it should tell him very little, and he makes no efforts to gain any juster views than he has at first, of his relations to the world around him and to his Creator. Thus he apprehends part, and part only, of the moral law; has scarcely any idea at all of sanctity; and, instead of tracing actions to their source, which is the motive, and judging them thereby, he measures them for the most part by their effects and their outward aspect. Such is the way with the multitude of men everywhere and at all times; they do not see the Image of Almighty God before them, and ask themselves what He wishes: If once they did this, they would begin to see how much He requires, and they would earnestly come to Him, both to be pardoned for what they do wrong, and for the power to do better. And, for the same reason that they do not please Him, they succeed in pleasing themselves. For that contracted, defective range of duties, which falls so short of God's law, is just what they can fulfil; or rather they choose it, and keep to it, *because* they can fulfil it. Hence, they become both self-satisfied and self-sufficient;—they think they know just what they ought to do, and that they do it all; and in consequence they are very well content with themselves, and rate their merit very high, and have no fear at all of any future scrutiny into their conduct, which may befall them, though their religion mainly lies in certain outward observances, and not a great number even of them.

So it was with the Pharisee in this day's Gospel. He looked upon himself with great complacency, for the very reason that the standard was so low, and the range so narrow, which he assigned to his duties towards God and man. He used, or misused, the traditions in which he had been brought up, to the purpose of persuading himself that perfection lay in merely answering the demands of society. He professed, indeed, to pay thanks to God, but he hardly apprehended the existence of any direct duties on his part towards his Maker. He thought he did all that God required, if he satisfied public opinion. To be religious, in the Pharisee's sense, was to keep the peace towards others, to take his share in the burdens of the poor, to abstain from gross vice, and to set a good example. His alms and fastings were not done in penance, but because the world asked for them; penance would have implied the consciousness of sin; whereas it was only Publicans, and such as they, who had anything to be forgiven. And these indeed were the outcasts of society, and despicable; but no account lay against men of well-regulated minds such as his: men who were well-behaved, decorous, consistent, and respectable. He thanked God he was a Pharisee, and not a penitent.

Such was the Jew in our Lord's day; and such the heathen was, and had been. Alas! I do not mean to affirm that it was common for the poor heathen to observe even any religious rule at all; but I am speaking of the few and of the better sort: and these, I say, commonly took up with a religion like the Pharisee's, more beautiful perhaps and more poetical, but not at all deeper or truer than his. They did not indeed fast, or give alms, or observe the ordinances of Judaism; they threw over their meagre observances a philosophical garb, and embellished them with the refinements of a cultivated intellect; still their notion of moral and religious duty was as shallow as that of the Pharisee, and the sense of sin, the habit of self-abasement, and the desire of contrition, just as absent from their minds as from his. They framed a code of morals which they could without trouble obey; and then they were content with it and with themselves. Virtue, according to Xenophon, one of the best principled and most religious of their writers, and one who had seen a great deal of the world, and had the opportunity of bringing together in one the highest thoughts of many schools and countries,—virtue, according to him, consists mainly in command of the appetites and passions, and in serving others in order that they may serve us. He says, in the well-known Fable, called the choice of Hercules, that vice has no real enjoyment even of those pleasures which it aims at; that it eats before it is hungry, and drinks before it is thirsty, and slumbers before it is wearied. It never hears, he says, that sweetest of voices, its own praise; it never sees that greatest luxury among sights, its own good deeds. It enfeebles the bodily frame of the young, and the intellect of the old. Virtue, on the other hand, rewards young men with the praise of their elders, and it rewards the aged with the reverence of youth; it supplies them pleasant memories and present peace; it secures the favour of heaven, the love of friends, a country's thanks, and, when death comes, an everlasting renown. In all such descriptions, virtue is something external; it is not concerned with motives or intentions; it is occupied in deeds which bear upon society, and which gain the praise of men; it has little to do with conscience and the Lord of conscience; and knows nothing of shame, humiliation, and penance. It is in substance the Pharisee's religion, though it be more graceful and more interesting.

Now this age is as removed in distance, as in character, from that of the Greek philosopher; yet who will say that the religion which it acts upon is very different from the religion of the heathen? Of course I understand well, that it might know, and that it will say, a great many things foreign and contrary to heathenism. I am well aware that the theology of this age is very different from what it was two thousand years ago. I know men profess a great deal, and boast that they are Christians, and speak of Christianity as being a religion of the heart; but, when we put aside words and professions, and try to discover what their religion is, we shall find, I fear, that the great mass of men in fact get rid of all religion that is inward; that they lay no stress on acts of faith, hope, and charity, on simplicity of intention, purity of motive, or mortification of the thoughts; that they confine themselves to two or three virtues, superficially practised; that they know not the words contrition, penance, and pardon; and that they think and argue that, after all, if a man does his duty in the world, according to his vocation, he cannot fail to go to heaven, however little he may do besides, nay, however much, in other matters, he may do that is undeniably unlawful. Thus a soldier's duty is loyalty, obedience, and valour, and he may let other matters take their chance; a trader's duty is honesty; an artisan's duty is industry and contentment; of a gentleman are required veracity, courteousness, and self-respect; of a public man, high-principled ambition; of a woman, the domestic virtues; of a minister of religion, decorum, benevolence, and some activity. Now, all these are instances of mere Pharisaical excellence; because there is no apprehension of Almighty God, no insight into His claims on us, no sense of the creature's shortcomings, no self-condemnation, confession, and deprecation, nothing of those deep and sacred feelings which ever characterize the religion of a Christian, and more and more, not less and less, as he mounts up from mere ordinary obedience to the perfection of a saint.

And such, I say, is the religion of the natural man in every age and place;—often very beautiful on the surface, but worthless in God's sight; good, as far as it goes, but worthless and hopeless, because it does not go further, because it is based on self-sufficiency, and results in self-satisfaction. I grant, it may be beautiful to look at, as in the instance of the young ruler whom our Lord looked at and loved, yet sent away sad; it may have all the delicacy, the amiableness, the tenderness, the religious sentiment, the kindness, which is actually seen in many a father of a family, many a mother, many a daughter, in the length and breadth of these kingdoms, in a refined and polished age like this; but still it is rejected by the heart-searching God, because all such persons walk by their own light, not by the True Light of men, because self is their supreme teacher, and because they pace round and round in the small circle of their own thoughts and of their own judgments, careless to know what God says to them, and fearless of being condemned by Him, if only they stand approved in their own sight. And thus they incur the force of those terrible words, spoken not to a Jewish Ruler, nor to a heathen philosopher, but to a fallen Christian community, to the Christian Pharisees of Laodicea,—"Because thou sayest I am rich, and made wealthy, and have need of nothing; and knowest not that thou art wretched, and miserable, and poor, and blind, and naked; I counsel thee to buy of Me gold fire-tried, that thou mayest be made rich, and be clothed in white garments, that thy shame may not appear, and anoint thine eyes with eye-salve, that thou mayest see. Such as I love, I rebuke and chastise; be zealous, therefore, and do penance."

Yes, my brethren, it is the ignorance of our understanding, it is our spiritual blindness, it is our banishment from the presence of Him who is the source and the standard of all Truth, which is the cause of this meagre, heartless religion of which men are commonly so proud. Had we any proper insight into things as they are, had we any real apprehension of God as He is, of ourselves as we are, we should never dare to serve Him without fear, or to rejoice unto Him without trembling. And it is the removal of this veil which is spread between our eyes and heaven, it is the pouring in upon the soul of the illuminating grace of the New Covenant, which makes the religion of the Christian so different from that of the various human rites and philosophies, which are spread over the earth. The Catholic Saints alone confess sin, because the Catholic Saints alone see God. That awful Creator Spirit, of whom the Epistle of this day speaks so much, He it is who brings into religion the true devotion, the true worship, and changes the self-satisfied Pharisee into the broken-hearted, self-abased Publican. It is the sight of God, revealed to the eye of faith, that makes us hideous to ourselves, from the contrast which we find ourselves to present to that great God at whom we look. It is the vision of Him in His infinite gloriousness, the All-holy, the All-beautiful, the All-perfect, which makes us sink into the earth with self-contempt and self-abhorrence. We are contented with ourselves till we contemplate Him. Why is it, I say, that the moral code of the world is so precise and well-defined? Why is the worship of reason so calm? Why was the religion of classic heathenism so joyous? Why is the framework of civilized society all so graceful and so correct? Why, on the other hand, is there so much of emotion, so much of conflicting and alternating feeling, so much that is high, so much that is abased, in the devotion of Christianity? It is because the Christian, and the Christian alone, has a revelation of God; it is because he has upon his mind, in his heart, on his conscience, the idea of one who is Self-dependent, who is from Everlasting, who is Incommunicable. He knows that One alone is holy, and that His own creatures are so frail in comparison of Him, that they would dwindle and melt away in His presence, did He not uphold them by His power. He knows that there is One whose greatness and whose blessedness are not affected, the centre of whose stability is not moved, by the presence or the absence of the whole creation with its innumerable beings and portions; whom nothing can touch, nothing can increase or diminish; who was as mighty before He made the worlds as since, and as serene and blissful since He made them as before. he knows that there is just One Being, in whose hand lies his own happiness, his own sanctity, his own life, and hope, and salvation. He knows that there is One to whom he owes every thing, and against whom he can have no plea or remedy. All things are nothing before Him; the highest beings do but worship Him the more; the holiest beings are such, only because they have a greater portion of Him.

Ah! what has he to pride in now, when he looks back upon himself? Where has fled all that comeliness which heretofore he thought embellished him? What is he but some vile reptile, which ought to shrink aside out of the light of day? This was the feeling of St. Peter, when he first gained a glimpse of the greatness of his Master, and cried out, almost beside himself, "Depart from me, for I am a sinful man, O Lord!" It was the feeling of holy Job, though he had served God for so many years, and had been so perfected in virtue, when the Almighty answered him from the whirlwind: "With the hearing of the ear I have heard Thee," he said; "but now my eye seeth Thee; therefore I reprove myself, and do penance in dust and ashes." So was it with Isaias, when he saw the vision of the Seraphim, and said, "Woe is me . . . I am a man of unclean lips, and I dwell in the midst of a people that hath unclean lips, and I have seen with my eyes the King, the Lord of Hosts." So was it with Daniel, when, even at the sight of an Angel, sent from God, "there remained no strength in him, but the appearance of his countenance was changed in him, and he fainted away, and retained no strength." This then, my brethren, is the reason why every son of man, whatever be his degree of holiness, whether a returning prodigal or a matured saint, says with the Publican, "O God, be merciful to me"; it is because created natures, high and low, are all on a level in the sight and in comparison of the Creator, and so all of them have one speech, and one only, whether it be the thief on the cross, Magdalen at the feast, or St. Paul before his martyrdom:—not that one of them may not have, what another has not, but that one and all have nothing but what comes from Him, and are as nothing before Him, who is all in all.

For us, my dear brethren, whose duties lie in this seat of learning and science, may we never be carried away by any undue fondness for any human branch of study, so as to be forgetful that our true wisdom, and nobility, and strength, consist in the knowledge of Almighty God. Nature and man are our studies, but God is higher than all. It is easy to lose Him in His works. It is easy to become over-attached to our own pursuit, to substitute it for religion, and to make it the fuel of pride. Our secular attainments will avail us nothing, if they be not subordinate to religion. The knowledge of the sun, moon, and stars, of the earth and its three kingdoms, of the classics, or of history, will never bring us to heaven. We may "thank God," that we are not as the illiterate and the dull; and those whom we despise, if they do but know how to ask mercy of Him, know what is very much more to the purpose of getting to heaven, than all our letters and all our science. Let this be the spirit in which we end our session. Let us thank Him for all that He has done for us, for what He is doing by us; but let nothing that we know or that we can do, keep us from a personal, individual adoption of the great Apostle's words, "Christ Jesus came into this world to save sinners, of whom I am the chief."

Select Bibliography

1. PRIMARY SOURCES

Newman collected his works in a uniform edition of 36 vols. (1868–1881). Until his death in 1890 he continued making minor textual changes in reprints of individual volumes in this edition, of which all the volumes from 1886 were published by Longmans, Green, and Co. of London. This edition includes *Parochial and Plain Sermons* (8 vols., 1868), *Sermons Bearing on Subjects of the Day* (1869), *Sermons Preached on Various Occasions* (1870), and *Discourses Addressed to Mixed Congregations* (1871). A number of other writings important for Newman's spirituality have been published posthumously:

Meditations and Devotions of the Late Cardinal Newman. London and New York: Longmans, Green, 1893.
Sermon Notes of John Henry Cardinal Newman, 1849–1878. Edited by Fathers of the Birmingham Oratory. London: Longmans, Green, 1914.
John Henry Newman: Autobiographical Writings. Edited by Henry Tristram. London and New York: Sheed and Ward, 1956.
Catholic Sermons of Cardinal Newman. Edited at the Birmingham Oratory. London: Burns and Oates, 1957. Also published as *Faith and Prejudice and Other Unpublished Sermons of Cardinal Newman.* New York: Sheed and Ward, 1956.
The Letters and Diaries of John Henry Newman. Edited by Charles Stephen Dessain et al. Vols. i–vi, Oxford: Clarendon Press, 1978–1984; xi–xxii, London: Nelson, 1961–1972; xxiii–xxxi, Oxford: Clarendon Press, 1973–1977.
Newman the Oratorian: His Unpublished Oratory Papers. Edited by Placid Murray, OSB. Dublin: Gill and Macmillan, 1969.

SELECT BIBLIOGRAPHY

John Henry Newman: Sermons 1824–1843, vol. 1. Edited by Placid Murray, OSB. Oxford: Clarendon Press, 1991.

2. SECONDARY SOURCES

Biemer, Günter, and Fries, Heinrich, eds. *Internationale Cardinal-Newman-Studien*, Vol. 12. *Christliche Heiligkeit als Lehre und Praxis nach John Henry Newman/Newman's Teaching on Christian Holiness*. Sigmaringendorf: Verlag Glock and Lutz, 1988.

Blehl, Vincent Ferrer, S. J. "Divine Call and Human Response: John Henry Newman on Prayer," *The Way*, Oct. 1982, pp. 297–306.

Bouyer, Louis. *Newman: His Life and Spirituality*. London: Burns and Oates, 1958.

———. *Newman's Vision of Faith*. San Francisco: Ignatius Press, 1986.

Boyce, Philip. *Spiritual Exodus of John Henry Newman and Thérèse of Lisieux*. Dublin and Manchester: Carmelite Centre of Spirituality/Koinonia, 1979.

Davies, Horton. *Worship and Theology in England: From Newman to Martineau, 1850–1900*. Princeton: Princeton University Press, 1962.

Dessain, Charles Stephen. *John Henry Newman*. London: A. and C. Black, 1966.

———. *The Spirituality of John Henry Newman*. Minneapolis: Winston Press, 1977. Also published as *Newman's Spiritual Themes*. Dublin: Veritas Publications, 1977.

———. "Newman's Spirituality: Its Value Today." In Charles Davis, ed., *English Spiritual Writings*. London: Burns and Oates, 1961. Reprinted from *The Clergy Review* 45 (May 1960): 257–82.

Graef, Hilda. *God and Myself: The Spirituality of John Henry Newman*. London: P. Davies, 1967.

Griffiths, Eric. "Newman: The Foolishness of Preaching." In Ian Ker and Alan G. Hall, eds., *Newman after a Hundred Years*. Oxford: Clarendon Press, 1990, pp. 63–91.

Ker, Ian. *John Henry Newman: A Biography*. Oxford: Clarendon Press, 1988.

———. *The Achievement of John Henry Newman*. Notre Dame: University of Notre Dame Press, 1990; London: Collins, 1990.

———. *Newman on Being a Christian*. Notre Dame: University of Notre Dame Press, 1990.

SELECT BIBLIOGRAPHY

Lamm, William R. *The Spiritual Legacy of Newman.* Milwaukee: The Bruce Publishing Company, 1934.

Reidy, James. "Newman and Christian Humanism," *Renascence* 44 (Summer 1992): 249–64.

Rowell, Geoffrey. "The Roots of Newman's Scriptural Holiness: Some Formative Influences on Newman's Spirituality." In Heinrich Fries and Werner Becker, eds., *Newman Studien* 10, pp. 13–20. Heroldsberg, Nürnberg: Glock and Lutz, 1978.

Tristram, Henry. "With Newman at Prayer." In *John Henry Newman: Centenary Essays.* London: Burns, Oates and Washbourne, 1945.

White, W. D., ed. *The Preaching of John Henry Newman.* Philadelphia: Fortress Press, 1969.

Index to Foreword, Preface, and Introduction

Arianism, 39
Athanasius, Saint, 7, 28, 39
Atonement, 29, 39
Augustine, Saint, 28
Authorized Version, 11, 12

Balaam, 10, 42
Bramhall, John, 4
Bull, George, 7
Bunyan, John, 7

Christianity, real, 14–16, 17
Church Fathers, 1, 7, 28–41
Consistency, 51–52
Cosin, John, 7

Dessain, Charles Stephen, 55

Eliot, George, 13–14, 21

Faber, F. W., 5
Faith: and obedience, 51; and works, 16–20
Froude, Hurrell, 3
Froude, James Anthony, 12–13

Greek Orthodoxy, 7

Habits, 23–24, 43, 47, 48
Holiness, 48–49

Holy Spirit: indwelling of, 34–37, 49; and redemption, 32–33; work of, 16–17

Imitation of Christ, 8n
Incarnation, 28–30
Introspection, 20–26

John of the Cross, Saint, 8n
John Paul II, 6
Justification, by faith, 5, 17, 20, 21, 27, 36–37

Keble, John, 3, 5
Ker, Ian, 7

Liguori, Alfonso, 8n

Manning, H. E., 5
Mayers, Walter, 28
Milner, Joseph, 28
Mystery, 39–41

Newman, John Henry: *Apologia*, 5; *Arians of the Fourth Century, The*, 28; *Callista*, 1, 38; "On Consulting the Faithful in Matters of Faith," 6; *Discourses Addressed to Mixed Congregations*, 1;

INDEX TO PREFACES

Dream of Gerontius, The, 1; *Essay in Aid of a Grammar of Assent, An*, 15; *Essay on the Development of Christian Doctrine*, 28; influence of the Greek Fathers on, 28–41; *Lectures on Justification*, 3; *Letter to the Duke of Norfolk*, 6; *Meditations and Devotions*, 1; *Parochial and Plain Sermons*, 1, 10, 16, 28, 45; *Prophetical Office of the Church, The*, 3; reaction against evangelicalism, 13–28; scriptural background of, 9–13; spirituality of, 41–52

Obedience, 18, 22, 45–52
Oriel College, Oxford, 3, 28
Oxford Movement, 4, 28

Papal infallibility, doctrine of, 6
Pentecost, and the resurrection, 32–34
Pilgrim's Progress, 7
Prayer, 7, 46
Private Devotions, 7
Prodigal Son, 10
Pusey, E. B., 3

Realism, 41–45

Religion: and emotion, 18–20; of the world, 26–28
Repentance, 17, 44
Resurrection: and the crucifixion, 33; and the incarnation, 31; and Pentecost, 32–34
Routh, M. J., 7

Sacraments, 5, 38–39
Scotus, Duns, 29
Self-deception, 24–26, 42
Self-denial, 18
Sin, 41, 43

Taylor, Jeremy, 4
Thirty-Nine Articles (1571), 3, 4: subjects not covered in, 8
Thomas à Kempis, 8n
Thomas Aquinas, Saint, 28, 29
Thorndike, Herbert, 4
Tractarian Movement. *See* Oxford Movement
Tracts for the Times, 3

Ullathorne, Bishop, 6

Vatican Council I, 6

Whately, Richard, 3
Wiseman, Cardinal, 5
Works, and faith, 16–20

Index to Texts

Abraham, 80, 180–81, 343, 351
Accomplishments in the arts and literature, danger of, 152–58
Acts, 1:14, 370; 2:1, 370; 2:12–13, 220; 2:46, 370; 3:1, 370; 4:28, 258; 4:32–35, 371; 7:53, 147; 9:4, 252; 9:26–27, 137; 9:40, 177; 10:1–3, 370; 10:35, 221; 11:24, 136; 13:2–3, 177; 13:48, 220; 15:37–38, 138; 16:25, 370; 17:32–34, 220; 18:10, 287; 21:5, 370; 23:1, 317; 24:16, 317; 24:25, 348
Adam, 131, 308, 309–10, 313
Ahab, 233
Aloysius, Saint, 396
Ananias, 376
Angels, work in nature, 146–51
Anna, 136, 349
Apollos, 136

Balaam, 105, 197–208, 264–65, 296, 310
Balak, 199, 200
Barnabas, 80, 137–39, 174, 220
Bezaleel, 128, 153

Cain, 310
Caiphas, 296
Christianity, real, 304, 306–8, 367–77

1 Chronicles, 21:16, 150
2 Chronicles, 30:18–19, 100
Church: as the Body of Christ, 251–52; visible, 219–29
Colossians, 1:3, 177; 1:10, 298; 1:24, 166, 273; 1:27, 294; 3:2–4, 369; 3:3, 234; 3:4, 273; 3:22, 187; 3:24, 187; 4:2, 176
Communion with God, moral effects of, 237–44
Consistency, 109
1 Corinthians, 1:7, 273; 1:30–31, 287; 3:13, 81; 4:4, 90; 4:7, 290–91; 4:11–13, 374; 6:11, 294; 6:19, 129; 6:19–20, 130; 7:22–23, 187; 7:29, 372; 8:5, 61; 9:21, 187–88, 215; 9:22, 220; 9:24, 367; 9:27, 90, 93; 13:2, 263; 13:12, 281; 14:3, 177; 16:13, 158, 271; 16:22, 114
2 Corinthians, 1:7, 90; 1:12, 317; 1:22, 129, 318; 4:6, 314; 4:10, 90, 167, 273; 4:17, 168; 5:5, 129; 5:10, 281; 5:16–17, 372; 5:17, 130; 6:6, 306; 6:16, 129; 7:1, 285; 7:7, 319; 7:9, 319; 7:11, 319; 8:9, 322, 340; 8:12, 302, 304; 10:5, 133, 188; 11:24–27, 219–20; 11:27, 82; 13:5, 294
Cornelius, 178, 349, 370

INDEX TO TEXTS

Custom, 83–84

Daniel, 180, 182, 284, 299, 340, 403
Daniel, Book of, 10:2–14, 182; 10:8, 284
David, 79–80, 149–50, 299, 310, 340, 343
Death, 331–33
Demas, 343–44
Deuteronomy, 4:24, 116; 28:65, 212

Ecclesiastes, 2:16, 233; 3:19, 332; 9:3, 290; 9:10, 330
Eli, 266
Elijah, 162, 179, 340
Enoch, 238
Ephesians, 1:14, 129; 1:16, 177; 2:2, 358; 4:22, 188; 4:26, 341; 5:9, 294; 5:13, 308; 5:14, 314; 5:14–17, 65; 6:10–13, 271; 6:18, 176
Eve, 300, 359
Exodus, 19:10–12, 285; 19:16–18, 147; 20:12, 182; 28:3, 153; 31:2–5, 153; 31:3–4, 128; 31:6, 152; 33:20, 257; 34:8, 257; 35:5–10, 153
Ezekiel, 18:20, 160; 33:30–32, 158

Faith: and love, 263–69, 305–6; and works, 91, 106–7, 123; and the world, 357–66
Faults, secret, 77–85
Fear, of God, 117–18
Felix, 348

Galatians, 1:4, 222, 358; 1:24, 223; 2:12–13, 138; 3:1, 217; 3:19, 147; 4:6, 129, 316; 5:7, 367; 5:17, 296; 6:14, 372; 6:17, 90
Genesis, 6:3, 128; 6:5–6, 290; 6:11, 289–90; 11:6–8, 290; 15:6, 181; 18:17–19, 180; 19:13, 147; 28:11–17, 256; 28:17, 216; 32:30, 256; 42:36, 257; 47:9, 230
Gideon, 256
God, contemplation of, 313–21
Grace, state of, 209–18

Habits, 83, 98–99, 211–12, 298
Hagar, 108
Hebrews, 2:1, 163, 275; 4:12–13, 306; 4:13, 316; 4:15, 172; 8:10, 266; 10:22, 95; 11, 263–64; 11:6, 161; 12:2, 120, 329; 12:11, 169; 12:28–29, 110; 13:14, 369
Herod, 348
Hezekiah, 80, 100, 310
Holiness, and religion, 266–67
Holy Seasons, 285
Holy Spirit, 251: as Comforter, 138, 254; giving glory to God, 254–55; indwelling of, 127–35; in sanctification, 292–94; witness of, 317–18
Hypocrisy, and sincerity, 304–12

Ignatius, Saint, 396
Ignorance, as sin, 95–102
Immortality, 61–68, 234–36
Incarnation, 133, 245–47, 248–49
Infirmity, sins of, 296–303
Intercession. *See* Prayer, as intercession

411

INDEX TO TEXTS

Introspection, 77–85, 120–26
Isaiah, 403
Isaiah, Book of, 1:4, 348; 3:16, 158; 26:3, 134, 241; 26:3–4, 68; 26:11, 207; 33:17, 279; 37:14, 310; 40:8, 84; 40:31, 196; 43:2, 168; 51:12–13, 165; 51:15–16, 165; 53:2, 245; 56:4–5, 145; 63:10, 128; 64:6, 105, 290

Jacob, 216, 230, 256, 257, 345
James, the apostle, 137, 167, 174, 387, 389
James, Book of, 2:8, 263; 2:10, 192; 2:14, 85; 2:26, 106; 3:17, 306; 4:4, 358; 5:13, 237; 5:16, 179
Jeremiah, 17:9, 290; 23:21, 367; 31:14, 314; 31:25, 314; 33:3, 226, 352; 35:18–19, 182
Jeroboam, 310
Jesus Christ: as hidden from the world, 245–53; as manifested in remembrance, 254–62; passion of, 381–91; privations of, 322–29; return of, 244, 270; sufferings of, 166–67, 171–72, 322–29
Job, 179–80, 328, 403
Job, Book of, 19:26–27, 281
John, the apostle, 136, 137, 142–43, 167, 174, 250, 328, 387, 389
John, the Baptist, 89, 136, 309, 343, 352, 368
John, Book of, 1:5, 245; 1:12, 130; 3:7, 290; 3:16, 340; 3:21, 308; 4:14, 131, 314; 5:4, 147; 5:35, 89; 7:38–39, 131; 9:31, 178; 11:8, 171; 12:16, 256; 12:27, 328; 13:7, 256; 13:14, 374; 13:17, 69; 13:27, 171; 14:9, 245; 14:23, 132, 316; 14:27, 374; 15:5, 290; 15:7–15, 179; 16:7, 129; 16:14, 254; 17:9, 222; 18:2, 171; 18:4–5, 171; 20:22, 129; 21:9, 326
1 John, 1:3, 132; 1:5–9, 307; 2:8, 307; 2:15, 358, 372; 2:17, 84; 2:20–21, 242; 2:27, 242; 2:28, 91; 3:1, 243; 3:2, 243, 281; 3:9, 242; 3:14, 263; 3:20, 316; 3:20–21, 307; 3:21, 90; 3:22, 179; 3:24, 307–8; 4:4, 130; 4:7, 264; 4:16, 264; 5:3, 266; 5:10, 308
3 John 1, 143
John Mark, 137
Jonah, 117
Joseph, 257–58
Josiah, 202, 233
Judas Iscariot, 70, 326, 386
Judges, 6:22, 256; 13:20, 256; 13:22, 256
Judgment, of God, 74, 81, 116, 144–45, 280–81, 365
Justification, by faith, 121, 181, 209–18

2 Kings, 19:35, 147; 20:12–19, 80
Knowledge, of God's will, 69–76

Lamentations, 1:12, 329
Law, Old Testament, importance to Christians of, 96–97
Law of Christ, strictness of, 186–96

INDEX TO TEXTS

Lazarus, 327
Leviticus, 5, 97; 5:2, 97; 5:6, 97; 14:1–32, 97
Life, human, 230–36
Literature, reading of, 154–58
Lord's Prayer, 73, 132
Lot, 84
Love, and faith, 263–69, 305–6
Luke, the apostle, 136, 152
Luke, Book of, 2:35, 167; 5:8, 283; 6:23, 373–74; 8:3, 327; 8:13, 265; 9:23, 91, 339; 9:51, 171; 9:58, 325; 12:15–20, 371–72; 12:33–35, 372; 12:37–38, 278; 12:39, 270–71; 13:24, 115, 339; 14:18–20, 371; 14:26, 339; 14:26–27, 91; 14:27, 167; 15:29, 159; 16:13, 308; 16:19, 371; 16:25, 374; 17:27–29, 338, 371; 18:8, 290; 21:19, 374; 21:28, 281; 21:36, 271; 22:15, 328; 22:44, 328; 22:53, 328; 23:42, 335; 24:32, 256; 24:53, 370

Malachi, 3:18, 312
Manoah, 256
Mark, 3:21, 246; 6:31, 326; 8:34, 91; 9:29, 182; 9:43–47, 91; 10:21, 192–93; 10:23, 372; 10:24, 192–93; 13:33, 270; 13:35–37, 271, 369; 14:37, 271
Martha, 136, 326
Mary, the Blessed Virgin, 136, 167, 246, 250
Mary, sister of Lazarus, 136
Mary, wife of Cleophas, 136
Mary Magdalene, 136

Matthew, the apostle, 65, 136
Matthew, Book of, 3:6, 89; 5:3–10, 374; 5:19–20, 192; 5:37, 374; 6:22–23, 370; 6:31, 372; 6:33, 227; 6:34, 318; 7:1, 374; 7:3, 374; 7:14, 115, 339; 10:9–10, 372–73; 10:22, 373; 10:24–25, 373; 10:37, 372; 10:41–42, 221; 12:32, 250; 12:34–35, 370; 13:43, 233; 14:3, 348; 14:30, 310; 15:19, 290; 16:26, 61; 17:2, 217; 18:5, 252; 18:8–9, 373; 19:29, 372; 20:22, 167; 20:26–27, 342; 21:25, 352; 21:28–30, 103; 22:40, 263; 23:26, 370; 24:37–39, 371; 24:42, 369; 24:44, 369; 25:5–6, 282; 25:6, 369; 25:13, 271, 369; 25:31–32, 281; 25:35–40, 252; 25:44, 113; 25:46, 115; 26:39, 328; 26:64, 281; 27:46, 329; 28:2, 147
Meditation, on Christ's sufferings, 323–25, 329
Micah, 6:8, 200
Michael, the archangel, 129–30
Mortality, 230–33: proper attitude toward, 233–35
Moses, 80, 128, 180, 257, 283, 285, 343

Naaman, 75
Nature, powers of angels in, 146–51
Nehemiah, 9:20, 128
Noah, 180
Novels, effects upon the mind of, 154–55

INDEX TO TEXTS

Numbers, 11:17, 128; 11:25, 128; 22, 199; 22:38, 197; 23, 199; 24:17, 281

Obedience, 90–91, 214–15, 277–78: aspects of, 108–9; daily, 91–92; to the law of Christ, 186–96; without love, 197–208; and knowledge of God's will, 69–76

Paul, the apostle, 80, 90, 93, 136, 137, 138, 152, 173, 174, 178, 220, 227, 243
Pelagianism, 291
Peter, the apostle, 70, 79, 133, 136, 137, 138, 174, 177–78, 182, 220, 255, 256, 300, 303, 310, 328, 387, 389, 403
1 Peter, 1:8, 324; 1:17, 209; 1:22, 306; 1:24–25, 84; 4:7, 369; 4:12–13, 167; 4:18, 81; 6:7, 271
2 Peter, 1:4, 130
Philip, the apostle, 256
Philip Neri, Saint, 396
Philippians, 1:3–4, 177; 1:13, 220; 2:12, 209; 2:13, 289; 3:9, 215; 3:10, 273; 3:20, 238, 369; 4:4, 237
Pilate, 386
Prayer, 73, 75, 95, 101, 132: definition of, 238; effects of, 238–40; as intercession, 176–85; as mark of the Christian, 369–70
Prodigal Son, 308, 312, 319
Promise, false, 103–9
Proverbs, 2:3–5, 351; 4:18, 105, 354; 4:19, 353; 11:21, 357; 16:14, 200
Providence, secret nature of, 254–62
Psalms, 1:6, 160; 11:7, 160; 14:2–3, 290; 16:8, 312; 17:1–3, 307; 18:25–27, 160; 19:1, 147; 19:12, 77; 22:14, 171; 26:2, 317; 27:4, 237; 31:5, 307; 31:24, 237; 32:10, 160; 36:8–9, 314; 37:5–6, 307; 46:4, 131; 49:2–10, 331; 51:4, 307; 63:5, 314; 63:8, 307; 69:8, 243; 73:12–13, 160; 73:14, 93; 73:24–26, 307; 73:25–26, 321; 90:8, 312; 104:4, 146; 119:1–2, 354; 119:89–91, 147–48; 123:1–2, 163; 125:4, 161; 131:2, 337; 139:1–2, 307; 139:4, 307; 139:23–24, 317

Regeneration, 130–31
Religion: contracted views in, 159–65; and emotion, 104, 106, 162–63, 165, 209–10; and holiness, 266–67; as an instrument of Satan, 110–19; of the world, 71–72, 87–88, 110–19, 140–42, 143–45, 189–92, 202, 203–4, 206–8, 213–14, 225–26, 241, 274–77, 304, 338–39, 348, 350, 395, 404
Remorse, 319–20
Repentance, 318–20
Revelation, 1:7, 281; 1:17, 283; 3:17–18, 314; 3:20, 316; 4:6, 131; 7:1, 147; 8, 147; 9, 147;

414

INDEX TO TEXTS

11:3, 173; 12:6, 173; 16, 147; 16:10-11, 169; 16:15, 126, 271; 20:12, 334; 22:4, 281; 22:11, 224
Reward, 181-82
Romans, 1:1, 187; 2:11, 160; 2:20, 62; 5:1-2, 209; 5:2, 183, 237; 5:3, 318; 5:3-4, 90; 5:3-5, 374; 5:5, 129, 318; 6:18, 186; 7:24, 298; 8:1-4, 192; 8:3-4, 215; 8:9, 127, 129; 8:10, 294; 8:11, 129; 8:15, 313; 8:16, 129, 308, 318; 8:17-28, 273; 8:19, 233; 8:29, 224; 9:1, 317; 12:2, 358, 372; 12:9, 306; 13:2, 86; 13:10, 263; 13:11-12, 271; 14:10-12, 281; 15:16, 294
Rose, Saint, 396

Sacraments, 101, 130, 217-18, 252-53, 260-61, 273, 284-85
Salvation, as a divine gift, 287-95
Samaritan woman, 136-37, 326
Samson, 348
Samuel, 180, 206, 266, 310
1 Samuel, 13:12, 310; 17:37, 79
2 Samuel, 12:7, 80; 24:14, 311; 24:15-17, 147
Sapphira, 376
Satan: lack of discernment, 258; temptations of, 98; and worldly religion, 110-19
Saul, 79, 206, 310
Self-deception, 83, 104
Self-denial, 86-94: duty of, 337-45
Self-love, 82

Simeon, 136, 349
Simon the Zealot, 136
Sin: from the devil, 300; habits of, 298; of ignorance, 300-301; original, 97-98, 291, 297-98, 313-14; of lack of self-command, 298-300; sudden, 300; from unworthy motives, 301; of weaknesses, 301
Sincerity, and hypocrisy, 304-12
Slavery, to Christ, 186-88
Solomon, 80, 344
Soul, immortality of. *See* Immortality
Stephen, the martyr, 174
Suffering: adverse effects of, 168-71; of Christ, 166-67, 171-72; partaking of Christ's, 167-68, 171, 172-75

Theology, natural, 115, 116
1 Thessalonians, 1:2, 177; 2:19, 224; 4:18, 318; 5:2-3, 281-82; 5:6, 271; 5:16-18, 237; 5:25, 177
2 Thessalonians, 3:1, 177
Thomas, the apostle, 137, 250
Time, lapse of, 330-36
Timothy, 305
1 Timothy, 1:5, 266; 2:1-2, 177; 2:8, 177
2 Timothy, 2:4, 372; 2:5, 367; 2:10, 219; 2:21, 130; 3:13, 89; 3:16, 197; 4:2-4, 158; 4:4, 346
Titus, 2:14, 222
Tolerance, of religious error, 136-45
Truth, seeking of, 346-54

INDEX TO TEXTS

Watchfulness, 75, 126, 270–78, 285–86, 369
Weakness, as sin, 95–102
Wisdom of Solomon, 5:1–5, 244
Works, and faith, 106–7, 123
World: and faith, 357–66; proper attitude toward, 235–36; separation from, 371–73
Worship, 101: as preparation for Christ's coming, 279–86

Xenophon, 399

Other Volumes in this Series

Julian of Norwich • SHOWINGS
Jacob Boehme • THE WAY TO CHRIST
Nahman of Bratslav • THE TALES
Gregory of Nyssa • THE LIFE OF MOSES
Bonaventure • THE SOUL'S JOURNEY INTO GOD, THE TREE OF LIFE, AND THE LIFE OF ST. FRANCIS
William Law • A SERIOUS CALL TO DEVOUT AND HOLY LIFE, AND THE SPIRIT OF LOVE
Abraham Isaac Kook • THE LIGHTS OF PENITENCE, LIGHTS OF HOLINESS, THE MORAL PRINCIPLES, ESSAYS, AND POEMS
Ibn 'Ata' Illah • THE BOOK OF WISDOM and Kwaja Abdullah
Ansari • INTIMATE CONVERSATIONS
Johann Arndt • TRUE CHRISTIANITY
Richard of St. Victor • THE TWELVE PATRIARCHS, THE MYSTICAL ARK, AND BOOK THREE OF THE TRINITY
Origen • AN EXHORTATION TO MARTYRDOM, PRAYER, AND SELECTED WORKS
Catherine of Genoa • PURGATION AND PURGATORY, THE SPIRITUAL DIALOGUE
Native North American Spirituality of the Eastern Woodlands • SACRED MYTHS, DREAMS, VISIONS, SPEECHES, HEALING FORMULAS, RITUALS AND CEREMONIALS
Teresa of Avila • THE INTERIOR CASTLE
Apocalyptic Spirituality • TREATISES AND LETTERS OF LACTANTIUS, ADSO OF MONTIER-EN-DER, JOACHIM OF FIORE, THE FRANCISCAN SPIRITUALS, SAVONAROLA
Athanasius • THE LIFE OF ANTONY, A LETTER TO MARCELLINUS
Catherine of Siena • THE DIALOGUE
Sharafuddin Maneri • THE HUNDRED LETTERS
Martin Luther • THEOLOGIA GERMANICA
Native Mesoamerican Spirituality • ANCIENT MYTHS, DISCOURSES, STORIES, DOCTRINES, HYMNS, POEMS FROM THE AZTEC, YUCATEC, QUICHE-MAYA AND OTHER SACRED TRADITIONS
Symeon the New Theologian • THE DISCOURSES
Ibn Al'-Arabi • THE BEZELS OF WISDOM
Hadewijch • THE COMPLETE WORKS
Philo of Alexandria • THE CONTEMPLATIVE LIFE, THE GIANTS, AND SELECTIONS
George Herbert • THE COUNTRY PARSON, THE TEMPLE
Unknown • THE CLOUD OF UNKNOWING
John and Charles Wesley • SELECTED WRITINGS AND HYMNS
Meister Eckhart • THE ESSENTIAL SERMONS, COMMENTARIES, TREATISES AND DEFENSE
Francisco de Osuna • THE THIRD SPIRITUAL ALPHABET
Jacopone da Todi • THE LAUDS
Fakhruddin Iraqi • DIVINE FLASHES

Menahem Nahum of Chernobyl • THE LIGHT OF THE EYES
Early Dominicans • SELECTED WRITINGS
John Climacus • THE LADDER OF DIVINE ASCENT
Francis and Clare • THE COMPLETE WORKS
Gregory Palamas • THE TRIADS
Pietists • SELECTED WRITINGS
The Shakers • TWO CENTURIES OF SPIRITUAL REFLECTION
Zohar • THE BOOK OF ENLIGHTENMENT
Luis de León • THE NAMES OF CHRIST
Quaker Spirituality • SELECTED WRITINGS
Emanuel Swedenborg • THE UNIVERSAL HUMAN AND SOUL-BODY INTERACTION
Augustine of Hippo • SELECTED WRITINGS
Safed Spirituality • RULES OF MYSTICAL PIETY, THE BEGINNING OF WISDOM
Maximus Confessor • SELECTED WRITINGS
John Cassian • CONFERENCES
Johannes Tauler • SERMONS
John Ruusbroec • THE SPIRITUAL ESPOUSALS AND OTHER WORKS
Ibn 'Abbād of Ronda • LETTERS ON THE SŪFĪ PATH
Angelus Silesius • THE CHERUBINIC WANDERER
The Early Kabbalah
Meister Eckhart • TEACHER AND PREACHER
John of the Cross • SELECTED WRITINGS
Pseudo-Dionysius • THE COMPLETE WORKS
Bernard of Clairvaux • SELECTED WORKS
Devotio Moderna • BASIC WRITINGS
The Pursuit of Wisdom • AND OTHER WORKS BY THE AUTHOR OF THE CLOUD OF UNKNOWING
Richard Rolle • THE ENGLISH WRITINGS
Francis de Sales, Jane de Chantal • LETTERS OF SPIRITUAL DIRECTION
Albert and Thomas • SELECTED WRITINGS
Robert Bellarmine • SPIRITUAL WRITINGS
Nicodemos of the Holy Mountain • A HANDBOOK OF SPIRITUAL COUNSEL
Henry Suso • THE EXEMPLAR, WITH TWO GERMAN SERMONS
Bérulle and the French School • SELECTED WRITINGS
The Talmud • SELECTED WRITINGS
Ephrem the Syrian • HYMNS
Hildegard of Bingen • SCIVIAS
Birgitta of Sweden • LIFE AND SELECTED REVELATIONS
John Donne • SELECTIONS FROM *DIVINE POEMS*, SERMONS, *DEVOTIONS AND PRAYERS*
Jeremy Taylor • SELECTED WORKS
Walter Hilton • *SCALE OF PERFECTION*
Ignatius of Loyola • *SPIRITUAL EXERCISES* AND SELECTED WORKS
Anchoritic Spirituality • *ANCRENE WISSE* AND ASSOCIATED WORKS
Nizam ad-din Awliya • MORALS FOR THE HEART

Pseudo-Macarius • THE FIFTY SPIRITUAL HOMILIES AND THE *GREAT LETTER*
Gertrude of Helfta • *THE HERALD OF DIVINE LOVE*
Angela of Foligno • COMPLETE WORKS
Margaret Ebner • MAJOR WORKS
Marguerite Porete • *THE MIRROR OF SIMPLE SOULS*